Other Destinies

◆

American Indian Literature
and
Critical Studies Series
Gerald Vizenor, General Editor

Other Destinies

Understanding the
American Indian Novel

◆

By Louis Owens

University of Oklahoma Press : Norman and London

*elists: An Annotated Critical

, Georgia, 1985)
Land (Boston, 1989)
Wolfsong (Albuquerque, 1991)
The Sharpest Sight (Norman, 1992)
Other Destinies: Understanding the American Indian Novel (Norman, 1992)

This book is published with the generous assistance of The McCasland Foundation, Duncan, Oklahoma.

Owens, Louis.
    Other destinies : understanding the American Indian novel / by Louis Owens.—1st ed.
       p. cm.—(American Indian literature and critical studies series ; v. 3)
    Includes bibliographical references.
    ISBN 0-8061-2423-7 (permanent paper)
    1. American fiction—Indian authors—History and criticism.
2. Indians of North America—Intellectual life. 3. Indians in literature.   I. Title. II. Series.
PS153.I52O74   1992   92-3507
813.009′897—dc20   CIP

Other Destinies: Understanding the American Indian Novel is Volume 3 in the American Indian Literature and Critical Studies Series.

The paper in this book meets the guidelines for permanence and durability of the Committee on Production Guidelines for Book Longevity of the Council on Library Resources, Inc. ∞

For mixedbloods, the next generation

Yes, we are between two fires, the Red and the White. Our Caucasian brothers criticize us as a shiftless class, while the Indians disown us as abandoning our own race. We are maligned and traduced as no one but we of the despised "breeds" can know.

—Mourning Dove, *Cogwea, the Half-Blood*

Mixedbloods loosen the seams in the shrouds of identities.
—Gerald Vizenor, "Crows Written on the Poplars"

Contents

Acknowledgments

♦

A work such as this depends on the aid and insights of many. My gratitude goes to the National Endowment for the Humanities for a grant that allowed me time to research and write, to the University of New Mexico for providing funds for travel and research, and to the University of California at Santa Cruz for the support that enabled me, at very long last, to complete this study. I am indebted to Kimberly Wiar of the University of Oklahoma Press for her enthusiam and encouragement and to Fred Hoxie and the staff of the D'Arcy McNickle Center at the Newberry Library for their patient assistance.

The individuals to whom I owe debts of gratitude are numerous: N. Scott Momaday, for a conversation more than twenty years ago that planted the seed of this study and for his generosity with both time and words; Gerald Vizenor, for friendship and wisdom as well as the generous access to unpublished materials he has provided over the years; LaVonne Ruoff, for being an invaluable font of knowledge; Michael Dorris, for providing me with copies of unpublished materials and for his unceasing kindness; Terry Wilson, for his careful and informed reading of this study and valuable suggestions as well as humor; Dorothy Parker, for her friendship and for sharing her rich knowledge of D'Arcy McNickle with me; Jay Miller, for allowing me to read and quote from work in progress; Susan Scarberry-Garcia, for providing me with a manuscript copy of her excellent study of *House Made of Dawn*; Luci Tapahonso and Patricia Clark Smith, for their friendship, advice, and encouragement; and

Evelina Lucero, for her shared insights into American Indian fiction and Pueblo culture as well as her prayers.

Needless to say, I owe an enormous debt to all of the critics, such as Paula Gunn Allen, Charles Larson, Alan Velie, Kenneth Lincoln, Kenneth Roemer, Jack Davis, and others too numerous to name, who have done such valuable work in this area and to my students who have taught me so much about American Indian literature. Finally, my deepest gratitude must go to my mother and father, Ida and Hoey Owens, for never letting their children forget who they are, and to my wife, Polly, for years of wisdom and patience with mixedblood metaphors.

Other Destinies

◆

1

Other Destinies, Other Plots

An Introduction to Indian Novels

♦

To begin to write about something called "the American Indian novel" is to enter a slippery and uncertain terrain. Take one step into this region and we are confronted with difficult questions of authority and ethnicity: What is an Indian? Must one be one-sixteenth Osage, one-eighth Cherokee, one-quarter Blackfoot, or full-blood Sioux to be Indian? Must one be raised in a traditional "Indian" culture or speak a native language or be on a tribal roll? To identify as Indian—or mixedblood—and to write about that identity is to confront such questions. The fact that, as D. H. Lawrence clearly recognized, at the heart of America's history of Indian hating is an unmistakable yearning to *be* Indian—romantically and from a distance made hazy through fear and guilt—compounds the complexity. The fact that so many people throughout the world have a strangely concrete sense of what a "real" Indian should *be* adds still greater stress to the puzzle; woe to him or her who identifies as Indian or mixedblood but does not bear a recognizably "Indian" name or physiognomy or life-style, as the cases of the Lumbee or Mashpee or the innumerable mixedbloods in the United States testify. Discussing the controversial 1976 land claim of the Mashpee Wampanoag Tribal Council, James Clifford has pointed out that "in court they were not helped by the fact that few of them looked strongly 'Indian.' Some of them could pass for black, others for white." With only some simplification, Karen I. Blu argues:

> For Whites, blood is a substance that can be either racially pure or racially polluted. Black blood pollutes White blood absolutely, so that, in the logical extreme, one drop of Black blood makes an otherwise

White man black. . . . . White ideas about "Indian blood" are less formalized and clear-cut. . . . It may take only one drop of Black blood to make a person a Negro, but it takes a lot of Indian blood to make a person a "real" Indian.[1]

Identity for Native Americans is made more complex yet by the fact that the American Indian in the world consciousness is a treasured invention, a gothic artifact evoked like the "powwows" in Hawthorne's "Young Goodman Brown" out of the dark reaches of the continent to replace the actual native, who, painfully problematic in real life, is supposed to have long since vanished. Even individuals seemingly well informed about American Indian literature can exhibit this tendency to relegate "real" Indians to an absolute past, as when we see a writer for the *New York Times*, reviewing James Welch's *Fools Crow*, stating in the simple past tense that "Indians *applied* revelations from the world beyond to the workings of this one, for they *believed* that by tapping into the spiritual they could gain power over everyday occurrences." Such statements leave no room for the Indian today who still applies such revelations and believes in the compelling force of the spiritual.[2] In fact, the Indian in today's world consciousness is a product of literature, history, and art, and a product that, as an invention, often bears little resemblance to actual, living Native American people.

It is at this disjuncture between myth and reality that American Indian novelists most often take aim, and out of which the material of their art most often arises. "I'm still educating an audience," the Chippewa writer Gerald Vizenor has explained. "For example, about Indian identity I have a revolutionary fervor. The hardest part of it is I believe we're all invented as Indians. . . . The inventions have become disguises. . . . This occurs in invented Indians because we're invented and we're invented from traditional static standards and we are stuck in coins and words like artifacts." Vizenor would go still further, agreeing with Paul Watzlawick that what is considered the real world "is an invention whose inventor is unaware of his act of invention . . . the invention then becomes the basis of his world view and actions."[3]

For American Indians, the problem of identity comprehends centuries of colonial and postcolonial displacement, often brutally enforced peripherality, cultural denigration—including especially a harsh privileging of English over tribal languages—and systematic oppression by the monocentric "westering" impulse in America. It comprehends the fact that on reservations today, more than 90 percent of Native American children up for adoption are adopted into non-Indian families, an institutionalized "mainstreaming" of Indian children into Euramerica that results in widespread loss of cultural identity as well as a feeling by Indian people that their children are being systematically stolen away.[4] The recovering or rearticulation of an identity, a process dependent upon a rediscovered sense of place as well as community, becomes in the face of such obstacles a truly enormous undertaking.[5] This attempt is at the center of American Indian fiction.

For Vizenor, who celebrates with "agonistic" humor his own mixed blood, or what he refers to as "torsion in the blood," fiction becomes a process of deconstructing the verbal artifacts of Indian— or mixedblood—identity. For other writers who identify as Native American, the novel represents a process of reconstruction, of self-discovery and cultural recovery. In Laguna author Paula Gunn Allen's term, it is a *re-membering* or putting together of identity. What is put together is rich and complex, like Spiderwoman's wondrous web of creation that appears again and again in American Indian writing, particularly in works by Native American women. For the contemporary Indian novelist—in every case a mixedblood who must come to terms in one form or another with peripherality as well as both European and Indian ethnicity—identity is the central issue and theme, and, as Clifford has suggested, ethnic identity is always "mixed, relational, and inventive." "We are what we imagine," N. Scott Momaday has written. According to Momaday, "An Indian is an idea which a given man has of himself." Writing of his mother's identification as Indian, Momaday says simply, "She imagined who she was."[6]

Whether, to borrow catchy phrases from Alain Robbe-Grillet's *Jealousy*, the writer is "taking apart" in the deconstructionist mode of Vizenor or "taking a part" in the (more high modernist) fashion of an N. Scott Momaday, who carefully crafts an Indian identity through language, in their fiction American Indian novelists confront, inevitably and absorbingly, this question of identity. This issue of contextual identity is one virtually every contemporary Native American—mixedblood or fullblood—is aware of. Chippewa artist Sam English, whose paintings often feature traditionally costumed and confident Indians wearing sunglasses and seeming to challenge the viewer to attempt a cultural definition, has explained, "I'm trying to paint Indians who are making it in both worlds, guys who have jobs like everybody else in the country but who go home at five and become traditional Indians again." Like Vizenor, English locates indices of Indian identity in humor: "Humor that's kept us all going during the bad times. A lot of people don't realize that, and I try to show it." [7]

To comprehend the extraordinary challenge faced by Indian authors and by those who would come to some kind of understanding of Indian fiction, it may help to turn to the ubiquitously useful Russian critic Mikhail Bakhtin, who wrote:

> Indeed, any concrete discourse (utterance) finds the object at which it was directed already as it were overlain with qualifications, open to dispute, charged with value, already enveloped in an obscuring mist—or, on the contrary, by the "light" of alien words that have already been spoken about it. It is entangled, shot through with shared thoughts, points of view, alien value judgments and accents. The word, directed toward its object, enters a dialogically agitated and tension-filled environment of alien words.[8]

For a Native American storyteller or writer working within an awareness of traditional, oral American Indian literatures and cultures, Bakhtin's contention that in the dialogic process context is crucial to understanding would seem self-evident. Within traditional Native American literatures, speaker and listener are coparticipants in the telling of a story.

Barre Toelken and Tacheeni Scott, discussing the storytelling of Yellowman, a "Navajo raconteur," have made this point effectively, writing that "the audience plays a central role in the narrative style; without an audience, his tales are almost entirely lacking in the special intonations, changes in speed, pacing, and dramatic pauses which are so prominent [in the 'told' story]." Arnold Krupat has further pointed out that "there simply were no Native American *texts* until whites decided to collaborate with Indians and make them."[9] While Krupat's declaration omits such Native American "texts" as the traditional winter counts or calendars, it nonetheless underscores the complexity of the task confronting the novelist who would write as an Indian about Indian concerns. For the Indian author, writing within consciousness of the contextual background of a nonliterate culture, every word written in English represents a collaboration of sorts as well as a reorientation (conscious or unconscious) from the paradigmatic world of oral tradition to the syntagmatic reality of written language.[10]

Discussing literature written in English by "natives" under colonial pressures, Ashcroft, Griffiths, and Tiffin, authors of *The Empire*

Writes Back, state: "The producers signify by the very fact of writing in the language of the dominant culture that they have temporarily or permanently entered a specific and privileged class endowed with the language, education, and leisure necessary to produce such works."[11] Contemporary American Indian writers have indeed most often permanently entered that class, possessing as they do a consistently high level of education (almost always at least one college degree) and mastery of English, a fact that certainly adds complexity to the overarching question of cultural identity.

Native American authors face constantly the dilemma of a privileged discourse already "charged with value" and "alien." The dilemma begins with the word *Indian*. Perhaps no other utterance in American language is so "enveloped in an obscuring mist," so "entangled, shot through with shared thoughts, points of view, alien value judgments and accents." In spite of its wide acceptance, even appropriation, by Native Americans, it should be borne in mind that the word *Indian* came into being on this continent simply as an utterance designed to impose a distinct "otherness" upon indigenous peoples. To be "Indian" was to be "not European."[12] Native cultures—their voices systematically silenced—had no part in the ongoing discourse that evolved over several centuries to define the utterance "Indian" within the language of the invaders. Although Native Americans have appropriated that term to make it serve their own, separate needs, the end result as non-Indians understand it is a signifier that comprehends Euramerican responses to the "New World" but has little to do with the native inhabitants of that world. When a character in Vizenor's *Bearheart* demands of Belladonna Darwin Winter-Catcher, "What does Indian mean?" the question cuts to the heart of the predicament illuminated and explored and, to varying degrees, resolved in works by contemporary Indian authors. By deconstructing the utterance, writers such as Vizenor are redefining American Indian identity, and they are doing so in the face of often stunning ignorance of American Indian cultures on the part of the rest of the world.

This ignorance ranges from such typical confusion as English historical novelist Antonia Fraser's succinct explanation that Pocahontas was "a member of the Sioux tribe, who were all about six feet tall," to Ashcroft, Griffiths, and Tiffin's ground-breaking 1989 study of postcolonial literatures that omits any mention at all of American Indian writing, though the authors do consider the Euramerican colonial and postcolonial experience. Similarly, in a re-

cently published article in which a teacher describes his praisewor-
thy attempts to introduce Navajo students—on the Navajo
reservation—to "post colonial" literature, the author of the article
stresses works from Africa, the Caribbean, and the Pacific but fails
to mention literature actually written by American Indians such as
Navajo poets Luci Tapahonso and Nia Francisco or the Pawnee-
Otoe novelist and short fiction writer Anna Lee Walters, who is
employed by Navajo Community College.[13]

The nature of the confrontation permeating Native American
fiction is intensely political. "A particular language in a novel is
always a particular way of viewing the world, one that strives
for a social significance," Bakhtin writes,[14] and within the novels
discussed in my study are to be found particularly "Indian" ways
of viewing the world, worldviews that are almost always in direct
conflict with the dominant *ideologemes* of Euramerica. Again and
again in this fiction, this conflict is epitomized through conflicting
discourses, through breakdowns in communication and understanding, failures in articulation. Confronted with the authoritative,
privileged voice of European America, the Indian resorts to subversion or often falls silent. We see the former response most clearly
in a work such as John Rollin Ridge's *Joaquin Murieta*, in which this
Cherokee mixedblood author thinly disguises his outrage in a story
of Mexican-American conflict in California. The latter response is
ubiquitous in these novels, in characters such as Archilde, who
extends his hands in silence at the end of D'Arcy McNickle's *The
Surrounded*, or in Abel in N. Scott Momaday's *House Made of Dawn*.
These Native American mixedbloods approach the condition Fredric Jameson, following Jacques Lacan, has described as a schizophrenia characterized by a "breakdown in the signifying chain of
meaning."[15]

Conversely, confronted with the alien nonanthropocentric and
ecologically oriented world-view of the Indian, the white culture
shown in fiction by Native Americans relies more heavily upon
privileged discourse to assert its dominance, like James Fenimore
Cooper's Natty Bumppo dismissing a Pawnee description of heaven
with his own privileged, European version. Such privileging supports the contention that "language becomes the medium through
which a hierarchical structure of power is perpetuated, and the
medium through which conceptions of 'truth', 'order', and 'reality'
become established." Elaine Jahner has described this epistemological crisis: "Translating what they [Native Americans] sensed into

terms that might communicate interculturally was impossible because such translation requires knowledge of two ways of knowing,
but beyond that it requires that the issue itself make sense to the
people to whom it is being addressed. Until the twentieth century,
few European intellectuals radically questioned their own epistemological foundations."[16]

Native American novelists confront the additional challenge of
making themselves understood in a prose form quite foreign to
traditional Native American discourse. Before their "corruption"
into written English, American Indian texts were oral and communal. Primary to this transition is a fundamental shift in the conception of language as well as knowledge. The coercive power of
language in Native American oral traditions—that ability to "bring
into being" and thus radically enter into reality—intersects with
what has been called "the development of historic consciousness"
as a result of written language.[17] With written literacy, language
becomes descriptive/historic and begins to lose its unique power as
creator of reality.

Just as significant is the fact that the concept of a single author
for any given text, or of an individual who might conceive of herself
or himself as the creative center and originating source of a story,
or of the individual autobiography, would have made as little sense
to pre-Columbian Native Americans as the notion of selling real
estate.[18] For the traditional storyteller, each story originates with
and serves to define the people as a whole, the community. This
fact, of course, does not preclude the essential adaptation and
evolution of each story as it is told, for as Dennis Tedlock has
explained in regard to the Zuni of New Mexico, "the storyteller-
interpreter does not merely quote or paraphrase the text but may
even improve upon it, describe a scene which it does not describe,
or answer a question which it does not answer." Tedlock goes on
to explain: "For the Zuni storyteller-interpreter, the relationship
between text and interpretation is a dialectical one: he or she both
respects the text and revises it."[19] Traditional storytelling is a syncretic process, necessary to the adaptive, dynamic nature of American Indian cultures—that quality requisite for cultural survival.
The ease and subtlety with which Indians incorporated European
mythology into their own highly syncretic oral tradition has often
been documented and commented upon. The brilliant and ideosyn-
cratic anthropologist Jaime de Angulo provides the example of a Pit
River/Klamath storyteller who says, "This here Jesus, he and his

wife Mary, and they had a little boy with them, they traveled all over the world, they made mountains and trees, they made trees, they made springs everywhere, *teeqaade toolol.* . . . This here Jesus he was a great man; he was the best gambler in the whole United States!"[20]

The emphasis in such storytelling falls nonetheless not upon the creative role of the storyteller but upon the communal nature of the stories, with the "outcome" of each story already being known to the audience.[21] Within the oral tradition, literature is authorless, lacking what Michel Foucault, describing the modern concept of "author," has called "the principle of thrift in the proliferation of meaning." John Bierhorst has commented upon the collective nature of traditional Indian literatures, explaining that "the Indian poet does not consider himself the originator of his material but merely the conveyor. . . . Indian poetry, then, is usually attributed not to an individual but to his culture." About the concept labeled "author," Foucault has written, "The coming into being of the notion of 'author' constitutes the privileged moment of *individualization* in the history of ideas, knowledge, literature, philosophy, and the sciences."[22] The birth of the novel, as Ian Watt and others have shown, parallels and owes much to the new emphasis upon the individual in Western societies,[23] and it is perhaps worth noting that the modern novel was being created by Cervantes in Spain at the same time that Native Americans—belonging to radically diverse cultural groups speaking more than 250 distinct languages— were receiving their intense introduction to the Old World through colonialism. The privileging of the individual necessary for the conception of the modern novel (and for the conception of the American Myth) is a more radical departure for American Indian cultures than for the Western world as a whole, for Foucault's "moment of individualization" represents an experience forced harshly, and rather unsuccessfully, upon Native Americans. In this sense, while contemporary American Indian poets, regardless of their consciousness of influence, may imagine themselves part of an ancient oral tradition of singers or storytellers, the Native American novelist works in a medium for which no close Indian prototype exists. The novelist must therefore rely upon story and myth but graft the thematic and structural principles found therein upon the "foreign" (though infinitely flexible) and intensely egocentric genre of the written prose narrative, or novel.

Regardless of how effectively a novel may incorporate the cyclical, ordered, ritual-centered, and paradigmatic world of traditional oral literatures, try as he or she may, the Native American novelist can never step back into the collective anonymity of the tribal storyteller. Ironically, for the novelist writing with a consciousness of responsibility as a member of a living Native American culture, this irreversible metamorphosis from oral, communal literature to the written commodity of published work may be an essential objectification. The form of the novel may thus represent a necessary "desacralization" of traditional materials, a transformation that allows sacred materials—from ritual and myth—to move into the secular world of decontextualized "art" and one that resembles the transformation of ceremonial dance by the highly choreographed American Indian Dance Theater. This transformation can be problematic, as the mixedblood Laguna Pueblo writer Paula Gunn Allen points out when she writes that "to use the oral tradition directly is to run afoul of native ethics." The risk, however, is one that many Indian authors appear ready to assume.[24]

The transformation may be problematic in other ways as well, putting into particular focus the dilemma of identity and authenticity which, while common to inhabitants of the modern Western world, is particularly intense for Native Americans and, especially, mixedbloods. As writers such as Silko, Erdrich, Vizenor, Momaday, and virtually all contemporary authors identifying as "Indian" to one degree or another inscribe their authorial signatures to published works, they enter into what Foucault has termed the realm of the author as "ideological product," that "certain functional principle by which, in our culture, one limits, excludes, and chooses." Native American writing represents an attempt to recover identity and authenticity by invoking and incorporating the world found within the oral tradition—the reality of myth and ceremony—an authorless "original" literature. Yet through the inscription of an authorial signature, the Indian writer places him- or herself in immediate tension with this communal, authorless, and identity-conferring source, at once highlighting the very questions of identity and authenticity the new literature attempts to resolve: "Who really spoke? Is it really he and not someone else? With what authenticity or originality?" One paradoxical result can be a sense, in writing by contemporary Indian authors, of the oral tradition as what Jacques Derrida has termed "the absent origin," a "sad, negative, nostalgic" response that contradicts a Nietzschean "joyous affirmation of freeplay." In every case, however, the Native

American novelist plays off of and moves beyond (and challenges the reader to likewise move beyond) this faint trace of "Rousseauist" ethnostalgia—most common to Euramerican treatments of Native American Indians—toward an affirmation of a syncretic, dynamic, adaptive identity in contemporary America.[25]

In addition to the "foreign" genre of the individually authored, egocentric text (a concept often discounted, of course, in contemporary theory), the Native American writer, like almost all colonized people, must also function within an essentially appropriated language. For behind the modern Indian author's fluent mastery of English lies a centuries-old history of assimilation, not merely the painful, forced assimilation of a marginalized people into the cultural mainstream (the federal government's infamous and disastrous answer to the "Indian Problem"), but also the assimilation of "alien" discourse by an oppressed people. "The ideological becoming of a human being," according to Bakhtin, "is the process of selectively assimilating the words of others." The contemporary American Indian, and particularly the mixedblood, is the product of generations of such selective assimilation. "The tendency to assimilate others' discourse," Bakhtin writes, "takes on an even deeper and more basic significance in an individual's ideological becoming, in the most fundamental sense. Another's discourse performs here no longer as information, directions, rules, models and so forth—but strives rather to determine the very basis of our behavior; it performs here as *authoritative discourse*, and an *internally persuasive discourse*." Native Americans have had several centuries of experience with authoritative discourse, having had their native languages ruthlessly suppressed to the extent that punishment for speaking "Indian" represents a common denominator among Native Americans who have "gone to school" (often in boarding schools where the process of displacement was most rapid and intense). Indian writers have consistently recognized this inescapable struggle with language. Like Rocky in Leslie Marmon Silko's *Ceremony* and Benally in N. Scott Momaday's *House Made of Dawn*, both victims of the American Dream, Native American writers repeatedly demonstrate to some degree this conflict between an authoritative "alien" discourse and an internally persuasive worldview articulated by traditional values. Like the school books Rocky believes wholeheartedly, the dominant language insists upon its authority and "demands that we acknowledge it, that we make it our own; it binds us, quite independent of any power it might have to persuade us internally; we encounter it with its authority already fused to it." Language "indissolubly fused with its authority—with political power" is a central concern in the novels discussed in this study, a concern evidenced again and again in the themes of articulation and inarticulateness.[26]

For Momaday, a lifelong quest for a fully realized Kiowa identity began precisely with language. Momaday has said:

> I think of myself as an Indian because at one time in my life I suddenly realized that my father had grown up speaking a language that I didn't grow up speaking, that my forebears on his side had made a migration from Canada along with . . . Athapaskan peoples that I knew nothing about, and so I determined to find out something about these things and in the process I acquired an identity; and it is an Indian identity, as far as I am concerned.[27]

Like his fellow Indian writers, Momaday discovered that the task before him was not simply to learn the lost language of his tribe but rather to appropriate, to tear free of its restricting authority, another language—English—and to make that language accessible to an Indian discourse. The task is herculean—sometimes, as McNickle seems to suggest in his two major novels, almost impossible—and it is, of course, immensely complicated by considerations of audience.

Traditionally, a storyteller's audience consisted of tribe or clan members who could be counted on to contribute a wealth of intimate knowledge to the telling of any story, to thus actively participate in the dynamics of the story's creation. Bakhtin explains: "Whatever kind it be, the behavioral utterance always joins the participants in the situation together as *co-participants* who know, understand, and evaluate the situation in like manner." Addressing Native American traditional literatures specifically, Dell Hymes explains further: "When things were said or sung within the native culture, explicit analysis—a detailed meta-language for dealing with form—was not needed. Performer and audience shared an implicit knowledge of language and ways of speaking." Papago autobiographer Maria Chona explains most succinctly: "The song is very short because we understand so much." In the oral tradition, context and text are one thing; Hymes writes: "The joy, the understanding, the language are all of a piece." The oral tradition assumes that, as deconstructionists would have it, both "producers [conveyers?] and consumers of 'texts' (cultural artefacts) participate in the production of significations and meanings." Today, however, the Native American novelist's audience will likely consist of a heteroglot gathering, including tribal relations (who might be expected, for example, to know—to be immanent participants in—the Laguna and Navajo myths operative in Silko's *Ceremony* or the Blackfoot stories of Old Man and Old Woman important in James Welch's *Winter in the Blood*); Indian readers from the same or other tribal cultures who may not be familiar with the traditional elements essential to the work but who may recognize the coercive power of language to "bring into being"; and non-Indian readers who approach the novel with a completely alien set of assumptions and values.

"Every discourse," Bakhtin writes, "presupposes a special conception of the listener, of his apperceptive background and the degree of his responsiveness; it presupposes a specific distance."[28] For the Native American novelist, that presupposition is a complex conundrum. While writing for the Indian reader, the Indian novelist who desires publication must also write for the non-Indian. The relativity of specific distance becomes dizzying. Again, Bakhtin, though unaware of Native American writing nascent during his lifetime, has defined the predicament of the contemporary Native American writer rather neatly:

> The more a poet is cut off from the social unity of his group [tribe, clan], the more likely he is to take into account the external demands of a particular reading public. Only a social group alien to the poet can determine his creative work from outside. One's own group needs no such external definition: It exists in the poet's voice, in the basic tone and intonations of that voice—whether the poet himself intends this or not.[29]

The effect is a richly hybridized dialogue aimed at those few with privileged knowledge—the traditionally educated Indian reader—as well as those with claims to a privileged discourse—the Eurocentric reader. One effect of this hybridization is subversive: the American Indian writer places the Eurocentric reader on the outside, as "other," while the Indian reader (a comparatively small audience) is granted, for the first time, a privileged position. On the one hand, by consciously identifying her- or himself as "Indian" the writer seeks to establish a basis for authoritative, or externally persuasive, discourse; on the other hand, the writer must make that discourse internally persuasive for the non-Indian reader unaccustomed to peripherality. At the same time, the writer is appropriating an essentially "other" language and thus entering into dialogue with the language itself. The result of this exquisite balancing act is a matrix of incredible heteroglossia and linguistic torsions and an intensely political situation.

For American Indian novelists, the "special conception of the reader" is obviously complicated, much more so than for mainstream American writers. While American modernists such as T. S. Eliot and Ezra Pound chose to deliberately narrow their audiences via the obstacle course of extreme literacy—classical erudition and obscurantism—their work was nonetheless aimed at a remarkably homogeneous readership defined by the metropolitan center. The same can be said for mainstream postmodernist writers such as Donald Barthelme or Robert Coover, regardless of whatever levels of difficulty they propose for the conventional reader through their polysemous texts.[30] The same cannot be said, however, for Native American authors. Many novels by Indian authors involve difficulties common to traditional Native American literatures precisely because they depend upon those literatures so profoundly. As Karl Kroeber has written of traditional materials, Native American novels "are not so accessible; and most create doubts, difficulties, and frustrations for a serious reader trying to understand in depth, wishing to gain something more than a superficial, and therefore patronizing, 'appreciation' of Native American literary art." Readers who fail, for example, to bring at least some knowledge of traditional Chippewa trickster tales to the fiction of Gerald Vizenor—not to mention an openness to trickster discourse—are very apt to find themselves confused and perhaps appalled. Unaware of the crucial role of play and humor in Native American cultures, readers groomed by stoic stereotypes will miss much in Vizenor and most other Indian novelists.[31] Likewise, as Alan Velie has pointed out, readers who do not have at least an inkling of poststructuralist theory may well be simply put off and confused by such Vizenoresque fantasies as the "Bioavaricious Regional Word Hospital."[32] Of course Vizenor, who, in his rapid-fire approach to deconstruction, is fond of citing such theorists as Foucault, Lacan, Derrida, Roland Barthes, Bakhtin, Tzvetan Todorov, and Paul Ricoeur among a multitude of others,[33] has insisted that "some upsetting is necessary." In that spirit, Vizenor anticipates this somewhat narrow "apperceptive background" as essential to the dialogic of his text and, rather like his modernist predecessors, agrees to the inevitable narrowing of audience for the sake of intensification of effect.

As of yet, literature by Native Americans has met with only begrudging and at best slight acceptance into the American canon. (The same, of course, could be said for ethnic literature as a whole in this country, and claims of Eurocentric–white–male–East Coast bias have also been made convincingly in support of literature from women and from the entire region of the American West.) More than any other particular segment of American literature, like the peoples who have produced it, Native American literature— whether materials from oral traditions or works by contemporary authors—has been routinely marginalized. One obvious reason for this exclusion may be the almost singularly urban nature of modernism, the sensibility and obsession dominant during the nascence of Native American written literature. Ashcroft, Griffiths, and Tiffin suggest that New Criticism "had a profoundly negative impact" upon indigenous writers: "The assimilation of post-colonial writers into a 'metropolitan' tradition retarded consideration of their works within an appropriate cultural context, and so seriously militated against the development of a 'native' or indigenous theory." [34] Modernism was "an art of cities" designed to "confront the psychological, sociological, technical, organizational, and political problems of massive urbanization." While the local color movement of the nineteenth century and the "revolt from the village" that propelled itself into the early decades of twentieth-century American writing did focus attention upon the nonurban experience (in first romantic and later mostly negative, naturalistic fashion), this concern was at best a sideshow on the cultural midway of the American canon. In the New Critical and modernist context dominant through the first half of this century, Native American literature—almost always concerned primarily with rural existence and as far removed from the mechanical concerns of modern life as was possible—simply did not figure. [35] Simultaneously, traditional American Indian epistemology had little in common with the empiricism of the Enlightenment inheritance of the late nineteenth and early twentieth centuries or with the logical positivism that flowered along with high modernism. Thus, literature—oral or written—by Indians was, with the exception of a few individuals, such as Yvor

Winters at Stanford, universally shuffled aside into the realm of folklore and anthropological "local color" by literary professionals.

If we approach the concept of a literary canon with what Krupat and others have called "hermeneutical suspicion" and define the canon as "that body of texts which best performs in the sphere of culture the work of legitimating the prevailing social order," the rationale behind the exclusion of minority texts, including especially Native American texts, should be even more apparent. The general absence of Native American texts from university English departments is further understandable if we consider Barbara Herrnstein Smith's suggestion of the bifurcated aims of scholars:

> The reasons for the general neglect and exile [of marginalized texts] . . . are more complex, reflecting among other things, the fact that literary studies in America, from the time of its inception as an institutionalized academic discipline, has been shaped by two conflicting and mutually compromising intellectual traditions and ideologies, namely . . . positivistic philological scholarship and humanistic pedagogy. That is, while professors of literature have sought to claim for their activities the rigor, objectivity, cognitive substantiality, and progress associated with science and the empirical disciplines, they have also attempted to remain faithful to the essentially conservative and didactic mission of humanistic studies: to honor and preserve the culture's traditionally esteemed objects—in this case, its canonized texts—and to illuminate and transmit the traditional cultural values presumably embodied in them.[36]

Native American literature lends itself to neither of these schizophrenic pursuits, being tainted according to the positivists' light with the label of folkloric mysticism while failing utterly to reinforce traditional cultural values embodied in canonical texts. In short, the famous Vanishing American has always been in the best interests of this country's "prevailing social order." Works that both resuscitate the beleaguered and maltreated original inhabitant—who was supposed to have disappeared along with the passenger pigeon— and provide a countertext to the national meta-narrative of westering and millennial materialism are not likely to be selected into the canonical tradition. As Roy Harvey Pearce has put it so well, "Studying the savage, trying to civilize him, destroying him, in the end they [European-American intelligentsia] had only studied themselves, strengthened their own civilization, and given those who were coming after them an enlarged certitude of another, even happier destiny—that manifest in the progress of American civilization over all obstacles." The Indian's role in this millennial drama was supposed to be romantic, tragic, and epic, and as Bakhtin has written, "The epic and tragic hero is the hero who, by his very nature, must perish." The noble savage's refusal to perish throws a monkey wrench into the drama: "Outside his destiny, the epic and tragic hero is nothing; he is, therefore, a function of the plot fate assigns him; he cannot become the hero of another destiny or another plot." With few exceptions, American Indian novelists—examples of Indians who have repudiated their assigned plots—are in their fiction rejecting the American gothic with its haunted, guilt-burdened wilderness and doomed Native and emphatically making the Indian the hero of other destinies, other plots.[37]

As everyone knows, it has never been in the vested interests of the literary establishment to embrace voices that undermine the monologic authority of hard-won civilization and challenge the traditional cultural values embodied in the accepted canon; American intellectuals have always prefered to look eastward, striving like Henry James's Christopher Newman to establish irreproachable bonds with the old world where values originate. (Recall how eager the "make-it-new" crowd was to go back to the "center" of colonial privilege, to relocate from the New World to the Old at the beginning of this century, and how, as Krupat has pointed out, amidst the literary fragments T. S. Eliot—the most visible "icon" of literacy in modernist art—busily shored against his and the Western world's spiritual and intellectual ruin in *The Waste Land* there is not a single American shard.[38] Recall also how late in American history it was before even mainstream American literature was allowed a place in hallowed halls.) Clifford, tracing this pattern of marginalization and erasure of the minority voice or identity in the Western world, suggests that this process "occurs whenever marginal peoples come into a historical or ethnographic space that has been defined by the Western imagination. 'Entering the modern world,' their distinct histories quickly vanish." Arguing more directly against this pattern of exclusion as it relates to the literary canon, Krupat writes: "For the canon of American literature, secular heterodoxy on an empirical level means something very specific: it means that any proposed canon of American literature that does not include more than merely occasional examples of the literatures produced by red and black people as well as white people—men and women, of indige-

nous and African, as well as European origins—is suspect on the
very face of it." Krupat elaborates:

> It is not simply that these texts should be read in the interest of fairness
> or simply because they are available; nor is it because they provide
> charming examples of "primitive" survivals: they should be read be-
> cause of their abundant capacity to teach and delight. But for that
> capacity to be experienced and thus for the excellence of these texts
> to be acknowledged, it will be necessary . . . to recognize that what
> they teach frequently runs counter to the teaching of the Western
> tradition, and that the ways in which they delight is [sic] different
> from the ways in which the Western tradition has given pleasure.[39]

Today, thanks in part to critics such as Foucault and Lyotard,
marginalized literatures are moving onto the center screen of critical
concerns. The exurban, suburban, and even rural subjects of a
considerable body of postmodern fiction, such as that of Raymond
Carver, and the rise since the sixties of a new and more comprehensive wave of environmental literature are also giving Native American literature a new currency. However, it is accurate, I think, to
say that Native American writers have their reservations; they work
for the most part consciously outside the concerns of postmodern
theorists, at times working at odds with the aims of deconstructionist theory. The postmodern insistence upon the fragmented
sense of self finds its reflection in the radically deracinated
mixedblood of much Indian fiction—figures such as Abel in *House
Made of Dawn*, Ephanie in *The Woman Who Owned the Shadows*,
and many others—characters who truly find themselves between
realities and wondering which world and which life might be theirs.
In many cases, Indian protagonists resemble the typically displaced
modernist figure who "finds himself in a situation he recognizes
structurally as an inquiry into significance, but he is no longer sure
what he is supposed to be looking for."[40] Repeatedly in Indian
fiction, though, we are shown the possibility of recovering a centered sense of personal identity and significance.

It can be said of the protagonists in American Indian fiction that
they suffer from alienation in the Marxist sense, for the self from
which they are alienated is, in fact, shown to be potentially coherent
and dependent upon a continuing and coherent cultural identity.
While these characters may, like Abel in *House Made of Dawn* or the
unnamed narrator in *Winter in the Blood*, suffer from something like
"schizophrenia in the form of a rubble of distinct and unrelated

signifiers," their authors more often than not move them through narrative toward a "temporal unification of the past and future with the present" and, even more crucially, toward an ability to "unify the past, present and future of our own biographical experience or psychic life"—or toward a coherent personal identity entirely dependent upon a coherent cultural identity.[41] Ultimately, whereas postmodernism celebrates the fragmentation and chaos of experience, literature by Native American authors tends to seek transcendence of such ephemerality and the recovery of "eternal and immutable" elements represented by a spiritual tradition that escapes historical fixation, that places humanity within a carefully, cyclically ordered cosmos and gives humankind irreducible responsiblity for the maintenance of that delicate equilibrium. Such a generalization would seem at first glance to exclude a writer like Vizenor, who joyously embraces the writerly text and the chaos of play that inhabits the gap between signifier and signified, but a close examination of Vizenor's trickster discourse will easily discover an intense didacticism and insistence upon certain immutable values—precisely the aim of traditional trickster discourse. Thus, in Vizenor we may find something rather like the paradox of reform in naturalism.

In 1979, Michael Dorris, at that time professor of Native American studies at Dartmouth College, wrote that "there is no such thing as "Native American literature," though it may yet, someday, come into being." One of the requisites for a Native American literature, Dorris suggested, was a reflection of "a shared consciousness, an inherently identifiable world-view."[42] More than a decade later, it seems that there is indeed such a thing as Native American literature, and I would argue that it is found most clearly in novels written by Native Americans about the Native American experience. For, in spite of the fact that Indian authors write from very diverse tribal and cultural backgrounds, there is to a remarkable degree a shared consciousness and identifiable worldview reflected in novels by American Indian authors, a consciousness and worldview defined primarily by a quest for identity: What does it mean to be "Indian"— or mixedblood—in contemporary America? Michael Dorris, with his 1987 novel *A Yellow Raft in Blue Water*, has helped to define and expand this literature, introducing the first dual-minority protagonist in the person of Rayona, his half-Indian and half–African American protagonist.

There is no need here to belabor the long history of confusion, theft, and genocide everyone associates with Euramerican and Indian relations from the beginning. Suffice it to say that the struggle for an "Indian" identity—and a long battle between competing discourses—began with a European error that, in the fifteenth century, placed the North American continent, and the several hundred distinct native cultures contained therein, along the banks of the Indus River in European imaginations. Since that initial moment of entanglement in the metanarrative of Western expansionism, the identity of American Indians—or Native Americans[43]—has been ever subject to the psychic cravings and whims of the European colonizers. Kimberly W. Benston's definition of the "central crux of all black self-definitions" may apply also to the dilemma of self-determined identity for Native Americans: "how envision and name a people whose very existence was predicated upon expropriation of land, culture, and the binding imperatives and designations of what Ellison terms the 'familial past.' " Although Native Americans have lost far less of the "familial past" and self-defined identity than have African-Americans, in what Vizenor has called "word wars," stretching over almost half a millennium, Native Americans have fought an unending battle to affirm their own identities, to resist the metamorphoses insisted upon by European intruders and to hold to that certainty of self that is passed on through tribal traditions and oral literatures. Resisted most strongly has been the great Western myth of cultural extinction: the last Mohican stalked by the towering, epic shadow of Natty Bumppo westward into the sunset. Citing perhaps the most influential proponent of this myth in its enlightened version, Clifford declares:

> In Lévi-Strauss's global vision—one widely shared today—authentic human differences are disintegrating, disappearing in an expansive commodity culture to become, at best, collectible "art" or "folklore." The great narrative of entropy and loss in *Triste tropiques* expresses an inescapable, sad truth. But it is too neat, and it assumes a questionable Eurocentric position at the "end" of a unified human history, gathering up, memorializing the world's local historicities.[44]

Within this context of indigenous culture as vanishing, collectible commodity, the words of a popular guidebook for collectors of Indian "artifacts"—including ceremonial pipes and many other objects that have undoubtedly come from burial sites—offer American Indians a chilling insight. "It should be noted," the author of the guide admonishes, "that the listed value . . . is not an ultimate valuation. . . . Instead, it is judged by the possesser to be fair market value." The author goes on to encourage collectors: "Don't be upset by what may seem to be high prices; don't feel that American Indian items are beyond your financial reach."[45] What, we are led to ask, is the "fair market value" of a sacred object, what might be the "ultimate valuation" of a culture? When might American Indian identity finally be beyond the "financial reach" of commodifiers?

To borrow Clifford's wonderfully descriptive phrase, novels by Native American authors might be thought of as "local narratives of cultural continuity and recovery."[46] That "great narrative of entropy and loss" which is the Euramerican version of Native American history since the fifteenth century is being revised and rewritten in contemporary Indian literature from an Indian perspective. The consciousness shared in all of these works is that of the individual attempting to reimagine an identity, to articulate a self within a Native American context.[47] And in every case the mixedblood turns at the point of division back toward an Indian identity and away from the collective dream of white America. In arguing for a distinct Native American literature, Lester A. Standiford has emphasized this repudiation of the so-called American Dream and simultaneously articulated useful distinguishing characteristics of American Indian literature on a broader scale, emphasizing points that will be taken up in the various readings of novels in my study. Standiford writes: "Because many Native Americans view the notion of 'Manifest Destiny' as a form of genocide that still threatens them today; because they share an Oriental view of man as a creature of equal spirit stature with all other things in the world, striving to maintain harmonious balance; because they hold fast to the traditional belief in the very real power of the word; and because they build on the influence of the oral literary tradition, with its symbolic density and intricate patterns of repetition, contemporary poetry and ficiton by Indian Americans distinguishes itself from the so-called 'mainstream.' "[48]

This study is a modest attempt to further introduce novels by American Indian authors to the wider audience they deserve and to make readers more aware that for fiction about Indians they can go directly to Indian authors rather than to the immense American library of fiction about Indians by Euramerican writers. Recently, Native American fiction has begun to attract attention partly because of the stunning popularity of novels by Chippewa writer Louise Erdrich. With award-winning and best-selling novels—*Love Medicine, The Beet Queen, Tracks,* and *A Yellow Raft in Blue Water*—

Erdrich and her husband/collaborator Michael Dorris have made East Coast publishers and readers aware of the fact that Native Americans can write, quite well, about themselves. Kiowa author N. Scott Momaday—riding the crest of 1960s enthusiasm for Indians and all things "earthy"—had made a critical beginning in this direction when, in 1969, he won a Pulitzer Prize for the brilliant novel *House Made of Dawn*. Here, critics discovered, was a novel that displayed the craft and ambitious complexity expected of the major writers of modernism, a work by an Indian author who brought formidable skills to bear upon the subject of Indians. Perhaps most importantly, with its blatant echoes of Faulkner, Hemingway, even Emily Dickinson, *House Made of Dawn* seemed to be a novel that lent itself rather nicely to the conventional tools of modernist critique— never mind the subtle complexities of Pueblo and Navajo elements in the novel.

Prior to *House Made of Dawn*, most fiction about American Indians had been written by non-Indian authors in a process that resembled literary colonization. In the early nineteenth century, James Fenimore Cooper's stoic savage had padded out of the eastern forests (and, as Pearce has shown, out of an already well established tradition of "savagism") squarely into American romanticism, and as naturalism began to darken the glass of American literature later in that century, Cooper's noble stoic was joined by his close relative, the even more doomed, even more rapidly vanishing Native American. In spite of his inspired belief that "we cannibals must help these Christians," Queequeg in Herman Melville's *Moby-Dick*, upon whose coffin Ishmael surfaces and survives, represents one of the best-known examples of this doomed figure (as Erdrich subtly points out in *Love Medicine*). Mark Twain's tortured and torturing mixedblood, "Injun Joe," in *Tom Sawyer*, takes this cliché to the painful conclusion that would be seen again and again in American fiction and film all the way to Blue Duck, the pathological "breed" (a version of the conventional "renegade" of dime novels) in Larry McMurtry's 1987 novel, *Lonesome Dove*. In the twentieth century the modernists would delightedly appropriate the Indian as the quintessential naturalistic victim, and William Faulkner would add "Chief Doom" to the Vanishing American Hall of Fame, while the author and "Indian expert" Oliver LaFarge would reap great novelistic rewards with a Harvard anthropology student's filmy perspective on the Native American.[49]

As with all colonization, the native is made over in this fiction to reflect the psychic cravings of the colonialist—for the most part Indian characters in American fiction bear very little resemblance to the human beings who, whether living on reservations or in urban centers, identify with the many tribal cultures on this continent. Momaday, undoubtedly the best-known American Indian writer world-wide, takes a very broad view of this subject, saying, "I've read non-Indians who have written about Indian matters and done it very well, and of course that works the other way around, too. I've also read some things that were very bad because the writer was simply writing outside his experience."[50] However, the Native American writer, surveying what is surely a literary wasteland for the Indian, sees inexhaustible opportunity and need to "make it new."

Before 1968 only nine novels by American Indian authors had been published. The first was John Rollin Ridge's *Joaquin Murieta* in 1854, followed by Simon Pokagon's *Queen of the Woods* in 1899,[51] Mourning Dove's *Cogewea, the Half-Blood* in 1927, three novels by the Cherokee writer John Milton Oskison in the 1920s and 1930s, John Joseph Mathews's *Sundown* in 1934, and D'Arcy McNickle's *The Surrounded* in 1936 and *Runner in the Sun* in 1954. However, as if Momaday had triggered a long-dormant need among Indian writers, the 1970s saw the publication of a stream of novels by Indian authors including Janet Campbell Hale, Nasnaga (Roger Russell), Chief George Pierre, Ted Williams, Dallas Chief Eagle, Hyemeyohsts Storm, Denton R. Bedford, James Welch, Virginia Driving Hawk Sneve, Gerald Vizenor, Charles Penoi, and Leslie Silko. The 1980s and '90s have added novels by Louise Erdrich, Michael Dorris, Paula Gunn Allen, Anna Walters, Tom King, Linda Hogan, Craig Strete, and myself as well as new works by Momaday, Vizenor, and Welch.

In more than a century of American Indian novels, an evolution has taken place in the way Indian writers approach their subjects and the way these novels fit into the mainstream of American literature. In the beginning, the mixedblood Cherokee author John Rollin Ridge felt obligated to disguise his outrage at America's genocidal treatment of his tribe, accomplishing this disguise by writing a novel masquerading as a biography of a California bandit. Nearly three-quarters of a century later, Mourning Dove wrote of the bitter sense of isolation and estrangement felt by the mixedblood in *Cogewea*. Somewhat problematic in its editing, *Cogewea* reflects the bittersweet, romantic atmosphere that surrounds the Indian in much American literature. That romantic atmosphere begins to disappear from the Indian novel in the 1930s with the appearance of fiction by Mathews and McNickle. Writing of the nightmare time of new oil money and dissolution for the Osage, Mathews permeates his novel, *Sundown*, with a feeling of naturalistic despair as the protagonist, Chal Windzer, slips into the deracinated no-Indian's-land between Osage and white worlds. In spite of subtle invocation of sacred geography and patterns out of the oral tradition, both of which hint at continuity and survival, McNickle, like Mathews, reflects the grimness of the Hemingway era of naturalism in his first novel, *The Surrounded*. Like Chal Windzer, McNickle's protagonist Archilde Leon never has a chance within a civilization bent on turning Indians into Europeans.

The next generation of Indian novelists begins with Momaday, the spiritual father of today's Native American writers. And in *House Made of Dawn*, Momaday picks up where Mathews and McNickle leave off. Abel, the protagonist of Momaday's novel, is as alienated and fragmented as either Chal Windzer or Archilde Leon. Returned from the trauma of a white-man's war, Abel is dislocated from his cultural roots. He cannot articulate his identity as an Indian. However, in this novel Momaday takes the next crucial step for Indian writers: he brings Abel full circle, back home to his Southwestern pueblo and a secure knowledge of who he is. For Chal and Archilde there is no coherent world to return to, but Abel has his grandfather and the ancient home of his people. Though like his predecessors he focuses upon the agony of the Indian seemingly trapped between worlds, with this circular journey toward identity Momaday establishes a new pattern that will continue to inform Native American novels up to the present time. With Momaday, American Indian fiction becomes a kind of vision quest, with the writing reflecting the journey of its author toward a rich self-recognition as Indian (in Momaday's case, as specifically Kiowa). Momaday's writing illustrates a process of becoming, and demonstrates Bakhtin's contention that "one's own discourse is gradually and slowly wrought out of others' words that have been acknowledged and assimilated."[52]

In his mixed-genre masterpiece, *The Way to Rainy Mountain*, Momaday illuminates brilliantly this process of self-articulation. James Welch reflects this new direction in *Winter in the Blood* (1974) when he allows his alienated protagonist a glimpse of the meaningful, ordered world of his ancestral Blackfeet and thus begins the healing process for his nameless narrator. In *The Death of Jim Loney* (1979),

Welch moves nearer the patterns of *Sundown* and *The Surrounded*, creating in Jim Loney a mixedblood trapped inexorably between identities and worlds. With a knowledge of his Indian heritage held tantalizingly just out of reach, Loney drifts toward his demise. With *Fools Crow* (1986), Welch completes his own act of recovery as he moves all the way back to the traditional Blackfoot world only glimpsed by the narrator of *Winter in the Blood*. In *Fools Crow*, Welch "re-members" his Blackfoot heritage and makes it whole and accessible. Simultaneously, though writing in English, Welch becomes the first author to grant privilege and authority to an Indian discourse by demanding that the reader adapt to, or assimilate, a Blackfoot world-view. Throughout the novel, the almost exlusively Blackfoot context as well as abundant literal translations of Blackfoot terms creates an unmistakable awareness of Indian language as what Bakhtin terms a "social language," or "a concrete socio-linguistic belief system that defines a distinct identity for itself. . . ." The result is, more obviously in *Fools Crow* than in any other novel by an Indian author, an unmistakable hybridization, or "a mixture of two social languages [Indian and Euroamerican English] within the limits of a single utterance, an encounter, within the arena of an utterance, between two different linguistic consciousnesses."[53] Thus *Fools Crow* becomes, in form as well as content, a powerfully political work, one that may herald a new confidence and new direction for Indian authors. In *The Indian Lawyer*, Welch's most recent novel (1990), the protagonist is a Native American caught up in the kind of sex-and-politics entanglement long familiar to soap-opera fans; here, though Indian elements permeate the novel, Welch's subject is primarily the common, domestic human drama rather than anything peculiarly "Indian."

Leslie Silko, in *Ceremony* (1977), writes again of a mixedblood protagonist lost between cultures and identities. However, in the character of Tayo, Silko turns the conventionally painful predicament of the mixedblood around, making the mixedblood a metaphor for the dynamic, syncretic, adaptive qualities of Indian cultures that will ensure survival. As she leads Tayo through a healing ceremony in mythic time, in a novel that becomes a ceremony for its reader, Silko makes it clear for the first time in American Indian literature that the mixedblood is a rich source of power and something to be celebrated rather than mourned. In *Darkness in Saint Louis Bearheart* (1978), Gerald Vizenor goes still further in his celebration of mixedbloods. Writing a postapocalyptic allegory, Vizenor challenges those who would insist upon static definitions of the concept "Indian" or of anything else.[54] With the wild, satiric humor of *Bearheart* and his more recent novels—*Griever* (1987) and *The Trickster of Liberty* (1988)—Vizenor rejects entirely the conventional posture of mourning for the hapless mixedblood trapped between worlds, identifying the mixedblood with the shape-shifting visage of trickster, who requires that we reexamine, moment by moment, all definition and discourse.

Paula Gunn Allen, in *The Woman Who Owned the Shadows* (1983), and Janet Campbell Hale, in *The Jailing of Cecelia Capture* (1985), introduce the first novels since Mourning Dove's *Cogewea* to be both by and about American Indian women. Both of these novels feature mixedbloods at odds with surroundings and self, and both allow their protagonists to put the pieces of their identities back together through discoveries—in very different manner and degree—of their Indian selves. Louise Erdrich adds to this emerging body of fiction by Native American women with *Love Medicine* (1984), *The Beet Queen* (1986), and *Tracks* (1988), novels that move easily within the marginal zones where fullbloods, mixedbloods, and non-Indians meet and merge. With wry humor and an emphasis upon discontinuous and multiple narratives, Erdrich creates a fiction that is more familiar to non-Indian readers and critics than is much of the fiction of other Native American writers. Collectively, these first three books of a planned quartet constitute an ordering or putting together of a contemporary Chippewa identity. *Love Medicine*, with its numerous narrators and almost inextricably confused genealogies, bares the contemporary reservation world, where the rules of politics and survival seem to change daily. At the center of the novel is Lipsha Morrissey, the character circling gradually toward self-knowledge—knowledge that will come in the form of a traditional Chippewa trickster, Nanapush. In *The Beet Queen*, Erdrich shifts her focus to a small Dakota town inhabited primarily by Anglo-Americans, a place where the reservation is merely some kind of mute outback and Indians just another thread in the very bare fabric of society. *Tracks*, on the other hand, moves back in time to the generation preceding *Love Medicine* and *The Beet Queen* to show, primarily through the narration of another Nanapush-trickster, how the world of the two later novels came to be. In these novels, Erdrich goes beyond the long-established pattern of making cultural conflict and mixedblood angst the thematic center. Instead, she writes of the more universal trials of characters who just happen to be Indian or Indian-and-white, setting the multiple minidramas against a recognizable Indian world.

Erdrich's husband and collaborator, Michael Dorris, follows a similar path in his first novel, *A Yellow Raft in Blue Water* (1987), using multiple narrators to triangulate in on the mixedblood identity of Rayona, a half-African American, half-Indian girl. Anna Walters opens up still a new region for Native American fiction with her 1988 novel, *Ghost Singer*, a book that weaves Navajo history and mythology into a story of "ghosts" and anthropological desecration. Walters picks up a thread from D'Arcy McNickle's posthumous 1976 novel, *Wind from an Enemy Sky*, and makes the violation of Indian "artifacts" central to her plot. She illustrates powerfully James Clifford's contention that "collecting—at least in the West, where time is generally thought to be linear and irreversible— implies a rescue of phenomena from inevitable historical decay or loss."[55] Simultaneously, Walters introduces a story of a Navajo woman's search for her identity, embedding that story in a grimmer tale of Navajo enslavement and mutilation. Though other Indian writers have dealt with the subject, Walters is the first novelist since McNickle to make the highly controversial appropriation of American Indian remains a central theme.[56] Most recently, Linda Hogan has taken up the thread of Mathews's Osage material in *Mean Spirit* (1990), writing of the dangerous times of oil money and murder among the Osage, while Tom King, in *Medicine River*, has shifted the ground of the Indian novel across the "medicine line" into Canada in a complex and very funny tale of mixedbloods and mixed lives.

American Indian novelists are revising fundamentally the long-cherished, static view of Indian lives and cultures (or noncultures) held by people around the world. Of Cooper's nineteenth-century fiction, Roy Harvey Pearce declared, "The interest is not in the Indian as Indian, but in the Indian as a vehicle for understanding the white man, in the savage defined in terms of the ideas and needs of civilized life." The same words might apply to most literature about Indians by non-Indian authors. In Native American fiction, for the first time, the interest is always and intensely in the Indian defined in terms of Indian ideas and needs as those have evolved into the late twentieth century. In contemporary literature, and, I would argue, the novel in particular, Native American writers are producing what Pearce longs for in his postscript to *Savagism and Civilization*: "a study of the Indian image of himself, a study of the idea of Civilization as it at once has been introjected into the Indian psyche and helped to shape it."[57]

The cardboard cliché that has trod stealthily through American literature from its inception has been replaced by Indian characters with the complexity, depth, and drama of characters we have been taught to think of as "real"—a distinction reserved usually for nonethnic characters in fiction. The "zone of consciousness," as Hugh Kenner might phrase it, or, to use Bakhtin's term, the *character zone*, is an Indian one, where the privileged utterance is refreshingly "other" for the non-Indian reader. The stoic, humorless, pancake-flat Indian of fiction and film has given way to a gallery of characters who can laugh at themselves and others, who are fully capable of cowardice as well as heroism, and whose lives can be every bit as tangled and messy as the worst scenario dreamed up by a John Updike or Eudora Welty. And, perhaps most significant, American Indian novelists have introduced to the world a new and ancient mythology. Just as the major figures of modernism—T. S. Eliot, Ezra Pound, et al.—demanded that readers know Greek and Roman mythology and the literary history of their western culture, Indian writers today have come to expect, even demand, that readers learn something about the mythology and literary (oral) history of Native Americans. Dell Hymes, writing about traditional Native American literatures, has expressed this point neatly, saying, "As with Beowulf and The Tale of Genji, the material requires some understanding of a way of life."[58]

The wealth to be drawn from an understanding of *Ceremony*, *Bearheart*, or *Fools Crow* will remain always just out of reach to anyone who does not take the trouble to learn something about Navajo, Pueblo, Chippewa, or Blackfoot mythology and culture. And just as Eliot—looking forthrightly toward Europe—attempted to piece together the cultural and mythological resources needed in a time of deracination and despair, Native American writers are offering a way of looking at the world that is new to Western culture. It is a holistic, ecological perspective, one that places essential value upon the totality of existence, making humanity equal to all elements but superior to none and giving humankind crucial responsibility for the care of the world we inhabit. Vine Deloria, Jr., has stated, "In seeking the religious reality behind the American Indian tribal existence, Americans are in fact attempting to come to grips with the land that produced the Indian tribal cultures and their vision of community."[59] Simply put, as the world begins at last to confront the increasingly unavoidable fact of ecological disaster, the Native American world view comes to make more and more sense.

In addition to some basic knowledge of the tribal histories and mythologies of the Indian cultures at the heart of these novels, readers should be aware of crucial moments in Native American history of the last two centuries. Such moments, or historical facts, figure prominently in writing by Indian authors and inform the actions and responses of characters within the works I will discuss in this study.

One of these disastrous moments for Native Americans was the Indian Removal Act of 1830, which stipulated that the tribes of the Southeast and what was then called the Old Northwest be moved to the wilderness west of the Mississippi River. When the Cherokee tribe, trying to avoid the loss of ancestral homelands, took its case for self-government to the U.S. Supreme Court under Chief Justice John Marshall and won the case, President Andrew Jackson's response was, "John Marshall has made his decision; let him enforce it." The Cherokees, along with the Choctaws, Chickasaws, Creeks, Seminoles, and other tribes were forced to relocate, a trauma including months in concentration camps and finally the long march of the Cherokee people that resulted in thousands of deaths and came to be called the "Trail of Tears."

A second historical catastrophe for the American Indian came with the General Allotment Act (Dawes Act) of 1887, an act designed to end traditional ways of life for Indian tribes by breaking communal tribal lands into individual allotments of 160 acres for each family head, 80 acres to single persons over eighteen and orphans under that age, and 40 acres to each tribal member under eighteen. Indians who accepted allotment or agreed to adopt "the habits of civilized life" were granted citizenship, something most native Americans would not enjoy until 1924. A key provision of the Dawes Act allowed the federal government to purchase "surplus" Indian lands—what was left over after all eligible individuals received their allotted shares. The major effect of allotment was to take land away from Indians so effectively that in the forty-five years following the Dawes Act's passage 90 million acres passed from Indian ownership.

Still another major trauma for Indian tribes in their relations with the federal government came in the form of the House Concurrent Resolution 108. Passed in 1953, this resolution stipulated that the policy of Congress was the unilateral termination of the trustee relationship between the federal government and Indian tribes. The goal was to solve the centuries-old "Indian problem" by terminating tribes and thus forcing Indians to join the American mainstream. The result was catastrophic for a number of tribes that were thus "terminated," and the pressures brought to bear by the policy did not abate until the Kennedy administration in the sixties.

Other federal actions, such as the Indian Reorganization Act of 1934, have continued to significantly affect Indian tribes up to the present. The most profound changes reflected in novels by Indian authors, however, have come about because of the movement of Indian people from rural reservations into urban cities. Spurred first by the heavy enlistment of Indian men in both world wars, this movement received greater momentum through the government's relocation program of the 1950s. With twenty-five thousand American Indians enlisting in World War II, the Indian veteran became a common sight in urban Indian gatherings and back on the reservations. Suffering the same kinds of trauma experienced by all soldiers at war, the Indian veterans had the added pains of discrimination and, more crucially, the eventual return to an Indian world where identity had been difficult for a long time. The results are seen in such characters as Abel in *House Made of Dawn*, Tayo and the other veterans in *Ceremony*, and Russell in *The Beet Queen*. Following the displacement initiated by the world wars, the relocation program—designed to move Indians from poor reservations to jobs and greater prosperity in the cities—helped to create a generation of displaced urban Indians, people like Benally in Momaday's *House Made of Dawn*.[60]

All constructions must have boundaries—especially books, given publishers' understandable concern with textual dimensions. The result of such parameter-drawing is my reluctant exclusion from this study of a number of significant works. Among these are Paula Gunn Allen's *The Woman Who Owned the Shadows*, Janet Campbell Hale's *The Jailing of Cecelia Capture*, Tom King's *Medicine River*, and Anna Lee Walters' *Ghost Singer*—each of which represents a powerful, original voice in Native American fiction. Some works, such as Hogan's *Mean Spirit*, Welch's *The Indian Lawyer*, Vizenor's *The Heirs of Columbus*, and Erdrich and Dorris's *The Crown of Columbus*, simply appeared in print too late to be included. In selecting as I have, my goal has been to include works that serve to illustrate the beginnings and major evolutions in what I call the Native American Indian novel. The reader will find a complete list of novels by Native American writers in my bibliography at the end of this volume.

2

Origin Mists

John Rollin Ridge's Masquerade and Mourning Dove's Mixedbloods

◆

John Rollin Ridge

John Rollin Ridge, the first American Indian to publish a novel, arrived in California in 1850, a mixedblood Cherokee fleeing the turmoil set loose by the injustices of the Removal Act. If the "Indian Territory" that would become Oklahoma was a displaced setting wrought out of violence and confusion, however, the gold-fevered place to which Ridge fled was no promised land for Native Americans. The same year that Ridge arrived in California—a new state with an already well established history of genocide against Indians—California's governor, Peter H. Burnett, announced what amounted to a war of extermination against California's native population.[1] In the midst of this intense Indian-hating (exemplified by the bitter racism against "Digger" Indians in Mark Twain's *Roughing It*), in 1854 the half-Cherokee Ridge published *The Life and Adventures of Joaquin Murieta, the Celebrated California Bandit*, a wild and bloody fiction purporting to be the biography of a notorious Mexican American bandit.

In this, his only novel, Ridge transforms himself and his bitterness against the oppression and displacement of Indians, becoming a haunted shapeshifter writing between the lines. The result is a deeply encoded work filled with dialogic tension, a subversive narrative in which the surface plot rides over the subtext like a palimpsest. It is a novel that stands as fascinating testimony to the conflicts and tensions within the mixedblood author, who moves easily inside the dominant white culture but cannot forget or forgive the denigration by that culture of his indigenous self. It is also a work that marks the thinly camouflaged beginning of a long campaign by Native American writers to wrench a new genre—the novel—free from the hegemony of the dominant and (to Native Americans especially) destructive culture of European America. Ridge's *Joaquin Murieta* is a disguised act of appropriation, an aggressive and subversive masquerade.

In considering Ridge's novel, the first question that arises is why an author who experienced first-hand some of the most painful oppression of Native American people in the nineteenth century should have chosen to write about a Mexican American bandit in California, a subject that seems so distant from American Indian concerns. The most obvious answer to this question is, of course, that Ridge's choice was determined by the literary marketplace: like many authors he hoped to make money quickly from a sensational potboiler. With the Gold Rush and the completion of America's transcontinental march had come a vivid interest in the far West, the frontier. Ridge's acute judgment of his audience's "apperceptive background" would have led him to expect a profitable response to the romantic tragedy of a colorful "Californio." It is also significant, however, that in the western United States at midnineteenth century, American Indians had not yet taken their stylized place in the epic drama of extinction favored in the East. There were too many actual Indians living very visible lives in California in 1854, and their removal—primarily by disease, but often through simple slaughter—was a messy and unromantic business. As the terminus for the metanarrative that provided a context for domination of the continent, California was too close to the ugly underbelly of the millenarian enterprise to find the central victim of that enterprise very charming. Ridge, a successful journalist, would certainly have recognized the poor marketabililty of Indian outrage in the West, and, like Native Americans and other marginalized authors writing today, he would also have recognized the necessity for writing the kind of literature that would be acceptable and publishable. To be published, he would have to mimic the discourse of the privileged center. By writing about the fictionalized Joaquin Murieta, however, Ridge could have it both ways: he could write his romantic potboiler in the language of monocentric, Euramerican consciousness while simultaneously including a not-very-veiled protest against America's treatment of Native American people.

Ridge attempts his masquerade with a straight face. "The author," declares Ridge in his "Editor's Preface" to *Joaquin Murieta*, "in presenting this book to the public, is aware that its chief merit consists in the reliability of the ground-work upon which it stands and not in the beauty of its composition." According to Ridge, "In the main, it will be found to be strictly true."[2] In spite of this disingenuous preface, the publisher of Ridge's novel cleverly alerts readers to the narrative doubling in *Joaquin Murieta*, attempting to ensure that the epic tragedy of the American Indian would loom portentously behind the surface text. "The following production," Ridge's publisher wrote in a "Publisher's Preface," "aside from its intrinsic merit, will, no doubt, be read with increased interest when it is known that the author is a 'Cherokee Indian,' born in the woods—reared in the midst of the wildest scenery—and familiar with all that is thrilling, fearful, and tragical in a forest-life" (2). Less dramatically, Ridge's publisher ends his preface with the suggestion that "the perusal of this work will give those who are disposed to be curious an opportunity to estimate the character of Indian talent. The aboriginal race has produced great warriors, and powerful orators, but literary men—only a few" (3).

Despite his publisher's appeal to the reader's gothic sensibility, Ridge, who published his work as "Yellow Bird," the name under which he had also contributed a stream of poems and sketches to northern California newspapers, had not exactly been "born in the woods." Born in 1827, the grandson of the prominent and wealthy Cherokee leader Major Ridge, John Rollin Ridge had spent his first eight years in extremely privileged surroundings, in a house which, according to a visitor, swarmed with seventeen servants.[3] If, as Bakhtin suggests, "the ideological becoming of a human being is the process of selectively assimilating the words of others," John Rollin Ridge had ample opportunity—rather rare for Native Americans at the time—to thoroughly assimilate the privileged discourse of Euramerica. In this process of "ideological becoming," the "other" discourse, writes Bakhtin, "strives . . . to determine the very basis of our behavior; it performs here as *authoritative discourse*, and an *internally persuasive discourse*."[4] On one hand, as his publisher observes, John Rollin Ridge writes in language assimilated from the authoritative discourse of privileged "literary" America; on the other hand, the internally persuasive discourse of the oppressed and marginalized minority continually subverts the authority of the dominant discourse. As a result, like the traditional Native American trickster, the author of *Joaquin Murieta* gives ample evidence of being divided within and against himself; he embodies cultural fragmentation. In this light, Ridge's *Joaquin Murieta* can be seen as intensely dialogic, a hybridized narrative within which the author is in dialogue with himself, within which two distinct linguistic consciousnesses, two kinds of discourse, coexist in a "dialogically agitated and tension-filled environment."[5]

To understand the tensions underlying Ridge's prose, some history is required. John Ridge, the author's father, had been sent north to the Cornwall Indian School in Connecticut for his education, there he met and married Sarah Northrup, the daughter of the school's white principal. Returning to Georgia, where John Rollin Ridge was born in 1827, John Ridge set his wife up in the style becoming a well-to-do southerner. As is common knowledge today, the prosperity and large landholdings of the so-called Five Civilized Tribes, the Cherokee and Choctaw in particular, led to conflict with whites who wanted what the Indians possessed. In 1830, Congress bowed to this pressure by passing the Indian Removal Act ordering the removal of the tribes to "Indian Territory" in the west, most of what would become Oklahoma.

In the face of increasing hostility and violence from whites, Major Ridge declared that resistance to removal was futile, a stance that put him into conflict with Cherokee leader John Ross as well as the largest portion of the Cherokee tribe. In 1835, the Ridges, their cousin Elias Boudinot (a successful journalist), and a few other prominent Cherokees signed the New Echota Treaty agreeing to the removal as the only hope for the tribe. In signing, the Ridges and others defied a tribal law making it a capital offence for any Cherokee to enter into a treaty with the United States—a law Major Ridge himself had drawn up in 1829.

Despite the opposition of the majority faction under John Ross, the largest portion of the Cherokee population was moved into stockades and concentration camps and then force-marched to Oklahoma, with as many as four thousand deaths resulting from the move. Meanwhile, a number of families of means, such as the Ridges—the core of what came to be known as the Treaty Party—had sold their Georgia holdings and moved comfortably to the Indian Territory ahead of the mass exodus, settling on choice lands and setting themselves up in livestock, farming, and merchandising businesses in the new country.

As a result of the conflict between the Ridge and Ross followers, on June 22, 1839, twelve-year-old John Rollin Ridge found himself watching as a group belonging to the antitreaty faction rode up to the family home and stabbed his father to death in the front yard. The decree of death for signers of the New Echota Treaty had been enforced. Later that night the family learned that Major Ridge and Elias Boudinot had also been murdered.[6] Thus, by the time he was twelve years old the future author had been witness to the federal government's theft—against the ruling of the U.S. Supreme Court and by military force—of his tribe's ancestral homeland and his people's brutal removal to what was considered a worthless region. He had seen his father murdered by a political faction born from that removal and had learned of the simultaneous murders of his grandfather and cousin.

Of the murder of John Rollin Ridge's father, Franklin Walker wrote in the noble-savage tones common to literature about American Indians: "The boy learned that the avenging spirit of a noble line of savages was bequeathed to him that night. The deed darkened his mind with an eternal shadow; retribution for that deed remained his chief purpose in life." Joseph Henry Jackson, in his introduction to the 1955 reprint of Ridge's novel, suggests similarly that "ideas of violence, sudden death, and—more important—long-cherished revenge, might well enough have been planted in an impressionable boy's mind by such events" (xiii). Though it is tempting to see the familiar "invention" of the gothic Indian in such descriptions, Ridge apparently did nurture thoughts of revenge, writing from his New England college to a famous cousin, Stand Watie, to request "an article I wish extremely that you would get for me—a Bowie knife." Before he turned twenty, Ridge had returned from his mother's home in Fayetteville, Arkansas, to the Indian Territory and, in a dispute, had killed Judge D. Kell, one of the rival faction. Subsequently, in 1850, Ridge traced the route of what had already become an American archetype: he fled westward to California, arriving at the height of the gold rush and at the birth of a California literary scene energized by such figures as Samuel Clemens and Brett Harte.[7]

While physical and cultural displacement has been the common experience for American Indians since the sixteenth century, for Ridge's Cherokees and the other tribes "removed" to the territory, displacement was particularly abrupt and traumatic, an experience giving rise to an acute version of what has been called a "postcolonial crisis of identity": "the concern with the development or recovery of an effective identifying relationship between self and place."[8]

When Ridge was forced to remove himself yet again from Cherokee culture, he placed himself still more fully within a tense, liminal position of suspension between dialectically opposed indigenous (Indian) and colonial (Euramerican) realities. It is this intense liminality that illuminates *Joaquin Murieta's* transparent text.

Ridge's Joaquin Murieta arose, apparently, out of the specters of several minor California bandits named Joaquin, bearing the various surnames of Murieta, O'Comorenia, Valenzuela, Bottelier, and Carillo, all of whom Ridge collapses into two Joaquins, these two being the brilliant bandit leader Murieta and his lieutenant Valenzuela (xxi). Ridge selected one of the Joaquins—Murieta—and from scraps of information created a legend.

Again and again, throughout his novel Ridge makes it clear that Joaquin Murieta has been driven to his bloody outlaw life because of mistreatment by Anglo-Americans. As a precipitating factor, Ridge notes the Foreign Miners' Tax Law, an 1850 statute by the California legislature which made it virtually impossible for Latin Americans to mine in the state. Having been beaten and tied up and forced to watch while his young wife was raped, at age eighteen Murieta is driven from his mining claim. "They left him," Ridge writes of the scene, "but the soul of the young man was from that moment darkened. It was the first injury he had ever received at the hands of the Americans, whom he had always respected, and it wrung him to the soul as a deeper and deadlier wrong from that very circumstance" (10).

Despite his darkened soul, Murieta swallows his rage and, with the patience of Job, settles with his beautiful Sonoran wife on a small farm in a Sierra Nevada valley. But like the agrarian Cherokees who had obligingly made room for Europeans and tolerated generations of abuse in the Southeast, Joaquin is finally driven from his homestead by whites who want the "fertile tract of land." Twice humiliated and forced out by the more powerful whites, Murieta still pursues a peaceful life, becoming a professional monte dealer in "Murphy's Diggings" in the gold fields, where "he was considered by all the very beau ideal of a gambler and the prince of clever fellows" (12). Almost immediately, however, he is falsely charged with complicity in horse-stealing and is flogged while his half-brother, wrongly accused of stealing the animal, is hanged "without judge or jury." "It was then," writes the author, "that the character of Joaquin changed, suddenly and irrevocably. Wanton cruelty and the tyranny of prejudice had reached their climax. . . . Then it was that he declared to a friend that he would live henceforth for revenge and that his path should be marked with blood" (12).

In spite of the superhuman carnage the noble Joaquin and his followers spill across the state, Ridge reminds us repeatedly that the bandits' actions are no more than a response to the "tyranny of prejudice" in Mexican Americans' treatment by racist whites, a race Murieta, like many American Indians, had begun by admiring and welcoming. Ultimately, Ridge explains, the young bandit would die "not as a mere outlaw, committing petty depredations and robberies, but as a *hero* who has revenged his country's wrongs and washed out her disgrace in the blood of her enemies" (80). And finally, when his splendid bandit dies at age twenty-two, the age at which Ridge himself had become a fugitive, Ridge declares that

> in the few years which were allowed him, he displayed qualities of mind and heart which marked him as an extraordinary man, and leaving his name impressed upon the early history of this State. He also leaves behind him the important lesson that there is nothing so dangerous in its consequences as *injustice to individuals*—whether it arise from prejudice of color or from any other source; that a wrong done to one man is a wrong to society and to the world. (158, emphasis is Ridge's)

The authorial voice here is that of the dime-novel romance, a discourse arising from the Eurocentric conflation of heroic quest and manifest destiny, and one that Ridge appropriates to make it "bear the burden" of his subtext. Ridge's Joaquin belongs to that gothic tradition described by Michel Foucault: "the character of the black, cursed hero devoted to making the world expiate the evil done to him."[9] It does not require a leap of imagination to conclude that Ridge, having seen his people robbed of their land and heritage and having had his father, grandfather and cousin murdered as a result, is acting out his often-sworn desire for revenge in the form of the invented bandit. At the same time, that the increasingly successful author would choose this heavily veiled medium for protest against America's treatment of Indians is not surprising. After all, with his thick black beard and urbane dress, Ridge passed easily as a Euramerican, and, more importantly, with his education and talents he was distinguishing himself amongst his "white" peers and seeing his name appearing repeatedly in association with those of the leading literati of San Francisco. Ridge, like many mixedbloods who "pass" and who have succeeded within the parameters of the dominant culture, must have felt the conflict deeply.

More direct treatment of Indians in the novel underscores the complexity of the mixedblood author's feelings, as when Ridge introduces the "half-breeds and others at the Cherokee House" in a settlement called Cherokee Flat. Gold fever had sent a large number of Cherokees to the mountains of California. Even the prominent leader John Ross had set himself up as a dry-goods dealer proposing to sell supplies to his fellow Cherokees headed for the gold fields.[10] In Ridge's novel, these mixedbloods eagerly and energetically assist the whites in capturing and hanging various unlucky Mexicans with little evidence of the captives' guilt. And when Ridge comes to mention the native inhabitants of California, he easily embraces the nineteenth century's racist stereotypes that reduced the many Indian cultures in California to the status of "Diggers." After referring to California Indians as "naked savages" and "ignorant Indians," Ridge describes "old Sapatarra," chief of the Tejon Nation, "seated upon his haunches in all the grandeur of 'naked majesty,' enjoying a very luxurious repast of roasted acorns and dried angle-worms." Ridge continues: "His swarthy subjects were scattered in various directions around him, engaged for the most part in the very arduous task of doing nothing. The little, smoky-looking children were sporting, like a black species of water-fowl" (36). These Indians, he declares, always act "with great skill and caution; which last, by the way, is a quality that particularly distinguishes California Indians, amounting to so extreme a degree that it might safely be called cowardice" (39). Finally, Ridge sums up this particular tribe as the "poor, miserable, cowardly Tejons."

While the well-educated Ridge, grandson of a tribal leader and member of the highly cultured and militantly proud Cherokee Nation, might easily look down on the oppressed and destitute California Indians, the absence of any sense of irony in his descriptions of the Tejons or "Diggers" suggests that Ridge thought primarily and perhaps almost exclusively of his own people when he addressed the concern of racial injustice through the example of Joaquin Murieta. Ridge paradoxically both embraces the racist values of his fellow Californians and protests social and racial injustice at the same time. He is divided against himself, an internal conflict further suggested in the fact that although there can be no doubt that Ridge thought California Indians to be vastly inferior to the Cherokee and other tribes to the east, he did at times defend the "Diggers" in print against Californians' depredations.[11]

The Life and Adventures of Joaquin Murieta is at times abominably written, mimicking the romantic horrors in prose common to much nineteenth-century fiction. Nonetheless, Ridge's book marks an important moment in the development of American Indian fiction. This first novel by an Indian author demonstrates in fascinating fashion the tension arising from conflicting identities that would emerge as the central theme in virtually every novel by a Native American author to follow. Writing to his Cherokee cousin, Stand Watie, Ridge could identify himself as Indian and swear vengence and redemption for his Cherokee relatives. When he turned to face his more privileged audience, however, Ridge was forced to veil his Indianness, to inscribe his identity within a context of sublimation and subterfuge. Following in Ridge's wake, American Indian authors would face again and again the dilemma of audience and identity, being forced to discover ways to both mimic and appropriate the language of the center and make it express a different reality, bear a different burden. Nearly a hundred years would pass before a novel written by a Native American could address the issues of injustice and genocide more directly, and even more time would pass before a work by an author recognizably Indian would gain critical acceptance. And in the novels of later generations of Indian writers, the character of the mixedblood behind the mask—Ridge himself—would move into the novel as protagonist and central concern.[12] Out of the explosion of blood in Ridge's psychodrama of Mexican banditry and revolution would emerge a subgenre in American literature: the American Indian novel with its unceasing investigation of cultural dialectics, competing discourses, fractured identities, and historical genocide.

Mourning Dove

The publication of *Cogewea, the Half-Blood: A Depiction of the Great Montana Cattle Range* in 1927 brought into print the third novel by an American Indian author and the first by an American Indian woman.[13] With its introduction of Cogewea as "a 'breed'!—the socially ostracized of two races," Mourning Dove's novel announced explicitly what was to become the dominant theme in novels by Indian authors: the dilemma of the mixedblood, the liminal "breed" seemingly trapped between Indian and white worlds. And with its focus upon Cogewea, Mourning Dove's work would remain the only novel by an Indian woman to feature a female protagonist until Paula Gunn Allen published *The Woman Who Owned the Shadows* more than half a century later. Looking at *Cogewea* from a feminist perspective, Rayna Green has suggested that while the novel is no "feminist tract and flawed as a 'Western,' this book nevertheless deserves a feminist and literary audience, certainly one interested in some very different perceptions about Indians, Native women, the West, and half-breeds."[14]

Mourning Dove, born according to her own report in a canoe while her mother was crossing the Kootenay River in Idaho, was named Christine Quintasket, a name she later changed to Christal and then, as her pen name, Mourning Dove. Joseph Quintasket, Mourning Dove's father, was an orphan from the Nicola tribe, while her mother, Lucy, was a member of an important family of the Colville tribe in eastern Washington. As a child, Mourning Dove was taught to read by a white orphan her father had brought home to live with the family—a fascinating inversion of the standard practice of ensuring cultural hegemony by "kidnapping" Indian children and placing them in boarding schools. Mourning Dove's formal schooling consisted of eight fragmentary years at various mission schools and two years of clerical training at Calgary College. At Goodwin Catholic Mission, in 1894, the young Okanogan girl shared the common Native American experience of being punished for speaking "Indian" instead of English, and by age fourteen, according to an interview with a Washington newspaper, she had advanced only as far as the third grade in the Colville public school.[15]

"There are two things that I am most grateful for in my life," Mourning Dove announced in the autobiography left unpublished at her death. "The first is that I was born a descendant of the genuine Americans, the Indians; and second, that my birth happened in the year 1888." Of her ancestry, Mourning Dove writes in the autobiography: "Father's mother was a Nicola Indian, with a strain of Okanogan in her family. His father was a white man, a Scot named Andrew, who, at one time, was in the employ of the Hudson's Bay Company." In his introduction to this autobiography, editor Jay Miller complicates this simple picture of Mourning Dove's mixedblood status, suggesting that Mourning Dove may have invented this ancestral miscegenation in order to make more convincing the heteroglossia of her voice: "Her appeal to a white ancestry, denied by her family and the tribal census, indicates how strongly she saw herself as a mediator between white and red. It was an appeal that was both emotional and melodramatic." Miller adds,

"Mourning Dove said [her father's] father was a Scot, but his other children deny this. Evidently, Christine provided a white ancestor to appeal to her readership."[16]

Mourning Dove shows subtle understanding of the dialogic that would come to be called heteroglossia in her insistence upon mixedblood status and in her attempt, at the same time, to establish her position within a privileged, authoritative discourse as Indian:[17] "I speak the Indian language of my own tribe better than I do the adopted lingo of the English-Americans," she declares in her autobiography, adding that, because of her traditional upbringing within the Colville Confederated Tribes of eastern Washington, "I had the opportunity to learn the legends, religion, customs, and theories of my people thoroughly." In her novel, Mourning Dove creates a female protagonist firmly in control of a language that is at the same time liminal, emerging from the thresholds of both Indian and white worlds, and forceful.

In 1909 Mourning Dove married Hector McLeod, a member of the Flathead tribe in Montana, and moved with McLeod to Polson at the tip of Flathead Lake, where in 1908 Mourning Dove had witnessed the roundup of the last free-ranging buffalo, the Michel Pablo herd—the same roundup watched by the young D'Arcy McNickle, an adopted member of her husband's tribe (who would write about the fenced buffalo in *The Surrounded*). Within four years of the bison roundup, Christine Quintasket was separated from McLeod and living in Portland, Oregon, where she began to write the first draft of *Cogewea* in pencil and where she assumed the pen name of Morning Dove, or Hu-mi-shu-ma in Okanogan, a name she later changed to Mourning Dove. By 1921 she had divorced McLeod and married Fred Galler, a mixedblood Colville with whom she worked as a fruit tramp, following the apple and hop harvests around the Northwest and working on her novel at night in a tent, often after ten hours of labor.

In 1914, two years after she had begun her novel, Mourning Dove met Lucullus Virgil McWhorter at a Walla Walla, Washington Frontier Days celebration and confided in him her desire to collect and publish the history of her people. Soon, McWhorter, a writer and editor with a commitment to Indian materials, was writing to Mourning Dove to urge her to record tribal tales:

Why should this young woman hesitate . . . I see in her vast possibilities. I see a future of renown; a name that will live through the ages, if only she will decide to take the right-hand trail. Helping hands are held out to her, and the trail will not prove so rough as it appears. Her race-blood will be of actual benefit to her in this work. It is a duty she owes to her poor people, whose only history has been written by the destroyers of her race.[18]

Ultimately, McWhorter would become the editor of *Cogewea*, the "Sho-pow-tan" through whom, according to the novel's title page, the book is "Given" and the contributor of notes and a biographical sketch. McWhorter would add cloyingly romantic epigraphs (from "Hiawatha" among other works) to each chapter and, according to critic Dexter Fisher, insert "into the narrative innumerable didactic passages about the injustices suffered by Indians at the hands of government agencies, as well as historical facts about other tribes that are hardly relevant to the story" (xiv).

Eleven years after the completed collaboration between Mourning Dove and McWhorter, and fifteen years after she began the work, *Cogewea* was published. Of the completed novel, Mourning Dove wrote somewhat poignantly to McWhorter: "I have just got through going over the book *Cogewea*, and am surprised at the changes that you made. I think they are fine, and you made a tasty dressing like a cook would do with a fine meal. . . . I felt like it was some one elses book and not mine at all. In fact the finishing touches are put there by you, and I have never seen it" (xv). In reading the novel, it is not difficult to discover the "tasty dressing" of inflated language, gratuitous anthropological and historical information, and allusions very likely added by McWhorter. Fisher suggests that "in a sense, Mourning Dove is herself the 'half-blood,' standing between an Indian world that seems to be rapidly disappearing and a white world that is either indifferent or bent on government control of Indians. She wants not only to save the heritage that is slipping away, but also to present her way of life in a manner that is intelligible and acceptable" (xxiv). Jay Miller concurs: "She saw herself as the voice of her people in the wilderness of continued misunderstanding, trying to bring the two races closer together."[19]

One of the most fascinating elements of Mourning Dove's novel is precisely this complex voice. Not only does Mourning Dove's utterance enter what Bakhtin termed a "dialogically agitated and tension-filled environment of alien words," but because of the recognizable presence in the novel of McWhorter's more privileged discourse, appealing as it does to the power of cultural hegemony with its high degree of literacy, Mourning Dove's voice exists for us within a text that is itself "entangled, shot through with shared

thoughts, points of view, alien value judgments and accents."[20]
Because, as Bakhtin writes, a "particular language in a novel is
always a particular way of viewing the world, one that strives
for social significance," the reader feels throughout *Cogewea* the
presence of a political disturbance permeating the text as the voices
of Mourning Dove and McWhorter struggle to be heard one over
the other—with Mourning Dove's easily winning out. On one level
the reader feels the internal persuasiveness of Mourning Dove's
depiction of a mixedblood reality, and on another level we respond
to the authority of McWhorter's liberal discourse as it demonstrates
a remarkable knowledge of literature, the Bible, world geography,
and diverse Native American cultures while appealing to the reader's sympathy for a displaced people. Mourning Dove's "Indian"
voice vanishes even in such uncomplicated lines as, "If the Malady
is deep seated, an abatement must not be expected in so short a
time. An absorption remedy of any nature is usually slow of results
and a persistent and potent application is oftimes necessary" (82–
83).

Cogewea is a halfblood, daughter of an Okanogan mother and a
white father. With her mother dead and her father having deserted
the family for the Alaskan gold rush, Cogewea and her sisters Julia
and Mary are raised by their Indian grandmother, the "Stemteemä,"
before going to live with Julia and her white husband on a Flathead
Reservation ranch in Montana. Of the missing father, Mourning
Dove writes: "During all the long years no word had come from the
silent North, and it was supposed that this father had succumbed to
death in the realms of storms and ghastly whiteness" (15). In the
mixedblood world of the novel—as it is in works by other marginalized writers such as Richard Wright and Ralph Ellison—whiteness
is a threat.

The ranch is a transitional world, suspended between Indian and
Euramerican realities, where the owner may be white but where
the cowboys are Indians, or "breeds," who are presented in wonderfully hybridized portraits. The halfblood hero of the novel and
patient suitor for Cogewea's hand is the strong, often-silent James
LaGrinder, epitome of the western hero who prefers shooting to
talking. Among the other cowboys are "Rodeo Jack," a blond quar-
terblood Texan "of uncertain qualities," and "Celluloid Bill," a half-
blood Cheyenne who "got his range sobriquet wearing a white
celluloid collar when he first came to the ranch" (36). So ubiquitous
do mixedbloods seem on the heterogeneously populated ranch that

Densmore, the white city slicker and villain of the novel, has serious problems identifying the world he has entered: "Where were these picturesque Indians that he was promised to meet? Instead, he had been lured into a nest of half bloods, whom he had always understood to be the inferior degenerates of two races" (48). The fact that the cowboys, in Indian fashion, engage in ceaseless verbal and physical pranks—often at Densmore's expense—makes the easterner still more suspicious of their authenticity. Where did the noble, stoic Indian go? the easterner seems to wonder.

Cogewea is recognizable as a typical romantic story of betrayed love, stoic loyalty, and sentiment—like *Joaquin Murieta* a narrative right out of the pulp-fiction tradition. It is also recognizable as an impressive attempt by a Native American writer to appropriate this vehicle and make it bear the burden of a different and peripheralized reality. And it is the first novel by an Indian writer to attempt to define the complex dilemma of the mixedblood: "Regarded with suspicion by the Indian; shunned by the Caucasian; where was there any place for the despised breed!" (17). In this attempt, the authorial voice is complicated even beyond the conflicting utterances of Mourning Dove–McWhorter by dialogism within utterances that might be identified most closely with Mourning Dove. Mourning Dove's novel introduces code switching and a system of complex hybridization. Speaking to a rattlesnake, for example, an animal feared and respected by Okanogans, Cogewea says, "Your 'medicine' is strong and my grandmother would not hurt you. But *I* am *not* my grandmother! I am not a full-blood—only a *breed*—a *sitkum* Injun and that breaks the charm of your magic with me. I do not fear you! Besides, I happen to know of the machinations of one of your progenitors in a certain garden several thousand years ago, where he deceived and made trouble for two of my ancestors" (26). Cogewea's speech here is a fascinating concatenation of appropriated *e*nglish and authoritative English, one the voice of the denigrated culture ("medicine," "*sitkum* Injun") and the other the voice of the privileged center.[21] As Cogewea's utterance, rich with ironic humor, plays across this wide range of what feels like a transcultural dialogue, the reader easily hears the conflict between internally and authoritatively persuasive discourse. This "dialogue" is emphasized in the conflation of Indian and white mythologies, underscoring Cogewea's unstable position between both cultures. This cultural conflict is sharpened when Cogewea refers to Columbus, telling James LaGrinder: "I may surprise you yet. . . . even if I am a 'squaw' as you call me. . . . I may use the pen! The wiseheads laughed at the theories of Columbus. . . . Columbus is now honored by all nations for the correctness of his ideas" (34). Cogewea ignores the fact that Columbus is not honored by the many nations of Native America. Cogewea's voice is that of the dominant Eurocentric culture. Though later in the novel she will muse bitterly upon the destruction introduced by the "discovery" of America, in this scene she demonstrates no consciousness of the portents to Native Americans of Columbus's historical and geographical accident.

Of mixedbloods, Mourning Dove writes: "The rising generation was educating, while the half-bloods, brought up more like the white children, enjoyed some business advantages over their full-blooded relations. But then, they were just a go-between people, shut within their own diminutive world. There seemed no place for them among either race" (41). And Cogewea muses, "Yes, we are between two fires, the Red and the White. Our Caucasian brothers criticize us as a shiftless class, while the Indians disown us as abandoning our own race. We are maligned and traduced as no one but we of the despised 'breeds' can know. If permitted, I would prefer living the white man's way to that of the reservation Indian, but he hampers me" (41). Even within Cogewea's mixedblood family there are divisions. Julia, the elder sister, married to a sympathetic and successful white rancher, approves of Cogewea's courtship by Densmore because the easterner is white, while Mary, the younger sister, correctly suspects the white man's motives because Cogewea is Indian. In a wry emphasis upon what James Clifford calls the "mixed, relational, and inventive" nature of ethnic identity, Mourning Dove describes Mary, who remains closest to traditional Indian values learned from the Stemteemä, as having eyes "of the deepest blue" and fair skin. In this extraordinarily subtle comment upon ethnic authenticity, Mourning Dove demonstrates a complex and sophisticated understanding that would not be matched in American Indian fiction until Leslie Marmon Silko's *Ceremony* a half century later. Similarly, as Rayna Green has suggested, in the figure of the Stemteemä, Mourning Dove introduces a figure who embodies the traditional grandmother we have come to expect in Indian fiction but who "becomes more than the wise old lady—she is an important female character rarely allowed to emerge in most works."[22]

In the novel's most blatant symbolism, Cogewea enters two

Fourth of July horse races, both the "Squaw" race and the "Ladies" race. Cogewea's decision to enter both competitions evolves out of her determination to define herself in both worlds and to control her own destiny—and it arises just as certainly out of her often humorous and determined sense of irony. As is to be expected, the mixedblood is refused entry into both races. "You have no right to be here," the Indian women tell her. "You are half-white! This race is for Indians and not for *breeds!*"

Mourning Dove even inserts a moment of literary self-consciousness when she causes Cogewea to read a novel about a halfblood "brave" in love with a white girl. Cogewea is disgusted and reflects "bitterly how her race had had the worst of every deal since the landing of the lordly European on their shores; how they had suffered as much from the pen as from the bayonet of conquest." Cogewea shows here a sophisticated understanding of the political power of language to determine conceptions of "truth" and "reality," of language as "the medium through which a hierarchical structure of power is perpetuated."[23] As she ponders the injustice of such fiction, the villain Densmore appears: "Cogewea was startled from her reverie by a shadow falling across her lap. The broad shoulders of Densmore barred the rays of the low hanging sun" (91–92). In this symbolic scene, the dishonest white suitor, who gives no other indication in the novel of having broad shoulders or being physically imposing, seems almost to rise out of the text she is reading. He comes between her and life, the sun, paradoxically darkening the sun with his whiteness and forming a stark image of the power of privileged discourse to dominate and displace the indigenous personality.

Ultimately Mourning Dove's romantic novel allows for the inevitable betrayal of the "breed" girl by the shallow easterner and her rescue and awakening to true love with the mixedblood hero Jim LaGrinder. She turns, thus, back toward the mixedblood Indian world, where a greater opportunity for coherence and self-knowledge exists. However, Cogewea's survival is assisted by her induction into the ranks of questers after the American dream when she learns that her long-vanished father has died and that she and her sisters have, through a flaw in his will, each inherited a quarter of a million dollars. And the novel concludes ambiguously with the prospect of a wealthy Cogewea and Jim living happily ever after, a matched pair of mixedbloods in the lap of luxury. While we may agree with Rayna Green that in the end Cogewea "gets everything she really wants, and some besides,"[24] it is also apparent that the true privileged discourse of Euramerica—that of commodification—has been appropriated to bring this story of perpherality to closure. Nonetheless, Mourning Dove accomplishes a great deal in this novel, not the least of which are the creation of an independent, forceful mixedblood woman and the illumination of the kind of teasing humor that permeates American Indian communities and is universally ignored in writing about Indians. Together with her complex treatment of identity within this "cowboys and Indians" world, these accomplishments underscore Mourning Dove's refusal to succumb to the stereotypes that have informed most writing about American Indians.

Mourning Dove's ambivalence about the future of Indian people, and the outcast mixedblood in particular, is registered again and again in this novel. At one point Cogewea thinks, "A few more generations at most, and the full-blooded Indian shall have followed the Buffalo" (139), while at another she refers to her people as "my vanishing race" (109). On the other hand, she prophesies, "The day will dawn when the desolate, exiled breed will come into his own; when our vaunting 'superior' will appreciate our worth" (95). With the conclusion, the dilemma of the mixedblood poised between red and white worlds remains unsolved. Very literally allowed a place in neither the Indian nor white races, Cogewea will marry Jim LaGrinder and produce children who will, like the parents, be halfbloods. The novel ends on a note of stasis, with nothing resolved, none of the many questions answered.

3

Maps of the Mind

John Joseph Mathews
and D'Arcy McNickle

◆

John Joseph Mathews

With the publication of *Sundown* in 1934, the mixedblood Osage writer John Joseph Mathews introduced the modern American Indian novel, laying out a pattern for novels by Indian writers that would be confirmed two years later when D'Arcy McNickle published *The Surrounded* (1936) and again and again during succeeding decades. Like *The Surrounded*, *Sundown* is the story of a mixedblood living both in and out of his tribal culture, and it is a nearly fatalistic tale that at a superficial glance seems to mesh neatly with the popular naturalism of the twenties and thirties. While Hemingway had chosen to emphasize at least an earthly continuum in his title for *The Sun Also Rises*, another novel of deracination and despair, at first glance Mathews would seem to focus starkly upon the other end of daylight, showing us the tragic results of the oil boom in Osage County—what had until only recently been the Osage Reservation.[1]

Mathews himself served as an unlikely model for his protagonist, Challenge Windzer. Like Chal, Mathews was born on the Osage Agency of mixedblood parents,[2] and like Chal, the author studied at the University of Oklahoma and went on to become a pilot during World War I. Like Chal, Mathews came of age amidst the oil boom that brought wealth and disaster to many Osage people, but unlike his character, Mathews graduated from the University of Oklahoma, served in France during the war, and later received degrees from both Oxford and the University of Geneva. Mathews, described by his publisher, Savoie Lottinville, as possessing "many of the qualities of the English gentleman blended with those of the gentleman Osage," may be in fact the most acculturated of all Indian novelists. After completing his degree in international relations at Geneva, where the League of Nations was in session, he toured France by motor bike and bummed around Europe. It was while on a big-game hunting trip in North Africa that, after encountering a wild group of Arab horsemen, he decided to return to his home and learn about his Osage relations.

With impressive tenacity and foresight, the Osage opposed the Dawes Severalty Act of 1887 (the General Allotment Act), which had such disastrous consequences for other tribes. According to Terry Wilson, "By steadfastly resisting a hasty application of the Dawes Act to its reservation, the tribe was able to protect the valuable mineral resources beneath the surface from individualization and to avert the loss of any of its territory through the expropriation of 'surplus' land by white settlers as had happened to Oklahoma tribes whose land was alloted earlier" so that when the Osage at last submitted to pressures for allotment in 1906 the tribe was able to keep its reservation holdings intact. Eventually, Osage County in Oklahoma retained the outline of the Osage Reservation boundaries. As an allotted member of the tribe, Mathews received 560 acres and a headright, and he came to take a deep interest in his heritage, writing about his people in *Wah'Kon-Tah: The Osage and the White Man's Road* (1932), in his autobiographical *Talking to the Moon* (1945), a kind of Osage *Walden*, and in *The Osages: Children of the Middle Waters* (1961). From 1934 through 1942 Mathews also served on the Osage Tribal Council.[3]

Sundown seems to offer a quintessential postcolonial scenario, as described by the authors of *The Empire Writes Back*: "A valid and active sense of self may have been eroded by *dislocation*, resulting from migration, the experience of enslavement. . . . Or it may have been destroyed by *cultural denigration*, the conscious and unconscious oppression of the indigenous personality and culture by a supposedly superior racial or cultural model." Like others in such a postcolonial drama, including nearly all Native Americans, Mathews's characters are beset by "a pervasive concern with . . . identity and authenticity."[4] Prior to the opening of *Sundown*, the Osage, like Ridge's Cherokees and many other tribes, had been forcibly relocated by the federal government. Their culture had been exposed to the denigrating pressures of missionaries, including schools, and disruptive Euramerican values. And with the discovery of rich oil fields on tribal lands, this process had been accelerated enormously. The Osage in Mathews's novel are finally overwhelmed by outsiders who (with their extreme sense of racial and cultural superiority) consciously and unconsciously destroy traditional values and attempt to displace the Indians yet further—through miscegenation, marriage, and simple murder in order to gain control of headrights and, thus, oil money.

Sundown begins with Chal Windzer's birth at a critical point of transition for the Osage Nation between old and new worlds. "The god of the great Osages was still dominant over the wild prairie and the blackjack hills when Challenge was born," writes Mathews in the novel's opening line. "He showed his anger in fantastic play of lightning and thunder that crashed and rolled among the hills; in the wind that came from the great tumbling clouds which appeared in the northwest and brought twilight and ominous milk-warm silence."[5] The ecosystemic world of the Osage is intact in this scene and can be comprehended mythically. From these first sentences to the final lines of the novel, associations with the natural world—the sacred geography of the Osage people—will serve as an index to Chal Windzer's character and well-being. During those moments when, for a brief time, he is immersed in nature, he will feel nearly whole and close to something instinctual and sustaining; when he is removed from intimate contact with the natural world, he will become ever more displaced and confused.

"On this birthnight," Mathews continues as the novel begins, "the red, dim light which shone from the narrow window of the room where his mother labored, seemed faint and half-hearted in the moonlight; faint as though it were a symbol of the new order, yet diffident in the vivid, full-blooded paganism of the old; afraid, yet steady and persistent, and the only light in the Agency on this tranquil, silver night of silence" (1–2). Associated with the sun, for the Osage the most powerful manifestation of the creator, the color red figures as a crucial link to the traditional Osage world in which the sun was honored in virtually every aspect of life. In this birth scene, the color seems to emanate from Chal's fullblood mother—the "only light in the Agency"—whose Indianness remains steadfast throughout the novel as a touchstone to unchanging and essential values. However, in its half-heartedness in conjunction with the sacred moonlight—also symbolic of the older, immutable Indian world—the red light underscores the tenuousness of even the mother's hold on traditional identity. Cast into this uncertain light at birth, Chal Windzer is born into the easily recognizable postcolonial and modernist position of deracination, alienation, and confusion.

Mathews's opening scene introduces the dialectic that will inform the novel's plot: the struggle between old and new—Indian and Euramerican—"orders." In keeping with this dialectic, the color red becomes sacred to Chal almost from birth, when he reaches out for the red dress of the Euramerican "har'd" girl. Red, Chal learns later, is the color of the Sun "who was Grandfather, and of Fire, who was Father, and of the Dawn, sacred to Wah'Kon-Tah" (13).

John Windzer, Chal's father, declares at his son's birth, "He shall be a challenge to the disinheritors of his people. We'll call him Challenge" (4). Ironically, however, Chal never overtly challenges the new order, attempting instead to mold himself according to the new, non-Indian values, which he accepts but never comprehends. This attitude he inherits from his mixedblood father, who sits at home reading "Childe Harold"—a canonized artifact of the privileged culture and a romantic narrative that reinforces the Euramerican's "epic" and thus entropic view of the vanishing, historic past. This *"triste tropiques"* myth of cultural ruin and decay dovetails neatly, and ironically, with the Euramericans' desire to brush the Osage aside while appropriating Osage oil and land. Chal's father, one of the rapidly growing population of politically influential mixedbloods amongst the Osage, is proud to be a descendant of British nobility in the form of Sir John Windzer, an artist who lived among the Osage, and he boasts that "if it hadn't been for the progressives on the council, they never would have been any allotment, if it was left up to the fullblood party" (45). With this declaration, Mathews is illuminating the bitter division between fullbloods and mixedbloods within the tribe, with the former generally struggling to retain traditional ways of life while the latter pushed increasingly for adoption of "civilized" values.

Serving as a pawn in the whites' maneuvers to control and rob the Osages, John Windzer actually facilitates the disfranchisement of the son he named Challenge. In the end, it is Mathews's depiction of Chal Windzer's descent toward ruin which challenges "the disinheritors of his people," a descent culminating when Chal swears to himself, "I wish I didn't have a drop of God damn' Indian blood in my veins" (160).

In a recurring pattern throughout the novel, Chal identifies with animals and the natural world. As a child he imagines himself consistently as animal: "a panther lying lazily in his den" or "a redtail hawk circling high in the blue of the sky" or "an indefinite animal in a snug den" or a coyote stalking the prairie. On an almost unconscious level, he remains aware of the older Indian world outside of his parents' comfortable house and the increasingly civilized town:

> And then sometimes, when he waked early in the morning, he could hear some mourner on the hill which bordered the creek, chanting the song of death, and always some inscrutable sorrow welled and flooded him; something that was not understandable and was mysterious, and seemed especially fitting for the dense dark hours just before dawn; the hours most fitted for that questing, that feeble attempt to understand. (44)

Chal's own unstated quest in this passage is for the impossible: an understanding of a world that has been made remote from him at birth. The song of death and the "inscrutable sorrow" are for the Osage world disappearing at astonishing speed in the course of Chal's life as oil money pours into what had been the reservation. This is the romantic posture toward American Indian existence adopted and celebrated by the non-Indian world. Writers from Freneau and Cooper to Faulkner and LaFarge would stop here, with a crocodile tear for the dying noble savage. Writing from within the supposedly "dying" culture rather than from the outside, however, Mathews goes beyond such a stock response, making of Chal's story a more complex narrative of cultural survival. The "dark hours just before dawn" are Mathews's subject; a "feeble questioning" of the dilemmas of Indian existence and identity in the twentieth century is his method; and an awakening to a renewed sense of self—authenticity—for Native Americans would appear to be his goal.

Central to Chal's childhood is the nearby creek, where he swims and about which his life seems to revolve. And it is the creek which serves as an index to how far the destruction has progressed in the name of progress. Even as the oil boom is just beginning, Chal notices a change: "It had been several years since he had heard the wild turkeys flying up to roost along the creek, and he could scarcely remember what the howl of the wolf was like" (64). As the "civilized" values of the town grow too intense for Chal, he invariably returns to the creek, still searching for that "something that was not understandable and was mysterious." One night he rolls up in his blankets to sleep beside the creek only to be awakened by the abrupt howling of coyotes: "There was the moon, large and white, hanging in a gleaming sycamore. The coyotes stopped as suddenly as they had begun. A great unhappiness filled him, and for the briefest moment he envied the coyotes, but he didn't know why" (71). He rises and studies the moon and then

> he crossed the creek and climbed a little hill in the full flood of the ghostly light. He stood there, then spread his arms toward the moon. He tried to think of all the beautiful words he had ever heard, both in Osage and English, and as he remembered them he spoke them aloud to the moon, but they would not suffice it seemed; they were not sufficient to relieve that choking feeling. (71)

Chal envies the coyotes because they know, instinctively, how to celebrate the sacral significance of the moon—nature—something he cannot do. In his desire to utter a polyphony of "beautiful words," Chal is attempting to create a prayer that would comprehend the potentially rich heteroglossia of his world, to fuse the "internally persuasive" language of his Osage heritage with the "authoritative" discourse of English in a syncretic utterance, and by speaking this hybridized utterance to the sacred Osage moon, to put the parts of himself together in an identity that can comprehend both worlds. Could Chal conflate the "beautiful" in both discourses, he might solve the painful dilemma of his inauthenticity and achieve a "temporal unification of the past and future with the present" that leads to a coherent sense of self.[6] He is, with his desire to "think of all the beautiful words he had ever heard" and to speak them, attempting to emulate the coyotes. But Chal's dissociated sensibility cannot speak in one voice; he is choked into silence by his inabilty to articulate—to put the pieces of the self together into a coherent utterance. "But this mysterious unhappiness came to him only at times," Mathews writes, "and never except when he was alone on the prairie" (72). At other times, Chal achieves a kind of transcendent awareness of his place in the natural order of the traditional, sacred Osage world:

> The sun was setting and the west looked like leaping flames that had been suddenly solidified. . . . Then, very suddenly, that mysterious feeling came over him. A mild fire seemed to be coursing through his veins and he felt that he wanted to sing and dance; sing and dance with deep reverence. He felt that some kind of glory had descended upon him, accompanied by a sort of sweetness and a thrilling appreciation of himself. (73)

As the oil boom draws more of the "civilized" world to the Osage country, Chal grows more distant from the natural world. When he leaves for the state university with his friends, Sun-on-His-Wings and Running Elk, his disinheritance from his Osage identity becomes almost complete. From the beginning, he is annoyed with his childhood friends "for acting like Indians" (94). When he flees the university to walk along the river, he daydreams about his future: "He couldn't dream fast enough to visualize all the honors that came to him. He even visualized a great feast and dance held in his honor by the Osages when he arrived back home for Christmas. They had made a song and invented a dance especially for him, and they gave him a name, but he couldn't decide what the name should be." In Indian cultures a name is earned—as Chal's father has told him earlier in the novel—and most crucially a name comes from the community to both confer an identity and confirm one's place within that community. Indian identity is communal, and Chal has lost his place within his Osage community; thus he cannot conceive of an Osage name. At this point the daydream evaporates, and in place of a rich heteroglossia Chal is left with only the authoritative discourse represented by the American dream of being "self-made": "As pleasant as the dream was, he decided to leave the Osage part of it out. He didn't want to call attention to the fact that most of his blood was of an uncivilized race like the Osages. He believed that they didn't have any backbone, and he certainly wanted to make something of himself" (153). Chal's reflection mimics the observation of one J. E. Jenkins, an inspector for the Indian Office, who reported approvingly in 1906 that the Osage mixedbloods—who by the turn of the century outnumbered fullbloods—"act like white people, well educated and intelligent." A year earlier, however, Frank Frantz, the Osage agent from 1904 to 1905, had reported that if the fullbloods were an improvident lot, the mixedblood was "a worse proposition" and did not "deserve any efforts in his behalf."[7]

As Chal prepares to go to a college dance, he remembers his reflection: "At the last impression of his face in the mirror that evening, he had seen a bronze face in the black-and-white; the white making the bronze stand out, and he had wondered if he wasn't too dark" (124). By the (white) values of the privileged culture, Chal finds himself unacceptable. However, Mathews does not allow Chal to completely repress his Osage way of viewing the world. As Chal dances with Blo, his beautiful (white) date, Mathews writes: "But this was a new experience, merging with someone in such fervency; someone like the Moon Woman, who, like many things beautiful, lived briefly. Like the Moon Woman of his child- hood who reigned over the forgetfulness of the night; over the tranquil world of dreams; the world of Wah'Kon" (124). Mathews adds later: "He wondered why he had a feeling that was something like a religious emotion when he thought of Blo. Of course it never occurred to him that it might be the tribal heritage of religion associ- ated with beauty and dreams" (155). For a moment, Chal's Osage self has achieved the upper hand in this political struggle, reversing the pattern that denigrates an Indian world-view, removing his date from the referential context that had made him feel "too dark" and displacing her into an Indian system of reference. She is made beautiful and given significance within the mythic paradigms of his tribal heritage.

Chal leaves the university to enlist in the Army Air Corps, and upon graduation from ground school, "he thought of himself as being separated by a great abyss from Sun-on-His-Wings and Run- ning Elk, and from the villages and the people moving among the lodges" (208). So separated is he that he tells a female admirer that he's Spanish rather than have her guess his real identity. Nonetheless, Chal is still profoundly Indian, and his ambivalence is underscored when he looks down from his airplane: "He had a feeling of superiority, and he kept thinking of the millions of people below him as white men" (218). In the air, radically displaced, alone and controlling the most sophisticated example of American machinery, Chal fuses his resentment of the white man with a sense of having beaten the whites at their own game of individualism and machinery. Still, when he begins to gain self-assurance brought on by the admiration of women, "he felt that he had begun to be gilded by that desirable thing which he called civilization. He was becoming a man among civilized men" (230).

When his father is murdered,[8] Chal returns home and becomes another of the directionless Osages drinking and driving fast cars. In this aspect of Chal's malaise, Mathews reflects an accurate picture of the cultural disintigration besetting the Osage. In fact, while the bootleg liquor Chal drinks was a major problem among the Osage as among other portions of the American population, even drugs had become a scourge of the newly wealthy Indians, with mor- phine, cocaine and marijuana provided by an influx of "pushers." A seizure of fifty thousand dollars' worth of drugs in a single cache in Osage County in 1929 was reportedly the largest single drug seizure in Oklahoma prior to World War II.[9] On a drinking spree, Chal goes in search of the old special place by the creek only to find that "several black wells stood about on the prairie above the trees and from each a path of sterile brown earth led down to the creek, where oil and salt water had killed every blade of grass and exposed the glaring limestone. Some of the elms had been cut down, and the surface of the water had an iridescent scum on it" (250). Again, nature mirrors the condition of the Osage. Later, after an all-night drunk, Chal returns to the creek to try fishing, but "the water was lifeless" (285).

While Chal was away, his friend Running Elk has also been murdered by whites trying to gain control of allotments. Before his murder, however, while drying out in a detoxification ward, Running Elk provides a vivid nightmare image of what has befallen his people. When Chal visits him, Running Elk describes a terrifying dream in which a "fat white man, completely naked and glistening, would stand at the door of his room with a spear in his hand" (273). This nightmare vision illuminates the displacement of the Indian by the avaricious (fat) white man who has, as the spear and blocked doorway suggest, both looted Indian culture and trapped the Indian. The particularly deadly displacement of Indian males—which will be a concern of the next generation of Native American novelists—is suggested in the sexually aggressive posture of the naked white man with the phallic, appropriated spear. There would appear to be no place left for the Indian male except escape through alcohol and unconsciousness.

As foils for Chal, Running Elk and Sun-on-His-Wings stand at opposite ends of the spectrum of possibilities for the Osage. While Running Elk has sought oblivion through alcohol, Sun-on-His-Wings has turned toward Osage tradition and the new peyote church. Visiting his childhood friend, Chal takes part in a Sweat Lodge ceremony and is moved by the experience. After the ceremony, "they went back into the lodge, picked up their blankets, and dispersed. Chal drew his blanket closely around him" (277). To Chal, as for others, the blanket has always been a sign of traditional, "primitive" Indians, and as such something to be scorned. Here, following the sweat and the prayers of the ceremony, Chal becomes, briefly, one of those scorned "blanket Indians." With this brief touch, Mathews hints at a potential return to traditional, immutable values through the new, syncretic peyote ceremonies.

The promise seems short-lived, however. During the Sweat Lodge ceremony, Watching Eagle, the Road Man, has told a man named White Deer: "Your son and those People who have been killed by these white men, followed that road which they thought was white man's road. Your son married white woman. You have children of your son, but they are not your children. They can never have a name among their people. They have no people" (273–74). On a literal level, Watching Eagle is referring to the fact that according to tribal laws the offspring of Osage men and white women could not receive allotments or headrights, though children of Osage women married to white men could.[10] Even though his mother is Osage, Chal, too, has no name among his people. As a mixedblood, he seems, in fact, to very nearly have no people. When he takes a group of drunken whites to see an Osage dance, Chal feels a strong urge "to go down on the floor and dance." He does not dance, however, because, as Mathews writes, "he had never danced with his people" (260). Chal's alienation is further emphasized when shortly after the Sweat Lodge ceremony he thinks that "he wanted to be identified with that vague something which everybody else seemed to have, and which he believed to be civilization" (285).

Near the end of the novel, after drinking all night, Chal dances alone as he had in childhood:

> He stopped the car suddenly and climbed out and started talking to himself; talking nonsense. He kept repeating to himself, "Extravaganza," without reason, as the word was not associated with his frothy thoughts. . . . He arose with difficulty, with an intense urge for action. Suddenly he began to dance. He bent low over the grass and danced, and as he danced he sang, and as he sang one of the tribal songs of his people, he was fascinated by his own voice, which seemed clear and sonorous on the still air. He danced wildly and his blood became hotter, and yet that terrific emotion which was dammed up in his body would not come out; that emotion which was dammed up and could not be exposed. As he danced he wondered why that emotion which had begun to choke him did not come out through his throat. He was an Indian now and he believed that the exit of all spirit and emotion was the throat, just as the soul came out through the throat after death. (296–97)

Chal's solitary dance is an extravaganza, a frenzied celebration of nothingness rather than a ceremonial act expressive of one's place within the tribal community and natural world. In its frenzy, his dance contradicts the traditional poise and dignity of Osage dances, which never embraced the wilder "fancy dancing" of Plains tribes.[11] Mathews's irony is heavy when he writes, "He was an Indian now," for in his extravagance (that is, *extra*, "outside," and *vagant*, *vagari*, "to wander about") Chal is far from his Osage people. He still cannot fathom that mystery he sensed as a child: "He wanted by some action or some expression, to express the whole meaning of life; to declare to the silent world about him that he was a glorious male; to express to the silent forms of the blackjacks that he was a brother to the wind, the lightning and the forces that came out of the earth" (297). Drunk and without the teachings of his people, Chal has no language for such expression. He is inarticulate. His performance is, from the white perspective he has learned to value, simply another "extravaganza."

Sundown does not end on a fatalistic note. In the final scene, Chal boasts foolishly to his mother (while correctly associating linguistic facility with political power), "I'm goin' to Harvard law school, and take law—I'm gonna be a great orator." He then falls asleep with his head on his arms. Around him, in the novel's final lines, nature comes alive: "The nestlings in the nest above settled down to digest their food. A flamewinged grasshopper rose in front of Chal's still form, and suspended there, made cracking sounds like electric sparks, then dropped to the grass and became silent. The flapping and splashing of the mother robin, as she bathed in the pan under the hydrant, was the only sound of activity." The natural imagery of this conclusion, enveloping the sleeping Chal, strikes a positive note. Thus far, Chal has failed as a challenge to the disinheritors of his people. He has been disenfranchised culturally and is adrift in a wasted land. However, the novel, within which natural imagery has served consistently as an index to whatever is positive in Chal's world, ends with the purifying image of the bathing robin. A few lines earlier, a sparrow has pushed from the nest and killed one of the robin's young, but the mother goes on; she has other young and proceeds to cleanse herself. It is a small story of loss followed by renewal and hope. The flamewinged grasshopper sounds a more portentous note, rising like a warning before the sleeping Chal. In the grasshopper may also be seen a sign of hope, however, for in this image Mathews merges the natural world of the Osage—the sacred red, or flame color—and the "civilized" world of electricity. As the novel ends, unlike Running Elk, Chal is alive and sleeping peacefully near his mother in whom Osage values still live. The natural world, represented by bird and insect, remains intact.

Sundown ends on a somewhat ambivalent note, leaving the future of its mixedblood protagonist and of the Osage people unresolved. Just as the strong identity and self-assurance of the more traditional Sun-on-His-Wings balances the despair of Running Elk's disintegration and death, the novel depicts starkly the consequences of oil and acculturation for the Osage while simultaneously refusing to accept the familiar pattern of simple doom for the Indian, the "vanishing American" pattern so familiar to American literature and thought. In *Sundown*, Mathews leaves open the possibility of "another destiny, another plot" for the American Indian, refusing any romantic closure that would deny the immense difficulties confronting the displaced Native American, but simultaneously rejecting the cliché of the Vanishing American as epic, tragic hero. In this repudiation of the simple, entropic plot assigned to the American Indian by Euramerican myth-making, Mathews anticipates the major direction of Indian fiction into the 1990s. Perhaps the author saw other possibilities for Chal in the model that he, John Joseph Mathews, had to offer as a sophisticated, worldly, educated mixedblood and member of the Tribal Council. Perhaps Mathews is anticipating the possibility articulated by a member of a succeeding generation of Osages, Kenneth Jump, who wrote in 1979: "Could it be that Indian blood mixing with other bloods will create a new type of Indian? If this be true then the Osages will not be engulfed by present society but a new type of Osage Indian will emerge from this propagation."[12] Chal may indeed represent the "new type of Indian" who figures so prominently in contemporary American Indian fiction.

D'Arcy McNickle

On April 6, 1929, Harcourt, Brace and Company rejected a novel manuscript by D'Arcy Dahlberg entitled "The Hungry Generations." Addressed to "Miss Dahlberg," the rejection letter quoted a confidential reader's report: "The story of an Indian, wandering between two generations, two cultures; excellent. . . . A new territory to be explored: ancient material used for a different end. Perhaps the beginning of a new Indian literature to rival that of Harlem." More than five years later, with the novel entirely rewritten, McNickle would receive another editor's manuscript report even more favorable:

"It [*The Surrounded*] will be one of the best novels ever written about the American Indian, and the essential poignancy and beauty of its theme and background will find a wide audience. Moreover, it is becoming easier and easier as time goes on to put across books with the primitive American appeal. I think we could work up a good ballyhoo for this novel, lining up such people as Oliver La Farge, Ruth Benedict, Blair Niles, John Collier, Robert Gessner, and others behind it."[13]

Again, despite this reaction (and despite its vaunted "primitive American appeal" and promised "ballyhoo"), the novel would be rejected before finally being accepted for publication by Dodd, Mead & Co. in December of 1935. In 1936, with the titles of both novel and author radically different, the novel would be published as *The Surrounded*, by D'Arcy McNickle. And, despite their confusion over the author's gender, Harcourt, Brace's declaration would prove prophetic: along with Mathews's *Sundown*, *The Surrounded* would mark the beginning of "a new Indian literarature" that would come, by the 1980s, to more than rival the famous Harlem Renaissance in black literature. More than any other Indian writer, D'Arcy McNickle would prove to be a seminal figure in the new American Indian fiction, publishing three novels over a span of forty years while turning himself into one of the nation's most articulate and knowledgeable spokesmen for Indian concerns.

Born on the Flathead Reservation in northern Montana, D'Arcy McNickle was métis, part Cree on his mother's side and adopted into the Flathead tribe. In a letter to Professor William Gates at Johns Hopkins University two years before the 1936 publication of *The Surrounded*, McNickle explained his blurred ancestry:

I am an Indian then, a breed, rather, for I had a Scotch-Irish father and a French-Canadian (that is, French-Cree) mother. I do not know the proportion in which the bloods are mixed on my mother's side, and probably no one will ever resolve the question, for her people were a long time beyond the pale in the United States and Canada. Her father was one of Louis Riel's rebels in the uprisings of 1873 and 1885 and was finally chased off British soil with a bounty on his head. He died in poverty, his large ranch and herds of stock swallowed in the onward rush.[14]

McNickle's certainty of the quantum of Indian blood in his veins would never become any more clear, although in 1934, while seeking a position in the Interior Department's Indian Bureau, whose requirements for Indian preference were that applicants be at least one-quarter Indian, he would write to John Collier to say, "I am a native of the Flathead Indian Reservation in Montana, and I believe the records there show me to be a quarter-breed. The Indian blood comes through my mother, who was really of Cree descent." His allotted status as a "quarter-breed" on the Flathead Reservation was never questioned, and McNickle went on, during the desperate Depression-bound thirties, to join the bureau and begin to forge for himself an impressive career in Indian Affairs.[15]

When his mother divorced William McNickle and married a man named Dahlberg, D'Arcy informally adopted his stepfather's name and became D'Arcy Dahlberg. It wasn't until 1933 that, in the midst of trying to publish his first novel and land a job in the Bureau of Indian Affairs, D'Arcy Dahlberg reclaimed the name by which he was listed on the Flathead rolls and became once again D'Arcy McNickle.

While being read and rejected by more than a dozen publishers, and even getting as far as a tentative contract with Covici, Friede, Inc., before being rejected, "The Hungry Generations" went through enormous changes, evolving into a version briefly titled "Dead Grass" before becoming, finally, *The Surrounded*.[16] In these changes, particularly in the substantial revisions made by McNickle between the lengthy final version of "The Hungry Generations" and the shorter, more concise version published as *The Surrounded*, can be seen the author's transformation from a writer who wanted merely to write "of the West, not of Indians primarily, and certainly not the romantic West,"[17] to a writer whose subject was very specifically the Indian caught up in the oppressive and often brutal attempts of a militant and millennially minded culture—that of Euramerica—to eradicate totally the native cultures they were displacing. And McNickle, more than any writer before him, would recognize and write about the crucial role of language and epistemology in the Indian's struggle for identity, authenticity, and survival.

The Surrounded begins with Archilde Leon, half-Salish and half-Spanish, returning to his home on the Flathead reservation from a brief spell of wandering and fiddle-playing in Oregon. Archilde's venturing forth into the "other" world outside of Salish culture resembles a "wandering time" or vision quest common to Native American cultures. Such a journey—requiring temporary separation from community—is a search for identity, for a profound understanding of one's place within the world, and, if the quest is successful, results in a newly forged sense of intimate relationship with the whole—a relationship cemented most often through the assistance of spirit helpers from the natural world. Archilde, however, returns home with the appearance of being both assimilated and disoriented, dressed in a blue suit, his shoes polished and his attitude toward his Indian past one of indifference bordering on embarrassment. The disjuncture between worlds is emphatic: "When you came home to your Indian mother," McNickle writes, "you had to remember that it was a different world."[18]

Archilde's immersion in the Euramerican world has caused him to question the very reality of his Salish relations: In a positivistic, historically conscious order, the ritually centered tribal world has no place. Of the feast his mother gives in his honor, Archilde thinks, "You gorged yourself on meat until you felt sick, and a lot of old people told tiresome stories" (4). At the feast, Archilde listens to and watches his mother and Modeste, an old, blind elder, and Archilde thinks: "Actually, in the way he was learning the world, neither Modeste nor his mother was important. They were not real people. Buffaloes were not real to him either, yet he could go and look at buffaloes everyday if he wished, behind the wire enclosure of the Biological Survey reserve. . . . To him they were just fenced up animals that couldn't be shot, though you could take photographs of them" (62). In this powerful juxtaposition, McNickle subtly underscores Euramerica's centuries-long attempt to turn the Indian into an artifact, an unthreatening image that, like a photograph of the buffalo, can be contained and controlled within the national metanarrative.[19] For Archilde, the Indian part of the self has come to represent such a static, meaningless image. A decentered drifter, Archilde is radically displaced and unable to make the association between place and self that confers an Indian identity.

In the course of the novel, beginning at the feast as he listens to the old Salish stories, Archilde moves toward a new understanding of the world of his mother and her people—the world that has nearly vanished from the valley. Though at first his Indian relatives—and by extension that side of himself—make Archilde sick, and though he at first insists that the old ways are "gone, dead" (63), he soon comes to listen to the stories and to understand the lessons they teach. As Archilde hears Modeste tell of the old ways and the lost world of the people, McNickle writes: "A story like that, he realized, was full of meaning" (69). In spite of the alienation so obvious as the novel opens, in the context of his temporary separation from the Salish community and his wandering and repudiation of traditional values, Archilde's slow recognition of what is "full of meaning" in his heritage suggests a positive coming of age. This resembles the process Bakhtin describes when he writes that "consciousness awakens to independent ideological life precisely in a world of alien discourses surrounding it, and from which it cannot initially separate itself. . . . When thought begins to work in an independent, experimenting and discriminating way, what first occurs is a separation between internally persuasive and authoritarian enforced discourse."[20] Archilde has already rejected the authoritarian discourse of the Church, and the Euramerican discourse of his father, and now he is turning back to the internally persuasive discourse of the Salish culture. Like other mixedbloods in Native American fiction, Archilde is a walking battleground for political struggle between conflicting discourses, that struggle defined by Foucault when he argues that "we cannot exercise power except through the production of truth."[21] In the end Archilde will withdraw into silence.

As Archilde is beginning to comprehend what it means to be Indian—or, more specifically, to be mixedblood with the heterogeneous potentials inherent in that condition—his Spanish father, Max Leon, lies in his big ranch house listening to the sounds of the Indian feasting, "swearing at the noise and wondering what it signified" (60). Despite, and because of, his place in a privileged monocultural center, like the invisible narrator in Alain Robbe-Grillet's *Jealousy*—and perhaps all colonial functionaries—Max can approach the indigenous reality of his appropriated world only through a highly frustrated sense of his own "otherness" in relation to that reality. The utterances of that marginalized world—in this case physically marginalized on the periphery of Max's property—are epistemologically unapproachable for Max, with a barrier between signifier and signified so impenetrable that he can hear only "noise." In "The Hungry Generations," McNickle wrote of Max: "Every time his mind confronted an Indian boy he felt baffled. He could not see into the enigma. They were not animals for they could think—but their ideas were always of no value; their actions born of their thinking were always contrary and childish."[22]

The barrier that has developed between Archilde's two worlds is further underscored by the fact that while Max lives in the ranch house, Archilde's Indian mother, Catharine, remains in a sod-roofed cabin set off from the big house. Husband and wife do not communicate. In spite of the fact that Max can speak Catharine's Indian language, as he listens to his wife's people in the distance, Max thinks, "Why was it that after forty years he did not know these people and was not trusted by them? . . . What were they saying? Why didn't they talk to him?" (75). Dialogue apparently has no place in the world Max has thus far conceived of in purely monologic terms. Catharine's Salish world remains impenetrably "other" to Max, the conceptual horizon inexorably "alien" and obscure. Paradoxically, however, Max's world is, in fact, very intensely "a dialogically agitated and tension-filled environment of alien words."[23] Max, as a Spaniard and therefore also an "other" in the Anglo-European society of the valley, fails to understand everyone, mistaking the admiring glances of his white neighbors for scorn and misunderstanding the attempts of the storekeeper, Moser, to be friendly. McNickle writes, "Max didn't understand. He mistrusted them. Their smiles he misinterpreted" (28). In spite of their privileged discourse, whites, too, suffer from confusion in this "dialogically agitated" postcolonial environment. Moser, a desperate and grasping man, is equally confused by Max's hostility: "He could not understand it" (29).

McNickle weaves the theme of fatal misunderstanding skillfully through the novel. Catharine thinks of her life, and "she could not understand the ruin that had overtaken her" (22). Max cannot understand what has happened to his sons, all of whom started out well but soon went inexplicably "bad." Father Grepilloux, the priest at the nearby mission, cannot understand what has happened to the Indian "children" of the church, telling Max, "Somehow or other the bad Indians . . . have come upon the scene. Who turned them loose I don't know" (45).

Again and again in the novel, understanding fails and something goes inexplicably wrong for the Indians, as if they are in the grip of an incomprehensible fate—as if, in fact, McNickle's Indians are playing out their tragic roles in the American epic, roles that simply require that they perish and that deny them what Bakhtin calls "another destiny or another plot." Archilde thinks of an Indian String Quartette from the government school in Oregon, remembering that at first the group had flourished, but then for some incomprehensible reason "something had gone wrong with them and even they had lost the track" (96). Archilde's nephews, Mike and Narcisse,[24] are sent to the mission school much against their wills, and we are told that "When Mike and Narcisse returned from the mission school something was wrong" (175). Archilde thinks about the disastrous twists of his own fate in the valley of his people, and he realizes, "But something had gone wrong, uselessly, without reason" (150).

The Indian characters in this novel seem both helpless to control their own destinies and hopelessly trapped in that condition. The symbol of the Indians' entrapment is the mountain range that surrounds them, cutting off the valley from the outside world. And in Archilde, McNickle illustrates the impossibility of escaping from the present Euramerican-dominated world into an Indian past. McNickle underscores the futility of escape when Archilde finds Mike and Narcisse hiding in the woods, drumming and dancing around a pagan pole, and McNickle writes, "Take care, he tried to tell them. The game was gone from the mountains; even the fish were getting fewer each year; and they could not always stay in the woods and dance" (247). Inevitably, McNickle acknowledges, the Indians will have to engage in dialogue with their conquerors; however, the dialogic deck is stacked infinitely in favor of the dominant culture. "A particular language in a novel is always a particular way of viewing the world, one that strives for a social significance," Bakhtin warns us, and the Salish language/ worldview in *The Surrounded* seems to have little chance against the power of the discourse leveled against it.

The "something" that goes wrong for the Indians in this novel involves the Catholic priests, who, impressing their own metamyth upon the Salish world, have tried to turn this paradise into a garden, complete with a Christian concept of sin, the serpent the Indian paradise lacked.[25] "Only one thing they didn't understand," Father Grepilloux tells Max, in a statement that reverberates through American history, "and that was sin. We taught them, and that was the beginning of their earthly happiness" (136). McNickle's irony here is subtle and splendid. Along with the narrative of the Fall comes a plunge out of mythic and into historic time. "Earthly happiness" in the priest's interpretation, cuts the Salish people off from the eternal moment of mythic time, from the traditional sense of self that comes from participation in the ordered, cyclical world that has defined their existence prior to the intrusion of the Church. Father Grepilloux places the Indian squarely within the millennial myth of America and obliterates the Indian conception of reality.

McNickle's irony at the expense of the Church is sharp. One of the first things the Sisters of Providence at the mission school teach young Catharine, Archilde's mother, involves the question of signification: "where to find dirt and how to get rid of it" (170). The mission school has a deadly effect on the Indian children. Catharine thinks of her son, Louis, who is hunted by the local sheriff for horse stealing: "Then he went to school to the Fathers, and there was a change. . . . She knew the Fathers had not done it, but it started after he went to school. She could not understand it" (131). McNickle makes it clear that the Fathers have attempted to impose a new reality upon the Salish people, with the result that the old world is lost without a new world to take its place. Old Modeste sums up the problem when he says, "the old law is not used and nobody cares about the new" (207). Designed to eradicate the Indian reality and replace it with a completely foreign conception of the world, beginning with the imposition of a privileged and alien language, the mission school serves to displace and alienate the students almost irreparably.

Just before his death, Max ponders what has been done to the Indians of the valley: "As for the Indians who had been taught to understand sin, certainly they offer no satisfaction. Instead one had to ask of them—were they saved or were they destroyed?" (139). Finally, Max places the blame for the pathos squarely where it belongs, crying out to the white storekeeper, "You and me and Father Grepilloux were the ones that brought it on" (146).

Though the Euramericans in the novel never move closer to a comprehension of the Indian world, in the mixedblood Archilde the Indian and white realities begin to merge in a rich, hybridized understanding as Archilde rediscovers the essential value of his Salish heritage while simultaneously becoming reconciled to his father. "We'll make a new beginning!" Max tells Archilde (in an ironic echo of the deadly Euramerican Adamic myth upon which American colonization was founded). Together with Father Grepilloux, Max makes plans for his son to travel to Paris to study the violin—a journey that would, of course, take Archilde closer to the originating center of Euramerican culture and thus further from his indigenous identity. This apparent (if precarious) reconciliation of Indian and white worlds within Archilde is paralleled by the reconciliation Archilde brings about between Max and Catharine. Just as the promise of a new beginning unfolds, however, McNickle abruptly denies the fruition of this promise. Archilde, against his own and his father's wishes, takes his mother on a last, ritualistic hunt in the mountains. There they meet Louis, who shoots a doe out of season, and suddenly the fate which hangs over the Indians appears "with ghostlike unaccountableness" (124) in the form of the game warden. Because of a misunderstanding, the warden kills Louis, and as Archilde shouts, "You're wrong! It's a mistake—" (127), Archilde's mother kills the game warden.

In constructing this crisis point, McNickle is writing from an accurate knowledge of Indian-white relations in an area where conflicts over hunting rights had long been a source of strain between the Flathead tribe and surrounding whites. In 1898, a letter to a local newspaper declared, "The state ought to offer a bounty on these worthless Indians that infest this part of the country. . . . They destroy more game and stock than the lions and coyotes."[26] Regardless of the rationale, once the warden has been killed, the Indian's inevitable fate is personified in the snakelike sheriff, Quigley, the serpent in this paradise from whose coils Archilde cannot escape. It is as if the metanarrative of American colonization, founded upon the myth of the reclaimed Garden that allowed Europeans to impose their own order and excused all inhumanity in the process, has taken fatal form in Quigley. Finally, in the shelter of the confining mountains Archilde becomes an accessory to the murder of the sheriff as well and is, in the novel's final scene, captured by the Indian agent who had trusted Archilde.

The Surrounded ends on a grim note of futility and frustration. With the novel's protagonist, Archilde Leon, about to be led away and charged with complicity in not just one but two murders, the Indian agent says bitterly, "You had everything, every chance, and this is the best you could do with it!" And as Archilde's two young nephews, Mike and Narcisse, escape further into the mountains, the agent adds, "It's too damn bad you people never learn that you can't run away. It's pathetic—." The novel's final line underscores a profound sense of entrapment and futility as McNickle writes: "Archilde, saying nothing, extended his hands to be shackled."

In *The Surrounded*, it would seem, communication between Indian and white worlds is impossible—heteroglossia is ruthlessly subordinated to the monologic language of authority. Repeatedly in the course of the novel understanding fails, communication leads to confusion, and individuals find themselves trapped in a kind of mute isolation.

As the plot unfolds, however, the novel's final outcome does not seem inevitable. Change in the novel does not always portend disaster, it seems, as Father Grepilloux tells Max Leon: "It was inevitable that a new age would come. It is beginning now. And your boy is standing there where the road divides. He belongs to a new time. He may not stay in this valley, and it makes no difference whether he does or not; it's what he makes of himself that will count" (108). To understand this novel, and to comprehend D'Arcy McNickle's fiction as a whole, it is important to solve the dilemma posed here. If Archilde Leon stands at the place where the road divides, we need to ask where those divided paths lead, to what end. And why, in the end, doesn't Archilde actually possess the ability to determine his own life, to assume control over his own destiny and make of himself what he will?

In this novel, the metaphorical road begins to divide at the juncture of Indian and white worlds. From the point of view of the dominant culture, a choice must be made: the white man's road or the Indian's? That this is the choice the old priest has in mind seems clear, given the Church's single-minded desire that the Indian become as Europeanized as possible. On that road lies full acculturation and disengagement from the last vestiges of the Indian world as represented in the novel, a complete subordination of the self to the will of the colonial power. The priest's complete failure to understand the Indian world is illustrated in his declaration that it makes no difference whether Archilde stays in the valley or not; such a statement ignores the essential ties between Indian identity and place, the significance of both community and sacred geography to cultural identity. Grepilloux's perspective is purely Euramerican and valorizes the individual above all else, a perspective diametrically opposed to a Native American value system. In this light, Archilde's flight into the mountains, even as nondeliberate as it is, may be seen as a positive attempt to flee from the authoritative center of cultural hegemony. It is an escape into the cyclic, ritual-centered natural world of the Salish. But McNickle does not allow the reader a great deal of satisfaction in Archilde's transient flight.

If assimilation lies along one fork of this road, what waits on the other, the road Archilde actually takes? The answer suggests that the old priest's metaphor is somewhat misleading, for what lies just around the first bend on the Indian road in this novel would appear to be a dead end. From the beginning, almost all hope for a vital and viable Indian world is undercut by a mysterious force. There really is no choice. In one direction lies success and life; in the other lies failure and death. And all possibilities for communication across the median strip between the two roads are denied.

Again and again in the novel, in spite of glimpses of a promising future, understanding fails and something goes inexplicably wrong for the Indians. How do the Indians, like the hapless members of the Indian String Quartette, lose the "track," and where does that track lead? Clearly, the track is that fork in the road leading away from the Indian world toward the world defined by Anglo-European values. In McNickle's posthumously published third novel, *Wind from an Enemy Sky*, a reform-minded Indian agent muses to himself about the failure of Indian-white relations: "The problem is communication. . . . The answer, obviously, is that we do not speak to each other—and language is only part of it. Perhaps it is intention, purpose, the map of the mind we follow."[27] In *The Surrounded*, Archilde stands where not just the road but the maps— the "conceptual horizons" in Bakhtin's words—divide. One fork would seem to lead toward a past that is irretrievable, the other toward a world in which Indian values have no meaning.

That the Indian road is no longer viable appears indisputable in *The Surrounded*. The mountains are described by Archilde as dead and empty, and the traditional values—signposts on the map of the Indian world—lead only to disaster. Louis, after all, has committed no crime according to an Indian worldview. He has stolen horses from the enemy, an act once honored by his ancestors, and he has shot a young doe, which will be more tender than one of the old, antlered bucks prized by the white hunter. In a world governed by a different discourse, or mental map, both actions would be praised. In the white world, however, one action is punishable by hanging while the other leads to Louis's death.

Indian men in *The Surrounded* have been rendered impotent, incapable of "making" something of themselves in the priest's words. In the resulting role reversal, those who act forcefully and attempt with disastrous results to control events are the women, Faithful Catharine and Elise La Rose, both of whom coerce an unwilling Archilde into the mountains and in the mountains commit murder in defense of their men. And McNickle implies that this inability to control their own lives is to a large extent the result of the Church's attitudes toward the Indians. The priests' view of the valley as a garden paradise lacking only one thing—sin—recalls strongly the Puritan belief in the New World as a New Eden, New Canaan, or New Jerusalem. According to this immensely powerful metanarrative, if America were indeed such a prelapsarian Garden, the Indian must be the primal innocent awaiting baptism into the

Christian faith. Toward these innocent children not just the Church but the entire Anglo-European power structure quickly adopted a paternal stance. From the fathers in the Church to the "Great White Father" in Washington, the posture was very similar. That McNickle is thinking along these lines would seem amply clear in the parent-child motif of *The Surrounded*. In Father Grepilloux's journal, we learn that when "discovered" by the Jesuit priests, the Indians had "the hearts of children." Repeatedly, the old priest refers to the Salish as "Faithful Children," "Wilderness Children," or "Blessed Children." Even Louis, horse thief and outlaw, is described as "a child talking." Finally, in Archilde's very name McNickle subtly conflates the themes of disfranchisement and dialogism that permeate the novel, for while his name may suggest "Our Shield"—the Indians' protector—if anglicized this name would sound much like "Our Child." The effect of such paternalism is to render the child powerless to articulate or control his own destiny and to institutionalize dependence upon the paternal power. In the last major speech of his life, at the Northwest Indian Education Conference in 1977, McNickle approached this issue more formally, declaring, "When the educational function is taken over first by missionary societies—as early as John Elliot in New England and later by federal and state schools—the Indian tribes were deprived of their right to develop the leaders needed for growth and development. The Indian communities became less and less able to manage their affairs." This has been the primary direction of Anglo-European relations with American Indians from the beginning. The Indian—denied a credible discourse—becomes a helpless child in need of a stern father, a father who demands unconditional allegiance. In this same 1977 speech, McNickle strongly emphasized the crucial role of responsiblity in the traditional education of Indian children, offering examples from Papago, Hopi, and Navajo cultures and quoting an Oglala Sioux study: "The child was given responsible work with social results. With this came the development of autonomy. There was no supervision." As early as 1934, in a letter seeking employment with the BIA, McNickle had struck a very similar theme: "I am certain that Indians, if given responsibility, can contribute toward the making of a wiser Indian policy."[28]

The stern father in *The Surrounded*, of course, is Max Leon, the unbending Spaniard who fails abysmally to communicate with his own sons. Max's problem is that he has never attempted to understand his half-Indian sons, demanding simply that they obey and that they become "Americanized" ranchers. When they fail to become fully acculturated, Max becomes bitter. When Archilde devotes himself to working on the ranch, and shows an inclination toward the Anglo-American desire to "get ahead," Max is drawn toward this son. Like the Church, Max Leon expects unquestioning obedience from his children, and like the Church, Max does not comprehend the need to recognize another map of the mind than his own. When Father Grepilloux says of Archilde, "It is what he makes of himself that counts," he is failing to recognize that the entire thrust of his Church's relationship with the Indians, as well as the federal government's, has been to ensure that the Indian cannot make anything "of himself" but must be dependent, as a child, upon a higher authority.

Valiant attempts have been made by critics to read *The Surrounded*, as well as McNickle's other fiction, in terms that would deny such fatalism. In *Word Ways*, the only book-length critical study devoted exclusively to McNickle, John Purdy argues that "McNickle intended his words to be statements of the ability of Native cultures to endure despite consistent, and sometimes violent, efforts to destroy them." Purdy seems to have foundered somewhat against an unavoidable inconsistency in McNickle's writing. While his nonfiction does indeed argue for Native American cultural survival in convincing and confident terms, McNickle's fiction does not fully support such optimism. Ignoring the complexities of McNickle's own process of "becoming" in his evolving quest to come to terms with an Indian identity, Purdy simplifies both the man and his fiction, arguing ingenuously:

> On the surface, McNickle seems to have adopted fully the ways of life found in "mainstream" America, the "American values, culture, and aspirations" largely Anglo in origin. But one need not dig too deeply into McNickle's history and writings to find evidence that demonstrates the extent to which the cultures of his childhood (Cree and Métis, but also Salish) remained an inseparable part of his being, directing his values and aspirations throughout his life, *although their influence was not manifested in any material way.*

To support his claim that the novel should be read as a positive, "Indian" vision, Purdy makes such suggestions as this: "He [Archilde] travels into the mountains along the same trails as his ancestors and sees his surroundings as they had. He makes no effort to return. . . . From the townspeople's point of view, he is an Indian 'gone bad' and following in the footsteps of his criminal brothers; from the Salish point of view, he is a redeemed tribal member, an 'Indian going good.' "[29]

Such a glowing account ignores the fact that Archilde has been dragged helplessly into the mountains by Elise, a mixedblood who prefers white dances, drinking, and sex (with sensible fears of "syph") to the ceremonies of her Indian relations, and that once in the mountains he makes no choice at all but simply falls prey to circumstances manipulated by the impulsive Elise. The "Indian going good" is led away in handcuffs under the agent's ironic epithet. As noted above, Archilde's flight into the mountains might possibly be interpreted as a positive repudiation of the oppressive Euramerican power center, a kind of subversion of paternalistic authority. But McNickle makes it too clear that nothing is left for Archilde in the mountains for us to take the escape too positively. What hope for cultural survival remains is with the boys, Narcisse and Mike, who flee to the mountains and remain free at the novel's end. Mike and Narcisse have broken away from the oppressive machinery of white America that seeks to obliterate their identity as Indian—that much is indisputably positive. But McNickle has made it clear that survival will be at best painfully difficult. In the end, we feel that the next generation may benefit from Archilde's example, but Archilde himself is simply a victim of time and place.

More convincing is James Ruppert's reading of *The Surrounded*. Relying upon Wolfgang Iser's deconstruction of novelistic discourse, Ruppert argues that "while the character Archilde is doomed, the lasting transformation of *The Surrounded* is in the reader as he adopts new attitudes and adds them to his store of experience." While the "implied author" may believe Archilde is doomed, Ruppert suggests, the reader need not share the same belief or assume that McNickle himself believes in that doom. Writing about *Wind from an Enemy Sky*, Jay Vest makes a similar argument based upon an informed, culture-specific reading of that novel, an argument that can be applied to *The Surrounded* as well. *Wind*, Vest insists, "is a mythic narrrative composed in the trickster motif," a motif determined by the "anti-hero—a being who expresses the antithesis of normative cultural order and value." According to this reading, McNickle is playing trickster, presenting the reader with a narrative antithetical to his purpose of demonstrating how American Indian cultures can and will survive. With these two approaches we can exempt McNickle himself from a despairing outlook on Native American survival, a move that places McNickle's fiction in greater harmony with his nonfiction. Neither argument, however, can redeem Archilde or the other Indian characters in the novel from the dead end that confronts them.[30]

The Surrounded did not always end on such a note of despair. In the earlier draft of the novel entitled "The Hungry Generations," a version much longer than the published manuscript and very different in its implications, McNickle allowed Archilde to live happily ever after. In this draft, Archilde actually travels to Paris and experiences the heady atmosphere of the Lost Generation's milieu. After falling in love with Claudia, a young lady of excellent breeding, Archilde returns to his Montana home, where the murder is discovered and he is brought to trial. The trial of Archilde Leon sheds interesting light on D'Arcy McNickle's evolving attitude toward his protagonist and, more importantly, toward Indian identity.

As he lies in jail awaiting trial, Archilde thinks of his mother's people as "inhabitants of a bleak world into which the sunlight had not yet penetrated. . . . Dull, naked, savage, the breath of their nostrils was fatalism—these were the hundred generations who stood behind Archilde." And in the trial, the state prosecutor accuses Archilde of being ungrateful, willful, and spoiled. The prosecutor adds:

> The defendant is an Indian breed. . . . If the Indian is to form a part of our state he must learn the duties and the qualities of a citizen. How is he to get this knowledge? By granting him special privileges and dealing leniently with him when he defies our laws? Is this the way we treat our children when they disobey our wishes and wander from the straight path? Or hasn't our axiom always been—"Spare the rod and spoil the child"? We come from a race of sturdy Pilgrim fathers who owned the virtues of discipline. They built for us a great nation on that very principle.[31]

Here, as in the published novel, the Indian becomes an errant child in the eyes of the state, to be treated with harsh justice for his own good. Here the Pilgrim fathers are invoked explicitly, and here we find McNickle recognizing that "language becomes the medium through which a hierarchical structure of power is perpetuated, and the medium through which conceptions of 'truth', 'order', and 'reality' become established."[32]

In his defense, Archilde's lawyer notes Max Leon's relationship with his sons: "If there was ever a man who was ashamed of his sons—who hated his sons—Max was that man. We know that he had some reason for his hatred." The defense lawyer invokes the different conceptual horizons, different maps of the mind: "An Indian boy is brought up under influences that we don't begin to touch with all our laws and government provisions." And finally, as the clincher in his argument that the mother rather than her half-breed son has killed the game warden, the lawyer implies the Euramerican myth of the Indian as well as the cultural center's desire to eradicate "Indianness" from indigenous peoples: "If you have noticed the defendent you must be struck with how few of the Indian characteristics he has; his father is present in him. But his mother was a full-blood—simple in her hate and love; quick to avenge a wrong—loyal to her race and her sons."[33]

In this unpublished version of the novel, the charges against Archilde are dismissed. He returns to the ranch his father has willed him, sole owner and master. He sits in his dead father's favorite chair and gazes at his property as McNickle writes: "He hadn't looked forward to his homecoming; he did not know that there was magic in the earth beneath his feet. . . . All this world would be his—when he recaptured it again. He must walk out soon and make a survey of everything, asserting his command once more." Proudly, he remembers that the judge "had shook his hand after the trial and commended his stolid qualities that would, no doubt, make him a splendid citizen." And he thinks of his rebellious nephews:

> Mike and Narcisse would be kicking over the traces again, he told himself. They were working hard today but who knew what they'd be doing tomorrow? One thing he knew, *he'd waste no words on them hereafter.* They could make their own choices and his shoe would be ready to boot them through the door the first time they strayed too far. He was standing now in the footprints his father had left twenty-five years ago. Already he had said in his mind, *"If they will not live on my terms*—then they will get out and stay out! As for himself, he would live in his father's house and bring to pass such of the dream as he had caught from the old man—and his own in its time.[34]

Here, Archilde has embraced the monologic authority of his father's Euramerican posture: he will dictate privileged language that will define the nephews' world; if they cannot conform to his authoritative narrative, they will be evicted. In the meantime, he will inscribe his father's dream/colonial vision upon the landscape, replacing the sacred geography of the Salish with the utopian appropriation of the European.

"The Hungry Generations" ends on an ironic note as Archilde recalls a Salish song linking man and rain:

> Clouds not of water!
> I have seen my dream of power
> walking the clouds of water!
> He was a valiant god, a red warrior.
> He buckled to his breast a bright robe
> And strode over the tops of hills,
> Walking the clouds of water!

As he chants the words, he is awaiting the arrival of Claudia, his love from New York. Together, we are led to assume, they will live happily ever after in profitable stewardship of Archilde's domain.

Upon a superficial first glance it would seem, in this earlier version of the novel, that within Archilde the two worlds—Indian and white—have come together in fruitful merger. On the one hand he has accepted his responsibility as a good, productive citizen, and, as the Salish song suggests, on the other he has found a strength in his Indian self. However, it takes only a moment's scrutiny to recognize that what Archilde has become is merely a younger version of Max Leon. In place of the Salish sense of a profound relationship with the land, Archilde has embraced his European father's attitude of dominion over the land. His will alone shall make the land productive. In place of the profound need for understanding and communication even this unpublished version of the novel has made so painfully evident, Archilde adopts the role of authoritarian father figure with his nephews. He has accepted fully the prosecuting attorney's axiom, "Spare the rod and spoil the child," precisely the approach which isolated Max Leon from all of his family. In short, the Archilde we see at the end of this version of the novel has become fully acculturated. In this version of the novel, the road divided and Archilde took the fork that promised a future. Evidence suggests that McNickle is fully aware of the irony of this conclusion, an irony at the expense of those readers who would accept this as a "happy" ending.

"The Hungry Generations" and *The Surrounded*, with their different versions of the same story, seem to represent the two roads Father Grepilloux defines in the published novel. There can be no doubt that in McNickle's mind Archilde—and the author himself—

stood at the dividing of ways between Indian and white worlds. In the more extensive and unpublished novel Archilde takes the white man's road toward success and happiness, his father's path but one abetted by a wife with whom he, unlike his father, can communicate: the lovely, cultured, very white Claudia. In the revised novel, Archilde is hijacked from this heavenly course by a wild "breed" girl named Elise La Rose before he can leave for Paris. It is Elise rather than Archilde who selects the other fork in the road, the one which dead-ends in another killing in the lifeless mountains.

It would be comforting to be able to draw from McNickle's novels an "Indian" reading that would challenge the entropic stereotype dominant in American fiction through the 1930s. To do so, however, strains the evidence of McNickle's fiction. What McNickle illustrates in *The Surrounded*, and as will be seen below in *Wind from an Enemy Sky*, is the Euramerican view of the Indian, as Roy Harvey Pearce has suggested, "as the state of one almost entirely out of contact, for good or bad, with the life of civilized man. . . . The American Indian had long been out of contact with the main stream of civilized life, so long that he could never participate in that life unless by some miracle he should stop being an Indian."[35] Subtly and at times brilliantly, McNickle demonstrates how such thinking affects the Indian; when Archilde extends his hands to be cuffed, the shackles are those of this national myth; he is imprisoned by America's image of the Indian. In his first novel, McNickle does not appear to see a promising route of escape from this damning image.

In electing to revise as he did, D'Arcy McNickle chose to underscore the predicament of the mixedblood trapped irretrievably between worlds and identities. Ultimately following a different "map of the mind," and thereby failing to take the path whose signposts point toward the American dream, Archilde in *The Surrounded* becomes the prototype for the protagonist in novels written by Indian authors. Mourning Dove's Cogewea lived happily ever after in a kind of mixedblood heaven with plenty of inherited wealth from the great white north, balanced eternally, it seems, between her two fires. John Joseph Mathews's Chal Windzer was left straddling two worlds with only the faintest note of hope echoing in the Indian world he had left. Following *The Surrounded*, however, American Indian authors would almost invariably create protagonists who are poised, like Archilde, at the dividing point. And, like the author of *The Surrounded*, they would send their characters—in nearly every case a mixedblood—down the Indian road and away from the American dream. For characters such as Momaday's Able, Silko's Tayo, Welch's Jim Loney and unnamed narrator, Hale's Cecelia Capture, and Allen's Ephanie, results will vary, but the quest will be the same: a search for Indian identity and order in the chaos between worlds.

In October of 1936, NcNickle's agent, Ruth Rae, who had labored long and loyally to place *The Surrounded*, received a letter from E. H. Dodd, Jr., that novel's publisher, stating, "We all feel very partial to Mr. McNickle and his work but THE SURROUNDED, in spite of its quality and excellent reviews, sold so few copies that the net result was a pretty bad loss to us." Thus, wrote Dodd, they were unable to offer an advance on the novel NcNickle already had underway. Dodd added, however, "We are looking forward eagerly to seeing the manuscript." So poorly did *The Surrounded* sell that out of the first royalty statement, dated August 1, 1936, after his $50.00 advance and merchandising costs were deducted, McNickle was paid $8.33, while his tireless agent earned $0.93 for that period.[36]

In March of 1937, Dodd wrote to McNickle again to enquire about the second novel and to say that Ruth Rae had told him McNickle "had completed one chapter of the new novel and expected to get a lot of work done on it presently. This was good news indeed and I am hoping that you will have it done in time for fall publication." By that time, however, McNickle was launched on his new career with the Bureau of Indian Affairs and had little time for the novel, complaining repeatedly from November, 1937, through the spring of 1940 that he had no time to complete the novel. "I have continued work on the Indian Agent book and have cherished the hope of some day bringing it to a conclusion," he wrote to Dodd in March of 1940, adding a month later that he hoped to have "the first half of the manuscript sent to you by the first part of June as you suggest." Finally, in May of 1944 the novel, now called "The Flight of Feather Boy," was rejected by Dodd, Mead and Company, who complained with delightfully unconscious irony, "We would all . . . like a little more Indian in it," adding, however, "we know from previous experience that Indians aren't a particularly popular subject."[37]

"The Flight of Featherboy" would be put on the back burner for years while McNickle became ever more deeply involved in his BIA career and went about the task of turning himself into a nationally prominent authority both in the field of anthropology and in Indian affairs. In November, 1944, McNickle helped found the National

Congress of American Indians, assisting in the writing of its consti-
tution. The same year, he signed a contract to write the study of
Indian culture and history which was published in 1949 as *They
Came Here First*, a book dedicated to John Collier, the creator of the
Indian New Deal. Before McNickle would return to "The Flight of
Featherboy," he would be increasingly caught up in his BIA work
in the Southwest and he would publish additional books: a novel,
Runner in the Sun (1954);[38] a study of Indian cultures and federal
Indian policy co-authored with Harold Fey, *Indians and Other Ameri-
cans: Two Ways of Life Meet* (1959); a narrative of Indian history, *The
Indian Tribes of the United States: Ethnic and Cultural Survival* (1962,
revised and republished in 1973 as *Native American Tribalism: Indian
Survivals and Renewals*); and *Indian Man*, a biography of novelist
Oliver LaFarge (1971). During this period he had also received an
honorary doctorate from the University of Colorado and accepted
an invitation to join the faculty of the University of Saskatchewan's
Regina campus to head its new department of anthropology.

In April, 1937, Henry Dodd, Jr., sent McNickle a copy of a *New
York Herald Tribune* review by Lewis Gannett of a book called *The
Amerindians*. In the review, Gannett ended with a suggestion that
"perhaps the great book that will realize the drama of the American
Indian is close at hand." In his note accompanying the review,
Dodd exclaimed to McNickle: "I want to call your attention to the
last sentence and tell you that I am betting the book he is referring
to is the one you are going to write when you finish your novel."[39]
McNickle's unfinished novel, tentatively entitled first "The Indian
Agent" and then "The Flight of Feather Boy," would not be truly
finished and published until 1978, a year after the author's death
and more than four decades after it was begun. And while McNickle
would never produce "the great book" that Dodd hoped for, *Wind
from an Enemy Sky*, as it was finally called, would assume an important place amidst the sudden outpouring of novels by Indian writers
in the seventies, an outpouring for which John Joseph Mathews
and D'Arcy McNickle had prepared the way in the 1930s.

In a letter to Douglas H. Latimer, an editor at Harper & Row,
McNickle explained something of his motivation in *Wind from an
Enemy Sky*: "I guess the most general thing I can say is that I wanted
to write about the Indian experience as objectively as possible; not
just the usual story of the wronged Indian, but the greater tragedy
of two cultures trying to accomodate each other." And, in the same
letter, McNickle went on to explain, "I would like the reader to see

the Little Elk episode not as an isolated tragedy, about which one need not get too concerned, but as a critical statement about the quality of human behavior when people of different cultures meet." About the doomed but well-intentioned Indian agent, Rafferty, McNickle declared: "Most critics of government policy in Indian affairs seem unaware of their own involvement in support of the very morality which informs that policy; and this is part of the argument of the book. The incidents in the chapter [chapter 23 of manuscript] describe what actually happened on the Flathead reservation in western Montana."[40]

Whereas McNickle set *The Surrounded* on a clearly recognizable Flathead Reservation and *Runner in the Sun* in the precontact Southwest of four thousand years ago, *Wind from an Enemy Sky* features a purely fictional tribe and place disguised but drawn from the author's knowledge of his adopted Flathead Reservation. By fictionalizing the Little Elk people, McNickle was free to be creative with the historical events upon which the story turns, and he was, more importantly, able to achieve the generalized statement he described to his publisher.

The roots of *Wind from an Enemy Sky*, as McNickle suggested to Latimer, began with the Salish people of the author's childhood. In 1936, just as *The Surrounded* had made its appearance to very favorable reviews, McNickle had proposed an article to the *New Republic* on a Salish water-rights conflict, eliciting the following statement from editor Malcolm Cowley: "We have so little space in the *New Republic* at present—what with the election and the counter revolution in Spain—that we couldn't possibly print an article about the Flathead Indians and the Rocky Mountain Power Company dam." Cowley had suggested instead the possibility of an "editorial paragraph containing the essential facts—not more than 200 words."[41] It is likely that the offending dam in *Wind from an Enemy Sky* grew out of McNickle's interest in this confrontation, and it is just as likely that in the central story of the lost Feather Boy bundle in *Wind* that he had in mind the experiences of the Gros Ventre Tribe of North Dakota. In 1938, as he was attempting to make progress on this second novel, members of the Water Buster Clan of Gros Ventre journeyed to Washington, D.C., and New York to reclaim their clan's prized sacred bundle. In exchange for the sacred bundle, the tribe presented the Museum of the American Indian with a Sacred Buffalo Medicine Horn, also invaluable and centuries old. With the return of the Water Busters' sacred bundle, the threat of drought was removed from tribal lands. As a government representative, McNickle participated in the 1937-38 negotiations for the return of the medicine bundle.

The sacred bundle of the Water Busters Clan, thought to have contained two skulls of Thunderbird deities who had come to earth many generations before, had fallen into neglect during the late nineteenth century when pressures from missionaries and the federal government were brought to bear upon Indian ceremonial practices. Finally, the medicine bundle was sold to a Presbyterian minister who in turn sold it to New York City's Museum of the American Indian before it finally made its way back to the tribe.[42] The happy ending to this Gros Ventre exchange is mirrored in an unpublished draft of *Wind* entitled "The Indian Agent." In this version, the agent, Toby Rafferty, arranges the successful return of the Feather Boy bundle. Before the bundle is unwrapped, Bull makes a speech:

> I would like our Superintendent to be the one to unwrap this thing. He came to us when the road was crooked and we could not see our way. He talked to us when we would not talk. He held us in his hand. We are ignorant Indians believing in things which my white man friends cannot believe in. Our Superintendent was not too proud to listen to our stories and to let us keep what was ours. We did not ask him to believe and he did not make us feel foolish by trying to tell us that our stories are better than his own. Let the Indian keep what is his and the white man keep his own. Only let us be friends. I think that is how it is best for men to live together. Our Superintendent will decide who is to be the keeper of this bundle and his hands should be the first to touch it.[43]

Like "The Hungry Generations," the unpublished version of *The Surrounded*, this early draft of *Wind* ends on a positive, highly romantic note of easy resolution. Rafferty has a love interest, an anthropologist named Hortense Abernathy who is "making an acculturation study of the Little Elk Indians" and is fully accepted by the Little Elk people. Even Adam Pell, well-intentioned villain of the published novel, is accepted in this romantic version, smiling and holding hands with Bull. As the novel ends, the restoration of the bundle has brought rain to the drought-stricken land.

Like *The Surrounded*, *Wind from an Enemy Sky* underwent a complex transformation in its revision from "The Indian Agent" to the published novel, a transformation that darkened the novel significantly. It is interesting to note that McNickle at one time planned to darken the novel even further by including an additional character which McNickle described as

> one Clarence Fleury, a mixed-blood "professional" Indian and agitator par excellence. His type (every reservation has a rich assortment) has not been dealt with in the literature of the Indian, and he offers a make-up rich in conflicts and desperate compensations. The "half-caste" or the "mixed-breed" is a familiar enough figure, a pitiable misfit, inheritor of vices and weaknesses, redeeming himself only by the pathos of his situation. But Clarence Fleury is a different kind of animal. He has learned to make a business, a trade, out of his ill favor.[44]

At the same time, the published novel demonstrates even more clearly than did *The Surrounded* McNickle's sophisticated comprehension of the crucial role language plays in the struggle for power between cultures. In *Wind from an Enemy Sky*, the conflict centers explicitly around discourse and, therefore, conflicting epistemologies. Here, McNickle illustrates brilliantly the belief that "language becomes the medium through which a hierarchical structure of power is perpetuated, and the medium through which conceptions of 'truth', 'order', and 'reality' become established."[45] And in the dialogical tensions within this novel, he illuminates the predicament Elaine Jahner has defined as epistemological crisis between Native American and Euramerican cultures: "Translating what they [Native Americans] sensed into terms that might communicate interculturally was impossible because such translation requires knowledge of two ways of knowing, but beyond that it requires that the issue itself make sense to the people to whom it is being addressed. Until the twentieth century, few European intellectuals radically questioned their own epistemological foundations."[46] In this novel, only the Indian agent—the potential agent for an integration of worlds, for achievement of heterogeneity—is capable of sincerely questioning the epistemological foundations of his dominant cultural center. Others, most conspicuously Adam Pell, simply cannot comprehend that "other" way of knowing that values a sacred valley instead of a dam or that finds identity in being rather than acquiring.

Unlike the romantic early draft, *Wind from an Enemy Sky* picks up the central theme of *The Surrounded* and presents the reader with again a dialogically agitated and tense world of mistrust, misunderstanding, and death. Once again, communication between all individuals is difficult at best, while between Indian and white worlds it would appear nearly impossible, a schism emphasized in the novel's opening pages as Bull, chief of the fictional Little Elk tribe, looks down from his mountain retreat to "the open valley far below, a white man's world. A world he sometimes passed through but never visited" (2). Bull, a man "who 'lives inside,' " has kept his people apart from the whites, isolated in the mountain camp, while his older brother, Henry Jim, has chosen the white man's way and a farm in the valley. The brothers and the Little Elk people have been split for thirty years—nearly the period of time McNickle had been working on and thinking about this novel—neither communicating nor understanding one another. McNickle develops the theme of misunderstanding in *Wind* in the barrier of silence between Indian brothers, in the miscommunication between Indian and white, and in the seeming impossiblity of dialogue between all men (with Hortense Abernathy revised out, women play no significant role in this novel).

Early in this novel, we learn that Antoine, Bull's young grandson, has, like McNickle himself, returned home from the Indian boarding school in Oregon. Antoine, like Mike and Narcisse and all the others in *The Surrounded*, has experienced the authoritative privileging of English that marked the central concern of Indian boarding schools. Approaching the Indian agency with trepidation early in the novel, Antoine thinks of the government people he has known: "They had loud voices," he remembers (106). He recalls a terrified Eskimo girl who had subverted the monocentrism of the boarding school by simply becoming mute in the face of the white world: "Antoine never heard her speak a word" (109). In leaving school and returning to Bull's camp in the mountains, Antoine is escaping to reclaim an Indian identity. However, Antoine will become an interpreter for his people, a fact of significance in our reading of the novel.

Soon after the novel begins, Bull takes Antoine to see a dam the government has constructed in a meadow sacred to the Little Elk Indians, a "place of power." When Bull realizes that the whites have indeed "killed the water," he shoots at the dam: "He raised the gun waist-high and fired into the concrete dam. Once. Twice. Nothing moved. . . . Not even a flash of a splinter. If the lead-nose bullet smacked against the structure, no one heard it. The sound of whining machinery and the thunder of water even smothered the bark of the gun" (7). In Bull's gesture, McNickle symbolizes the futility of resistance to the world of machinery and power and foreshadows the novel's conclusion, when Bull will once again fire into the seemingly impenetrable wall of white machinery. In the end, however, the machinery will be represented by two men, Adam Pell and Rafferty, the Indian agent.

McNickle's primary theme in this novel is what it was in *The Surrounded*: the difficulty, verging on impossiblity, of communication and the tragic consequences this entails. And again, while communication is particularly difficult between worlds—Indian and white—it is a problem common to all characters. Not only do Bull and Henry Jim refuse to talk to one another for thirty years, even Featherboy, the incarnation of powerful Thunderbird, cannot talk to the Indian people he has come to help, because they fear him: "The only one he could talk to was his own mother, which wasn't the way Thunderbird had planned it, and it almost spoiled everything" (206). Bull admits early in the novel, "I never learned how to talk to the white man" (19), a statement he will echo many times, later confessing, "I didn't know how a white man talked, because I never went to listen" (180). When he is forced to talk to the agent, Rafferty, Bull says, "When I talk to a white man, what does it matter what I say?" (167). Bull's brother, Louis, underscoring the political struggle involved in every discourse and especially within the "dialogically agitated and tension filled" environment of competing Indian-white discourses,[47] declares even more bitterly, "We learned a long time ago that when we talk to the strangers from across the mountains, we lose something" (225). Bull and Louis have discovered the unequal power struggle inherent in dialogue between Indian and Euramerican worlds. Watching their world being appropriated by the invader, they have learned rather painfully the power of language as a weapon of conquest.

Henry Jim has alienated his people not only by turning onto the white man's path, but even moreso by attempting to turn his people from the old ways by giving away Featherboy, the most powerful of the tribe's medicine bundles. Henry Jim's action is a deliberate and miscalculated but well-meaning attempt to divert the Indians from their mythic world into the historic consciousness of the white culture. In gratitude, the government has built a fine house and farm for Henry Jim, but in the end Henry Jim rejects the white world whose "prize" Indian he has been. He moves out of his house into a tepee to die. Henry Jim's final rejection of the white world is indicated by the fact that before he dies he can no longer speak English. And it is this rejection of the language of the dominant culture that most surely subverts the hegemony of monologic Euramerica. In the beginning, Henry Jim had tried to decode the invaders' discourse, "to discover what the white men were saying, and what they meant beyond the words they used" (26). He had tried heroically to assimilate an alien discourse into his own conceptual system, and he remembers that "the words were a marvel of obscurity, but in the days of telling they seemed important" (30). After years of lonely exile in a white world he can never fully understand, and which demands unconditional allegiance without acknowledging the significance of his inherited world-view, Henry Jim returns to his people.

"How to translate from one man's life to another's" writes McNickle, "—that is difficult. It is more difficult than translating a man's name into another man's language" (26). In these words, McNickle articulates wonderfully the epistemological crisis between Indian and European America. In The Boy, the tribal policeman, McNickle illustrates the point he makes here. The Boy's Indian name is Son Child, but as he is translated from one world to another, this man of great tact, understanding, and courage is diminished, "loses something" as Louis would put it, and becomes The Boy, an implement manipulated by the machinery of the dominant (paternally authoritative) government. In the translation of Son Child, McNickle illustrates the force of authoritative discourse arrayed against the Indians, a discourse Bakhtin defines as "indissolubly fused with its authority—with political power."[48] Such discourse "demands our unconditional allegiance," the kind of allegiance that will force The Boy to kill Bull at the novel's end.

Language not only defies translation in this novel, but it also defines character. The Indians approve of Rafferty because he does not insist upon "talking at once" when someone comes to see him (27), and The Boy praises Rafferty by saying, "I guess he's all right. He talks good" (87). To talk good in this novel is to engage dialogically, to acknowledge at least slightly "two ways of knowing." As Henry Jim prepares to tell Rafferty the history of the medicine bundle, Henry Jim thinks, "Today talks in yesterday's voice" (28), a statement that underscores the duration of the Indian world-view through time and space. This durational emphasis is something far different from Bakhtin's assertion that "in ancient literature it is memory, and not knowledge, that serves as the source and power for the creative impulse. That is how it was, it is impossible to change it." Within the oral tradition, regardless of the paradigmatic nature of reference, the stories are continually and contextually modified, adapted, restored to significance within an immediate context.[49] Henry Jim also thinks that "it was so important this time—so much depended on a good understanding" (28). In drawing nearer to the Indians, Rafferty is learning to hear "yesterday's voice," admitting to himself, "Maybe I wasn't listening before" (39). Later, as he is gaining the confidence of the Little Elk people, Rafferty senses the difficult reality of competing discourses, musing that "there seemed to be still a larger aspect, and this he did not yet understand. It had to do with their way of talking" (176).

Adam Pell, the man who has designed the dam, is also the director of the Americana Institute to which Featherboy was given. And in Adam—a name suggestive of the mythic American Adam so prominent in American literature and so deadly to Indian culture—McNickle presents his most stark example of the consequences of misunderstanding. Adam has "made a hobby of Indians" (104) and has even gone to Peru to help descendants of the Incas (among history's greatest engineers) build their own hydroelectric project.[50] Although Adam's sister says, "He may even be planning to talk to those Indians—he's always talking to Indians" (104), it is apparent that while Adam may talk to Indians, he has never engaged in dialogue with Indians. Adam makes the fatal mistake of attempting to make the Little Elk people conform to his static stereotype of "primitives."

Bull's nephew, Pock Face, shoots Adam Pell's nephew, who happens to be working on the dam. A young, angry Indian, Pock Face is caught between two worlds, competing languages. He wears cowboy boots and can "talk about horses like a white man" (41). He listens to what the old men of the tribe say, but he fails to understand the voice of the past, as is evident when he tells his side-kick, Theobold, that he had been to the dam before but that he hadn't understood the significance of the place: "Somebody said the old-timers used to go there all the time. But I didn't know why that was" (41). Adam's nephew dies because of a lack of understanding on both sides, and when Adam learns why his nephew has been shot, he recognizes his own culpability: "The enormity of his misapprehension swept over his mind and silenced him" (169). The shock awakens Adam to a faint glimmer of comprehension of the competing discourses symbolized both by language and, more powerfully, by the Euramerican attempt to impose a utopian order upon the landscape by means of the dam. He reflects perceptively that "they worked with different data and a different order of reality" (210), and he thinks that if only he could have returned the destroyed Featherboy bundle, "we could have worked together. They shot that young man, my nephew, because nobody tried to talk to them, not in their terms" (211). But Adam and his new-found understanding are both short-lived, and Adam brings about the final tragedy through the enormity of his misapprehension of the Indian world. Earlier, Bull had prophesied Adam's role: "Maybe he is a good man . . . and yet he will destroy us" (187).

When the Little Elk Indians, led by Bull, come to the agency expecting the return of the medicine bundle from Adam's museum, Adam tells them that Featherboy, valueless in the white world, has been destroyed by mice in the museum's basement. Earlier, he had told Rafferty, "There is nothing left to restore" (232), and now he attempts to replace the lost medicine bundle with a gold fertility figure from the Incan world, attempting, as Rafferty says, to "restore a lost world by a simple substitution of symbols" (249). Pell's action is highly significant. It calls to mind the large-scale commodification of culture found in galleries and museums throughout the Western world. "Collecting," James Clifford writes, "—at least in the West, where time is generally thought to be linear and irreversible—implies a rescue of phenomena from inevitable historical decay or loss." Ironically, once removed from a mythic context, the Featherboy bundle succumbs to that non-Indian reality of linear and historical decay from which it had previously been exempted. As an autonomous "art" object, the bundle has no life; as sacred fetish, it has eternal life. The decontextualization and commodification of the Featherboy bundle should call to mind the same process being applied on an enormous scale to Native Americans—and all "primitive" cultures worldwide—by powerful and increasingly homogeneous Western societies. Clifford explains that "we need to be suspicious of an almost-automatic tendency to relegate non-Western peoples and objects to the pasts of an increasingly homogeneous humanity." In this process, Native American cultures become frozen "icons" shored against the cultural ruin of America, while Indian people are decontextualized into oblivion. The traditional camp of Bull's Little Elk Indians tucked away in the mountains—distanced from the threatening language of the whites below—even suggests the localized "language games" invoked positively by Jean-François Lyotard, but the isolated camp offers little consolation. Inevitably, as McNickle makes clear, the Little Elk people—and all Native Americans—will have to find a voice (or be allowed a voice) within the national narrative.[51]

When the Indians realize that Featherboy is lost forever, Bull seizes a rifle and shoots both Adam and Rafferty, shooting into the machinery of the white world he does not understand just as he earlier shot into the heart of the concrete dam. Bull, in turn, is killed by The Boy, who shouts, "Brother! I have to do this!" (256) Again, just as in *The Surrounded*, McNickle has given us a tantalizing glimpse of the possibility of a merger of white and Indian worlds. As Rafferty and Bull draw closer toward one another, as the white world seems to be moving for the first time to meet the Indian world halfway, McNickle suggests a possibility for dialogue rather than monologue, and for mutual understanding. And just as in *The Surrounded*, McNickle pulls the rug out from under his characters, suggesting that the schism between worlds is simply too enormous. The "dog-faced man," the minister who has taken the medicine bundle and given it to the museum, sums up the barrier between white and Indian when he tells Rafferty: "The Indian people start from origins about which we speculate but know next to nothing. We do know they are a people who are unlike us—in attitude, in outlook, and in destination, unless we change that destination. . . . Regardless of what we white men have attempted, the Indian has always remained beyond our reach. . . . He's always slipping away into the distance" (51). For the "dog-faced man," the Indian is resolutely "other," lurking beyond an impenetrable "conceptual horizon" and approachable only via the vehicle of authoritative discourse: "unless we change that destination." The minister represents the unyielding stance of privileged discourse, in the face of which the Indian retreats into silence.

In the character of Antoine, Bull's nephew, McNickle posits whatever hope for cultural survival his novel offers. Antoine can interpret between Indian and white worlds. Discussing the colonial enterprise, Ashcroft, Griffiths, and Tiffin have written:

> The interpreter always emerges from the dominated discourse. The role entails radically divided objectives: it functions to acquire the power of the new language and culture in order to preserve the old, even while it assists the invaders in their overwhelming of that culture. In that divided moment the interpreter discovers the impossibility of living completely through either discourse. The intersection of these

two discourses on which the interpreter balances constitutes a site both exhilarating and disturbing.[52]

In a sense, Antoine takes up the combined burdens of Henry Jim and Bull at the novel's end. Identified with the mountain camp, where his tribe's culture remains much more intact and less subject to the annihilating forces of Euramerica, Antoine is simultaneously dialogical: he can talk with the "others." Thus, in Antoine, McNickle has left us with an element of hope for cultural heterogeneity and cross-cultural survival. It may not be too much to suggest that in Antoine, McNickle saw a reflection of his own role as a voice for cultural survival and dialogue.

McNickle offers some hope for future generations in both *Wind from an Enemy Sky* and *The Surrounded* in the forms of Mike and Narcisse in *The Surrounded* and Antoine in *Wind*: the children who spin away toward some kind of freedom and the boy who can interpret between worlds and who bears witness to the cataclysm. But those elements of future promise are nearly hidden by the sheer enormity of failure in both books. *Wind from an Enemy Sky* ends with the line, "No meadowlarks sang, and the world fell apart." Published posthumously, these are D'Arcy McNickle's last words. While Purdy, striving to read a "happy" ending into this novel, suggests wistfully that "one might question whether they [the final words] were McNickle's or his publisher's addition," this final phrase makes a hauntingly fitting epigraph for McNickle's life and fiction.[53] For this important and seminal figure in American Indian literature and politics, the world he had spent his lifetime trying to make whole—the Indian-white world of America and the mixedblood world within himself—fell finally and, it seems, inexorably apart. And language, McNickle insists, is the darkling plain upon which Native and Euramerican cultures clash.

Acts of Imagination

The Novels of N. Scott Momaday

◆

When, in 1969, *House Made of Dawn* was awarded the Pulitzer Prize for fiction, the Pulitzer jury, quoting one of its members, declared that "an award to its author might be considered as a recognition of 'the arrival on the American literary scene of a matured, sophisticated literary artist from the original Americans.' " At last, it seemed, N. Scott Momaday had produced the American Indian novel that reviewers had been anticipating since, in 1937, Lewis Gannett had prophesied: "Perhaps the great book that will realize the drama of the American Indian is close at hand."[1] But how should we interpret the juror's definition of a "matured, sophisticated literary artist from the original Americans"? Could it be that at last an indigenous writer had emerged who could emulate and imitate the discourse of the cultural center—Euramerica—so well that he could be accepted, perhaps canonized? Implicit in the juror's declaration, of course, is the fact that neither Mathews nor McNickle (much less Ridge or Mourning Dove) had "arrived." It is unlikely that the juror had ever heard of these forerunners of Momaday. Also implicit is the notion of a privileged center, that "literary scene" upon which an "original American" could "arrive" from what such highly affective language suggests must be truly epic distance: from the periphery comes a voice that may be recognizably part of a privileged discourse. Finally, this juror's words seem uncomfortably similar to the words of the publisher of John Rollin Ridge's *Joaquin Murieta* more than a century earlier: "The aboriginal race has produced great warriors, and powerful orators, but literary men—only a few." It doesn't require a great deal of stretching to see within this acknowledged "literary scene"—or accepted canon—an extension of colonial authority that has been described as follows: "The institution of 'Literature' in the colony is under the direct control of the imperial ruling class who alone license the acceptable form and permit the publication and distribution of the resulting work. So, texts of this kind come into being within the constraints of a discourse and the institutional practice of a patronage system which limits and undercuts their assertion of a different perspective."[2]

It can indeed be argued that with the appearance of *House Made of Dawn*, for the first time a novel by an American Indian author—a member of the "aboriginal race"—both portrayed with full power "the drama of the American Indian" (note the implication of theatrical performance, something to be observed from a safe distance) and displayed a talent and sophistication that placed it in the ranks of successful mainstream American novels. While *The Surrounded* told Archilde's story with penetration and force, it was, in the words of one publisher's rejection, somewhat "ingenuous and artless." And while the story of Chal Windzer in *Sundown* flowed with a smoothness suggestive of Osage oil, Mathews's novel lacked the formal sophistication, scope, and ambition of Momaday's.[3] But most significantly, it seemed that at last, with *House Made of Dawn*, an American Indian writer had produced a novel of a type well-schooled readers could both recognize and sink their teeth into, and the critical feast touched off by a Pulitzer Prize was a result in part of the fact that Momaday's novel is even at first glance recognizably modernist and thus deceptively easy fare for a New Critical approach. *House Made of Dawn*, the work of an author educated in a doctoral program at Stanford University under the tutelage of Yvor Winters, would seem, in fact, to contain the requisite elements of a work assimilable into the modernist canon: an alienated, deracinated protagonist who appears to fit the conventions of naturalism (which had long embraced the Indian as victim); a fragmented cultural context, suffering from a loss of order or structure; a formally experimental, discontinuous narrative replete with multiple perspectivism, stream of consciousness, and so on; and a dependence upon mythic structure to provide a way of ordering what T. S. Eliot had called the anarchy and futility of modern existence.

Once into the novel, however, a perceptive reader may begin to realize that sophistication in *House Made of Dawn* is of a different order from that in canonized texts. It is a sophistication of "otherness," a discourse requiring that readers pass through an "alien conceptual horizon" and engage a "reality" unfamiliar to most readers. What has matured with Momaday is not merely an undeniable facility with the techniques and tropes of modernism, but more significantly the profound awareness of conflicting epistemologies that had been suggested by Mathews and made explicit by McNickle. With Momaday the American Indian novel shows its ability to appropriate the discourse of the privileged center and make it "bear the burden" of an "other" world-view.[4] Momaday's novel represents more fully than any Native American novel before it the "assertion of a different perspective."

Born Navarro Scotte Mammedaty, according to the Office of Indian Affairs, in the Kiowa and Comanche Indian Hospital at Lawton, Oklahoma, on February 27, 1934, N. Scott Momaday would seem to have much in common with his predecessors. Like McNickle and Mathews, Momaday is a mixedblood. Like McNickle and Mathews, Momaday is well educated. On his father's side (Alfred Momaday, who had actually changed the family name from Mammedaty to Momaday in 1932), Momaday is Kiowa. On his mother's side, Momaday is primarily of European ancestry, with a distant infusion of Cherokee blood.

With Momaday, the question of identity that was masked in John Rollin Ridge's *Joaquin Murieta* and foregrounded in novels by Mourning Dove, Mathews, and McNickle becomes an obsession. It is out of the search for an identity that Momaday's writing grows. Again and again, more eloquently than any other Indian writer, Momaday has addressed this topic in essays, lectures, poetry and fiction. In his autobiographical work *The Names*, Momaday says of his mother's decision as a teenager to identify with her remote Cherokee ancestors: "She began to see herself as an Indian. That dim native heritage became a fascination and a cause for her. . . . She imagined who she was. This act of imagination was, I believe, among the most important events of my mother's life, as later the same essential act was to be among the most important of my own."[5] Elsewhere, Momaday has said, "The Indian, . . . by virtue of his diversity, has been rather more difficult to identify than have other Americans. His ethnic definition, whatever it is, consists in an intricate complex of experience." And, to a group of students, he once explained, "I think of myself as an Indian because at one time in my life I suddenly realized that my father had grown up speaking a language that I didn't grow up speaking, that my fore-bears on his side had made a migration from Canada along with . . . Athapaskan peoples that I knew nothing about, and so I deter-mined to find out something about these things and in the process I acquired an identity; it is an Indian identity, as far as I am con-cerned."[5]

Identity is acquired through an act of self-imagination, Momaday has explained: "We are what we imagine. Our very existence con-sists in our imagination of ourselves. Our best destiny is to imagine, at least, completely, who and what, and that we are. The greatest tragedy that can befall us is to go unimagined." Finally, Momaday has told critical biographer Mathias Schubnell, "I believe that I fashion my own life out of words and images, and that's how I get by. . . . Writing, giving expression to my spirit and to my mind, that's a way of surviving, of ordering one's life. . . that's a way of making life acceptable to oneself." John Rollin Ridge writing out his rage in a bloody romance, Mourning Dove exploring an identity between two fires, Mathews and McNickle illuminating mixedblood entrapment and conflicting discourse—all were "making life accept-able" for themselves as Indians and mixedbloods forced to imagine their existences in new ways. Momaday takes this quest for identity to a new level.[6]

Set in Walatowa, the native name for the Jemez Pueblo located an hour's drive north and west of Albuquerque, New Mexico, *House Made of Dawn* begins with the traditional invocation of Jemez storytellers: "*Dypaloh*." With a word, the author shifts his novel away from the mainstream of American fiction into a current new to our written literature, the American Indian oral tradition, a shift-ing that has important implications. While McNickle had invoked the oral tradition implicitly in many and subtle ways, Momaday clearly announces to the reader that he is privileging a particular kind of discourse, one which is "other" to the non-Indian reader. "*Dypaloh*" signals a transformative act, a subtly subversive process that runs counter to the internationalist orientation of modernism with modernism's emphasis upon a placeless iconography. With this invocation, Momaday is announcing what Ashcroft, Griffiths, and Tiffin have labeled a "strategy of appropriation," with its intent to "seize the language, re-place it in a specific cultural location, and yet maintain the integrity of that Otherness, which historically has been employed to keep the post-colonial at the margins of power, of 'authenticity,' and even of reality itself." With a single word,

House Made of Dawn assumes a place within a Native American
literary tradition in which stories have serious responsibilities: to
tell us who we are and where we come from, to make us whole and
heal us, to integrate us fully within the world in which we live and
make that world inhabitable, to compel order and reality. On this
subject, Linda Hogan has written that *House Made of Dawn* "uses
the traditional Native American oral concept of language where
words function as a poetic process of creation, transformation, and
restoration." Pointing out the novel's reliance upon the form and
language of the Night Chant ceremony, Hogan says, "The author,
like the oral poet / singer is 'he who puts together' a disconnected
life through a step-by-step process of visualization."[7]

Following the invocation, *House Made of Dawn* starts with a prologue opening with a vision out of the Navajo Night Chant that will
appear later in the novel: "There was a house made of dawn. It
was made of pollen and of rain, and the land was very old and
everlasting. There were many colors on the hills, and the plain was
bright with different-colored clays and sands. Red and blue and
spotted horses grazed in the plain, and there was a dark wilderness
on the mountains beyond. The land was still and strong. It was
beautiful all around." This paragraph shifts the actual landscape of
Walatowa, or Jemez, recognizable even in such a lyrical description,
into the timeless realm of myth. Ending with a declaration suggestive of the healing ceremony of the Night Chant, this first paragraph
underscores a feeling of coherence and permanence. The voice is
that of the oral tradition. The time and place are mythic, the mythic
dimension that takes its existence from the actual landscape of
Jemez but transcends the temporal landscape toward what Momaday has termed "the realization of the imaginative experience."
The reader is thus oriented away from historic consciousness into
mythic time.[8]

The second paragraph of the prologue introduces the novel's
protagonist: "Abel was running. He was alone and running, hard
at first, heavily, but then easily and well." The third and final
paragraph of this section tells us that "for a time the sun was whole
beneath the cloud; then it rose into eclipse, and a dark and certain
shadow came upon the land. And Abel was running. . . . Against
the winter sky and the long, light landscape of the valley at dawn
he seemed to be standing still, very little and alone." In the Jemez
Pueblo, as within many Native American Indian cultures, running
can have serious ceremonial applications. At Jemez, Abel's Wala-

towa, there are running ceremonies for each season, including the winter race for good hunting that Francisco remembers so vividly. As most critics have noted, the novel begins where it ends. This is Abel as we will see him at the end of the story, taking his grandfather's place in the race of the dawn runners, the runners after evil. Momaday himself has said, "I see the novel as a circle. It ends where it begins and it's informed with a kind of thread that runs through it and holds everything together."[9]

It is important to note, however, that the prologue removes Abel from time as the Occident conceives of it and shifts him into nonlinear, cyclical time of the pueblo in which "he seemed almost to be standing still." And like the earth itself, Abel is marked by the life-giving rain: "The cold rain slanted down upon him and left his skin mottled and streaked." To be integrated into the pueblo—the people, the place—is to be timeless, outside of time and part of the endless cycles of nature. It is also to be removed from the experience of ephemerality, fragmentation, and deracination that characterizes the modern predicament and, most significantly, to be defined according to eternal, immutable values arising from a profound integration with place. Although, like the typical modernist protagonist, Abel is first seen in isolation, and though Abel's "illness" will very shortly appear to resemble the shizophrenia theorists have identified as the postmodern condition—"schizophrenia in the form of a rubble of distinct and unrelated signifiers"—this prologue underscores the stable, coherent cultural and psychic center from which Abel is alienated and which may be recovered.[10]

As prologues are expected to do, this one lays out the "argument" of the novel. Because of the traditional invocation, we know that the story is to be conceived of as born from an older—timeless—oral tradition and bearing the responsiblities of that tradition. The allusion to the "house made of dawn" of the Night Chant suggests that a journey toward reintegration and healing will be part of the experience of the novel. Because at the conclusion of the prologue Abel is running and "seemed almost to be standing still," marked by the runnels of rain, we know that his reintegration has occurred, but only following the experience of a loss of sun—and thus vision—an eclipse and "a dark and certain shadow" upon the land and Abel. Thus the prologue tells us that Abel's quest will be complete and successful and that he will finally be integrated into the timeless landscape evoked in the first lines, but the "certain shadow" suggests that the journey will not be without danger and difficulty. As in traditional storytelling, we know the outcome of the story at the beginning, a fact that should shift our attention to the performance itself, to the way the story is told. An audience schooled in Native American storytelling will recognize in the prologue the typical pattern of the questing culture hero and realize that the well-known outline of a traditional story is being adapted to comprehend contemporary experience.[11]

The events of *House Made of Dawn* take place within a seven-year period. The novel is divided into four sections. Section 1, the most coherent portion of the novel, and that part which precipitates what will be the crisis in Abel's journey toward wholeness, constitutes nearly half of the novel and contains seven chapters. Sections 2 through 4 contain a total of seven chapters. Seven and four are powerful, sacred numbers within Native American cultures. Four is the number of the seasons, the cardinal directions, balance, beauty, and completion. Seven incorporates the cardinal directions as well as the center, zenith, and nadir. With its careful numerology, the very structure of the novel is designed to move us inward toward wholeness and well-being, echoing the centripetal forces dominant in the Indian world.

Section 1, "The Longhair," begins on July 20, 1945, with Abel's return from war. With this date, Momaday introduces the entropic pressures of colonial and modern history. July 20 marks the anniversary of Diego de Vargas's punitive campaign against the Jemez Pueblo in 1694 and the date upon which the Navajo were ordered to surrender at Fort Defiance in 1863.[12] Ironically, Abel is returning from a war in which he fought for the nation that upon each of these occasions had attempted to destroy the cultures—Pueblo and Navajo—that merge to form this novel. It is obvious that Abel's displacement is temporal as well as spatial.

Just as the prologue allowed us to enter a timeless, mythic dimension, the first paragraph of section 1 uses present tense and "to be" verbs to re-create this sense of timelessness: "The river lies in a valley of hills and fields. The north end of the valley is narrow, and the river runs down from the mountains through a canyon. The sun strikes the canyon floor only a few hours each day, and in winter the snow remains for a long time in the crevices of the walls. There is a town in the valley, and there are ruins of other towns in the canyon. In three directions from the town there are cultivated fields." Syntactically, Momaday creates a feeling of paradigmatic balance: this is the way it is, always.

In the third paragraph of this book the prose shifts from present tense to the simple past of the storyteller: "It is hot in the end of July. The old man Francisco drove a team of roan mares near the place where the river bends around a cottonwood." Here, we move suddenly out of mythic time into historic time as the old man drives out of the pueblo and into the world of Greyhound buses and events beyond the traditions of the people to meet his drunken grandson. Francisco has taken the "old road" to the nearby cross-roads village of San Ysidro, avoiding the higher paved road to the east and staying with the old ways as long as possible. Driving to meet Abel's bus, Francisco "glanced at the wagon and the mares to be sure that everything was in order." Order in the Jemez world, as in that of other American Indian cultures, signifies beauty and strength, but when Abel appears, all is not in order: "He was drunk, and he fell against his grandfather and did not know him" (13). In a world in which identity is derived from community, to not know one's grandfather is dangerous.

On the dawn of his first morning back, after sleeping a day and night, Abel goes out into the hills east of the pueblo in order to see the place, to be reintegrated into the landscape through vision. However, as he walks through the village, "all the dogs began to bark," a response that underscores Abel's strangeness. And it is a strangeness that derives not simply from the trauma of war. Abel had been alienated within the village even before he left for the war: "He did not know who his father was. His father was a Navajo, they said, or a Sia, or an Isleta, an outsider anyway, which made him and his mother and Vidal [his brother] somehow foreign and strange" (15). Coupled with the possibility, alluded to insultingly by Porcingula, that his grandfather, Francisco, may have been fa-thered by the corrupt priest, Nicolás, Abel's obscure parentage weakens his sense of self, setting him apart from the pueblo, even while it strengthens his implicit resemblance to the traditional cul-ture hero, whose parentage is often obscure.[13]

In a penetrating reading of this novel, Susan Scarberry-Garcia has discussed parallels between Abel and his brother Vidal and the Stricken Twins of the Night Chant. As Scarberry-Garcia notes,

Navajo story patterns reveal a hero or heroes (or occasionally heroines as in Mountainway and Beautyway), often "outsiders" from birth, forced by circumstances to leave home and combat numerous terrify-ing obstacles that confront them for reasons unknown. After undergo-ing a symbolic death experience and being reborn through the aid of the Holy People or spirit helpers, the heroes return home to their people to teach the healing ceremonial that remade them.[14]

Of names, Momaday has said, "I believe that a man is his name. . . . Somewhere in the Indian mentality there is that idea that when someone is given a name—and, by the way, it transcends Indian cultures certainly—when a man is given a name, existence is given him, too. And what could be worse than not having a name."[15] Abel's name, with its loud biblical resonance, emphasizes his position in tension between Indian and Euramerican cultures. From a mythic tradition "other" than that of Jemez, or Native American, the name "Abel" brings to the novel curious primal undertones that help to isolate Momaday's character from the matrix of pueblo culture described in the novel. Is the name designed to encourage European-Americans to think of the Indian as the slain brother, to consider themselves condemned for this primal sin? Such queries do not lead very far, but it is nonetheless impossible to ignore this obtrusive name already "charged with value" as it is, "shot through with shared thoughts, value judgments and accents."[16] The effect is centrifugal, decentering Abel further from Pueblo culture in the reader's mind.

Early in the novel, Abel's memory provides the reader with a coherent picture of his life before the war, including the powerful vision of snake and eagle as well as Abel's killing of the captured eagle, and Momaday writes, "This—everything in advance of his going—he could remember whole and in detail. It was the recent past, the intervention of days and years without meaning, of awful calm and collision, time always immediate and confused, that he could not put together in his mind" (25). Once outside of the continuum represented by life within the pueblo, Abel has no temporal referent; the cycles of Indian time vanish in a collision of incoherent time segments. Abel's condition, which involves an inability to articulate, suggests, as noted above, a postmodern schizophrenia: "If personal identity is forged through 'a certain temporal unification of the past and future with the present before me,' and if sentences move through the same trajectory, then an inability to unify past, present, and future in the sentence betokens a similar inability to 'unify the past, present and future of our own biographical experience or psychic life.' " Considering the "condition of postmodernity," David Harvey writes:

We can no longer conceive of the individual as alienated in the classical Marxist sense, because to be alienated presupposes a coherent rather than a fragmented sense of self from which to be alienated. It is only in terms of such a centred sense of personal identity that individuals can pursue projects over time, or think cogently about the production of a future significantly better than time present and time past. . . . Postmodernism typically strips away that possibility by concentrating upon the schizophrenic circumstances induced by fragmentation and all those instabilities (including those of language) that prevent us even picturing coherently, let alone devising strategies to produce, some radically different future.[17]

Back from the war, Able is unable to "unify past, present, and future in the sentence," unable to communicate even with his grandfather. Abel considers his inarticulateness:

His return to the town had been a failure. . . . He had tried in the days that followed to speak to his grandfather, but he could not say the things he wanted; he had tried to pray, to sing, to enter into the old rhythm of the tongue, but he was no longer attuned to it. And yet it was there still, like memory, in the reach of his hearing, as if Francisco or his mother or Vidal had spoken out of the past and the words had taken hold of the moment and made it eternal. Had he been able to say it, anything of his own language—even the commonplace formula of greeting "Where are you going,"—which had no being beyond sound, no visible substance, would once again have shown him whole to himself; but he was dumb. Not dumb—but inarticulate. (57)

Momaday plays upon the word *inarticulate* to suggest that Abel cannot speak because he is not whole; and he cannot imagine a future ("Where are you going") because such imagination is dependent upon an ability to unify past and present. As an archetypal questing hero, Abel must undertake a dangerous journey—from his home to war, to prison, to Los Angeles, and home again—and suffer greatly, to the point of annihilation, before he is made whole and knowledgeable. Crucial, however, is the fact that the center still holds in Abel's world; it is there to be recovered. Abel is alienated, but unlike many protagonists of postmodern fiction, Abel is not schizophrenic; he will achieve ultimately that "temporal unification of the past and future with the present" that forges identity.

During his trial for the murder of the albino, Abel realizes that "word by word these men were disposing of him in language, their language" (95). Recognizing the power of privileged language to deny him authenticity, by remaining silent Abel refuses to acknowledge the power of the court's language, that "medium through which a hierarchical structure of power is perpetuated, and the medium through which conceptions of 'truth', 'order', and 'reality' become established."[18]

Only one experience, "one sharp fragment of recall," stands out in Abel's recent memory: "He awoke on the side of a wooded hill. It was afternoon and there were bright, slanting shafts of light on all sides; the ground was covered with damp, matted leaves" (25–26). Abel's remembrance begins with a comforting sense of place, but it becomes a nightmare memory as a German tank enters this pastoral scene: "It moved into the wide wake of silence, taking hold of the silence and swelling huge inside of it. . . . The machine concentrated calm, strange and terrific, and it was coming." Six times in two paragraphs the tank is referred to as "the machine," never "the tank," and it becomes totemic: "It rose up behind the hill, black and massive, looming there in front of the sun. He saw it swell, deepen, and take shape on the skyline, as if it were some upheaval of the earth, the eruption of stone and eclipse" (26–27). The rather Faulknerian machine / tank rises up to represent everything that is threatening and alien in the non-Indian world surrounding Abel. It is another version of the machine in the garden so common in American literature. Like the "dark and certain shadow" in the prologue, the tank comes between Abel and the sun, denying light and vision. The repetition of the key word *eclipse* from the prologue assures that we will make a connection between the crisis presented metaphorically in the prologue and this dark war trauma.

Five days after his return, Abel rather surprisingly elects to participate in the contest of the chicken-pull, dressing in his old clothes for the first time and "making a poor showing, full of caution and gesture" (43). Obviously trying to force himself too quickly back into the ceremonial life of the pueblo, Abel is uncomfortable and awkward. He can no longer read the signs of the community, and he fails and is humiliated by the victorious albino. Seven days later, Abel and the albino speak softly in a bar and then go outside, where Abel kills his enemy with a knife. The albino is described as "large, lithe, and white-skinned. . . . The face was huge and mottled white and pink, and the thick, open lips were blue and violet. The flesh of the jowls was loose, and it rode on the bone of the jaws." Momaday's choice of the verb *rode* here echoes Emily Dickinson's startling image in the poem "A narrow fellow in the grass," in which the snake, an ambiguous symbol of evil and nature, is described as "riding" in / upon the grass. With a Guggenheim fellowship, Momaday had spent a year reading Dickinson in manuscript just before the publication of *House Made of Dawn*, and he has stated that from Dickinson he had learned "a good deal about language—and in the process a good deal about the art of intellectual survival." Such an allusion to Dickinson's serpent would certainly underscore the unfathomable ambiguity of the albino's evil.[19]

In the murder scene Momaday reinforces the disturbing qualities of the "white man":

> The white man raised his arms, as if to embrace him, and came forward. But Abel had already taken hold of the knife, and he drew it. He leaned inside the white man's arms and drove the blade up under the bones of the breast and across. The white man's hands lay on Abel's shoulders, and for a moment the white man stood very still. . . . Then he closed his hands upon Abel and drew him close. Abel heard the strange excitement of the white man's breath, and the quick, uneven blowing at his ear, and felt the blue shivering lips upon him, felt even the scales of the lips and the hot slippery point of the tongue, writhing. (77–78)

There can be little doubt that the albino, who in death "seemed just then to wither and grow old," is meant to be identified with the serpent and evil. Nor can the suggestion of witchcraft be avoided in the transformation of the youthful "white man" into the seventy-year-old he must be were he born in 1875 as Father Nicolás's journal indicates. Momaday himself has said, "He (the albino) is manifesting the evil of his presence. Witchcraft and the excitement of it is part of that too."[20]

The albino has intrigued critics of *House Made of Dawn* perhaps more than any other single aspect of the novel. The obvious reading is that he signifies the "white man" who has disenfranchised Indian people and Abel in particular—a simplistic reading that tells us little. Matthias Schubnell has suggested that "the killing of the albino is a symbolic representation of the cultural conflict which Abel is trying to resolve." In a rather ingenious reading, H. S. McAllister has argued that the albino is possessed by the witch, Nicolás *teah-wha*. The witch, the old priest Nicolás, and the albino are, says McAllister, "in a complex, magical way, three manifestations of a single person." Paula Gunn Allen has suggested vaguely that "Abel murders the witch because, for personal and historical reasons that become apparent as the plot develops, he believes that paganism is evil and that it must be destroyed."[21]

Momaday's own description of the albino may be the best directive toward an understanding of the "white man's" nature. In a letter to his editor at Harper & Row, Momaday said, "He is a white man, or rather 'white man' in quotes, in appearance, but in fact he is neither white nor a man in the usual sense of those words. He is an embodiment of evil like Moby Dick, an intelligent malignity."[22] In accepting the author's definition, however, it must be kept in mind that in Melville's *Moby-Dick* the white whale is "an intelligent malignity" only through the perception of Ahab, a thorough-going Calvinist—and monologist—whose imagination has achieved a Manichaean division of the world into a struggle between good and a very palpable evil. For Ahab, evil must be sought out and destroyed; there is no place in his world for ambiguity (or the polysemous text). The name of Ahab's ship, the *Pequod*, with its allusion to the Pequots slaughtered in their villages by the Puritans, is perhaps meant to remind us of the terrible consequences of such consciousness in this new world. Ahab's Calvinist dialectic has no place within the traditional paradigms of Native American cosmology.

However, while Momaday has obviously made his albino—with his scaly lips and pointed tongue—a much more unmistakable emblem of evil than is Melville's whale, there is a similar message in both *Moby-Dick* and *House Made of Dawn*. Melville's Ishmael is able to accept the "riddling blankness" of the whale, to look upon it nonteleologically without seeing a monomaniacal vision of evil. Ishmael is the "balanced man" who tells us at the beginning of his book: "Not ignoring what is good, I am quick to perceive a horror, and could still be social with it—would they let me—since it is but well to be on friendly terms with all the inmates of the place one lodges in."[23] Ishmael, spinning atop the final vortex, is the novel's only survivor, and Ishmael's philosophy sounds remarkably like Native American cultures' insistence upon balance and upon the necessity of both consciousness of and integration within all elements of this world. It is the *perception* of both good and evil that is humanity's responsibility, the *consciousness* of both that will ensure balance.

At his trial, Abel thinks, "He had killed the white man. It was not a complicated thing, after all; it was very simple. . . . A man kills such an enemy if he can" (95). However, it is not as simple as

Abel believes, for he has seriously erred in his murder of the albino. Acting in the manner of an Ahab, Abel attempts to destroy evil, and evil is turned back upon him as a result. Just as Ahab and the white whale are inextricably linked at the end of *Moby-Dick*, at the moment of his death the albino reaches out to embrace Abel. The murder scene is described, in fact, not as a struggle but as a kind of homoerotic self-sacrifice by the white man, who "raised his arms, as if to embrace him, and came forward." The albino embraces and kisses his killer, and Abel hears the "excitement of the white man's breath." The albino is excited by his triumph in this moment. In attempting to destroy evil, Abel has become one with it, accepted its seed.

It is Francisco who provides the clues to the real nature of Abel's confrontation with the albino. Francisco is the syncretic "balanced man" of the novel, he who has successfully fused the two worlds he inhabits. Of Francisco, the old priest Nicolás had written in a letter: "He is one of them & goes often in the kiva & puts on their horns & hides & does worship that Serpent which even is the One our most ancient enemy. Yet he is unashamed to make one of my sacristans" (50). This is the enduring strength of the Pueblo people of which Momaday has written: "Their invaders were a long time conquering them; and now, after four centuries of Christianity, they still pray in Tanoan to the old deities of the earth and sky. . . . They have assumed the names and gestures of their enemies, but have held on to their own, secret souls; and in this there is a resistance and an overcoming, a long outwaiting" (56). Francisco has no difficulty in bringing two worlds together into a vital, hetero-geneous unity—a crucial ability in a world where wholeness is essential and division or fragmentation causes illness. Unlike his grandson, Francisco knows who he is; like the Pueblo cultures as a whole, he subverts the language of the Church by assimilating it into his indigenous cosmology. By assuming the "names and gestures" of the colonizers, Native Americans for several centuries have abrogated the authority of the conqueror's most powerful weapon—language—and have appropriated the dominant dis-course by making it, in the words of Indian writer Raja Rao, "convey in a language that is not one's own the spirit that is one's own." This is the process Acoma Pueblo writer Simon Ortiz has described as making use of "foreign ritual, ideas, and material in their own—Indian—terms."[24]

Unlike Abel, Francisco knows the proper way to deal with the evil that is afoot in the world. As a child, Abel had been frightened by the witch, Nicolás *teah-whau*, who had appeared out of a cornfield as he was herding sheep and screamed a curse at him. He had run away "and waited for the snake-killer dog to close up the flock and follow." When the dog reaches the boy, however, it acts strangely: "The dog had quivered and laid back its ears. Slowly it backed away and crouched, not looking at him, not looking at anything, but listening. Then he heard it, the thing itself. He knew even then that it was only the wind, but it was a stranger sound than he had ever known. . . . The moan of the wind grew loud, and it filled him with dread" (16). Dogs, according to Pueblo and Navajo belief, are able to sense witches, and a ringing in the ears, like the moaning of the wind Abel hears, is a traditional sign of a witch presence.[25] The identification of the evil presence with the serpent is accomplished through the presence of the snake-killer dog (though the simple explanation, of course, is that sheepdogs are traditionally adept at killing rattlesnakes to protect their flocks).

Years later, after Abel's return from the war, Francisco experiences the presence of evil while hoeing his corn, a presence signified at first by whispers in the corn and then the warning of a ringing in the ears: "But now, at the end of long exertion, his aged body let go of the mind, and he was suddenly conscious of some alien presence close at hand. . . . His ears rang with weariness. . . . He was too old to be afraid. His acknowledgment of the unknown was nothing more than a dull, intrinsic sadness, a vague desire to weep, for evil had long since found him out and knew who he was" (64). After Francisco leaves the cornfield, the evil presence is confirmed: "And there the breathing resumed, rapid and uneven with excitement. Above the open mouth, the nearly sightless eyes followed the old man out of the cornfield, and the barren lids fluttered helplessly behind the colored glass" (64). Momaday appears to want us to identify the evil presence in the cornfield with the albino.

Unlike Abel, however, Francisco realizes the proper way with which to deal with evil. He acknowledges its presence and turns away, neutralizing its power. This is an important message of the novel: evil cannot be destroyed; to attempt to do so is to err seriously and dangerously. Particularly in the Navajo worldview, the universe from the time of creation has been a dangerous place balanced precariously between good and evil. Both Pueblo and Navajo healing ceremonies—such as the Night Chant in *House Made of Dawn*—are focused upon restoring harmony or balance within the individual and among natural, human, and supernatural elements that make up the world. In this vein, the rattlesnake is respected and feared by the Pueblo peoples and is considered a powerful, dangerous presence, but it is to be acknowledged and avoided, never killed. The identification of the witch, Nicolás *teah-whau*, and the albino with the serpent suggests that Francisco's is the only acceptable response. Abel, returned from a foreign war in which the adversaries were Hitler and fascism—embodiments to the Allied forces of an absolute evil that must be destroyed—and a war in which the atomic bomb (ultimate symbol of the world's destruction through fragmentation, the splitting of nuclei) came into being, has been severely wrenched from the Pueblo worldview.[26] He thus reacts incorrectly.

Another character divided against herself in the novel is Angela Grace Martin St. John, with whom Abel has a brief affair. If Abel's name comes laden with suggestive tensions, Angela's full name is a Christian labyrinth.[27] Come from Los Angeles to live in the Benevides ("good health") house and take the healing waters of Los Ojos, Angela is immediately identifiable with Mary, Our Lady of the Angels, who happens to be the patronness of the Bahkyush people of Walatowa, a patroness they also refer to as Porcingula. Porcingula, coincidentally, is also the name of the witch's daughter, with whom Francisco conceives a stillborn child. It would appear that, like Francisco, Abel is involved with a woman identified with Mary—Francisco's lover is a witch's daughter and Abel's a married, pregnant, white outsider. "Grace" underscores Angela's somewhat ironic identification with the Virgin, while her remaining names emphasize the conflict that has made her intensely unhappy. "Martin" calls to mind the great intellect of Calvinism, Martin Luther, while "St. John" evokes the great mystic—two poles of response to the world that signify the destructive split within Angela when she appears at Walatowa. The association with Calvinism again suggests the dualistic struggle between good and evil. While southwestern Native American cultures may also see the world as divided and balanced, the vital difference is one of teleology: to the Calvinist (and colonial American) mind the world is a millenarian battleground where Satan must, and inevitably will, be defeated, whereas to the Indian mind that balance constitutes a wholeness that must be precariously maintained through ritual and ceremony.

Angela's physical and spiritual selves are alienated from one another; to be healed she must be restored to wholeness, a restoration Abel will be able to effect. This division is attested to in her neurotic and contradictory feelings about the baby she is carrying when she arrives at Los Ojos. Angela has come to the canyon seeking vision, as her settling at Los Ojos indicates. The inability to see well, or clearly, is associated with vulnerability and "otherness" in the novel. In a lyrical evocation of the landscape, Momaday writes of the coyote, fox, bobcat, eagle, and other creatures—including the Indians—who "have tenure in the land." He excludes from this mystical "tenure," however, those elements associated with the white man: "The other, latecoming things—the beasts of burden and of trade, the horse and the sheep, the dog and the cat—these have an alien and inferior aspect, a *poverty of vision and instinct*, by which they are estranged from the wild land, and made tentative" (56; emphasis mine). Here, non-Indian reality is deprivileged, and reality is recentered in the Pueblo world. Angela cannot see what the Indians see and is aware of that limitation. Remembering the eyes of the dancers at the Cochiti Pueblo, she thinks that "their eyes were held upon some vision out of range . . . some reality that she did not know or even suspect" (37). Like the whites in McNickle's *Wind from an Enemy Sky*, Angela suspects a different "map of the mind," an alien epistemology from which she is excluded.

From the beginning, however, Angela watches, using her eyes to absorb and comprehend Abel's world. When Abel comes to split wood for her at the Benevides house, she watches him, looking down from an upstairs window, and Momaday's phallic description of Abel's wood-cutting, worthy of D. H. Lawrence at his least subtle, suggests that Angela has divined a transendent truth.[28] Like the runners who run as water, following the path of least resistance, Abel offers a lesson in wholeness for a brief moment to the distraught Angela, a lesson furthered when on another day she again watches Abel and identifies him with badger and bear: "Once she had seen an animal slap at the water, a badger or a bear. . . . She would have liked to cup her hand to the wet black snout, to hold for a moment the hot blowing of the bear's life. She went out of the house and sat down on the stone steps of the porch. He was there rearing above the wood" (34). Angela's vision of Abel here bodes well for this white woman who is learning to "see," for badger and bear are considered by the people of Jemez to be younger and elder brother, respectively, and powerful healers. Within the pueblo are both a badger clan and a bear curing society.[29]

Growing beyond her own "poverty of vision," Angela has seen within Abel the bear-power that came to Francisco when the bear gave itself to him during his youth; this is the power that will ensure Abel's survival on the dangerous journey ahead of him. Later, as they are making love, Angela thinks of "the badger at the water, and the great bear, blue-black and blowing" (63).

As Angela learns to see "beyond," to the interconnectedness of all things in the Indian world, she moves toward integration and health. This new, holistic vision is emphasized when she arrives home one night and sees the Benevides house in a new way: "There was no longer a high white house of stucco and stone . . . but a black organic mass the night had heaved up, even as long ago the canyon itself had been wrenched out of time." Momaday goes on in this paragraph to repetitively stress Angela's new sight: "She would see into the windows and the doors. . . . She would see whether the hollyhocks were bent with bees. . . . She would regard the house in the light of day. . . . And the Benevides house, which she had seen from the river and the road, to which she had made claim by virtue of her regard, this house would be the wings and the stage of a reckoning" (53).

A list of the psychologically and physically displaced includes nearly every character in the novel. Father Olguin's displacement is illuminated in a scene in which he inadvertently drives his car into the maze of the pueblo during a fiesta and comes face-to-face with an infant in a cradleboard: "The hair lay in tight wet rings above the eyes, and all the shapeless flesh of the face dripped with sweat and shone copper in the sunlight. Flies crawled upon the face and lay thick about the eyes and mouth. The muscles twitched under the fat and the head turned slowly from side to side in the agony of sad and helpless laughter" (69). In Father Olguin's vision the baby becomes a threatening sign of the priest's "otherness" in this world, one of the "grinning, unappeased, aboriginal demons" D. H. Lawrence saw in the guilty heart of Euramerica's fascination with wilderness and the Indian. The terror confronting Father Olguin in the form of the infant grows out of what Lawrence called America's "powerful disentegrative effect on the white psyche."[30] Like a character from a Joseph Conrad novel, the priest feels abruptly alien in an unfathomably pagan colonial outpost and mocked by the Indians' cultural persistence, by the subversiveness of their very survival in remoteness.

Near the end of the novel we will learn that the priest has become reconciled to his fate: "In the only way possible, perhaps, he had come to terms with the town. . . . To be sure, there was the matter of some old and final cleavage, of certain exclusion, the whole and subtle politics of estrangement, but that was easily put aside . . . (174). And when Father Olguin shouts after Abel in the novel's final paragraphs, "I understand, do you hear? . . . I understand! Oh, God! I understand—I understand!" it is apparent that, although this may be partly wish-fulfillment, the priest has indeed moved closer to the people of the pueblo. Unlike the priests in McNickle's *The Surrounded* or *Wind from an Enemy Sky*, Father Olguin has been finally allowed a measure of insight into the Indian world. That the insight will remain inevitably partial is suggested by his one opaque and sightless eye.

On one level, John Big Bluff Tosamah, the Priest of the Sun and Right Reverend of the "Holiness Pan-Indian Rescue Mission" in Los Angeles, is scarcely less alienated and displaced than Olguin. Section 2 of the novel begins with a description of the grunion spawning on California beaches, a description cast in the tones of a familiar nursery rhyme (a syncretic jingle about miscegenation, marriage of owl and pussycat): "They hurl themselves upon the land and writhe in the light of the moon, the moon, the moon; they writhe in the light of the moon." Momaday adds, "They are among the most helpless creatures on the face of the earth" (83). Immediately following this paragraph, the Priest of the Sun is introduced in his basement peyote church.

The helpless fish of the opening paragraph have been most often associated with Abel, whom we will soon see lying beaten and broken upon the beach under the light of the moon. The juxtaposition of Tosamah's introduction and the description of the fish makes it difficult not to connect the two, however, and the nursery jingle makes this connection even more intriguing, for the Priest of the Sun is both a trickster and a fraud, a manipulator of language the import of which is undercut systematically by a cynical superficiality that reduces his words at times to mere jingles or turns them against themselves. This aspect of Tosamah is hinted at in the description of paraphernalia for the peyote ceremony, the first of which is the alliteratively ludicrous "fine fan of fancy pheasant feathers." Tosamah's alienation, however, is tempered by his subversive role as trickster.

As a peyote priest, Tosamah is involved in the appropriation of biblical discourse to bear the burden of a new, syncretic American

Indian spirituality, a spiritual order that arose out of the darkest days for Indian cultures in the nineteenth century. As a trickster priest, Tosamah mocks, ridicules, and challenges every fixed meaning or static definition. Commenting upon Tosamah and in particular the priest's sermon based upon the Gospel of Saint John, Arnold Krupat has written: "Although the Gospel according to John may agree that the 'word gives origin,' inasmuch as 'In the beginning was the Word,' this is hardly what Native American cultures have believed nor is it what Momaday's own practice reveals. Words have power; they may indeed be sacred. But they do not come from 'nothing'; nothing is yet another category of the West whose Native American equivalents would be hard to specify." Krupat has an axe to grind with Momaday's art, declaring Momaday to be the "Native American writer most committed to hegemonic monologue"—the ultimate sin of the postmodern age—and even "absurdly racist." "There is very little," this critic complains, "in the way of wit or humor, no gossip or scatology, decidedly no self-criticism or criticism by others permitted to sound."[31] Krupat's indictment, seeming to accuse the Kiowa author of not writing like an Indian, demonstrates a significant misreading of Tosamah's character and role and of Momaday's art.

As a trickster, Tosamah functions in an antithetical mode—Native Americans in his audience would recognize this fact in the priest's declaration that words, with their generative power, come from "nothing." Tosamah's antic posturing, his deconstruction of his own discourse, his hilarious code-switching, are all trickster signs that his Indian congregation would read easily. Tosamah embodies precisely those elements Krupat finds missing from Momaday's work: he is witty, gossipy, scatological, and implicitly self-critical. In his role as spokesman for Momaday himself, Tosamah also represents a delightful self-parody on the part of his author. The connection between Tosamah and his author is at once obvious in the fact that Momaday has given the priest his own quasi-autobiographical remembrance from *The Way to Rainy Mountain*. Momaday has also admitted that Tosamah serves at times as the author's "mouthpiece" and that Tosamah is "far and away" his favorite character in the novel. "I think he's the most intricate," Momaday has explained. "He's much more interesting because he's more complicated and has many more possibilities. He has a strange and lively mind, and I find him, and did at the time I was writing the book, fascinating."[32]

Tosamah's voice functions primarily as an example of what Bakhtin would label "hybridization," defined as "a mixture of two social languages within the limits of a single utterance, an encounter, within the arena of utterance, between two different linguistic consciousnesses."[33] On the one hand, Tosamah believes what he says—his words carry the weight of internal persuasiveness—while on the other hand the priest implicitly acknowledges the presence of externally persuasive, authoritative discourse. Quoting the Bible, a prior discourse quite privileged in Western culture, and one very distinct from the sources of Native American cultures, Tosamah subverts the authority of that text by placing it in dialogic tension with a Native American *context*. Like the traditional trickster, Tosamah is in dialogue with himself, embodies contradictions, challenges authority, mocks and tricks us into self-knowledge. A reader who misses this crucial core of Tosamah's character may also fail to grasp the heterogeneous and dialogic nature of Momaday's novel and, in fact, all of Momaday's art.

In spite of the vital role he plays as the novel's trickster, the Priest of the Sun is also the most poignant figure in the novel. The embodiment of two linguistic consciousnesses, with his combination of insight and cynicism Tosamah is a fish out of water, helpless to help himself. While Abel can go home again, and Benally at least retains the world of his Navajo people intact within his imagination and memory, Tosamah—like the peripatetic trickster / creator of Native American mythologies—has nothing except imagination and language out of which to fashion his world. When he goes into the streets of urban Los Angeles with his eagle-bone whistle, we feel the ambiguity of his position: "In the four directions did the Priest of the Sun, standing painted in the street, serve notice that something holy was going on in the universe" (106).

In his sermon on the word, Tosamah echoes Momaday's thoughts expressed in "The Man Made of Words": "It seems to me that in a certain sense we are all made of words; that our essential being consists in language. . . . Man has consumate being in language, and there only. Only when he is embodied in an idea, and the idea is realized in language, can man take possession of himself." And, even more significantly, Momaday gives to the Priest of the Sun the author's own eloquent remembrance of his Kiowa grandmother, published earlier as an essay entitled "The Way to Rainy Mountain" and revised later as the introduction to *The Way to Rainy Mountain*.[34] Tosamah says,

My grandmother was a storyteller; she knew her way around words.
. . . She had learned that in words and in language, and there only,
she could have whole and consumate being. . . . I was a child and
that old woman was asking me to come directly into the presence of
her mind and spirit; she was taking hold of my imagination, giving
me to share in the great fortune of her wonder and delight. She was
asking me to go with her to the confrontation of something that was
sacred and eternal. It was a timeless, timeless thing. (88)

Despite the profundity of Tosamah's understanding of the oral
tradition, and despite the priest's appropriation of some his author's most sincere language, Tosamah deliberately violates his
grandmother's reverence for the power of the word as he distorts
and manipulates, committing the sin of which he accuses Saint
John: talking too much. "You see," the priest says of his grandmother, "for her words were medicine; they were magic and invisible" (88). The white man, says Tosamah, "takes such things as
words and literatures for granted. . . . He is sated and insensitive;
his regard for language—for the Word itself—as an instrument of
creation has diminished to the point of no return. It may be that he
will perish by the Word" (89). In the Priest of the Sun's parting
words, the neutralizing cynicism is obvious: " 'Good night,' he
said, at last, 'and get yours.' " As he illustrates the error he has just
described, Tosamah teaches by negative example.

Tosamah's dialogical tension is further evidenced in his relationship with Abel. As a trickster, Tosamah undertakes the appropriate
trickster task of mocking and taunting Abel into self-knowledge, a
painful process for Abel, but one that helps prepare him for his
return to the pueblo.[35] At the same time, Tosamah's dismantling of
Abel is inspired at least in part out of envy. When Tosamah complains about Abel, Benally, the displaced Navajo who is the "Night
Chanter" of section 3, questions the Priest of the Sun's perception:
"He was going to get us all into trouble, Tosamah said. . . . But,
you know, Tosamah doesn't understand either. He talks pretty big
all the time, and he's educated, but he doesn't understand" (135).
Ben recalls another speech Tosamah makes about Abel, a speech
that hints strongly at Tosamah's true feelings:

"You take that poor cat," he said. "They gave him every advantage.
They gave him a pair of shoes and told him to go to school. They
deloused him and gave him a lot of free haircuts and let him fight on
their side. But was he grateful? Hell, no, man. He was too damn dumb
to be civilized. . . . He turned out to be a real primitive sonuvabitch.
. . . They put that cat away, man. They had to. It's part of the Jesus

scheme. . . . They put all of us renegades, us diehards away sooner
or later. . . . Listen, here, Benally, one of these nights there's going
to be a full red moon, a hunter's moon, and we're going to find us a
wagon train full of women and children. Now you don't believe this,
but I drink to that now and then." (136–37)

Failing to decode the trickster discourse—and verbal irony—in the
priest's words, Benally dismisses Tosamah's talk, saying, "He's
always going on like that, Tosamah, talking crazy and showing off,
but he doesn't understand" (136). Tosamah understands more than
Benally realizes. Bernard Hirsch has suggested:

Seeing Abel through Indian eyes, Tosamah cannot help but admire
him as a kind of modern-day warrior who refuses to give in meekly
to the torment and tribulations of urban Indian life. But if Tosamah
as an Indian is vicariously elevated by Abel's integrity, he is at the
same time humbled by the lack of his own. Viewed from either perspective, then, white or Indian, Abel engenders in Tosamah self-
contempt so strong that it is beyond enduring.[36]

Deeply perceptive and sensitive to what it means to be a mixedblood
spiritual leader in barren Los Angeles, aware of his own offenses
against his grandmother's conception of the word as medicine,
Tosamah takes out his sense of loss and self-doubt upon Abel, for
Abel has what Tosamah can never have. Discussing his novel,
Momaday has underscored this aspect of Tosamah's character, saying, "He's a kind of riddle and he's extremely skeptical but has the
kind of intellgence that makes the most of it. But I think of him as
being in some ways pathetic, too. He's very displaced."[37] Unlike
Tosamah, Abel has a center to which he can return, a cultural
heritage intact and deeply imprinted upon him even in his most
desperate circumstances.

That Tosamah would like very much to identify with Abel is
evident in his reference to "all us renegades, us diehards." But,
straddling two worlds in antic disposition, Tosamah can't convince
even Benally. "He's a clown," Benally says of the priest, "he'll make
a fool out of you if you let him" (164). Benally's words, of course,
underscore Tosamah's trickster aspect and the priest's paradoxically healing effect upon his victim. As trickster does, however,
Tosamah tricks himself more often than not.[38] While Tosamah fur-
thers the disintegration that is a necessary step toward recovery for
Abel, Benally tries to help Abel to integrate into the new urban
reality. Ben, a product of the federal relocation policy of the fifties,
has bought into the American Dream with grim determination,

becoming literally dazzled by the city lights. About Abel, Ben says, "He was a longhair, like Tosamah said. You know, you have to change. That's the only way you can live in a place like this. You have to forget about the way it was, how you grew up and all" (135).

In spite of his statement, however, it is obvious that Benally has not forgotten the way it was. His memories recapture his childhood wholly and vividly. He remembers herding sheep for his grandfather: "And you were little and right there in the center of everything, the sacred mountains, the snow-covered mountains and the hills, the gullies and the flats, the sundown and the night, everything—where you were little, where you were and had to be." And he remembers returning to his grandfather's place from boarding school: "And at first light you went out and knew where you were. And it was the same, the way you remembered it, the way you knew it had to be; and nothing had changed. . . . It would always be the same out there. That was the way it was, that's all. It was that way on the day you were born, and it would be that way on the day you died" (154).

In Navajo country—a centripetal, spatially ordered world—Benally was centered, whole. Just as Abel went out at dawn to fix his home landscape within his vision upon his return from war, Benally went out to regard the country and re-place himself upon return from school. But Ben has lost the way. When he considers going home, he thinks "there would be nothing there, just the empty land and a lot of old people, dying off" (145). So he commits himself to the city: "It's a good place to live. . . . You wonder how you ever got along out there where you came from. There's nothing there, you know, just the land, and the land is empty and dead" (164). Ben has bought into the metanarrative of Euramerica with its historic, entropic definition of time and indigenous culture as well as place. But Benally nonetheless retains enough knowledge of his Navajo identity to serve as a healer to Abel. Having been beaten almost to death by Martinez, the corrupt cop—a physical disintegration paralleling his psychic disintegration—Abel has again made the mistake of confronting rather than acknowledging and avoiding evil. Called the "culebra," or "snake," by the Indians whom he persecutes, Martinez extends the evil presence of the albino. Abel's lesson is that evil cannot be killed.

As he lies upon the beach, close to death, Abel has the vision that leads to his restoration as he sees the dawn runners, "the old men running after evil. . . . full of tranquility, certitude." Momaday continues:

> The runners after evil ran as water runs, deep in the channel, in the way of least resistance, no resistance. . . . Suddenly he saw the crucial sense in their going, of old men in white leggings running after evil in the night. They were whole and indispensable in what they did; everything in creation referred to them. Because of them, perspective, proportion, design in the universe. . . . They ran with great dignity and calm, not in the hope of anything, but hopelessly; neither in fear nor hatred nor despair of evil, but simply in recognition and with respect. Evil was. Evil was abroad in the night; they must venture out to the confrontation; they must reckon dues and divide the world. Now, here, the world was open at his back. He had lost his place. He had been long ago at the center, had known where he was, had lost his way. (96)

Like Archilde Leon in *The Surrounded*, Abel cannot understand what seems to have gone inexorably wrong in his life: "He tried to think where the trouble had begun, what the trouble was. There was trouble; he could admit that to himself, but he had no real insight into his own situation" (97). However, with the new, nonteleological comprehension evident in his vision of the dawn runners, Abel is finally ready to return to Walatowa, to the center.

Abel has been prepared for his return by the healing powers of the Navajo chantways Benally has sung for him. At a "49" dance on a hill overlooking Los Angeles the night before Abel returns to the pueblo, Benally prays, chanting the "house made of dawn" prayer from the Night Chant, a prayer chanted by the singer, or healer, on the third day of the Night Chant ceremony and again at sunrise of the ninth day by the patient as he inhales the breath of the dawn.[39] The chant is a prayer for restoration of wholeness and balance, invoking the coercive power of language to compel change in the world. With the final lines of Benally's chant, the force of language to compel order and harmony is brought to fruition:

> May it be beautiful behind me,
> May it be beautiful below me,
> May it be beautiful above me,
> May it be beautiful all around me.
> In beauty it is finished. (135)

With the four iterations, the sacred number, the patient is centered and all is in balance and harmony in the universe. Abel, whose body has been broken by the brutal beating, and whose consciousness has been badly fragmented from our first meeting with him, is now able to return home, whole and on the path toward healing. Abel's healing has also been aided by the reappearance of Angela St. John, who comes to the hospital to see her former lover after he is beaten. While there, Angela tells Abel a story that she likes to tell her son, Peter. It is a story of a young Indian who "was born of a bear and a maiden" and who "had many adventures, and . . . became a great leader and saved his people." Angela tells Abel that "she always thought of him, Abel, when she told it" (169). Benally, who has been sitting in the hospital room and has heard Angela's story, thinks, "Ei Yei! A bear! A bear and a maiden. And she was a white woman and she thought it up, you know, made it up out of her own mind, and it was like that old grandfather talking to me, telling me about *Esdzá shash nadle*, or *Dzil quigi*, yes, just like that" (170). Ben then recounts the origin myth of the Mountain Chant, a story of the people fleeing from the frightening Changing Bear Maiden, and of Bear Maiden whose son by Bear becomes a culture hero.

A number of critics have discussed the figure of the bear in *House Made of Dawn*. Nora Baker Barry, examining the archetypal elements of the "Bear's Son," places Abel in the ranks of the "Bear's Son type" as "a universal hero." Peter Beidler suggests simply that in her "sexual fantasies" Angela has triggered a delayed awareness within Abel "of his own bear nature." The most thorough and worthwhile analysis of the bear figure in the novel, however, is that of Susan Scarberry-Garcia, who identifies Abel with Bear rather than Bear's son, thus making Peter, or the mythical young Indian of Angela's story, Bear's son and by implication the symbolic son of her union with Abel. Angela is identified both with the destructive Changing Bear Maiden and the more positive Bear Maiden of Navajo mythology. Scarberry-Garcia also relates a traditional Jemez bear story called the "Myth of the Mother Moon and the Great Bear," which "tells of a great bear who abducts the pregnant moon mother when she goes to get water for her husband the sun. In the bear's cave she gives birth to a son (stepson to bear) who emerges with great powers." As Scarberry-Garcia points out, structurally this myth fits neatly into events of the novel, making Peter stepson to Bear (Abel).[40]

Most importantly, Angela's story indicates that she has truly learned to "see" beyond; she has, through her experience in Los Ojos and Walatowa, seen into the mythic consciousness out of which is born the oral tradition. Benally recognizes the significance of this at once. And by bringing the healing forces of the Night Chant into the hospital room, with the powerful healing presence of Bear associated with Abel, Angela has joined with Benally in working to cure Abel.[41] More important than all of these associations is the fact that Angela has been able to achieve what Euramericans in McNickle's novels could not: she has shed the monologic authority of her privileged culture and broken through the "alien conceptual horizon" of another to realize a fertile syncretism. For Angela, Native American discourse has evidently become internally persuasive: "affirmed through assimilation, tightly interwoven with 'one's own word.'"[42] This is a process always demanded of those on the periphery and seldom accomplished by those from the privileged center.

The fourth and final section of *House Made of Dawn*, "The Dawn Runner," takes place seven years after Abel's return from the war. He has completed his journey of initiation, has had his illuminating vision of the dawn runners as he lay broken on the beach, and has come to sit beside Francisco as the old man dies. During the last seven mornings, Francisco talks to Abel. "The old man had spoken six times in the dawn," Momaday writes, "and the voice of his memory was whole and clear and growing like the dawn" (177). For Abel, however, the voice is not whole and clear: "He listened to the feeble voice that rose out of the darkness, and he waited helplessly. His mind was borne upon the dying words, but they carried him nowhere. His own sickness had settled into despair" (175).

Francisco is attempting to articulate and make whole the crucial experiences of his life, passing the story on to his grandson. He remembers the great race of his youth, the ritual bear hunt, Porcingula, and more, including his desire to teach Abel and Vidal about their world: "They must learn the whole contour of the black mesa. They must know it as they knew the shape of their hands. Always and by heart. . . . and they must live according to the sun appearing, for only then could they reckon where they were, where all things were, in time" (177). The Sioux lawyer, professor, and philosopher Vine Deloria, Jr., has distinguished between Native American and Euramerican worldviews by suggesting that "one group [Native American] is concerned with the philosophical problem of space and the other with the philosophical problem of time."

Deloria has further suggested that the "meaninglessness and alien-ation discernible in our generation results partially from our allowing time to consume space."[43] Abel has suffered just such a dislocation in time / space, a very modern predicament. In this remembered experience, Francisco had been attempting to place Abel and his brother very securely within the timeless space that defines their tribal identity.

Just before the seventh dawn, Abel awakens to find that his grandfather has died. Only at this moment does it seem that Abel has absorbed his grandfather's words, as Momaday writes: "He knew what had to be done." Abel prepares the old man ceremoni-ally for burial, doing everything correctly, and then goes to summon Father Olguin, the two actions recalling Francisco's ability to merge both religions and worlds during his lifetime. Instead of returning to his grandfather's house, Abel rubs himself with ashes and goes out into the dawn to join the "runners standing away in the dis-tance." The runners fix their vision upon "the clear pool of eternity," and Abel ends where he begins, by running after them: "All of his being was concentrated in the sheer motion of running on, and he was past caring about the pain." In motion Abel is no longer displaced. Of this figure of the runner with which the novel begins and ends, Momaday has said, "The man running is fitting himself into the basic motion of the universe. . . . That is simply a symbol-ism which prevails in the southwestern Indian world."[44] It would thus seem that Abel has recovered his place in an Indian world, mov-ing outside of the entropic, historical consciousness of Eurocentric America, with its voracious linear temporality and "fitting himself into the basic motion of the universe." Finally Abel breaks through the disorder of his conscious responses, and Momaday returns to the metaphor of vision once again: "Pure exhaustion laid hold of his mind, and he could see at last without having to think. He could see the canyon and the mountains and the sky. He could see the rain and the river and the fields beyond. He could see the dark hills at dawn." Abel achieves a coherent self-definition through his ability to see the space surrounding him, and see his place at the center. Silently Abel sings the prayer of restoration and healing he has learned from Be-nally: "House made of pollen, house made of dawn." And Momaday ends with the word "Qtsedaba," a convention of Jemez storytelling which, like the first word of the novel, places *House Made of Dawn* within the oral tradition that tells us who we are.

After two decades spent painting, traveling and writing nonfiction, including the multigenre masterpiece *The Way to Rainy Mountain*, Momaday returned to the interrelated themes of Indian identity and myth-making in a second published novel, *The Ancient Child* (1989). Featuring two protagonists, a young Navajo-Kiowa woman named Grey and a half-Kiowa artist named Locke Setman, or Set, *The Ancient Child* follows Set on a difficult and rather abrupt quest to discover who he is. Grey, self-assured and on her way to becoming a medicine woman, aids Set in his painful transformation. Underlying and informing the novel is the Kiowa myth of the boy who became a bear, the myth retold in the prologue to *The Way to Rainy Mountain* and again in the front pages of *The Ancient Child*. In 1986, Momaday had indicated the place of this myth in the novel—then a work in progress with the tentative title of "Set"—explaining that the myth of the boy who becomes a bear is central to the novel: "That's the basic myth, the one that I start with. That myth is very important to me personally, and I have thought about that story a lot and now it seems that it's time for me to expand upon it, to follow through on some of the possibilities that I've seen in it." At the same time, Momaday commented upon the place of myth in his second novel:

> I am very concerned to understand as much as I can about myth making. The novel that I'm working on now is really a construction of different myths. I've taken a Kiowa myth to begin with and am bringing it up to modern times. . . . My main character, Set, is the reincarnation of a boy who figures in Kiowa mythology, a boy who turns into a bear. And I'm also working with Billy the Kid in the same novel. And there will be other elements like that, other mythic elements that will inform the story in one way or another. I regard what I'm doing as an inquiry into the nature of myth making.[45]

Momaday suggests the essential place of myth in *The Ancient Child* with an epigraph from Borges: "For myth is at the beginning of literature, and also at its end."

The Ancient Child begins with the scene of Billy the Kid's death, fully imagined by Grey, a nineteen-year-old to whom visions come easily and frequently. Grey is infatuated with the myth of Billy, imagines him as her lover, and projects herself into the story of the young outlaw. For much of the novel, Grey's imagining of her life with Billy will form a motif punctuating Momaday's story of Set's identity quest and the developing relationship between Grey and

Set. The myth of the American West, starring Billy and appropriated by Grey, will be woven through the gradually revealed myth of the bear-boy. And as Grey outgrows the Euramerican western myth of eternal youth and irresponsibility—that for which the "Kid" stands—she grows into her role as medicine woman and helper in Set's realization of his place in the eternal Kiowa myth of transformation.

Grey is biculturally Native American and comfortable with her syncretic identity: "Her father was Kiowa and her mother Navajo, and the two cultures came together in her easily, more or less."[46] In addition, Native American and Euramerican worlds come together easily within Grey, as her fondness for Lewis Carroll's "Jabberwocky," Wallace Stevens's "Sunday Morning," Joyce's "The Dead," and Shakespeare, along with her growing awareness of her role as a traditional medicine woman, attest. All of these things, Momaday writes, she "had assumed, . . . appropriated them to her being" (185). In Grey, Momaday illustrates the act of appropriation essential to the marginalized culture that would wrest authenticity from the authoritative center. Within the rich heteroglossia of her Kiowa-Navajo-Euramerican life, Grey rejects the world's deadly narrative of epic "Indianness" with its tragic implications. Instead, Grey constructs her own destiny and plot as she invents her life imaginatively and mythically. Within Grey, the disturbing chasm between past and present, and between "civilization" and "savagism," that constitutes America's gothic self-image does not exist. She wrenches the American Myth—the Billy-the-Kid dream of perpetual, reckless youth that D. H. Lawrence understood—into a new context.

As she imagines life with Billy—the "lover, confidant, and hero of her girlhood, who had drawn her into the deepest mythic currents of the Wild West"—Grey articulates her place within the emerging myth in highly florid language: "I have enjoyed eighteen wondrous summers, all of them in the vastness of the wilderness, which is my incomparable element. I am tall and limber and well formed. . . . I am as trim and graceful as a doe, and I am free of the strictures of 'civilization,' so-called. I have dark, lustrous hair, gathered becomingly behind my shell-like ears. . . . My unpretentious attire is altogether appropriate" (18). The language of Grey's self-imagining here is that of a "prior discourse": the western romance. However, Grey is moving toward what Bakhtin described as "a free appropriation and assimilation" of this discourse. Whereas according to Bakhtin, "authoritative discourse permits no play with the context framing it, no play with its borders, no gradual and flexible transitions, no spontaneously creative stylizing variants on it," in Grey's myth-making we see a playful stylization of that privileged language. The metanarrative of Euramerican colonization, which, as McNickle recognized, requires the American Indian to play a specific role in the drama of redemption, is very much a political discourse "indissolubly fused," as Bakhtin wrote, "with its authority—with political power." In the character of Grey, Momaday is illustrating a process Bakhtin has described: "One's own discourse is gradually wrought out of others' words that have been acknowledged and assimilated, and the boundaries between the two are at first scarcely perceptible."[47]

Although the novel's narrative voice intrudes here to tell us that Grey's imagined self is not quite accurate, that voice ends the chapter with a description in even more admiring detail than Grey's own and with the declaration, "On the whole, she was beautiful beyond the telling." The result of this dialogue between narrator, text, and audience is an awareness for the reader of a rich layering of fictions: Grey's imagining of herself into the already imagined legend of Billy the Kid, and the novel's author's imagining of the character of Grey involved in this act of imagination.

Grey's fascination with and re-creation of the myth of Billy the Kid adds an interesting complexity to this novel, for into this nineteen-year-old visionary Momaday has visibly projected a significant part of himself. Grey's title for her memorial to Billy is "The Strange and True Story of My Life with Billy the Kid," a title borrowed straight from N. Scott Momaday, who had created it for his own cycle of poems and stories about the outlaw. The poems in Grey's memorial are Momaday's poems, some of which, such as "The Wound" and "He Would Place a Chair for Sister Blandina," are reproduced exactly in Grey's manuscript.[48] In an interview, Momaday explained his own fascination with Billy the Kid: "I grew up with Billy the Kid. I lived much of my life in New Mexico, which was his part of the world, and so I had heard stories about him all my life." About his Billy the Kid cycle, he added, "So this is a group of poems that bears upon his life, and upon my life, and the way in which those things come together in my imagination."[49]

Grey's Billy the Kid fantasies underscore the way in which we reimagine the world to make it give us back our own reflection. Momaday has defined storytelling as "an act by which man strives to realize his capacity for wonder, meaning and delight. It is also a process in which man invests and preserves himself in the context of ideas." In the course of the novel, however, as Grey matures into a medicine woman and enters into—invests herself within—older and deeper ways of knowledge, her fantasy world with Billy dissolves, a process Bakhtin has also described as that of consciousness awakening "to independent ideological life . . . in a world of alien discourses surrounding it." Grey represents a significant aspect of the character called N. Scott Momaday who has emerged as the central actor in Momaday's fiction. The author, who lived on the Navajo reservation as a child and who has said, "I feel closer to the Navajo than to other peoples," has invested his identification with Navajo people and culture, his fascination with the legend of Billy the Kid, and even his own identity as a poet, in the character of the young half-Navajo and half-Kiowa woman.[50]

The other half of Momaday in *The Ancient Child* is invested in the character of Locke Setman. Set, as Momaday has explained, is the reincarnation of the boy from the Kiowa myth, the "ancient child" who became the bear. Born to a Kiowa father and an Anglo-American mother, Set is orphaned when his mother dies in childbirth and his father is killed, when Set is seven, in an automobile accident. Through what can only be construed as malevolence on the part of his mother's family, Set is placed in an orphanage instead of being allowed to go to his father's Kiowa family. He is adopted by a retired philosophy professor and grows up in a privileged, enlightened household in San Francisco, cut off irrevocably, it seems, from his father's Kiowa culture and from any meaningful knowledge of who he is. Set is another in the long list of alienated mixedbloods seemingly trapped between worlds. A successful artist, he suffers an identity crisis when he is forty-four, feeling that he has sold out to the pressures of his agent and the demands of those who buy his art. Set is responding unconsciously to a condition Bakhtin has described: "The more a poet is cut off from the social unity of his group, the more likely he is to take into account the external demands of a particular reading public. Only a social group alien to the poet can determine his creative work from the outside. One's own group needs no such external definition: It exists in the poet's voice, in the basic tone and intonations of that voice—whether the poet himself intends this or not."[51] As Set recovers his original self in the course of the novel, his "own group"—his Kiowa identity—will surface in his painting.

Set's identity crisis intensifies when he is summoned to Oklahoma. At Cradle Creek, the suggestively named home of his father's people, Set finds both his father's grave and, as he is introduced to Kiowa relatives, the beginnings of an identity. When Set receives the telegram telling him of Kope'mah's death, he is "completely at a loss." He knows nothing of his father's people: "All that he had of his forebears was a sediment in his memory, the memory of words his father had spoken long ago—the stories his father had told him" (51). With the stories, words—more than just "memory in the blood"—Set has the necessary material to forge an identity, but like Abel, he must undertake a quest for this self.

"It was in Set's nature to wonder," Momaday writes rather explicitly, "until the wonder became pain, who he was. He had an incomplete idea of himself" (52). Set's idea of himself will not be complete until he enters the mythic reality of his Kiowa relatives and discovers his identity as bear; once he has journeyed to Cradle Creek, he begins the quest and the transformation that will bring him this knowledge.

Set's transformation begins when, at the home of his Kiowa relatives, he has a strange feeling "as if some ancestral intelligence had been awakened in him for the first time." There, he feels, "in the wild growth and the soft glowing of the earth . . . was something profoundly original. He could not put his finger on it, but it was there. It was itself genesis, he thought . . . not an Old Testament tale, but his genesis" (64). Set's transformational identity is engendered by place, suggesting what has been called the "special post-colonial crisis of identity," but a crisis particularly complex for Native Americans, who have, since colonial times, been systematically displaced. This special crisis is embodied in a "concern with the development or recovery of an effective identifying relationship between self and place."[52] This transformation becomes more determined when Grey presents Set with the bear medicine bundle, saying, "The grandmother, Kope'mah, wants me to give you back your medicine" (72). From this time until the end of the novel, Set will struggle with the bear within him, coming to terms with its overwhelming spiritual power and, in so doing, coming to terms with himself.

Momaday keeps the Kiowa myth of the bear-boy within the reader's consciousness throughout the novel by telling the story briefly at the novel's beginning and then elaborating upon the story at intervals as he (the authorial voice) imagines it more completely. The first of these elaborations comes when an old Kiowa woman watches fearfully as eight children move away from camp toward the distant forest. Much later, in another mythic interval, we are told that "no one ever saw the sisters again. . . . And when the stars came out and flickered on the black wash of the sky, the people were filled with wonder—and a kind of loneliness" (129). Between these two portions of the story, we hear through Set's memory his father's telling of the story of a strange boy who appears suddenly in a Piegan camp. As he tells the story, Cate Setman reimagines it, interpreting and bringing the story to life in the tradition of storytellers: "There must have been fires in the camp. There were always fires. And the fires shone upon the tipis and dimly on the trees beyond the camp. . . . Some of the people were outside, I suppose. Yes, some were outside tending the fires. And one of them saw the little boy" (119).[53] In the father's words we feel the existence of the oral tradition in an eternal present as he re-creates the story in his mind: "Some of the people were outside, I suppose. Yes, some were outside tending the fires." Because the boy does not speak their language, he has no identity to the Piegans, no name. "And do you see, Loki," Cate Setman says, using Set's boyhood name, "this matter of having no name is perhaps the center of the story" (121). So the people give the boy a name by creating a story: he is not a boy at all but a bear, "an extraordinary being." As Set's father completes his story, it becomes evident that he imagines the boy-bear to be the bear of the Kiowa transformation myth:

> And the boy, Loki, what became of him? What brought him to the camp of the Piegans in the first place? And what urged him away? . . . In the blackness again, did his tracks become the tracks of a bear: Did his lively, alien tongue fade into the whimper and growl of a beast? In his brain was there something like thought or memory? Did he feed upon his own boy's heart, and did he dream? Was there behind his eyes, like thought, the image of children playing? (121–22)

The paragraph quickly summarizes the significant events of the novel thus far and declares abruptly, dramatically, "The bear comes forth."

Set's search for his identity is haunted by the apparition of a young boy. The first time he sees him, "Set thought at first that the boy must be deranged, so strange and unsettling was his sudden and wild appearance" (60). Later, he thinks that the boy's eyes expressed "something like—well, foreboding, something ominous and . . . unimaginable" (66–67). The boy is Set's transformational self, the boy of the Kiowa myth. Set's "other" self is in conflict with the authoritative self Set has brought with him from Euramerican culture. The ominous and unimaginable is the bear power that overwhelmed and changed the boy in the myth and will do the same to Set. The "ancient child" may represent the elemental force of the natural world within us, the awesome power which the Kiowa myth articulates and which Set is rediscovering. It is this that causes Set to feel that "The presence . . . was strange and evasive. It inhabited another world, he thought. But it preyed upon him" (102). And it is a dim awareness of this reality that makes Set aware that what is happening to him did not begin at Cradle Creek but "was something that began a long time before that" (136).

As his change begins, Set feels that he is losing his mind, ex-claiming, "I am fighting for my life. . . ." Shortly afterwards, he adds, "It was as if I were trying to bring some crucial memory, deeply buried, to the surface of my mind" (137, 140). Set's paintings become more "elemental," with one picture that of "a creeping figure among the trees." "It's a self-portrait," he explains before going on to say, "Something seemed to be taking possession of me. . . . I wasn't myself" (144, 145). He paints a centaurlike picture titled "Venture Beyond Time," evoking the eternal present of the mythic world—and escape from history—that Momaday had earlier in the novel associated with Grey's evolving myth of herself and Billy which "was immediate, profoundly present: It remains that moment. . . . The next moment is forever to come" (13). Increas-ingly, Set's paintings are of "whirling depths, mysterious and pro-found as ancient rock paintings, beasts and anthropomorphic forms proceeding from the far reaches of time," and "there was insinuated upon his consciousness and subconsciousness the power of the bear. It was his bear power, but he did not yet have real knowledge of it" (213).

When Set finally breaks down, he is found in his studio sprawled unconscious next to the opened medicine bundle, with the bear medicine exposed. To an Indian, Set's madness and sickness would not be surprising. By placing the medicine bundle in the hands of one who is uneducated and uninitiated—one who does not know how to handle such a bundle and, more crucially, does not know the difficult and elaborate ritual required to open such a powerful medicine—Grey has put Set in enormous peril. In Kiowa culture, as in other Native American cultures as well, bear is extremely powerful, both a helper and potentially dangerous if dealt with incorrectly. According to one source, the bear in Kiowa culture is "the most powerful animal there was in a medicine way. Unless you were named for the bear, or were speaking to somebody that was, you mustn't even say the word bear. It was that powerful. Bears could drive you crazy, just for saying their name, and to look at them could almost kill a man. Nobody knew what would happen if you killed or ate a bear. People were afraid to try." If, of course, you are named for the bear, as Set is, and you have the bear spirit within you, as your helper, you have access to immense power and protection.[54]

The abrupt transfer of the bundle to Set seems to have been something of a make-or-break decision by Kope'mah; if Set survives his relatively unprotected exposure to the bear medicine, he will know who he is as a Kiowa. Set's survival, however, depends upon the aid of Grey, who, assisted by the spirit of the grandmother, is growing into a medicine woman of great power. It is Grey who tells him finally, "You are Set. Don't imagine that you have a choice in the matter. . . You are Set; you are the bear; you will be the bear, no matter what. You will act accordingly, in the proper way, because there is no other way to act" (271). Finally, it is Grey who takes Set back with her to the Navajo reservation and arranges an abbreviated bear healing ceremony for him. Immersed in his future wife's Navajo family, running daily on a ritualistic basis, Set regains his health, preparing for the last step in the self-imagining that will make him one with the bear spirit.

That final step comes when, like Momaday himself, Set retraces the migration path of his Kiowa ancestors all the way to Devil's Tower, Tsoai. Set fasts for four days and then, with a full moon, approaches Tsoai, "the rock tree" upon which the seven sisters had been thrust heavenward and saved from the bear-brother. Momaday's description of the scene provides essential insight into the method and purpose of his novel and into his comprehension of the myth-making impulse in the oral tradition and is worth quoting at length:

Tsoai, the rock tree, loomed before and above him in the moonlight. It was changing in the motion of the moon, and it *seemed* alive. Shapes and shadows shifted upon the great green igneous columns, upon the huge granite planes, across the long black vertical fissures. Set stood in awe of Tsoai. He could not take his eyes from it. He was stricken, spellbound. An awful quiet was in his heart; the thing before him was unimaginable, in some sense beyond knowledge and belief, and he knew that it was sacred. As he looked, the stars of the Big Dipper gradually appeared over it. They became brighter and brighter, riding over the north edge of the rock tree, revolving down the sky. And when he brought his focus back upon the monolith, a strange pitch-black shadow lay upon it, near the base. It was the image of a great bear, rearing against Tsoai. It was the vision he had sought. (313, emphasis mine)

As he did in *The Way to Rainy Mountain*, Momaday is re-creating here a crucial mythic moment in the history of the Kiowa. In *The Way to Rainy Mountain*, he wrote: "There are things in nature that engender an awful quiet in the heart of man; Devil's Tower is one of them. Two centuries ago, because they could not do otherwise, the Kiowas made a legend at the base of the rock." In this scene from *The Ancient Child*, the full moon sends shadows unfurling across the awesome striated tower, causing it to *appear* to move, to *seem* alive in the imagination of the perceiver. When the stars of the Dipper revolve down toward the tower, and a large shadow near the base rears in the form of a bear, the essential convergence is completed. Such a powerful vision requires a story so that it can take its place within the world that is ordered and made inhabitable through story, or myth. This experience, like the arrival of the strange boy in the Kiowa camp Set's father had told of, is the religious, or mythic, moment described by Deloria: "*Something* is observed or experienced by a community, and the symbols and sequences of the mythology are given together in an event that appears so much out of the ordinary experiential sequence as to impress itself upon the collective memories of the community for a sufficiently long duration of time."[55] Set is reenacting that moment in the mythic history of his Kiowa ancestors, and in embracing the vision, he enters into the myth. In the novel's final paragraph, the story of the bear-boy and his seven sisters is reenacted, with Loki / Set pursuing the fleeing sisters and entering into a new and infinitely more profound relationship with the natural world. Set's identity quest is complete; he has meaning and significance because he is part of a story that is ancient and essential, experienced within a space that is free of historic, entropic time. Like Abel, and like Momaday himself, Set is reintegrated into the mythic reality of his tribe; he has come home. In a novel that is more often explicit than subtle, it is a romantic ending—along with James Welch's *Fools Crow*, one of the only full recoveries in American Indian literature.

Earthboy's Return

James Welch's Acts of Recovery

◆

James Welch's first novel, *Winter in the Blood* (1974), is a tale told in the first person by a narrator whose name we never learn. The nameless narrator is frozen in time, caught in a wintry dormancy as he moves tentatively and torturously toward a glimmer of self-knowledge and a tenuous unification of past, present, and future. The landscape through which he moves is bleak, a Montana waste-land rooted immediately in the painful dislocations of Blackfoot and Gros Ventre history—the histories of Welch's own Blackfoot–Gros Ventre heritage—and, more indirectly and somewhat parodoxi-cally, in T. S. Eliot's *The Waste Land*. Within this drought-stricken landscape, mirroring in its sterility the inner state of the narrator, men and women seem at war with one another, communication fails repeatedly, and the present balances precariously between voids where past disappears and future cannot be imagined. The narrator's story unfolds in roughly sequential actions, the achrono-logical tradition of Native American storytelling entering the text only as Welch allows the surrealism of dreams to interpenetrate everyday reality and exploits the familiar technique of flashback to merge past and present.[1]

In the extraordinarily compact and suggestive first paragraph of the novel, Welch introduces the major themes of the story the narrator will tell:

In the tall weeds of the borrow pit, I took a leak and watched the sorrel mare, her colt beside her, walk through burnt grass to the shady side of the log-and-mud cabin. It was called the Earthboy place, although no one by that name (or any other) had lived in it for twenty years. The roof had fallen in and the mud between the logs had fallen out in chunks, leaving a bare gray skeleton, home only to mice and insects. Tumbleweeds, stark as bone, rocked in a hot wind against the west wall. On the hill behind the cabin, a rectangle of barbed wire held the graves of all the Earthboys, except for a daughter who had married a man from Lodgepole. She could be anywhere, but the Earthboys were gone.

A borrow pit is an excavation from which earth has been taken for use elsewhere, earth appropriated or "borrowed." We will learn later in the novel that the narrator's father, First Raise, has been found frozen to death in this same borrow pit, "pointing toward home"—an ironical direction arrow for his lost son. Just as the very earth itself has been taken, so we come to realize Blackfoot culture and identity have been appropriated by the dominant white culture, leaving a kind of nothingness in their place—a dormancy, winter in the blood. "Borrow" is also very close in its origin (OE *beorgan*, "to preserve") to the root of "bury." The novel begins and ends with graves, the Earthboys' and the grandmother's, as the last of those who knew what it meant to be Blackfoot in the old sense are buried. And in the language of Eliot's poem, the "dull roots" of the narrator's Blackfoot identity will, in the course of the novel, be stirred with "spring rain" as he awakens painfully from his winter in the blood.

Also entering the novel immediately here, through the image of the sorrel mare and her colt, is the mother-son motif which will run throughout the novel as the narrator halfheartedly attempts to wean the calf from its "wild-eyed" mother while Teresa, the narrator's mother, attempts simultaneously to wean her son and force him into the adult world. Near the mare and her colt, the decaying skeleton of a cabin and the tumbleweeds, "stark as bone," rocking in "a hot wind," introduce images of a wasteland which will merge with Blackfoot mythology to become a central metaphor in the novel. Similarly, the barbed wire enclosing the graves of the Earthboys will be echoed in the fences enclosing cattle throughout the novel, and in the grandmother's description of the Blackfeet being driven "like cows" to their reservation. Also suggested here are the facts of allotment, which, in 1907 broke the Blackfoot Reservation into allotted sections of 320 acres per individual and moved the Blackfeet closer to the cattle-ranching economy reflected in this novel.[2]

The suggestive name of the Earthboys hints at the traditional Indian males who have disappeared from the Blackfoot world

Welch describes—those Indians who once lived, secure in their identities, close to the earth. Throughout the novel, Welch will provide portraits and glimpses of Indian men who have ceased to know themselves or their places in the world, men directionless and powerless who leave vacuums that must be filled by desperate women. The lone survivor among the Earthboys, the daughter who had married an outsider and "could be anywhere," foreshadows the women of the novel, who, for the most part, are survivors forced to abandon (either literally or figuratively) their hopeless men and strike out alone.[3]

Nameless, the narrator would seem to be one of those lost mixedblood children described in Mathews's *Sundown*: "They can never have a name among their people. They have no people. . . ." He suffers from a condition N. Scott Momaday has described eloquently: "I believe that a man is his name. The name and the existence are indivisible. . . . Somewhere in the Indian mentality there is that idea that when someone is given a name . . . when a man is given a name, existence is given to him, too. And what could be worse than not having a name." It should also be noted that it was traditionally considered improper for a Blackfoot to tell his name if he could avoid it. Since the narrator is telling his own story, this might account for the absence of any reference to his name. However, the overwhelming absence of direction or identity within the narrator in conjunction with his apparent lack of traditional knowledge suggests that there are more complex reasons for his namelessness.[4]

Welch's narrator does not know himself and can therefore relate to no one else: "Coming home to a mother and an old lady who was my grandmother. And the girl who was thought to be my wife. But she didn't really count. For that matter none of them counted; not one meant anything to me. And for no reason. I felt no hatred, no love, no guilt, no conscience, nothing but a distance that had grown through the years." Describing the wasted landscape, the narrator adds: "It could have been the country, the burnt prairie beneath a blazing sun . . . the milky waters of the river. . . . But the distance I felt came not from country or people; it came from within me. I was as distant from myself as a hawk from the moon."[5]

The narrator's condition resembles what has been defined as a kind of postmodern schizophrenia, an inability "to unify the past, present and future of our own biographical experience or psychic

life." According to postmodern theorists, such a condition transcends familiar concepts of alienation, as David Harvey suggests:

> We can no longer conceive of the individual as alienated in the classical
> Marxist sense, because to be alienated presupposes a coherent rather
> than a fragmented sense of self from which to be alienated. It is only
> in terms of such a centred sense of personal identity that individuals
> can pursue projects over time, or think cogently about the production
> of a future significantly better than time present and time past. . . .
> postmodernism typically strips away that possibility by concentrating
> upon the schizophrenic circumstances induced by fragmentation and
> all those instabilities . . . that prevent us even picturing coherently, let
> alone devizing strategies to produce, some radically different future.[6]

Welch's narrator, however, is neither a victim nor a celebrant of
this kind of postmodern fragmentation and transience; he is, in
fact, alienated precisely in the sense described here. For Welch's
narrator there is a "coherent . . . sense of self" and a "centred sense
of personal identity" that may indeed be recovered. It is a recovery
dependent upon a renewed sense of identity as Indian, as specifically Blackfoot, and Welch's novel represents such a recovery project. Once the narrator has made significant progress toward that
rediscovery of a coherent, culturally determined identity, he will
be able to unify past, present, and future and begin finally to project
a future at least slightly, if not radically, different from the present.

Amidst the desiccation of the opening scene, the narrator says,
"My throat ached with a terrible thirst," and throughout the remainder of the novel we will be waiting for the cleansing rain that
will fall only near the end. "It never rains anymore," his mother
complains. "It never rains around here when you need it" (4). Even
the river water is suspect; everybody had blamed the sugarbeet
factory upstream for the river's milky color, but when the factory
shut down "the water never cleared."

Naturally associated with rain and water imagery throughout the
novel is another motif, that of fish. The fertility of the river is doubly
suspect because, in spite of the fact that the "white men from the
fish department came in their green trucks and stocked the river
with pike," there is no actual proof of fish in the river. "But the
river ignored the fish and the fish ignored the river," the narrator
explains, "The fish disappeared" (6). Archetypal symbols of fertility, fish will figure prominently in the novel, from the maddening
question whether fish may or may not be in the river or the lakes

in the surrounding country, to Fish, the medicine man who prophesied the tragedy of the Blackfoot people, to the narrator's girlfriend, Agnes, described as "a fish for dinner, nothing more," to the narrator's dream of his girlfriend and mother as victimized fish. The narrator's confusion concerning his own identity, his masculinity, and his spiritual sterility is epitomized in his bewilderment at various times about whether or not there might actually be fish in the waters.

Coming home to learn that his Cree girlfriend, Agnes, has taken two symbols of his masculinity, his gun and razor, the narrator goes fishing, casting an old, rusty lure lethargically until it catches on a snag and is lost. The line snaps and the narrator tells us that "a magpie squawked from deep in the woods on the other side of the river." With the first of several appearances by the trickster-magpie mocking the futile narrator, Lame Bull, the narrator's soon-to-be father-in-law, shows up, saying "You should try bacon. . . . I know these fish." Confused, the narrator asks, "Are the fish any good?" (8).

A case of arrested development, frozen in time by the traumatic death years before of his brother, Mose, the narrator has never matured. Reminiscing about a big flood, Lame Bull tells the narrator, "You, of course, are too young." The narrator responds, "I was almost twenty," and Lame Bull just laughs, "Ho. . . . You were not much more than a gleam in your old man's eye." Again and again in the course of the novel the narrator will desperately remind people of his age. The indications are that no one accepts him as an adult, and it is as an adult that a man in Native American culture earns his name. A thirty-two-year-old child, the narrator remains thus nameless. It is shortly after this exchange with Lame Bull that the narrator yells at the wild-eyed cow, shooing her calf away, "Get out of here, you bitch! . . . Don't you know we're trying to wean this fool?" (9–10). Later in the novel, when twice the narrator confesses, "I felt like a fool," his epithet for the calf will be echoed and his identification with the calf underscored.

While Blackfoot mythology plays a major role in *Winter in the Blood*, it would be a mistake to ignore another mythology operating here, that of the Fisher King from the grail romance, the central figure of Eliot's *The Waste Land* and much subsequent American literature. Welch both incorporates this myth into the fabric of the novel and has great fun parodying it. While a kind of wasteland is present from the opening lines, the grail mythology enters the novel most blatantly through an article the narrator is reading in a dog-eared copy of *Sports Afield*, an article he describes in some detail:

> I had read all the stories, so I reread the one about the three men in Africa who tracked a man-eating lion for four days from the scene of his latest kill—a prenant black woman. They managed to save the baby, who, they were surprised to learn, would one day be king of the tribe. They tracked the lion's spoor until the fourth day, when they found out that he'd been tracking them all along. They were going in a giant four-day circle. It was very dangerous, said McLeod, a Pepsi dealer from Atlanta, Georgia. They killed the lion that night as he tried to rip a hole in their tent.
>
> I looked at the pictures again. One showed McLeod and Henderson kneeling behind the dead lion; they were surrounded by a group of grinning black men. The third man, Enright, wasn't in the picture. (12)

In this hilarious paragraph, Welch seems to be having fun with Saul Bellow's *Henderson the Rain King*, a novel in which Bellow was having fun with Eliot's version of the grail romance. In Bellow's novel, Henderson, a wealthy and dangerously naive American, goes to Africa in search of himself. While there he falls into the patterned role of both grail knight and fisher king, riotously "freeing the waters" for a "primitive" people whose land—like Welch's narrator's—is suffering from drought. Furthermore, Henderson actually becomes, by befriending a young tribal prince, a sacrificial deity whose responsibility it is to bring rain and restore the wasted land. In the end, however, Henderson returns home happy and healthy, having confronted his own mortality in the form of a dangerous lion and learned who he is. Henderson sets his lands—or life—in order, and *Henderson the Rain King* ends "right." Bellow's novel is a farce and a romance, and it embodies the impulse to appropriate that has powered the American colonial enterprise from the beginning. The irrepressible Henderson goes into "wilderness" and appropriates an identity, subsuming the significance of that other, "primitive" world into the fabric of his own manifest destiny. Bellow's novel ends with Henderson's plane touching down in "Newfoundland" and Henderson running and leaping in joyous circles against a pure white background, possessor of a hybrid ("Persianized" American) child and a lion cub. In Welch's *Sports Afield* picture, Henderson, accompanied by a friend with a name easily associated with water—McLeod—is absurd, mocked in the photograph by the grinning natives. And in Welch's vignette "Enright"—the right, romantic ending—is not in the picture.[7]

Henderson will reappear in *Winter in the Blood* in the form of the "airplane man," whose plane touches down in the "new found" frozen wastes of Montana. Welch ensures that we will make this connection when the narrator describes this mysterious white man: "He had on one of those khaki outfits that African hunters wear. I thought of McLeod and Henderson in *Sports Afield*" (45). Here, however, the "primitives" will be the Indians of northern Montana, and the airplane man—who has no more identity than does the narrator—will find this heart of darkest America a place of confusion and no right endings. Whereas Bellow's Henderson had wandered into a world of order, of continuity with tradition and past, Welch's fugitive stumbles into a world already colonized, displaced, cut off from its past and the traditions that would offer meaning and order. The native prince he joins up with is our narrator, a wry, self-deprecating misfit for whom chaos is the order of the day.

The mocking story of the lion hunt in *Sports Afield* also suggests another theme in the novel: the conflict between mother and child. Like the black infant abandoned by the death of its mother, the narrator, who has elected to reread this particular story, feels abandoned by his own mother and is struggling with that feeling throughout the novel. An example of this struggle is the narrator's desire to repress the facts of Amos the duck's death. Amos, like the narrator, is the only survivor among its siblings, the others having drowned when the water in their tub fell too far below the rim. Feeling responsible for the ducks' deaths, just as he feels resonsible for Mose's, the narrator identifies with Amos, saying, "But he never went in. He must have been smarter than the others." Skeptically, Teresa replies, both reinforcing the narrator's identification and undercutting his rationalization: "He was lucky. One duck can't be smarter than another. They're like Indians" (15). Because he identifies with the survivor among the ducks, the narrator attempts to deny the fact that his mother has killed Amos, wanting, instead, to believe that a bobcat killed Amos and Teresa killed the turkey that had terrified the narrator as a boy. Teresa, however, will not allow the narrator this haven, insisting with flat finality, "I killed Amos." Shortly after this scene Teresa will tell the narrator, "There isn't enough for you here. . . . You would do well to start looking around."

The memory of Amos and the turkey also has a positive effect for the narrator in that he remembers his father's love. He recalls that as a child, when knocked to the ground by the turkey, "It was always my father bending over me." First Raise, the narrator's father, had provided the tenderness which Teresa never offered, and it will be the memory of First Raise's love, in part, that will trigger an awakening for the narrator later in the novel. Like his son and all of the other Indian men in *Winter in the Blood*—and men in other novels by Native American writers—First Raise was directionless, always "in transit." "He was a wanderer," Teresa tells the narrator, "just like all these damned Indians" (20). Displaced from the traditional male role of warring and hunting, First Raise still determined his life according to the traditional seasonal cycles. Explaining that his father was valued for his ability to fix farm machinery, the narrator remembers: "It was said that when the leaves turned, First Raise's yard was full of iron; when they fell, the yard was full of leaves." He also remembers his father's annual plans for the traditional fall hunt, a hunt that could only take place within the boundaries of a national park, where, like the Indians on reservations, the game had been sequestered. First Raise, however, has fully acknowledged the authority of the invader: "He inquired around, trying to find out what the penalty would be if they caught him. He had to know the penalty, almost as though the penalty would be the inevitable result of his hunt." First Raise never got caught, however, "because he never made the trip. The dream, the planning and preparation were all part of a ritual" (7).

Resistance for First Raise has taken the form of empty ritual. Incapable of meaningful action, First Raise represents a previous generation of displaced men. However, while he has no role in the society he occupies—dependent upon the landowning Teresa and upon the laughing white men whose equipment he fixes—he is sensitive and alive. His ability to demonstrate his love for his sons is vital to whatever chances the narrator has for renewal. And his care to introduce the narrator, as a child, to his real grandfather attests to his sense of the significance of the past and provides the impetus, years later, for the narrator's awakening.

The narrator's mother, of whom he says, "I never expected much from Teresa and I never got it," is, along with the other women in the novel, as much a victim of displacement as are the Indian men. As the men remove themselves more and more from their marginalized places within the daily workings of family life to wander aimlessly, Teresa and the other women move to fill the void created. Men like First Raise become mere retainers, or they become sexual clowns like Lame Bull and, at times, the narrator.

The tremendous decline in the significance and role of the Blackfoot male in this novel is even underscored by Lame Bull's name. In the mid-nineteenth century, at the height of Blackfoot power, a warrior named Lame Bull was head chief of the Pikuni (Piegan) and the first signer of the 1855 Treaty with the Blackfoot Nation, or, as the Blackfeet call it, Lame Bull's Treaty. That Welch's Lame Bull is far removed from traditional roles is underscored in his treatment of the grandmother as he speaks carelessly and somewhat mockingly to the old lady. For a man to meet his mother-in-law was a gross impropriety; to speak to her was unthinkable.[8] The men's confusion and failure embitters the women, resulting in detached cynicism such as Teresa's or aggressive masculinity such as that of Long Knife's mother, who castrates cattle with the men and "made a point of eating the roasted balls while glaring at one man, then another—even her sons, who, like the rest of us, stared at the brown hills until she was done" (24). Long Knife, whose name associates him with the Blackfeet's oppressors, is himself another example of radical displacement. "Long Knife came from a long line of cowboys," the narrator explains in unconscious irony.

The narrator's complex and conflicting feelings about his mother, about Agnes, and about his own sexual identity as well as his identity as Blackfoot surface in the disturbing dream he has after a surrealistic night of drunkenness and sex:

> Suddenly a girl loomed before my face, slit and gutted like a fat rainbow, and begged me to turn her loose, and I found my own guts spilling from my monstrous mouth. Teresa hung upside down from a wanted man's belt, now my own belt, crying out a series of strange warnings to the man who had torn up his airplane ticket and who was now rolling in the manure of the corral, from time to time washing his great pecker in a tub of water. The gutted rainbow turned into the barmaid of last night screaming under the hands of the leering wanted men. Teresa raged at me in several voices. . . . The men in suits were feeling her, commenting upon the texture of her breasts and the width of her hips. They spread her legs wider and wider until Amos waddled out, his feathers wet and shining, one orange leg crocked at the knee, and suddenly lifted, in a flash of white stunted wing, up and through the dull sun. (52)

By focusing on the leg "crocked at the knee," Welch makes sure that we identify Amos with the narrator, whose bad knee is the result of the accident that killed Mose. More importantly, Welch associates Amos, whose "wet and shining" feathers suggest renewal or rebirth, with the sun, the most sacred of Blackfoot deities. In discussing this dream, Lavonne Ruoff has suggested:

> By linking Amos, the survivor, to the sun, Welch may be alluding to the myth of the morning star in which A-pi-su'-ahs or Early Riser is the only one of all the many children of the sun and moon . . . who is not killed by pelicans. In Blackfeet traditional terms, Amos, the animal which has appeared to the narrator in his dream, has become his medicine or secret helper. Ironically, the instrument of Amos' death has become the means of his rebirth. By releasing her son, Teresa frees him to soar out of her grasp. The act foreshadows the rebirth later in the novel.[9]

The dream's association of Teresa and Agnes with fish, the recurrent symbol of fertility in the novel, suggests that this (a life in which fertility, or growth, is possible) is the fulfillment longed for by the narrator. The airplane man, cast as the aggressive "wanted men" as well as himself, would seem to pose a sexual threat to the narrator. When he rolls in manure and then washes "his great pecker in a tub of water," he appears to be conducting a bizarre fertility ritual in a parody of Bellow's white rain god. The dream both underscores the narrator's fear of the annihilation of his masculinity by the white world (whose goal has, for centuries, been to turn Native Americans into "faithful children") and hints at an unconscious awareness of Blackfoot tradition as a means of regeneration.

These tensions, preceding the narrator's awakening to a Blackfoot identity, all become highly evident in events following the dream. Hiding in his hotel room after having agreed to drive the airplane man to Canada, the narrator says, "I cursed the white man for being such a fool and my hotel room for being such a tiny sanctuary on a great earth of stalking white men" (54). And when a bartender says, "You're Teresa First Raise's boy," the narrator responds defensively, "I'm thirty-two." When the bartender calls Teresa "one of the liveliest little gals I know of," the narrator snaps back, "She's bigger than you are, bigger than both of us put together," his sexual jealousy triggered by the bartender's language and his sense of his mother's control dominating the response. A few paragraphs later the narrator contemplates an unopened letter from the Catholic priest to his mother which has fallen into the narrator's hands: "I wanted to read it, to see what a priest would have to say to a woman who was his friend." Instead of reading the letter, which might have disclosed disturbing details about his mother's relationship with the priest, the narrator says, "I felt vaguely satisfied as I tore up the letter between my legs and let the pieces fall to the floor" (58–59). The phallic implications of the letter-tearing—"between my legs"—suggest, again, the narrator's sexual jealousy.

Following his second return home, the narrator goes to see Yellow Calf. As he saddles Bird for the trip, he remarks that "he panted and rumbled inside, as though a thunderstorm was growing in his belly" (62). In his later novel, *Fools Crow*, Welch will make the significance of this thunder clear as he says of the protagonist in that novel: "He prayed to Thunder Chief, whose long rumbling voice foretold the beginning of life and abundance of the ground of many gifts."[10] Here, the thunderstorm growing in Bird's belly, through the association with Thunder Chief and with the coming rain, foreshadows a new beginning for the narrator. Upon dismounting from the horse, the narrator says, "My bad leg had begun to ache from the tenseness with which I had to ride out Bird's storm," a statement again connecting Bird with the coming rain. And as they ride across a rotten bridge toward Yellow Calf's cabin, the narrator comments, "There were holes in the planks and one could see the slow cloudy water" (63). Thunderstorm, storm, cloudy water—all hint at the cleansing rain, the wasteland freeing of waters, that is to come.

When he greets Yellow Calf, the narrator says, "I'm First Raise's son—I came with him once." With the kind of response the narrator should by now have come to expect, Yellow Calf says, "Ah, of course! You were just a squirt." And as soon as he returns home from the old man's cabin, the narrator will hear Lame Bull say to Teresa, "I was plenty wild myself when I was his age," evoking the familiar insistence from the narrator: "'I'm thirty-two,' I said. Sometimes I had to remind myself" (71).

Yellow Calf is old and blind and is closely associated with the earth and animal world. "His fingers were slick, papery," the narrator tells us, "like the belly of a rattlesnake" (67). Like Napi, Old Man, he can talk to and understand the animals.[11] "They can tell by the moon when the world is cockeyed," Yellow Calf says, and the narrator, in an indication of how far he is removed from Yellow Calf's traditional Blackfoot world, responds, "But that's impossible." As he leaves, he notes that the old man is "listening to two magpies argue" (70). A form of trickster, magpies reappear at key moments throughout the novel, observing and mocking the narrator's desperation. Here, if the old man can indeed understand animals, he is privy to the trickster's evaluation of the narrator. Earlier, the grandmother has been associated with the trickster by her hands, "small and black as a magpie's feet," and on the narrator's next visit Yellow Calf himself will become another trickster figure, suggesting the combined role of the grandparents as Old Man and Old Woman—wedded contraries.

The narrator is still a long way from balance and self-knowledge. He approaches male-female relationships with the curiosity and naiveté of a child. After meeting Larue Henderson, who says of an employee's mother, "His old lady'd cut my nuts off," the narrator encounters a barfly named Malvina. The narrator asks about a tattoo on Malvina's finger and when rebuffed says, "It was true that I was interested in her affairs" (79). He is curious about all male-female relationships. An Indian who has trained for two years at Haskell to be a secretary only to find there were no jobs for her, Malvina takes the narrator home with her. In her home are scores of pictures "of Malvina alone in various places" (83), more evidence of the isolation and wintry souls of not just the narrator but nearly all the characters of this barren landscape as well.

When he hooks up again with the airplane man—a fugitive from justice who has appropriated (the white man's crime) "something" that didn't belong to him—the airplane man asks, "Do you understand what's going on?" and the narrator says, "I shook my head" (87). No one seems to know what's going on, including the temporary bartender filling in for the regular bartender, who has taken time off due to "woman troubles." In the bar, the narrator goes into the bathroom, only to be reminded of his self-doubt by a graffito on the wall: *"What are you looking up here for? The joke's in your hand"* (92). When he returns, he notes that he has been displaced: "A large purple teddy bear was occupying my stool." And when they leave the bar he says, "I felt like a fool carrying the purple teddy bear through the streets of Havre," echoing his earlier statement after the old man had died in his oatmeal, "I felt like a fool." It is as if, just like colonial and federal policy for centuries, all events conspire to turn the Indian narrator into a foolish child. Spotting the girlfriend he has been rather aimlessly seeking, the narrator says, "I wanted to be with her, but I didn't move. I didn't know how to go to her" (102). The glimpse, however, awakens a flicker of life in him: "Seeing her in front The Silver Dollar had sparked a warmth in me that surprised me, that I couldn't remember having felt in years" (102).

Sparked by this momentary response, the narrator puts the air-plane man out of his life and then begins to recount events leading to his brother's death, beginning with more wasteland imagery of "heat that denied the regular change of seasons," "hot, fly-buzzing days," and alfalfa fields that "turned black beneath a black sky that refused to rain" (104). His memory begins with First Raise awakening him as he lies huddled beneath a star quilt, an image of tradition and security. Remembering their breakfast, the narrator says, "First Raise smiled. It was beginning to get light." He adds, "First Raise got us each a cup of coffee and watched us drink. It was beginning to get light. He loved us" (105–106). The repetition of "it was beginning to get light" suggests that this is a key moment in the narrator's movement toward awakening from his long dor-mancy and toward healing. By re-membering, reconstructing the past, he may be able to put it together into a meaningful whole—a "coherent rather than a fragmented sense of self." Thus far, significant pieces of the puzzle of identity have been withheld from him, but a crucial piece falls into place here with his realization that "he loved us." He introduces here the "wild-eyed roan. . . . like a spinster aunt" which will trigger the catastrophe that kills Mose and be mirrored in the "wild-eyed" cow that later leads to a crisis for the narrator.

Returned from the flashback, the narrator sits in a bar with a girl with green teeth, his girlfriend Agnes, and says, "You should learn a trade. . . . There's a crying demand for secretaries," a contradic-tion of the reality learned from Malvina. His awakening response to life is suggested in his description of Agnes's eyes: "They held the promise of warm things" (113). Following his flash of warmth for Agnes, however, the narrator—in a world "of stalking white men" and a stranger to white and Indian alike—is beaten and stumbles pathetically into bed with a woman named Marlene. After a drunken night he says, "The first light of dawn caught me draped over her belly. . . . Her breath was warm and pleasant like a child's" (121). The narrator falls asleep and awakens a second time, focusing again on Marlene's belly, which "rose taut and shiny." He feels pity for her naked body, which "seemed so vulnerable, so inno-cent," and he tries to burrow "down into her, trying to disappear into her flesh" (122–123). When Marlene wakes up and says, for the second time, "Kiss my pussy," the narrator slaps her. With Marlene, the narrator has attempted to regress all the way back through childhood and beyond. His desire to "disappear into her flesh," his fascination with the "taut and shiny" belly, and his sense of her vulnerability and innocence all suggest that he is regressing toward the womb, that his fascination with Marlene is that of child or infant with mother. The moment has twofold significance: On the one hand it represents the final triumph of "Indian policy" that has long sought to turn responsible Indian adults into helpless children. On the other hand it signals the nadir of the narrator's plunge into the self, and the disintigration of the self, that will prepare for his rebirth and reintegration. Her words are thus traumatic.

At the end of this scene the narrator says, "Everything had gone out of me, and I felt the kind of peace that comes over one when he is alone, when he no longer cares for warmth, or sunshine, or possessions, or even a woman's body, so yielding and powerful" (123). He would appear to have lost all sense of self, a possibility reinforced by the fact that as he walks out of town no self is reflected for him: "There were no mirrors anywhere." And as he hitchhikes home, it becomes apparent that he has regressed considerably. When he is given a ride by a couple "who spoke about the country-side as if it were dead," he says of the couple's sick daughter: "Her eyes were dull, like those of a sick calf," a comment that forges a complex identity between the narrator and the girl, given the repeated identification throughout the novel between the narrator and the calf that is being weaned. His identification is made certain when he says, "'How do you feel, honey?' asked the wife, but before I could answer, the girl said fine" (129). He is responding eagerly to human connectedness, reaching out even absurdly, as a child, toward the Anglo mother.

Arriving home, the narrator discovers that his grandmother is gone and, he concludes, dead. Glancing at her meager possessions, he realizes that "she must have had other things, things that would have been buried with her in the old days," an important thought because it illustrates at least a vague awareness of Blackfoot tradition and it foreshadows his final act of throwing the tobacco pouch into the grandmother's grave.[12] While digging the grandmother's grave with Lame Bull, the narrator climbs into and out of the grave in a hint of rebirth, saying, "I climbed out of the hole. It was going to be hot again, but from the southeast a few puffy white clouds

were beginning to build up. . . . There was little chance of rain—
it was the time of year when things grow stagnant (138–39). In spite
of his denial of rain, the encroaching clouds portend something
positive, at least a faint possibility for a freeing of the waters in this
stagnant world, like the distant thunder in Eliot's *The Waste Land*
and Bird's belly.

It is at this point in the novel that the narrator is finally able to
recount in full the events of his brother's death. In so doing, he is
able to forgive Bird for his part in the catastrophe, saying, "You
were born to eat grass and drink slough water, to nip other horses
in the flanks the way you do lagging bulls, to mount the mares. So
they cut your balls off to make you less temperamental" (144–45).
Implicit in this outpouring is the similarity between Bird and the
Indians of the novel, both of whom have been trained to be
cowhorse and cowboy, working within fences and emasculated in
the process. And following his remembrance of Mose's death and
his musing upon Bird, the narrator experiences a crisis: "'What
use,' I whispered, cried for no one in the world to hear, not even
Bird, for no one but my soul, as though the words would rid it of
the final burden of guilt, and I found myself a child again" (146).

Now that he has been able to confront the past and reexperience
it, he is ready for the final missing piece to appear to tell him who
he is, and Yellow Calf provides that element. Closer to rebirth, the
narrator is also closer to the rain for which we have been waiting.
"I feel it," Yellow Calf tells him when the narrator rides to the old
man's cabin again, "rain tonight maybe, tomorrow for sure, cats
and dogs" (149). And then Yellow Calf tells him in detail about the
starving time for the Blackfeet, when the narrator's grandmother
was cast out. In telling the story, Yellow Calf attempts to "bring into
being"—through the compelling power of language—the Blackfoot
world seemingly lost to the narrator. The narrator has an important
role in the story Yellow Calf tells: he, too, is Blackfoot and has
survived; through him past and future may merge in a coherent
present. However, the narrator seems inexorably distanced from
the world Yellow Calf describes: "I tried to understand the medicine, the power that directed the people to single out a young
woman, to leave her to fend for herself in the middle of a cruel
winter. . . . I didn't know it. I couldn't understand the medicine"
(155–56).

Bird, as was foreshadowed by the old horse's association with
thunder and storm, provides the narrator's epiphany: "Bird farted.

And then it came to me, as though it were riding one moment of the gusting wind. . . . 'Listen, old man,' I said. 'It was you!'" The narrator realizes that the old man is his grandfather. "I began to laugh," he says, "at first quietly, with neither bitterness nor humor. It was the laughter of one who understands a moment in his life, of one who has been let in on the secret through luck and circumstance" (158). Up to this point the narrator has thought himself to be the grandson of a half-white drifter; now, however, he realizes that he is the grandson of Yellow Calf. "And the half-breed, Doagie!" he says, "*He wasn't Teresa's father; it was you, Yellow Calf, the hunter!*" (159).

In this instant the narrator recognizes his role in the old man's story. Rather than being descended from a vague, halfblood drifter, another transient figure in this confused world, the narrator is the grandson of Yellow Calf, the hunter. A powerful link has been forged with the traditional world of the Blackfeet. And Yellow Calf assumes the guise of trickster: "His mouth had become the rubbery sneer of a jack-o'-lantern." In Blackfoot tradition, the original beings are Old Man (Na'pi) and Old Woman (Kipitaki). After forming the earth from a ball of mud brought from beneath the primal waters by muskrat, Old Man makes mountains, rivers, vegetation, animal life, and, finally, Old Woman herself as a mate. Together, Old Man and Old Woman design the people, with Old Man having first say and Old Woman second, and Old Man playing the trickster role in the process. [13] In *Winter in the Blood*, the narrator's repeated use of the names "Old Woman" and "Old Man" to refer to his grandmother and Yellow Calf associate the old people with the original beings, an appropriate association since it is from the pair that the narrator inherits identity and authenticity.

Returning from his discovery at Yellow Calf's cabin, the narrator is aware of "the smell of rain" and says, "I tried to imagine what it must have been like, the two of them, hunter and widow." With the revitalizing rain in the offing, for the first time the narrator engages his imagination in an attempt to comprehend a relationship involving deep commitment between man and woman, the only such relationship that exists in the novel. At the same time, through this act of imagination, he is bringing the past into "temporal unification" with the present, a crucial step in the recovery of a "centred sense of personal identity."[14]

Upon his arrival home, the narrator sees the wild-eyed cow stuck desperately in the mud. Associating the cow with the "wild-eyed spinster" that refused to go through the gate and precipitated the accident that killed his brother, the narrator is faced with a crucial decision: to attempt to save, and thus forgive, the cow just as he has pardoned Bird, or to walk away and retain his burden of guilt. "The two or three inches of stagnant water sent the smell of dead things through my body," he says, evoking the stagnation and dormancy, or living death, which has gripped him throughout the novel. In the midst of his effort to rescue the cow, he says, "I crouched and spent the next few minutes planning my new life." For the first time in the novel, the narrator thinks of a future, and for the first time he acts, at least in thought, to order that new life. He has transcended the "fragmentation and all those instabilities . . . that prevent us even picturing coherently let alone devising strategies to produce, some radically different future."[15] He has begun to move beyond alienation. He adds, "As I climbed aboard the horse, I noticed for the first time that it was raining" (170). The new identity, new life, and rain come together here in a convergence of promise. And, as at nearly all key moments in the novel, a magpie arrives to observe: "A magpie, light and silent, flew overhead, then lit on a fence post beside the loading chute. He ruffled his sleek feathers, then squatted to watch" (170). Trickster has arrived to view the transformation. It is trickster's role to challenge identities, to trick and probe and question and, above all, shatter stasis and stagnation. When Bird falls, never to rise again, the narrator notes, "The magpie must have flown closer, for his metallic *awk! awk!* was almost conversational" (172).

We see the changed narrator in the final scene of the novel, the burial of the grandmother. Through language, the narrator orders and controls the situation, using ironic deflation as a comic tool. In the tradition of Native American storytelling, the narrator has asserted some kind of order and significance within his own life by telling the narrative we have just read. He has, in Momaday's sense, articulated his existence and earned an identity: he is both the grandson of Yellow Calf, the hunter, and the storyteller of this narrative. Andrew Horton has called the narrator an "artist-trickster," arguing that "he has manipulated his experiences into words and those words into passages presented in a certain order to create the narrative we read. But he cannot 'trick' himself into happiness or fulfillment or satisfaction." At the same time, humor functions here as an important tool that has often been overlooked in Indian writing as well as Indian culture. Speaking of this novel in an interview, Welch noted that "many people . . . are afraid to laugh with that book, and I can't understand why. They think it's Indian and they think it's about alienation and so on and, therefore, there should be no funny moments in the novel. But I intentionally put comic stuff in there just to alleviate that vision of alienation and purposelessness, aimlessness, whereas in *The Death of Jim Loney*, by the very nature of its subject, there could be very little comedy. The guy is going to kill himself. No, that's not funny."[16]

Unlike *Loney*, *Winter* is very funny. "I had to admit that Lame Bull looked pretty good," the narrator says. "The buttons on his shiny green suit looked like they were made of wood. Although his crotch hung a little low, the pants were the latest style." Similarly, he praises his mother and then ironically undercuts the description: "Teresa wore a black coat, black high heels, and a black cupcake hat. . . . Once again she was big and handsome—except for her legs. They appeared to be a little skinny, but it must have been the dress" (174). The humor sharpens when he says, "The old lady wore a shiny orange coffin with flecks of black ingrained beneath the surface." And when Lame Bull must lower himself into the grave and jump up and down on the high end to make the coffin fit, the scene has arrived at slapstick.

The narrator also describes himself: "I was wearing a suit that had belonged to my father. . . . The collar and cuffs itched in the noonday heat, but the pant legs were wide enough so that if I stood just right I didn't touch them" (174). Old enough, finally, to wear his father's suit, the narrator still isn't quite mature enough to fill it. If the rain has finally come to the burnt landscape, and if the unnamed narrator has at last broken free of his stagnant and arrested life, Welch does not allow the stride to be a giant one. The narrator says, "The air was heavy with yesterday's rain. It would probably be a good day for fishing," and he thinks of Agnes, saying, "Next time I'd do it right. Buy her a couple of crèmes de menthe, maybe offer to marry her on the spot." The rain suggests renewal, and fish are associated with fertility and, through the medicine man, Fish, with vision into the future. Both are positive images. That the narrator is able this time to actually think of a commitment to Agnes, of marriage, indicates a significant change. And when, in the final gesture of the novel, he throws the grandmother's tobacco pouch into the grave, he assumes a role in the on-going story Yellow Calf has told, the Blackfoot story of the grandmother and Yellow Calf, Old Woman and Old Man. Like them, the narrator—and the Blackfoot people—has survived a "starving time."

The ending isn't exactly happy, however, and Welch told us early in the novel that it wouldn't be, for "the third man, Enright, wasn't in the picture." *Winter in the Blood* is no romance, with a "right" ending. The last time we saw Agnes, she had green teeth from drinking crèmes de menthe, and the narrator was about to be beaten. The circle may begin again, but the narrator will at least be alive this time, able to act—"offer to marry her on the spot"—and thus assert some control in his life. And he knows who he is: the grandson of "Yellow Calf, the hunter." Stressing the positive direction of this ending, Jack Davis has made an important connection between D'Arcy McNickle and Welch, writing that

> more than a generation later than McNickle's own first novel *The Surrounded* (1936), which graphically portrayed the disintegrating effect of white civilization upon another Montana tribe . . . *Winter in the Blood* brings that process up to date and then depicts a subtle reversal as the protagonist, in whom virtually all vestiges of Indian beliefs and customs appear to have been eradicated, reaches back toward prereservation culture and begins to reconstitute the tribal identity he had never possessed. [17]

The novel and the narrator's quest for authenticity take on still more positive significance if we consider them briefly in Brechtian terms. In his essay "Brecht and Rhetoric," Terry Eagleton quotes the Philosopher in the *Mesingkauf Dialogues*, who declares that "lamenting by means of sounds, or better still words, is a vast liberation, because it means that the sufferer is beginning to produce something. He's already mixing his sorrow with an account of the blows he has received; he's already making something out of the utterly devastating. Observation has set in." Eagleton adds, "If the child's trek from rhetoric to logic is part of the problem, the sufferer's transition from screaming to explaining is part of the solution. When lamenting becomes propositional it is transformed: it becomes, like theory, a way of encompassing a situation rather than being its victim."[18] The narrator of *Winter in the Blood* has made this transition from "screaming," or, in Indian terms, "crying for pity," to articulating or explaining. He is "mixing his sorrow with an account of the blows he has received"; he has ceased being merely a victim and has begun to "make something out of the utterly devastating." In this act of recovery, he has become a storyteller.

In *Winter in the Blood*, Welch delves into an Indian past, re-membering, putting together the fragments of that past into a significant whole which confers identity and meaning upon the protagonist. In Welch's next novel, *The Death of Jim Loney*, the author explores the predicament of a halfblood, a character trapped more fatally than the narrator of *Winter* could ever be in a wasteland between worlds.[19]

The protagonist's name, Jim Loney, with its pun on the name of the author, suggests that Welch may be exploring more desolate terrain farther out in the no-man's-land of Indian identity. What if the narrator of *Winter in the Blood* had been the son of a halfblood drifter and had had no grandmother to tell him stories of who he is, no Yellow Calf to trick him into self-knowledge? What if the narrator had been truly and inexorably a "stranger to both" Indian and white, made so by blood and circumstance? Such is the condition of Jim Loney, who resembles the figures in postmodern fiction who can "no longer contemplate how they can unravel or unmask a central mystery, but are forced to ask, "Which world is this? What is to be done in it? Which of myselves is to do it?"[20]

The Death of Jim Loney opens with a picture of both absurdity and pathos as Loney sits at a high school football game watching "the muddy boys bang against each other." With seconds to go, the home team attempts a fake kick:

> The holder scooped the ball off the ground and started to circle right. The kicker followed him, dancing behind him like a thin bird. The Chinook players fell back from the line to cover the end zone. Suddenly the holder stopped and cocked his arm and the thin player ran into him. The ball seemed to hang in the air as both players fell to the muddy field; then it, too, fell, landing on the thin player's back. He rolled over, pulled the ball into his midsection and lay there without moving.

Like the first paragraph of *Winter in the Blood*, this absurd vignette sets the tone of the novel, even introducing in the description of the doomed kicker as a "thin bird" the totemic image of the bird that will haunt Loney throughout the novel. And as he watches the game, Loney recalls a biblical passage: "Turn away from man in whose nostrils is breath, for of what account is he?"[21] Later we will learn that Loney has been troubled by this passage but has never looked it up because, as he tells his lover, Rhea, "I'm afraid I will find it and it will be bad." Loney has an Indian sense of language as a powerful, compelling force, and he fears the ability of that "other" language from the Bible to determine his life.

Loney fails to understand two crucial messages in the novel, one rising out of the Indian side of his unconscious and the other from his white consciousness. The bird will appear again and again to Loney, but he will never have the knowledge or training necessary to comprehend its message—the knowledge that finally enabled Momaday's Set Lockeman to recognize the vision of the bear and comprehend its significance. Loney cannot understand or believe in the mythic reality represented by the bird. Similarly, he does not look up the scripture from Isaiah to discover that it, too, warns him to look beyond human limitations toward the transcendent or spiritual. Welch has placed Loney amidst a world replete with hints of faith. Not only is Loney visited by dreams and visions from his Indian heritage, but he is also surrounded by fragments of Christianity: Christian holidays, a church (before the padlocked doors of which he stands in a dream), Mission Canyon, and much more, all of which is as unattainable to Loney as the meaning of his dark bird. Because he has no tradition and no teachers like Set's Grey, Loney lacks the necessary awareness and ability to believe in either world.

Loney's Montana is another Indian-and-white wasteland, a cold and barren landscape populated by displaced persons incapable of commitment to anyone or anything. When the novel begins, Loney is already far advanced along the road toward self-destruction, thinking as he walks from the bathos of the football game that "he was seeing things strangely. . . . It was as though he were exhausted and drowsy, but his head was clear." Though he can see and smell, he thinks, "I hear nothing, it is as quiet as death," and Welch adds, "and he did not hear the rain. The rain did not make a sound as it fell."[22] The long-awaited rain that ended the psychic drought in *Winter* falls unheeded here, suggesting that for Loney no renewal or rebirth may be possible.

Loney is not alone in his isolation and despair. Of Rhea, Loney's lover, Welch writes, "The malaise had fallen over her like a patch of winter fog and she thought it had to do with the onset of winter in a cold country" (7). Rhea is far from her Texas home and desperate. She tries to convince Loney to move to Seattle with her, a place she doesn't really know, and thinks ironically, "Maybe he wouldn't feel so displaced" (26). The town cop, Painter, longs for California and feels alien in the small Montana town, while Rhea's friend, Colleen, complains, "Living here is like being in exile. . . . Christ, I feel as if I hadn't a friend in the world" (123). The list is comprehensive: Loney's sister, Kate, lives alone and far from her birthplace in a sterile East Coast apartment; Myron Pretty Weasel lives friendless with his dying father, after his mother and sisters have left them; Loney's father, Ike, crouches in a decrepit trailer, miserable and friendless, mourning cynically for Loney's mother, who had left him just after Loney's birth; and the mother Loney has never seen exists in some undefined place—maybe a madhouse, maybe death—just outside the picture. Of Yellow Eyes, a basketball teammate and high school friend of Loney's and Pretty Weasel's, Loney thinks, "It was as though Yellow Eyes had disappeared without a trace" (118). Loney knows that Yellow Eyes was a body found beside the railroad tracks in another city, but he has never told anyone because no one ever cared enough to mention Yellow Eyes. Kenny, a bar owner in the novel, thinks at one point that he would never be questioned about Loney "because a man like Loney just wasn't that important to anyone" (98). Like Yellow Eyes, and like another anonymous former high school basketball star whom Loney sees in a bar, Loney just isn't significant.

The time is late fall and winter, seasons of dormancy and waiting, of lifelessness. And in an unmistakable echo of Eliot's *The Waste Land*, Welch causes Loney's sister, Kate, to ask, "What shall we do today?" and three paragraphs later, "What shall we do today?"[23] Rhea, comparing herself to a picture of a woman on her wall, thinks of them as "two passionless women waiting for something to happen" (8). In Eliot's poem—a search for spiritual significance and order in a time of deracination, alienation, and despair—the goal is to re-member, to put together the fragments and to rediscover the "roots that clutch" and thus recover a spiritual tradition that makes the world inhabitable (a shoring of fragments, however, remarkably Eurocentric even for an Anglo-American writer). The same is at stake in Welch's novels. In *Winter*, the protagonist is able to put the pieces together and thus survive. In *Loney*, the protagonist has only fragments and is so desperately deracinated and devoid of guidance that he cannot make connections—the roots do not clutch. Welch has said, "I think the novel is about looking back and looking forward, trying to make some sense of it all. Loney can't see anything beyond his death, the death of himself."[24]

Welch makes the source of Loney's plight glaringly obvious. "Do you ever think about your ancestors?" Rhea asks him as they sit together in Mission Canyon. "Which ones?" he responds, and she says enthusiastically, "Whichever you claim. Oh, you're so lucky to have two sets of ancestors. Just think, you can be Indian one day and white the next. Whichever suits you." Loney, however, thinks, "It would be nice to think that, but it would be nicer to be one or the other all the time, to have only one set of ancestors. It would be nice to think that one was one or the other, Indian or white. Whichever, it would be nicer than being a half-breed" (14). Whereas Momaday's half-Kiowa Locke Setman was able, with crucial assistance from Grey, to return to an Indian identity and be reintegrated into the mythic reality of his father's people, Loney cannot do this; he is, in fact, even more tragically cut off from the past than McNickle's Archilde Leon or Mathews's Chal Windzer. Loney, neither white nor Indian, abandoned by mother and father, has nothing. Like the schizophrenic who suffers from "a breakdown in the signifying chain of meaning" and who lives incoherently amidst "a rubble of distinct and unrelated signifiers,"[25] Loney cannot put the pieces of his past and present, and therefore his identity, together, with the result that he cannot project a future:

> Sometimes he felt like an amnesiac searching for the one event, the one person or moment, that would bring everything back and he would see the order in his life. But without the amnesiac's clean slate, all the people and events were as hopelessly tangled as a bird's nest in his mind, and so for almost a month he had been sitting at his table, drinking wine, and saying to himself, "Okay, from this very moment I will start back—I will think of yesterday, last week, last year, until all my years are accounted for. Then I will look ahead and know where I'm going." But the days piled up faster than the years receded and he grew restless and despondent. But he would not concede that his life had added up to nothing more than the simple reality of a man sitting and drinking in a small house in the world. (21)

We will see this image of the tangled past, like a bird's nest or tangled yarn, again in Leslie Silko's *Ceremony*. In that novel, however, the mixedblood protagonist will receive the guidance and support denied the isolated Loney.

Loney's sister, Kate, has been able to cut herself free of the past that pains Loney. Educated and working for the BIA, Kate has early "thought of learning as a kind of salvation, a way to get up and out of being what they were, two half-breed kids caught in the slack water of a minor river" (90). She has embraced conceptions of "truth," "order," and "reality" originating from the privileged center of white America. Wearing a squash blossom necklace "right from the heart of Navaho country," a turquoise blouse, and a sheepskin jacket from a boutique in Phoenix, Kate has become a professional pastiche, her authenticity derived from signifiers determined by the Euramerican culture that has commodified "Indianness." She has been able to survive only by cutting her losses. "Do you ever think about your past—our past?" Loney asks her, and Kate replies, "We have no past. What's the point in thinking about it?" (91). Trying to convince Loney to come back east with her, Kate says to her brother, "You have nothing left. . . . You have nothing." And Welch writes: "'I can't leave,' he said, and he almost knew why. He thought of his earlier attempts to create a past, a background, an ancestry—something that would tell him who he was. Now he wondered if he had really tried. He had always admired Kate's ability to live in the present, but he had also wondered at her lack of need to understand her past" (88).

Loney ponders his Indian ancestors without being able to imagine himself as Indian:

> It always startled Loney that when he stepped out of his day-to-day existence he was considered an Indian. He never felt Indian. Indians were people like the Cross Guns, the Old Chiefs—Amos After Buffalo. They lived an Indian way, at least tried. When Loney thought of Indians, he thought of the reservation families, all living under one roof, the old ones passing down the wisdom of their years, of their family's years, of their tribe's years, and the young ones soaking up their history, their places in their history, with a wisdom that went beyond age. (102)

He remembers Emil Cross Guns, a medicine man: "Emil was dead now and those days were gone to Loney. Everything was changed and the old ones did not exist." He thinks of Pretty Weasel's fullblood father: "Now he was old, but in a white man way, thrown away. Not like Emil Cross Guns. Loney thought this and he grew sad, not for Pretty Weasel's father, nor for Emil Cross Guns, but for himself. He had no family and he wasn't Indian or white. He remembered the day he and Rhea had driven out to the Little Rockies. She had said he was lucky to have two sets of ancestors. In truth he had none" (102). Loney is a victim of discourse that has turned "real" Indians into artifacts. Just as Kate has settled for the privileged white culture's surface significations of Indianness—squash blossoms and turquoise—in place of a personal sense of authenticity, Loney cannot move beyond the authoritative discourse's static definition of Indian identity. According to this definition, to have authenticity as "Indian," one must live in a way recognizable as Indian from the outside, as Loney's clichéd phrase suggests: "with a wisdom that went beyond age." For Loney, to whom this traditional role is inaccessible because "those days were gone" and "the old ones did not exist," there is no room for play, no flexible or creative stylizing within the signifier "Indian" that would allow him an inventive, coherent identity as a mixedblood in a contemporary Montana town. Loney, without community or family to teach him, with no trickster like Yellow Calf or Tosamah to shock him into self-awareness, has no syncretic capacities—precisely those qualities that have allowed Native Americans to change, adapt, and survive while retaining a coherent sense of self, whether mixed- or fullblood.

Myron Pretty Weasel, seemingly as isolated on his successful ranch as Loney in his despair, attempts to reestablish contact with his friend. Pretty Weasel remembers when Loney could control at least one aspect of his life, thinking that in high school Loney "had been the best ball handler and passer that Pretty Weasel had played with or against." And he wonders "how he and Loney could have drifted apart so absolutely. Loney was the last friend he'd had. Now he was gone, into the liquor store, into some kind of desperado life" (82). In the background, on the tape player in Pretty Weasel's truck, Hank Williams sings, "I'm so lonesome I could die," the theme song for this novel.

Pretty Weasel convinces Loney to go hunting with him on what turns out to be a kind of final, ceremonial hunt, beginning with the ritual smoke which Pretty Weasel, who "didn't smoke, ever," thinks of "as a kind of offering." On the night before the hunting trip, Loney muses, "After tomorrow I will have no future. . . . After tomorrow's slim purpose I will simply exist" (108). And during the hunt, a bear—a powerful medicine—appears to both men. Just as Loney cannot accept himself as Indian—or mixedblood—he cannot accept the presence of the bear: "He wanted to ask why that was a bear. There were no bears anymore." Pretty Weasel, however, has the ability, still, to fully imagine the bear's presence, exclaiming significantly, "Oh, yes. . . . *I believe* it is. *I believe it is what I think it is*" (117, emphasis mine).

Pretty Weasel identifies with the powerful bear spirit as Francisco had in *House Made of Dawn*, and he *becomes* the bear—as a successful hunter must—just before Loney shoots him: "Then he heard the brittle crashing of the dry stalks and he saw the darkness of it, its immense darkness in that dazzling day, and he thrust the gun to his cheek and he felt the recoil and he saw the astonished look on Pretty Weasel's face as he stumbled two steps back and sat down in the crackling cattails" (120). Having killed his former friend, Loney feels, as did Archilde in *The Surrounded*, that it has all been fated by some obscure and inexorable mystery:

> Loney saw the bear in the field, its head bobbing as though it beckoned to them. The image spooked him and he thought of the bear not as a bear but as an agent of evil—how else explain the fact that there hadn't been a bear in that valley for years and years?—and on Loney's last purposeful day he had succumbed to that evil.
> That it was an accident did not occur to Loney. That the bear, as rare and inexplicable as its appearance had been, was simply a bear did not occur to him either. And so he was inclined to think that what had happened happened because of some quirky and predictable fate. (129)

Like Archilde Leon, Loney thinks to himself that "somehow, at some time, everything had gone dreadfully wrong, and although it had something to do with his family, it had everything to do with himself" (134).

In shooting Pretty Weasel, Loney symbolically kills the Indian potential in himself—that which could believe in the bear. Next, he turns to his white father, the other side of himself, for whatever answers may be possible. Speaking with his father for the first time in fourteen years, he learns that his mother, Eletra Calf Looking, had been a fullblood Gros Ventre and traditional, "all dressed up in doeskin—dress, leggings, the whole works. She danced real slow, the way the women used to in those days." And when his father says, "I don't know what happened after those first couple of years. . . . She just sort of went to hell. Started drinking, running around," we hear an echo of Father Grepilloux in *The Surrounded*, the priest who is ironically unaware of his church's role in destroying Salish culture. From his vantage point outside of both identities, Loney recognizes what happened, telling his father, "It was because you made her that way. You ruined her," and adding, "You couldn't help yourself. You can't help the way you are" (142).

From his father, Loney learns nothing that will tell him who he is: "He had felt when he entered the trailer that there had to be an explanation to their existences, and his father had given him nothing." However, it is at this point in the novel that, for the first time, Loney begins to take control of his destiny. He tells his father about Pretty Weasel's death, and he carefully explains to his father that he plans to flee to Mission Canyon, knowing that "his father was the worst type of dirt—he would squeal and would enjoy the attention" (155).

Mission Canyon is a place Loney identifies with the old ones, the traditional Indians. When he arrives at the canyon, he thinks "about the Indians who had used the canyon, the hunting parties, the warriors, the women who had picked chokecherries farther up." Whereas earlier, the imagined faces of the vanished Indians had terrified him at Snake Butte, imagining the old "real" Indians now has a different effect: "These thoughts made him comfortable and he wasn't afraid" (168).

In the end, Loney is able to assert control over his life only by adopting a warrior's stance, by selecting and controlling the time, place, and manner of his death. By insuring that his father knows where he will be and then shooting the window out of his father's trailer, Loney knows that the tribal policeman, Quenton Doore, will come for him. And knowing Doore's brutality, he knows what the end will be. Quenton Doore also understands Loney. Whereas the white lawman, Painter, is totally confused until the final moments of Loney's life, Doore goes straight to Loney and shoots him just as Loney had planned. When Doore sees Loney standing clearly above the road, an obvious target, he grins and says, "That's the great Loney," recognizing in his cynical words that Loney has chosen a warrior's death, but a death that in the context is pathetic.

As Loney dies, "he felt a harsh wind where there was none and the last thing he saw were the beating wings of a dark bird as it climbed to a distant place." This is the "dark bird" that has haunted Loney throughout the book, the bird of which he has said to Rhea, "Sometimes I think it is a vision sent by my mother's people. I must interpret it, but I don't know how" (105). The totemic bird, which seems to hover about Loney throughout his decline, may well be

Loney's animal power, or spirit, sent according to traditional Indian belief in dreams and visions to provide a profound identification with the animal world and thus a special strength or power. Loney's lack of training, of knowledge necessary to interpret the vision, creates an unfathomable void between him and the bird, a barrier which he cannot cross. In the end, the spirit retreats into the distance, leaving Loney still more alone in death.

It is tempting to imagine that by choosing to die a warrior's death Loney has done something positive. Paula Gunn Allen takes this approach to the novel, arguing that Loney's vision quest is answered and "he obtains a vision that becomes the guiding force in his life and his death, and he dies like a warrior in a place and a time of his own choosing."[26] But in dying as he does, Loney simply remains victimized by the authoritative discourse that defines the utterance "Indian." In believing that the "real" Indian world is a thing of the dead past, Loney has adopted the Euramerican idea of the Indian as a figure of the epic, and therefore absolute, past. Of this epic past, Bakhtin has written: "One can only accept the epic world with reverence; it is impossible to really touch it, for it is beyond the realm of human activity, the realm in which everything humans touch is altered and re-thought." Thus, Loney cannot comprehend the attempts of mythic, Indian reality to interpenetrate his everyday, mixedblood world, the realm of human activity. By choosing to die "like a warrior," Loney adopts the stance of the Indian as tragic hero, that inauthentic, gothic imposition of European America upon the Native American. Loney enacts the fate of the epic Vanishing American: "Outside his destiny, the epic and tragic hero is nothing; he is, therefore, a function of the plot fate assigns him; he cannot become the hero of another destiny or another plot."[27]

If we read the ending as Allen does, as a positive statement by Welch concerning Loney's final identification as Indian, we have to assume it is the author, not the character, who has succumbed to this epic stereotype. Quenton Doore's cynical declaration, however, argues that Welch understands with sharp irony what he and his character are doing. Like Allen, Kathleen Mullen Sands has argued that *Loney* "is not a bleak novel, certainly not a nihilistic one as some critics have described it. . . . In Loney, Welch develops a deep structure of tribal traditions. . . . Though we resist Loney's journey away from life, we cannot regret his death; it is a foregone conclusion from the beginning, and there is a sense of release when it is accomplished."[28] Sands fails to make clear, however, what "deep structure of tribal traditions" remains for Loney, or how we can read Loney's utter alienation from coherent identity in anything but bleak terms. In fact, Loney stands in sharp and despairing contrast to the narrator of *Winter*, almost a parody of the Indian mixedblood as tragic victim caught between worlds.

The Death of Jim Loney would seem to offer no path that would lead to survival for its mixedblood protagonist unable to forge an identity between Indian and white cultures. Whereas in *The Surrounded* McNickle eventually took Archilde down what the old priest termed the Indian road toward a seemingly inexorable destruction, in *Loney* Welch allows his protagonist neither path. Loney's destruction grows out of a disintegration that is complete and irresistible.

In *Winter in the Blood* Welch examined the predicament of a fullblood who thought he was a mixedblood, an individual adrift in a world without definition. In the course of that novel, the narrator catches a fleeting glimpse of the way it used to be, of the Blackfoot world of traditional times when the people possessed a secure sense of place and therefore identity. With the assistance of Yellow Calf and the aid of his grandmother's stories—the assistance of Old Man and Old Woman—the narrator begins to understand who he is by comprehending where he has come from. It is at least a beginning for the still unnamed narrator. In *The Death of Jim Loney* Welch turned his focus upon a mixedblood protagonist for whom the past was inexorably unknowable and irretrievable, making the future impossible. Together the two novels represent opposing possibilities for contemporary Blackfeet and most Native Americans—two paths that lead in radically different directions.

In his third novel, *Fools Crow*, published in 1986, Welch returns to possibilities hinted at in *Winter in the Blood*, turning his fictional clock back a century to the Blackfoot world of the late 1800s. A historical novel, *Fools Crow* relies heavily upon documented Blackfoot history, merging actual events and characters with the author's creations. And in this work Welch attempts the full act of cultural recovery glimpsed only as a distant possibility by the narrator of *Winter*.[29] Welch reimagines the Blackfoot world here, and in so doing he replaces it, addressing for the Blackfeet—and for Native Americans more generally—what has been defined as the central "crisis of identity" in postcolonial literatures: "the concern with the development of an effective identifying relationship between self and place." Throughout his fiction, like nearly all American Indian novelists, Welch is deeply involved in this "dialectic of place and displacement." By reimagining, or re-membering the traditional Blackfoot world, Welch attempts to recover the center—to revitalize the "myths of identity and authenticity"—and thus reclaim the possibility of a coherent identity for himself and all contemporary Blackfoot people, that which was denied Jim Loney.[30]

To accomplish his goal, Welch, more fully than any other Native American novelist, explicitly seizes control of the language of the Blackfeet's oppressors, making English "bear the burden" of an "other" experience. The conceptual horizon—or "map of the mind"—through which the reader must pass in this novel belongs to the traditional world of the Blackfeet, and in this world the Euramerican is peripheral and alien. In *Fools Crow*, Welch inverts the Western. As early as *Winter in the Blood*, Welch had moved toward a redefining of this conceptual horizon for his reader. Discussing that first novel in a 1982 interview, Welch described his intentions: "If you were a tourist coming along Highway 2 there on the Highline, all you might want to do is get through this country as fast as possible. . . . I wanted to hijack a carload of those tourists. . . . I just wanted them to be immersed in this country so that they would see as much as I saw, because, to me, that was a whole world right there. . . ." In a later interview, Welch said of *Fools Crow*:

> I'm staying exclusively with the Blackfeet. I'm trying to write from the inside-out, because most historical novels are written from the outside looking in. My main character is a member of a particular band, and I'm talking a lot about camp life and ceremonial life, those day to day practical things that they did to survive—and to live quite decently, as a matter of fact. So I'm writing it from the inside-out. The white people are the real strangers. They're the threatening presence out there all the time.[31]

Like Welch's earlier novels, *Fools Crow* focuses on still another young Blackfoot male, but this protagonist differs greatly from Welch's previous central characters in that he is a fullblood immersed in a traditional world. Unlike the unnamed narrator of *Winter* and the directionless Loney, Fools Crow knows at all times precisely who and where he is: he is a Blackfoot in a world defined securely according to Blackfoot values and Blackfoot discourse. The Napikwans—white men—who a century later will become the "stalking white men" haunting the narrator's world in *Winter*, are only beginning to insinuate their power over the Blackfoot world as *Fools Crow* opens. The fact that these invaders are defined by Blackfoot language—as "Napikwans"—underscores the Indians' sense of still controlling their world, of being the privileged center within this world wherein the whites are "other."[32]

If language "becomes the medium through which a hierarchical structure of power is perpetuated, and the medium through which conceptions of 'truth', 'order', and 'reality' become established," the primary structure of power (and epistemology) in the world of *Fools Crow* still belongs to the Blackfeet. The protagonist's world is intact; there is no alienation—yet. However, by manipulating the syntax of the novel, by interpolating literal translations of Blackfoot utterances (for example, "sticky mouth," "real bear," "Cold Maker," and so on), and by rendering place so fully, Welch simultaneously makes his reader acutely aware of the "gap" his language attempts to overcome: that "resulting from the linguistic displacement of the pre-colonial language by English." Thus, as Welch attempts "to convey in a language that is not one's own the spirit that is one's own," the tensions—dialogism—within the very language of the novel become a radical indicator of the cultural denigration, displacement, even genocide that the novel is meant to demonstrate.[33]

Fools Crow is set in the late 1860s, as the protagonist's father, Rides-at-the-Door, indicates when he says, "It has been almost thirteen winters since the big treaty with the bosses from the east." Though twice ravaged by smallpox—in 1781, when more than half the Blackfoot population died, and again in 1837, when two-thirds of the tribe perished—as the novel opens the Blackfeet have regained their strength and are a powerful and confident people. White Man's Dog, as the protagonist is at first called, is a member of the Lone Eaters band of the Pikuni tribe of Blackfeet. The Blackfeet are historically divided into three main tribes: the Pikuni (Piegan), who are the focus of this novel; the Kainah (Blood); and the Siksika (Northern Blackfeet, sometimes called the Blackfeet proper). Throughout most of the year each tribe was further divided into bands of twenty to thirty families totaling one to two hundred individuals. The Lone Eaters are listed in Grinnell's *Blackfoot Lodge Tales* as one of two dozen Pikuni bands.[34]

Having undertaken an unsuccessful vision quest two years earlier, when he was sixteen, the young man still goes by the childhood name he earned by trailing Victory Robe White Man, an old story-teller, about camp. The name of White Man's Dog, conferred by the band, has given the protagonist an identity—though not one he relishes—and has replaced his birth name, Sinopa. However, he has yet to earn the name which will define his adult place within the tribe. The protagonist's first opportunity to prove himself comes when he is invited with four other young men on a horse-taking raid against the Crows. The group is led by the seasoned warrior Yellow Kidney and veteran scout, or "wolf," Eagle Ribs. Through-out the novel Welch incorporates a number of names from Blackfoot history. Eagle Ribs, for example, was an actual warrior who had boasted of killing white trappers and who was thought to be respon-sible for killing American Fur Company clerk Henry Vandenburgh, allegedly stripping the victim's flesh from his bones and throwing the bones in the Jefferson River. Mik-api, the "many-faces" man of the novel, bears the name of a figure from Blackfoot oral tradition: Mik-a'pi or Red Old Man, featured in Grinnell's *Blackfoot Lodge Tales* and about whom it is said, "Of all the great chiefs who had lived and died, he was the greatest. . . . It must be true, as the old men have said, that he was helped by the ghosts, for no one can do such things without help from those fearful and unknown persons." Often, Welch uses the actual names of both Blackfeet and whites involved in the historical events about which he is writing, such as the chiefs Heavy Runner, Little Dog, Mountain Chief, and Big Lake; the mixedblood scout Joe Kipp; and the white rancher Malcolm Clark. At other times, as with Eagle Ribs, he apparently borrows historical names for his fictional creations. Owl Child, for example, is a name borne by one of the most successful Blackfoot cattlemen in the 1880s and '90s, a name Welch ironically appropriates for his renegade warrior in the novel. Welch even borrows Grinnell's term for the traditional healer. "The doctor," Grinnell writes, "is named *I-so-kin'-uh-kin*, a word difficult to translate. The nearest English meaning of the word seems to be "heavy singer for the sick."[35]

During the horse-stealing expedition, White Man's Dog distin-guishes himself, while his more admired friend, Fast Horse, com-mits a foolish act leading to the capture and mutilation of Yellow Kidney. Having had a dream in which "Cold Maker" told him to move a big rock blocking an ice spring, and having failed to locate the spring, Fast Horse has first erred in not turning back from the raid. His second error comes in an act of individual aggrandize-ment—a shouted boast in the enemy camp—that endangers the success of the raid and the lives of the group. As a result, Yellow Kidney is captured by the Crows, who cut off his fingers and send him home as an example.[36] Before being captured and released, Yellow Kidney contracts smallpox, an event which White Man's Dog has foreseen in a dream. Welch's description of the dream suggests the historical arrival of smallpox among the Blackfeet in 1781, when a Blackfoot scouting party stumbled upon a seemingly deserted Shoshoni village only to find the inhabitants lying dead or dying within the lodges. Deciding that an evil spirit had afflicted their enemies, the Blackfeet took the best lodges and other possessions and left the Shoshoni to die. Thus the evil spirit of smallpox came among them.[37]

For the rough outline of his plot, Welch has relied almost entirely upon historical sources. The tribes raided in the novel are traditional Blackfoot enemies. The outcast Owl Child and the others who wage guerrilla war against the whites reflect those young men who, in the 1850s, resisted and killed the intruding whites throughout the territory. It was such a group that actually murdered the prominent former trader and successful rancher Malcolm Clark. According to Ewers, Clark was visited by twenty-five young Piegan warriors in 1869 and killed. Five of the warriors, recognized by Clark's children, were indicted for the murder by a grand jury, and warrants were issued for their arrest. Alexander Culbertson, a trader who knew the Blackfeet intimately, declared that the murders of Clark and other whites were committed by "a portion of the young rabble over whom the chiefs have not control," a declaration that is reinforced by Welch's treatment of the episode in his novel. According to historical accounts, in discussion with U.S. representatives the chiefs Heavy Runner, Little Wolf, Big Lake, and Gray Eyes agreed to "kill the murderers and bring in their bodies and all the stolen stock they could find."[38] This is the group represented by Owl Child's gang in the novel, the group which Rides-at-the-Door, speaking for the friendly chiefs, agrees to try to kill, saying, "It is the only way to avoid war." Similarly, the smallpox plague that sweeps through the villages late in the novel reflects the actual smallpox epidemic of 1869–70, the third major epidemic to devastate the tribes. The massacre of Heavy Runner's band is an event that actually took place on January 23, 1870, when the halfblood Joe Kipp, scouting for a large military command out to avenge the murders of Clark and other whites, mistook the friendly chief's village for that of the more hostile Mountain Chief. According to

Curlew Woman, a survivor of the massacre in Welch's novel, "Heavy Runner was among the first to fall. He had a piece of paper that was signed by a seizer chief. It said that he and his people were friends to the Napikwans" (383–84). Curlew Woman's account matches an Indian account of the actual attack, which states that "as soon as Heavy Runner learned troops were approaching, he walked out alone to meet them, and he was holding up his hand and waving his identification paper when a soldier shot him dead." Welch would also take the murder of Little Dog and the decline of the once-powerful Black Patched Moccasin band straight from history.[39]

Needless to say, Welch is accurate, according to historical sources, in reproducing Blackfoot life of the second half of the nineteenth century. At the core of this historical novel, however, is the fictional story of the young man who comes to be a warrior, healer, and visionary for his people. The protagonist's three names—in contrast to the nameless narrator of *Winter*—illustrate the essential process of maturation and integration into community in the Blackfoot world. Each new identity is conferred upon the individual from the community and thus tells everyone—Fools Crow as well as his fellow Pikuni—precisely who he is.[40]

Fast Horse acts as a foil to Fools Crow throughout the novel. Cast out of the Lone Eaters band, Fast Horse joins Owl Child's renegade gang. Like Fast Horse, Owl Child has lost his place within the Pikuni community because he has acted selfishly, falsely claiming a scalp taken by another warrior and killing the warrior in the argument. Ironically, the renegades who fight most vehemently against the intrusion of the whites are already the most displaced Indians in the world Welch describes, and in their alienation and displacement they come to resemble the displaced whites whom they kill. So dangerous to the Pikuni are the outcasts—individuals who are not controlled by community responsibilities—that Rides-at-the-Door and the other chiefs agree to kill Owl Child's renegades: "Tell this seizer chief that we will kill Owl Child," Fools Crow's father says. "It is the only way to avoid war."[41]

Following Fools Crow's journey to try to bring Fast Horse back to the Pikuni, Welch introduces another displaced American, a white deserter from the Confederate forces who serves as a guard for whiskey wagons passing through Blackfoot territory. While dreaming of home and family—the only myths of identity and authenticity left for perpetually outcast Euramericans—the young white man is abruptly murdered by Owl Child's warriors. In this chapter, chapter 25, Welch accomplishes a fascinating stylistic shift. Throughout the novel Welch has attempted to convey the texture and sense of Blackfoot speech not only by insinuating numerous literal "translations" of Blackfoot terms (for example, "sticky mouth," "real bear," and so on) but also through a careful manipulation of English syntax. Writing in predominantly simple declarative sentences and avoiding complex syntactical constructions, Welch attempts the nearly impossible feat of conveying a feeling of one language through another while simultaneously avoiding the clichéd formal pidgin of Hollywood Indians. The very first paragraph of the novel—while moving fluidly in order to propel the reader into the text—illustrates this deliberate style:

> Now that the weather had changed, the moon of the falling leaves turned white in the blackening sky and White Man's Dog was restless. He chewed the stick of dry meat and watched Cold Maker gather his forces. The black clouds moved in the north in circles, their dance a slow deliberate fury. It was almost night, and he looked back down into the flats along the Two Medicine River. The lodges of the Lone Eaters were illuminated by cooking fires within. It was that time of evening when even the dogs rest and the horses graze undisturbed along the grassy banks.

It is interesting to compare this paragraph with a paragraph from chapter 25 in which the point of view is that of the white man about to be killed: "The rolling prairies were as vast and empty as a pale ocean, and the sky stretched forever, sometimes blue, sometimes slate. The few small groups of mountains, like islands in this sea of yellow swells, only seemed to emphasize its vastness. In the winter, when snow covered the land and lay heavy in the bottoms, the man was filled with foreboding dreams of an even larger isolation" (289–90). Seen through Blackfoot eyes, the landscape has immediate presence; it is intimate and fully inhabited and its signs are read in direct relation to their interpenetration within the lives of the people and animals. Cold Maker and black clouds have imminent and practical significance for the illuminated lodges of the Lone Eaters and for the dogs and horses dependent upon them and at home in this place. In the lyrical rendering of the white man's thoughts, however, Welch suggests the imposition of an aesthetic valorization upon the landscape. For the white man, the landscape is vastly uninhabited, empty of local significance, mirroring, particularly in the key phrase "foreboding dreams of an even larger isolation,"

Heidegger's *Unheimlichkeit*, or "not-at-homeness," that informs postcolonialism.[42]

Having no history, no "place" within the landscape, the white man can only define it in abstract, broadly aesthetic terms that enable him to subsume it into his own romantic myth (compare Ralph Waldo Emerson's "not me" subsumed into the transcendental "me"). In his lyrical response, this naïve and doomed white man reenacts the symbolic depopulation of the continent ("vast and empty") necessary both as a first step toward appropriation and as a means of making the place accessible to the abstract language which is otherwise so inadequate to the task of description. At the same time, through this lyrically "placeless" language, the white man reenacts the colonial subsumption of the continent into the "manifest" destiny of the invaders. Like the African Americans in Ralph Ellison's *Invisible Man*, the Native Americans become invisible inhabitants of the strangely disturbing Promised Land surrounding the whiskey-trading, westering Euramerican. Emptiness characterizes this environment: the monochromatic sky stretches forever, while the prairies are a "vast and empty" sea, as if heaven and earth have merged to form an embryonic sea-space within which the romantic imagination may bring forth the new man, the isolate American. Very shortly, however, phantoms will rise up from that peripheralized reality to murder the young intruder.

When Fools Crow travels to the south, instructed by Nitsokan to go on his quest, he moves deeply into the mythology of the Blackfeet. So-at-sa-ki, or Feather Woman, the mythological figure whom he encounters, is also an outcast from her people. With a mixedblood's fair skin and pale blue eyes, Feather Woman confesses, "I do not live much in your world. . . . I do not fully understand the ways of the Pikunis anymore" (333). Sent back to earth with her son, Star Boy—Poia—Feather Woman becomes an outcast between earth and sky. "They say that you were never happy again," Fools Crow tells her, "that you rejected your people, that each dawn you would beg Morning Star to take you back" (352).

During his stay with her, Feather Woman allows Fools Crow a vision of the future, and he sees an apocalyptic vision in the dual forms of the halfblood Joe Kipp leading soldiers against the Blackfeet and the smallpox epidemic awaiting the people. "I do not fear for my people now," Fools Crow tells her. "As you say, we will go to a happier place. . . . But I grieve for our children and their children, who will not know the life their people once lived. I see them on the yellow skin and they are dressed like the Napikwans, they watch the Napikwans and learn much from them, but they are not happy. They lose their own way" (359).[43] Feather Woman's response is, "Much will be lost to them. . . . But they will know the way it was. The stories will be handed down, and they will see that their people were proud and lived in accordance with the Below Ones, the Underwater People—and the Above Ones" (359–60).

In *Fools Crow*, Welch is the storyteller committed to rediscovering and preserving this lost identity. Earlier in the novel, the chief Three Bears has said, "We will not become like the whitehorns that these white people herd from one place to another" (256), but in spite of that declaration this is almost precisely what the Blackfeet of *Winter in the Blood* have become. With the heavy analogy between cattle and Indians and the motif of fences in that first novel, Welch makes it clear that the Indians have become like the livestock herded and fenced by the white culture. However, in that novel the unnamed narrator, who as Fools Crow predicted has lost his way, is allowed a brief journey back in time, a glimpse if not a vision of the traditional Blackfoot world, and that glimpse provides whatever identity and hope the narrator finally possesses. In *Fools Crow* Welch himself has made a longer, more difficult journey home, delving into the depths of Blackfoot identity in order to make this world accessible to both himself and his contemporaries. The role of the storyteller is crucial to cultural and individual psychic survival, for stories confer meaning and identity in the Indian world. Bitterly, Fools Crow tells a survivor of the massacre of Heavy Runner's village: "It is good that you are alive. You will have much to teach the young ones about the Napikwans. Many of them will come into this world and grow up thinking that the Napikwans are their friends because they will be given a blanket or a tin of the white man's water. But here, you see, this is the Napikwan's real gift" (385).

Not only has Welch fully recovered the traditional Pikuni world in this novel, but he has also rendered the inhabitants of that world in the kind of convincing, fully human detail seldom allowed Native Americans in literature by Euramericans. The story of Running Fisher's adultery with his father's young wife, Kills-Close-to-the-Lake, for example, is a universally human drama. The pathos of the youngest wife's frustration and entrapment is poignant, and her movement toward first Fools Crow and then Running Fisher in search of warmth and love is developed as an inevitably human response. Rides-at-the-Door's response is also complex and compelling as he recognizes his own culpability and acts out of compassion and understanding.[44] In this subplot, Running Fisher and Kills-Close-to-the-Lake achieve a fully rounded dimension not available to Fools Crow. Whereas Welch allows these minor characters to act out of universally human impulse, his protagonist's role demands that he represent the Blackfoot world more completely and that he thus act more rigidly according to a role. As he matures toward his identity as warrior-healer-visionary, Fools Crow paradoxically never achieves the fully human dimensions of his younger brother and father's young wife. He is bound by a role, while they are free.

Fools Crow ends with a ceremonial procession through the Pikuni camp as the people celebrate the return of spring. Mik-api, the many-faces man, makes an offering to Thunder Chief, and the people pray "for long summer grass, bushes thick with berries, all things that grow in the ground-of-many-gifts." Having survived smallpox and the massacres of the U.S. Army, the people dance in a circle through the village with Butterfly, the child of Fools Crow and Red Paint, carried sleeping with the procession. In an unmistakable sign of renewal and promise, Thunder Chief sends rain to the village, and Welch concludes with a lyrical—almost Homeric— vision: "Far from the fires of the camps, out on the rain-dark prairies, in the swales and washes, on the rolling hills, the rivers of great animals moved. Their backs were dark with rain and the rain gathered and trickled down their shaggy heads. Some grazed, and some slept. Some had begun to molt. Their dark horns glistened in the rain as they stood guard over the sleeping calves. The black-horns had returned and, all around, it was as it should be."

Fools Crow—like the story of Feather Woman—is about returning, about going home to an identity, about looking back through the hole in time. And the world seen is one in which man is not an isolated, identityless drifter as he is in the first two Welch novels. *Fools Crow* presents a world endangered but intact, where men and women know who and where they are. In this world Raven flutters down to give advice and Nitsokan comes to a sleeper in a dream, and neither instance exemplifies what in contemporary fiction has come to be called "magical realism." In the Blackfoot world rendered so completely in this novel, there is no disjunction between the real and the magical, no sense that the magical is metaphorical. In the world Welch recovers, Raven talks to men and women, the sacred and the profane interpenetrate irresistibly, and this is reality.

If the reader can pass through that conceptual horizon, if the reader acknowledges and accepts this reality, he or she experiences an Indian world, that world forever distanced from the airplane man of *Winter* and, more tragically, from the doomed Loney. In *Fools Crow*, Welch has accomplished the most profound act of recovery in American literature.

"The Very Essence
of Our Lives"

Leslie Silko's Webs of Identity

◆

Like James Welch's *Winter in the Blood* and, more fully, *Fools Crow*,
Laguna author Leslie Marmon Silko's novel *Ceremony* is a remembering, a putting together of past, present, and future into a coherent fabric of timeless identity.[1] In Tayo, Silko's protagonist, the
novel features yet another in the long line of liminally displaced
mixedbloods who inhabit American fiction and fiction by Indian
authors in particular. Tayo's mother, whose death has preceded
the novel's opening, was Indian; the identity of his white father
remains a mystery. Seemingly abandoned between generations and
identities, Tayo lives with his aunt, grandmother, and uncle, his
internal and external landscapes equally barren. About her own
Laguna heritage, Leslie Silko has said: "The white men who came
to the Laguna Pueblo Reservation and married Laguna women
were the beginning of the half-breed Laguna people like my family,
the Marmon family. I suppose at the core of my writing is the
attempt to identify what it is to be a half-breed or mixed blooded
person; what it is to grow up neither white nor fully traditional
Indian."[2]

At the core of *Ceremony* is the author's attempt to find a particular
strength within what has almost universally been treated as the
"tragic" fact of mixedblood existence. The central lesson of this
novel is that through the dynamism, adaptability, and syncretism
inherent in Native American cultures, both individuals and the
cultures within which individuals find significance and identity are
able to survive, grow, and evade the deadly traps of stasis and
sterility. Simon Ortiz has accurately praised *Ceremony* as a "special

and most complete example" of "affirmation and what it means in terms of Indian resistance," particularly the characteristically Indian creative incorporation of "foreign ritual, ideas, and material in . . . Indian terms."[3] Rather than undertake a clear-cut recovery project such as that in Welch's fiction, Silko attempts to demonstrate the possibility for authenticity and a coherent identity available to those like herself who might otherwise fall prey to the familiar malaise of mixedblood alienation. In this aim, Silko's work most clearly resembles the more radically theoretical constructions of Gerald Vizenor. At the same time, Silko moves far beyond anything imagined by T. S. Eliot when he wrote of the usefulness of mythological structures in literature. Rather than a previously conceived metaphorical framework within which the anarchy and futility of "real" (as opposed to mythic) existence can be ordered, as often occurs in modernist texts, mythology in *Ceremony* insists upon its actual simultaneity with and interpenetration into the events of the everyday, mundane world. Holy Persons are not metaphors used to imply a "holistic" system of ecological values in this novel, like the sacrificial deities of Eliot's *The Waste Land*; they are very simply part of the reality into which Tayo is subsumed.

Throughout the novel, Silko works carefully to ensure that such binary oppositions are impossible to construct and that readers seeking to find distinct "realities," "planes," "dimensions," or "times" operating within her text will find that the text refuses to divulge such divisions. Rather than interweaving "planes" definable as "human," "myth/ritual," and "socio/cultural"—or working in several "dimensions" we might label "myth," "history," "realism," and "romance"—Silko spins an elaborate web that makes distinguishing between such concepts impossible. For example, Tayo's actions and experiences have "socio/cultural" significance only within the context of his mythic role, while history is shown to be the product of mythic consciousness and have no meaning outside of this consciousness. In the end, when the elders in the kiva recognize the mythic narrative that has determined Tayo's experience, they comprehend the timeless significance of Tayo's story for everyone. The romantic impulse that conventionally subsumes the "not me" into the transcendent "me"—that evolves into the heroic quester in all his individual glory—is inverted in the culture-hero paradigm operative in Tayo's story as the "me" is subsumed into the "not me" and Tayo discovers that the two are one. Tayo's individual identity disappears as he journeys toward the communal identity ultimately pronounced by the pueblo elders within the kiva—the center of their world.[4]

Ceremony begins with Ts'its'tsi'nako, Thought-Woman, "the spider," thinking and thereby creating the story we will read: "Ts'its'-tsi'nako, Thought-Woman, / is sitting in her room / and whatever she thinks about appears. / . . . I'm telling you the story / she is thinking." The feminine creative principle and form for thought or reason, Thought-Woman is regarded by the Keres (Pueblo) people as a supreme creator who has existed from the beginning.[5] Paula Gunn Allen has suggested that "Locating events within the ritual context that supports them, [Silko] relies on accretive structuring to build toward comprehensive significance in her novel, as do traditional storytellers."[6] Silko at once associates primal creation with storytelling, underscoring, like Momaday in *The Way to Rainy Mountain*, the essential creative power of story and discourse to "bring into being." Implicit within Silko's prefatory "poems" is the Indian certainty that through the utterance of stories we place ourselves within and make inhabitable an ordered universe that without stories would be dangerously chaotic. The complex webs of language called stories become ceremonial acts performed in order to maintain the world as both knowable and inhabitable.

By announcing in what amounts to textual superscript her own subordination as author to the story-making authority of Thought-Woman, or Spider Woman ("I'm telling you the story / she is thinking"), Silko effects a deft dislocation of generic expectations, placing her novel within the context of the oral tradition and invoking the source and power of language found within that tradition. She simultaneously, and self-consciously, rejects the egocentric posture of the modern author in favor of what could be defined as an ecocentric orientation and attempts a culturally determined heteroglossia in which her text serves as transmitter rather than originator of voices and meanings. As a result, *Ceremony*, more than any other novel I know of, approaches the category of "authorless" text. In response to Foucault's rehashed questions, "Who really spoke? Is it really he and not someone else? With what authenticity or originality?"—Silko's text points toward the polyvocal oral tradition that predates the "privileged moment of individualization" marked by the coming into being of the notion of author. In the oral tradition, stories are never original and always have the "duty of providing immortality"—of preventing the death of a culture; the very absence of author illuminates their authenticity. In the present age of author as icon, one can easily imagine a work such as *Ceremony* published with no author's name attached, a delightful possibility.[7]

By thus resituating her text and authority as author, Silko assumes a traditional role as storyteller in the context described by Dennis Tedlock (writing about the Lagunas' near neighbors, the Zuni), in which "the relationship between text and interpretation is a dialectical one: he or she both respects the text and revises it." Silko places the reader in the traditionally interactive position of coparticipant, taking part, as postmodern theorists would have it, "in the production of significations and meanings."[8]

More simply put, this framing device makes Silko—even moreso than Momaday in *The Ancient Child*—the vehicle for a story that is older than she, as old as the consciousness of the people. The unmistakable message is that though Silko, like a traditional storyteller, is remaking the story, reforming it, molding it to fit new situations and times, she is not inventing it. The story, and all of the stories within it, are part of the primal matrix that cycles and recycles infinitely, as Old Grandma indicates when at the novel's end she says, "It seems like I already heard these stories before . . . only thing is, the names sound different" (260).

In the second framing poem of the novel, one seemingly entitled "Ceremony," Silko introduces a second voice that explains, "I will tell you something about stories, / . . . They aren't just entertainment. / Don't be fooled. / They are all we have, you see, / all we have to fight off / illness and death. "He," possibly an anonymous clan elder, defines the role and significance of the story we are about to read under the title of *Ceremony*—Tayo's story. Within her story of Tayo's journey toward wholeness and health, Silko— as did Momaday in *House Made of Dawn*—conducts a healing ceremony for all of us, for the world at large. The implications are serious, not to be taken lightly. Self-reflexively, the life-giving story is within the belly of the storyteller while the rituals and ceremony from which the "he" voice arises are found within the belly of the story. A blurring of gender definitions, "he" both gives birth to the story and is born from the story, while both are contained within Thought-Woman. "She," possibly a clan mother or Thought-Woman reentering the text, responds in the final lines of this poem set apart on the facing page: "The only cure / I know / is a good ceremony, / that's what she said." The male-female dialogue here emphasizes the inextricable interrelatedness of story, ceremony and cure while also pointing toward the male-female balance that is the desired state in Pueblo ritual.[9] The dissolution of generic distinctions effected by Silko's interweaving of poetry and prose throughout the novel further underscores the permeability of all boundaries, the interpenetrability of "conceptual horizons" within all discourse.

At this point in the novel, Silko has given the reader sufficient clues to the fact that the novel they are already embarked upon is not within the conventions of the European-American genre. The novel is a multivalent ceremony, and it is designed to "cure." As an elder from the Tewa pueblo of San Juan has explained, the purpose of ceremonies in Native American cultures "is not entertainment but attainment. . . . Our dramas, our songs, and our dances are not performed for fun as they might be in the white world; no, they are more than that; they are the very essence of our lives; they are sacred."[10] Within the total context of the ceremony entitled *Ceremony* are other ceremonies: the story/ceremony charting Tayo's movements within the boundaries of the Keres world, the precisely orchestrated movements, events, and recognitions that lead to Tayo's being healed; the older story/ceremony of which Betonie is aware and of which Tayo's is merely a part; the healing ceremonies performed for Tayo by Ku'oosh and Betonie; the overall "witchery" ceremony woven by Emo and the destructive forces that would prevent Tayo from arriving at understanding and harmony and prevent balance from being restored within the Pueblo universe; and the several destructive ceremonies conducted in places such as bars and pickup trucks. Haunting the total ceremony of the novel, like figures in a sandpainting, are the dimly perceived physical presences of holy persons dispersed throughout the text in the physical dimensions of the poems/stories that bridge the distance between oral and written narrative. In an intriguing reading of *Ceremony*, David Hailey has taken this idea a step further, arguing that the structural—textual—forms of the oral materials placed in the novel as poems/stories actually evoke the presence of spiritual helpers within the text. "Silko fills *Ceremony* with a new dimension of conceptual life," Hailey suggests. "She adds more stories, being lived under the stories that are lived on the surface."[11]

Ceremony is a novel of demanding complexity, a work that, like other works by Native American writers, challenges readers with a new epistemological orientation while altering previously established understandings of the relationship between reader and text.

Finally, *Ceremony* is a "cure" for all of us—inhabitants of a Western world that has, for more than a century, been increasingly acknowledging and even embracing its own fragmentation, deracination, and inauthenticity—dangerously out of harmony with the world we inhabit. Carol Mitchell has discussed this aspect of *Ceremony* perceptively, declaring that "Silko's novel is itself a curing ceremony." Kenneth Lincoln also makes this point, writing that the novel "tells Tayo's story as a curative act."[12] Rather than functioning from a merely rhetorical basis, to inform the reader, Silko creates an accretive and achronological experience for the reader, placing us in the center of the ceremonial cycles like the patient in a Navajo sand painting.

Effective understanding of Silko's novel requires at least minimal familiarity with the Pueblo world. The universe of the Pueblos is a carefully controlled and balanced one with its boundaries precisely established by reference to the landscape in the four cardinal directions—most often marked by sacred mountains or, at times, bodies of water. Within these recognized boundaries the world is ordered and defined in reference to the center, the earth navel or, as the Tewa call it, the "Earth mother earth navel middle place."[13] As the Pueblos conceive of their world, all orientation is centripetal, toward the sacred center, an imaginative construct evoked in the inward-spiraling form of a ceremonial sand painting. Furthermore, things beyond the boundaries of the fully imagined Pueblo world are dangerous and defiling. This conceptual orientation stands in rather interesting contrast to the centrifugal energies identified by Mikhail Bakhtin at the core of the modern, heteroglossic novel, a fact that further underscores the unique direction of Native American fiction.

According to Pueblo cosmology, everything in the universe—whether animate or inanimate—is significant and has its ordered place and is knowable and therefore controllable. Such knowledge and control, however, require extreme vigilance and attention to detail coupled with proper action, thus the Pueblos'—like most other tribal peoples'—insistence upon formula, ritual, and ceremony. Implicit within the Pueblo world view is the belief that men and women have immense responsibility for the world we inhabit, a lesson that Tayo, along with the reader, will fully learn in the course of Silko's novel. And, concomitantly, the individual has little significance alone; an individual such as Tayo has identity and a coherent self only insofar as he is an integral part of the larger community. Discussing this communal basis for identity among Native American cultures, the American Indian writer and editor Elizabeth Cook-Lynn suggests that a Sioux greeting often translated as "What is your name?" should more correctly be translated as "Who are you in relation to all of us?" "When we ask each other this question," Cook-Lynn explains, "it's historical."[14] This is precisely the question confronting Tayo: "Who are you in relation to all of us?" By the end of his story, Tayo's ceremony will have moved him in a centripetal spiral toward the heart of his community until he is finally in the very center, within the kiva itself.[15]

Like *House Made of Dawn*, Tayo's story begins and ends with sunrise, a cycle suggestive of completion and wholeness. When we first encounter Tayo in the novel's opening lines, however, he is having a nightmare in which he is tormented by a confusion of voices rolling him "over and over again like debris caught in a flood." Amidst the voices he hears a refrain from "a familiar love song": "*Y volveré*." Immediately Silko has introduced the motif of water—the symbol of fertility and life which Tayo will seek throughout the novel—but water uncontrolled and dangerous. At the same time, in the words of the Spanish love song, she introduces the theme of cyclical, accretive time and recurrence, the continuum which Tayo must discover and consciously enter in the course of the novel. This discovery will come to Tayo through love and will simultaneously reawaken him to the possibilities of love; in that sense, like the song the novel is a "love story" of transcendent scope.

In addition to opening with a traditional Pueblo sunrise prayer, *Ceremony* begins in spring, the time when purification and healing ceremonies are held in the pueblos.[16] And it is at once obvious that Tayo is in need of both. Mixed up with the words of the Spanish song in Tayo's dream are Japanese voices and the Laguna words of his mother and his Uncle Josiah calling to him. The carefully ordered and infinitely interrelated world of the Pueblos has become confused and tangled for Tayo: "He could get no rest as long as the memories were tangled with the present, tangled up like colored threads from old Grandma's wicker sewing basket. . . . He could feel it inside his skull—the tension of little threads being pulled and how it was with tangled things" (6).

Another of the numerous Indian veterans in Native American fiction, Tayo has returned from World War II suffering from post-traumatic shock, what at the time was termed "shell-shock." Like the traditional culture hero in Native American mythology, Tayo has left his home and suffered almost to the point of annihilation. The experience of war has left him in a veterans' hospital seemingly schizophrenic. Like Abel in *House Made of Dawn*, Tayo is inarticulate, unable to put the pieces of himself back together in meaningful sentences. "He can't talk to you," he tells an Anglo doctor. "He is invisible. His words are formed with an invisible tongue, they have no sound." Silko adds: "He reached into his mouth and felt his own tongue; it was dry and dead, the carcass of a tiny rodent" (15). Tayo's sense of self has collapsed into a kind of bifurcated inarticulateness that has been defined as an almost quintessentially postmodern condition: "If personal identity is forged through 'a certain temporal unification of the past and future with the present before me,' and if sentences move through the same trajectory, then an inability to unify past, present, and future in the sentence betokens a similar inability to 'unify the past, present and future of our own biographical experience or psychic life.'" The effect of such a collapse, or "breakdown in the signifying chain" is to reduce experience to "a series of pure and unrelated presences in time."[17] Such a temporal breakdown is almost precisely what Tayo is experiencing. Before Tayo can be articulated, he must become articulate— he must be able to tell his story and thereby put his life into a coherent order—and by implication Silko suggests the same for all American Indians who must discover, once again, how to tell their stories. Tayo must discover, through the aid of an array of helpers, the relatedness and contemporaneity of all "presences in time." The order Tayo must come to understand is not a syntagmatic "signifying chain of meaning" but a paradigmatic signification of ceremonial, nonlinear time, a "web" of meaning.

Compounding Tayo's predicament is the fact that his cousin, Rocky, has been killed in the war. Like the unnamed narrator in *Winter in the Blood*, Tayo also suffers from survivor's guilt. Perhaps most significant here, however, is the possibility that Tayo's belief that his invisible self's words are formed "with an invisible tongue" and are without sound suggests his unconscious sensitivity to the enormous pressures brought to bear upon Native American speech by the monologic forces of colonization. Systematic, institutionalized attempts to eradicate Native American languages have formed a common denominator in Indian relations with European invaders from the colonial beginning to the present. Silence without cunning, "dry and dead" tongues are an easily anticipated result. In her writing Silko is attempting to return to Tayo, and to all Native Americans, the power of speech.

When, during Tayo's experience of war, American soldiers are ordered to shoot Japanese prisoners, Tayo believes that one of the executed men is his uncle, Josiah. To calm Tayo, Rocky says, "Hey, I know you're homesick. But, Tayo, we're *supposed* to be here. This is what we're supposed to do" (8). Although Tayo's vision of Josiah is dismissed as "battle fatigue," as Tayo comes to understand the world according to Pueblo values, he will realize that in a crucial sense the executed man actually was Josiah, that all men and women are one and all phenomena inextricably interrelated. What is dismissed as a form of insanity is, Silko ultimately argues in the novel, the only sane view of the world. The alternative is universal death. And in Rocky's words Silko introduces the "witchery" story/ceremony that works toward the destruction of the world. Rocky has fallen victim to the "authoritative discourse" of Euramerica, which "strives to determine the very basis of our behavior." This is the language of the privileged center Rocky encounters in school and in texts, a language "indissolubly fused with its authority— with political power"; the language of that privileged discourse tells a story, too, a metanarrative of westering, manifest destiny, and individualism that separates humanity from the world we inhabit. Precisely who, we are led to ask in this scene, has *supposed* Rocky and Tayo to be there in the midst of such evil? Whose story is this? Ultimately, Tayo must comprehend the web of meaning in his world through what Bakhtin calls "internally persuasive" discourse, that which is "affirmed through assimilation, tightly interwoven with 'one's own word.'"[18] Through ceremony, Tayo is able to "live into" the complex coherence of Pueblo reality and escape the metanarrative of the western world with its story of separation and ultimate destruction. Were he simply "told" the truth by Betonie or anyone else—instead of living into that truth—he would once again be the object of externally imposed "authoritative discourse."

As Rocky lies dying in the jungle, Tayo curses the rain: "He damned the rain until the words were a chant. . . . He wanted the words to make a cloudless blue sky, pale with a summer sun pressing across wide and empty horizons" (12). Though he has been excluded from traditional teachings because of Auntie's manipulations, Tayo knows nonetheless the power of words and stories: "He made a story for all of them, a story to give them strength" (12). When he returns home to his desiccated reservation, he believes that his words have caused the drought; by damning the rain in a chant, ritualistically, he has dammed the waters of life. "So he had prayed the rain away," Silko writes, "and for the sixth year it was dry; the grass turned yellow and it did not grow. Wherever he looked, Tayo could see the consequences of his praying. . . . and he cried for all of them, and for what he had done" (14).

Immediately following Silko's account of the war and Tayo's chanted curse, the author introduces the poem/story recounting a disagreement between Reed Woman and Corn Woman. Resentful of Reed Woman's constant bathing, Corn Woman becomes angry and drives Reed Woman away with the result that "there was no more rain then." By introducing this Pueblo myth at this point in the novel, Silko implies that Tayo has committed the same error as Corn Woman: through partial vision he has failed to see the necessity for every thread in the web of the universe, even the maddening jungle rains. His vision is unbalanced and has immediate effect upon his environment. The traditional story also underscores human responsibility for every aspect of existence, that responsibility Josiah had earlier explained to Tayo: "These dry years you hear some people complaining. . . . But the wind and the dust, they are part of life too, like the sun and the sky. You don't swear at them. It's people, see. They're the ones. The old people used to say that droughts happen when people forget, when people misbehave" (46). That Tayo and the land will be healed, that the vital rain will return once again to inner and outer landscapes, is clearly indicated here in the opening pages of the novel—as in *House Made of Dawn* and in traditional stories, we know from the beginning how this story will turn out. That the drought has continued for six years means that the number seven—in Pueblo tradition a powerful number comprehending the four cardinal directions plus zenith and nadir—will soon be invoked. Like Abel's journey in *House Made of Dawn*, Tayo's movement from fragmentation and alienation to wholeness and integration will require seven years. Furthermore, as Tayo steps outside the shack at his family's sheep camp, we are told, "The air outside was still cool; it smelled like night dampness, faintly of rain" (9). And as he wanders about the camp, Tayo steps inside a barrel hoop buried in the reddish sand. With the circle of the hoop, Silko suggests the continuum, the cosmos, the Native American concept of time and space and wholeness, the form of the sand painting that will figure later in Betonie's ceremony for Tayo. Tayo's brief step into the hoop, like the faint smell of rain, prefigures his eventual cure. In an interesting parallel to this passage, Hamilton Tyler suggests that "the place of the Pueblo in his cosmos might be compared to that of a hoop-dancer in relation to his numerous hoops which he must keep circling around himself."[19] As with traditional storytelling, our foreknowledge of how the story will "turn out" should shift our attention and interest to the performance of the story: How is this mixedblood storyteller adapting the traditional materials to fit the present context? How are we being involved in the story? Our interest shifts from the "telling of a story" to the "story of a telling."

Tayo's movement toward full comprehension of his role and responsibility starts at once as he begins "to understand what Josiah had said. Nothing was all good or all bad either; it all depended" (11). His memories of childhood, memories he has attempted to repudiate, also serve to open him to the understanding that will prepare for healing:

> Distances and days existed in themselves then; they all had a story. They were not barriers. If a person wanted to get to the moon, there was a way; it all depended on whether you knew the directions— exactly which way to go and what to do to get there; it depended on whether you knew the story of how others before you had gone. He had believed in the stories for a long time, until the teachers at Indian School taught him not to believe in that kind of "nonsense." But they had been wrong. Josiah had been there, in the jungle; he had come. Tayo had watched him die, and he had done nothing to save him. (19)

But witchery—the evil that strives to separate and thereby destroy—surrounds Tayo here in the beginning, as is suggested in the wind that "was getting stronger; it made a whirling sound as it came around the southwest corner of the ranch house" (21). This whirling sound, and whirling in general, as the reader will soon realize, is associated with witchcraft.

All of the veterans have returned from the war damaged and displaced. Ku'oosh, the Pueblo medicine man summoned for Tayo by his grandmother, says, "I'm afraid of what will happen to all of us if you and the others don't get well" (38). Earlier, the medicine man has explained:

> "But you know, grandson, this world is fragile." The word he chose to express "fragile" was filled with the intricacies of a continuing process, and with a strength inherent in spider webs woven across paths through sand hills where early in the morning the sun becomes

entangled in each filament of web. It took a long time to explain the
fragility and intricacy because no word exists alone, and the reason
for choosing each word had to be explained with a story about why
it must be said this certain way. That was the responsibility that went
with being human, old Ku'oosh said, the story behind each word
must be told so there could be no mistake in the meaning of what had
been said; and this demanded great patience and love. (35–36)

Words grow out of stories and stories out of words; stories tell the
people who tell the stories who they are. Tayo cannot be healed
alone, for no one and nothing within the cosmos has its existence
and meaning alone. "You understand don't you?" Ku'oosh asks
Tayo. "It is important to all of us. Not only for your sake, but
for this fragile world" (36). Thus Tayo is made to understand his
responsibility to his community and to all of creation; in this sense,
he becomes the archetypal questing hero familiar to Native American and world mythologies.

An outsider, a halfblood who, like the Old Woman K'yo's son in
one of the traditional stories in the novel, "didn't know who his
father was" (46), Tayo has not been taught the necessary rituals:
"He wished . . . they had taught him more about the clouds and
the sky, about the way the priests called the storm clouds to bring
the rain" (49). However, unlike Welch's Jim Loney, Tayo has unconsciously absorbed much from those around him, especially Josiah
and Old Grandma, who offer him humor as well as philosophy,
and he is ready for the teachings of the helpers who will soon enter
his life. He even anticipates Betonie's message when he tells the
white doctor about his illness, "It's more than that [the effects of
war]. I can feel it. It's been going on for a long time. . . . I don't
know what it is, but I can feel it all around me" (53).

Within the bar, the veterans conduct their own ceremonies. Emo
rattles his bag of human teeth and damns mother earth, saying,
"us Indians deserve something better than this goddamn dried-up
country. . . . They've got *everything*. And we don't get shit, do we?"
(55). In the spirit of witchery, Emo seeks to divide not only Indians
from mother earth (in a recognizably European pattern of thought)
but Tayo from the community and from himself: "He thinks he's
something all right. Because he's part white. Don't you, half-
breed?" (57). Led by Emo, the veterans tell stories of war and sex,
"But in the end, they always came around to it" (61). "It" is the
killing experienced in war. Taking on the form of stories from the
oral tradition, the bar stories—at times even structured typographi-

cally by Silko to resemble the oral materials interspersed throughout the novel—serve to define the veterans and their world. "They repeated the stories about good times in Oakland and San Diego," Silko writes; "they repeated them like long medicine chants, the beer bottles pounding on the counter tops like drums" (43). With words the world is made and remade, and the veterans' stories, paralleled by the stories of witchery Silko interjects in the form of oral material, become dangerous and threatening. When Tayo attempts to kill Emo, he commits the same error committed by Abel in *House Made of Dawn*; he believes foolishly that he can destroy evil: "He felt that he would get well if he killed him" (63). He still must learn the lesson Josiah had tried to teach him—that good and evil must coexist in a delicate balance.

Tayo's mother, Laura, has been lost to the world of white men, alcohol, and promiscuity and, finally, to death. The disappearance and death of his mother is an enormous loss for the half-white Tayo, for in a matrilineal culture such as that of the Pueblo, clan identity and a secure knowledge of one's identity within the community is conveyed most firmly through the mother.[20] Without that essential connection, and rejected by his mother's sister, Tayo seems cut adrift at the borders of his culture. In her shame—both at her sister's corruption and at her own failure to bring Laura back into the community—Auntie has ostracized Tayo from family and community, commiting essentially the same sin as Emo, that of separating what should be inseparable. "You know what people will say," Auntie tells Grandmother. "They'll say, 'Don't do it. He's not a full blood anyway'" (33). Like Corn Woman and Reed Woman, Auntie and Laura have quarreled, and, like Reed Woman, Laura has gone away. In this division, Silko suggests, may be found yet another reason for the drought afflicting the reservation.

Although Silko includes a variety of traditional stories in various permutations in the course of the novel, the primary unifying myth is the story of the people's failure to pay proper respect to the Corn Mother altar and the resulting anger of "Our mother / Nau'ts'ity'i." Drought and sterility are the result, and the people must seek help from Hummingbird and Fly in order to propitiate the Corn Mother and restore the rain and fertility of the earth. Like these mythic persons, the Indians of Silko's novel have failed to maintain the proper respect and understanding in relation to mother earth. Perhaps because of pressures from the dominant Euramerican culture, they have forgotten the stories that serve to reinforce correct behavior and to remind them of who and where they are. While no one has strayed as far as Emo, Tayo and the others have been taught in white schools that Indian beliefs are "nonsense." The stories have been confused; the orderly strands of Spider Woman's web have become tangled in the people's minds. Ironically, it is Tayo, the halfblood, who not only assumes responsibility for his people's well-being but also remembers, more effectively than the fullblood veterans, the traditional stories and, therefore, correct behavior. When he goes into a bar and sees flypaper "speckled with dead flies," for example, he leaves and closes the door "quickly so that no flies got in" (101). He is protecting Fly, the people's helper, because he remembers a story Josiah had told him as a child.

The difficult undertaking of Hummingbird and Fly obviously parallels Tayo's quest. Just as Hummingbird and Fly are seeking to bring back the Corn Mother, who has abandoned the people, Tayo is unconsciously awaiting the return of his own mother and thus his identity. At one point in the novel Tayo remembers the experience of living in the filthy squatters' camp of cast-off Indians in Gallup. When the camp is burned and sprayed (to kill flies and other unsanitary creatures) by whites, the infant Tayo hides in the tamarisk bushes, curled into a fetal position and thinking, "He would wait for her, and she would come back to him" (113). Like all abandoned children, the adult Tayo is still waiting, feeling that he has somehow offended his mother, that he is at fault, an attitude mirrored in the people's belief that drought is the result of a trespass they have committed against the Corn Mother.

Just as Hummingbird and Fly are the people's helpers and intermediaries with the Holy Persons, Tayo's helpers are Night Swan and Ts'eh Montaño. Night Swan, a Mexican with the distinctive hazel eyes of the mixedblood, has come from the New Mexican town of Socorro ("comfort") and has mysteriously appeared in Cubero at the edge of the reservation, drawn, she explains, to the vicinity of the sacred mountain, Tse-pi'na, "the woman veiled in clouds." Tse-pi'na (Mount Taylor on modern maps) is blue in the distance, the color associated by Keres people with west, the direction of rain. In Laguna Pueblo mythology, colors are associated with the fourfold underworld from which the people emerged through an opening the Laguna refer to as *shipap* and which is conceived of as filled with water. The lowest level of these worlds is white, and the succeeding levels red, blue, and yellow. Similarly, the Keresan Pueblos associate the six sacred directions with distinct colors, with north represented by yellow, west by blue, south by red, and east by white. The zenith is associated with darkness or black, while the nadir is identified as "all colors." With the addition of the center, the six directions form seven sacred reference points, a powerful orientation in Pueblo and Navajo cosmology.[21]

While the color blue figures as a positive motif throughout the novel (Ku'oosh, for example, wears a blue wool cap, the "good" cowboy who will later sympathize with Tayo wears a blue bandana, and it is a "blue lace shawl" that attracts the hunters' attention to Betonie's grandmother), Night Swan is most explicitly linked with this color and with rain itself. Wearing a "blue silk dress," the Night Swan lives in a room with a bright blue door. Josiah, Night Swan's lover before Tayo, drives to see her in a blue GMC pickup. When Tayo goes to her, she is wearing a blue kimono which outlines "her hips and belly" and she seats Tayo in a "blue armchair with dark wooden feet carved like eagle claws" in a room with "blue flowers" painted on the walls and blue sheets upon the bed. Tayo thinks of her as being "like the rain and the wind," and when they make love he feels "her rhythm merging into the sound of the wind shaking the rafters and the sound of the rain in the tree" (99).

Prior to his meeting with Night Swan, Tayo had speculated about prayer:

> He knew the holy men had their ways during the dry spells. People said they climbed the trails to the mountaintops to look west and southwest and to call the clouds and thunder. They studied the night skies from the mountaintops and listened to the winds at dawn. When they came back down they would tell the people it was time to dance for rain. Josiah never told him much about praying, except that it should be something he felt inside himself. (93)

In the course of the novel, Tayo will perform all these acts and will become one of the holy men. Following this speculation, he recalls a visit he had made before the war to a spring. He remembers watching as a spider comes to the water to drink: "He remembered stories about her. She waited in certain locations for people to come to her for help. She alone had known how to outsmart the malicious mountain ka't'sina who imprisoned the rain clouds in the northwest room of his magical house" (94). And he sees the frogs which are "the rain's children." "Everywhere he looked," he realizes, "he saw a world made of stories, the long ago, time immemorial stories, as old Grandma called them. It was a world alive, always changing and moving; and if you knew where to look, you could see it, sometimes almost imperceptible, like the motion of the stars across the sky" (95). He remembers also dragonflies that were "all colors of blue—powdery sky blue, dark night blue, shimmering with almost black iridescent light, and mountain blue," and he remembers seeing "a bright green hummingbird" (95).

It is following this passage with its intense association of the color blue with rain, its invocation of Grandmother Spider and, thus, Thought-Woman; and its introduction of the helper, Humming-bird, that Tayo first meets Night Swan. Just before going to Cubero, where she lives in a room over the bar, Tayo hears thunder from the direction of Tse-pi'na and sees rain "spinning out of the thunderheads like gray spider webs and tangling against the foothills of the mountain" (96). When he enters her room, she is playing a record with the refrain "Y volveré." And in her role as helper, Night Swan teaches Tayo about himself and his part in the larger ceremony. "I have been watching you for a long time," she tells him. "I saw the color of your eyes" (99). What she has seen are the tell-tale hazel eyes of the mixedblood—a hybrid color that results from the melding of blue and yellow, colors associated with rain and pollen.

Like other mixedbloods in Native American fiction, Tayo feels displaced. "I always wished I had dark eyes like other people," he tells Night Swan. She replies: "Indians or Mexicans or whites—most peole are afraid of change. They think that if their children have the same color of skin, the same color of eyes, that nothing is changing. . . . They are fools. They blame us, the ones who look different. That way they don't have to think about what has happened inside themselves" (98–99). Finally, she says, "You don't have to understand what is happening. But remember this day. You will recognize it later. You are part of it now" (100). When Tayo leaves the Night Swan's room, he sees that "the sacred mountain was a dusty, dry blue color" (101).

Through Night Swan, Silko lays out her rationale for the power of the mixedblood to introduce a new vitality into the Indian world. And in Night Swan's words, Silko makes it clear that the evolution of Indian people and culture is a part of this cosmic ceremony designed to ensure both spiritual and physical survival. Her message responds to the facts of contemporary Indian life that James Welch underscored in a 1986 interview: "The people are going to be getting further and further away from their culture, so actually the reservation will be just a place to live. There will always be

Indians, but they won't be very traditional, I don't think, on these small reservations."[22] It is a thesis in direct opposition to the more common image of the suffering halfblood caught between cultures.

The spotted cattle serve to further Silko's theme of renewed vitality and viability through a dynamic syncretism. The spotted "desert" cattle, crossed first with a Hereford and later with the yellow bull Josiah has acquired from rodeo stock, are mixedbloods. At the time of purchase, the cattle are branded with a mark that "looked like a big butterfly with its wings outstretched, or two loops of rope tied together in the center" (81). This Mexican brand is the symbol for infinity, the continuum. Butterflies are also identified with the Pueblo personification of Summer, Miochin, as well as Yellow Woman, a fact that will serve to associate Tayo more closely with this mythological figure when, later in the novel, Tayo encounters Ts'eh Montaño and her husband, the hunter.[23] To this Mexican brand Josiah and Tayo add Auntie's brand, a rafter 4, the number of completion, balance and harmony.

Like Thought-Woman, Josiah has made a story about the cattle that seems to compel the special breed into existence. "I'm thinking about those cattle Tayo," he says. "See things work out funny sometimes" (74), and Silko adds, "They would breed these cattle, special cattle, not the weak, soft herefords that grew thin and died from eating thistle and burned-off cactus during the drought. The cattle Ulibarri sold them were exactly what they were thinking about" (74). These cattle, repeatedly associated with deer and antelope (and therefore with rain), are physical and spiritual hybrids and survivors. For Tayo, the cattle hold a special place, for it is obvious that Tayo has a unique relationship with and a reverence for the deer.[24]

When Ku'oosh's ceremony is insufficient, Tayo is taken to Betonie, a mixedblood Navajo medicine man. An unusual medicine man—a mixedblood like Tayo, with the familiar hazel eyes—Betonie lives alone in a hogan cluttered with the paraphernalia of both traditional Navajo healing and modern American culture. And just as the patterns of a sand painting conform to the shape of a hogan and are formed centripetally, Tayo notes that "the boxes and trunks, the bundles and stacks were plainly part of the pattern: they followed the concentric shadows of the room" (120). Illustrating the nonlinear conception of time central to Native American cosmology—that time suggested in the infinity brand on the spotted cattle—the layers of old calendars in Betonie's hogan have "the sequences of years confused and lost as if occasionally the oldest calendars had fallen or been taken out from under the others and then had been replaced on top of the most recent years" (120).

In a monologue asserting the central theme of Silko's novel—the essential need for change and adaptation and the place of both within the traditional Indian world—Betonie confirms the sense Tayo has had all along that he is involved in a story much larger than himself:

> "You've been doing something all along. All this time, and now you are at an important place in the story." He paused. "The Japanese." The medicine man went on, as though he were trying to remember something. "It isn't surprising you saw him [Josiah] with them. You saw who they were. Thirty thousand years ago they were not strangers. You saw what the evil had done: you saw the witchery ranging as wide as this world." (124)

Like the Night Swan, Betonie teaches Tayo about himself and change: "The people nowadays have an idea about the ceremonies. They think the ceremonies must be performed exactly as they have always been done. . . . But long ago when the people were given these ceremonies, the changing began. . . . Things which don't shift and grow are dead things" (126). Tayo says, "I wonder what good Indian ceremonies can do against the sickness which comes from their wars, their bombs, their lies," and Betonie replies, "That is the trickery of the witchcraft. . . . They want us to believe all evil resides with white people. Then we will look no further to see what is really happening. . . . And I tell you, we can deal with white people. . . . We can because we invented white people; it was Indian witchery that made white people in the first place" (132).

Betonie's words and the story of witchery underscore an element central to Native American oral tradition and world-view: responsibility. To shirk that responsibility and blame whites, or any external phenomenon, is to buy into the role of helpless victim. We make our worlds, Silko is suggesting, and we thus have enormous responsibility. With this story, set in the same form as that of the stories from oral tradition in the novel, Silko also demonstrates how the stories evolve to meet new conditions and needs.

Following this recounting of the witchery ceremony responsible for the creation of whites and the ultimate destructiveness represented by the atomic bomb, Tayo rides deeper into the mountains with old Betonie and the medicine man's helper, Shush. Silko inserts here a story about a man transformed into a coyote and the precise actions necessary to bring the man back into the world of the people. Again, Big Fly is the messenger of the people, and the ceremony reenacts the emergence from the four worlds. At the end of this story/poem, Tayo is described sitting "in the center of the white corn sand painting" (141). Quite obviously, like the man stolen by the coyote, Tayo must be carefully brought back into the world of his people. The spirit of bear, the great curer for Keres peoples and (as we have seen in Momaday's *The Ancient Child*, other Indian cultures as well), is summoned to aid in Tayo's restoration, and the ceremony ends with the words "The rainbows returned him to his / home, but it wasn't over. / All kinds of evil were still on him" (144). Betonie reinforces this message when he tells Tayo, "One night or nine nights won't do it any more . . . the ceremony isn't finished yet," and he makes the extraordinary nature of Tayo's undertaking clear when he says, "Remember these stars. . . . I've seen them and I've seen the spotted cattle; I've seen a mountain and I've seen a woman" (152). When the sand painting ceremony is completed, Tayo sleeps and dreams of the spotted cattle, and when he awakens he comes to a cosmic understanding:

> He stood on the edge of the rimrock and looked down below: the canyons and valleys were thick powdery black; their variations of height and depth were marked by a thinnner black color. He remembered the black of the sand paintings on the floor of the hogan; the hills and mountains were the mountains and hills they had painted in sand. He took a deep breath of cold mountain air: there were no boundaries; the world below and the sand paintings inside became the same that night. The mountains from all the directions had been gathered there that night. (145)

Tayo is now living the ceremony fully, and Silko returns to the story of Fly and Hummingbird briefly at this point to remind us that the pattern of Tayo's quest has long been established in the oral tradition of the Pueblo.

As he heads home, Tayo is picked up by his friends and fellow veterans, Harley and Leroy, in their newly acquired truck. Also along for the ride is a young Indian woman named Helen Jean. An example of what must have gone wrong with Tayo's mother, Helen Jean is a long way from her tribal home, displaced and confused, drinking with drunken Indians in a battered pickup. When Harley says about Tayo, "Hey Leroy, this guy says he's sick! We know how to cure him, don't we, Helen Jean?" (156), and then repeats, "We'll give you a cure!" (158), we are given a sense of the inversions that constitute witchery in the novel and of the competing "stories" that seek to remake the world along opposing lines.

To make Tayo's role as questing hero still more obvious as he prepares to go into the mountains seeking the cattle, Silko interjects the traditional Pueblo story of Sun Man's journey into the mountains to rescue the stormclouds from the Gambler. Like the other stories, this one is about the restoration of proper order and a coming home to harmony and balance: "Come on out," Sun Man says to the stormclouds. "Come home again. / Your mother, the earth is crying for you. / Come home, children, come home" (176).

At the foot of the sacred mountain (Tse-pi'na, the home of the Keres rain deity), Tayo meets his second helper, Ts'eh Montaño. Ts'eh's eyes are ocher, her skirt is yellow (the color associated with the north) and silver rainbirds decorate her moccasins. On her blanket in four colors are patterns of storm clouds and black lightning. The constellations Betonie has foreseen revolve in the sky above her cabin. Dominating the imagery surrounding her are the colors yellow and blue, the colors of north and west, pollen and rain. So closely is Ts'eh identified with water that even the lovemaking between her and Tayo is described in water imagery culminating in a "downpour." And when she folds up the storm blanket to stop the snow, it is very obvious that Ts'eh is a supernatural being, a holy person.

At this point in the novel, another fragment of the story of Hummingbird and Fly enters the text and it is obvious that, since they have now acquired the necessary tobacco as an offering, they are close to the successful completion of their quest. By implication it seems that Tayo, too, as he heads up Northtop, is close to completion of his own quest. Looking for the cattle, Tayo stops by a lightning-struck tree, a powerful and sacred place, and he gains a clearer understanding of cyclical time, a kind of eternal present in which mythic and mundane, sacred and profane, are woven together like the inseparable strands of Spider Woman's web: "The ck'o'yo Kaup'a'ta somewhere is stacking his gambling sticks and waiting for a visitor; Rocky and I are walking across the ridge in the moonlight; Josiah and Robert are waiting for us. This night is a single night; and there has never been any other" (192). And as Tayo is abruptly overcome with a sudden sense of despair, a mountain lion appears, "moving like mountain clouds with the wind, changing substance and color in rhythm with the contours of the mountain peaks" (195–196). Tayo offers a prayer and yellow pollen to mountain lion, the hunter, "the hunter's helper."

Fleeing from the white cowboys who have stolen Josiah's cattle, Tayo is thrown from his horse and stunned. As he lies upon the pebbles and cinders of the mountain, "The magnetism of the center spread over him smoothly like rainwater down his neck and shoulders. . . . It was pulling him back, close to the earth" (201). Tayo has already journeyed in the four directions, and here at last he has reached a center—one of the mountaintop "earth navels" which, according to Alfonso Ortiz, "gather in blessings from all around and direct them inward toward the village."[25] He is reconnected with mother earth. And at this moment the mountain lion reappears to lead the threatening cowboys away from Tayo and allow him to escape. Subsequently, snow begins to fall, "filling his tracks like pollen sprinkled in the mountain lion's footprints" (204).

As he descends the mountain, Tayo meets a hunter who carries a deer slung across his shoulders and wears a cap that "looked like mountain-lion skin." The hunter is Mountain Lion, who has come to Tayo's aid. He is also Winter, who lives on North Mountain in Keres tradition, and in this particular story Tayo is Summer. Tayo is reenacting a role in a story from Pueblo mythology in which Yellow Woman, Winter's wife, meets Summer one day and invites him to sleep with her while her husband is out hunting deer. When Winter returns home in a "blinding storm of snow and hail and sleet,"[26] he is angry, and the two spirits withdraw to prepare for battle, the result of which is an agreement that Yellow Woman will spend part of the year with Winter and part with Summer. A reader familiar with the traditional paradigms of the story will recognize what is happening to Tayo and will know, of course, the outcome of the story. If he renders his role accurately, "remembers the story," Tayo will succeed in restoring balance to his world.

A reader familiar with this "time immemorial" story will understand why in March of the spring following his recovery of the cattle Tayo dreams of Ts'eh and "he knew he would find her again," and why Tayo and Ts'eh know instinctively where to find each other at the beginning of summer. If the story is told correctly, with whatever variations the storyteller may effect, it will always end this way. With his love for Ts'eh comes wholeness and health for Tayo, who now realizes that "nothing was lost; all was retained between the sky and the earth and within himself. . . . Josiah and

Rocky were not far away. They were close; they had always been close" (219). Silko repeats the word "love" four times: "And he loved them then as he had always loved them. . . . They loved him that way; he could still feel the love they had for him" (219–220). Harmony is achieved in both the four-part repetition and the careful balance of complementary pairs essential to Pueblo thought: "he loved them," "he had always loved them"—"They loved him," "the love they had for him."

Beneath "blue-bellied clouds," Tayo walks through flowers that are "all colors of yellow" as he gathers yellow pollen and moves toward the yellow and orange sandrock cliffs in the north. He sees a "yellow spotted snake"—a messenger to the people—and he meets Ts'eh "walking through the sunflowers, holding the blue silk shawl around her shoulders." In the distance the spotted cattle graze near Romero's yellow bull. Tayo sees the cattle "listening like deer" to his approach, and as he watches the calves play, "he could see Josiah's vision emerging, he could see the story taking form in bone and muscle" (226). He is almost fully integrated into the world of his people; even his hair "had grown below his ears and touched his neck" (229).

But Tayo's ceremony is not completed yet. Ts'eh tells him, "They have their stories about us—Indian people who are only marking time and waiting for the end. And they would end this story right here, with you fighting to your death alone in these hills" (232). "They" are the ones who would insist upon the Indian as victim, those who insist upon the "vanishing American" image of the Indian as incapable of change and invariably defeated. This is the impulse that drove Archilde down a naturalistic path in McNickle's *The Surrounded* and that left Jim Loney only the option of choosing "a good day to die" in *The Death of Jim Loney.* And like Archilde and Loney, Tayo is as yet not certain of who he is, a fact underscored when Ts'eh tells him that the elders in the pueblo "are trying to decide who you are" (233).

As the novel draws toward its end, it is clear that the drought is over, an end that was foreseen in the novel's beginning. The quest has succeeded and "the land was green again" (234); in an archetypal pattern Tayo, the questing hero, has "freed the waters." Tayo's story is not yet finished, however, for he must still learn the final lesson taught by Emo's evil witchery ceremony. Underscoring a supreme irony of the modern world, Silko brings Tayo to a realization of the place of the Pueblos within the destructive "story" of nuclear holocaust:

> He had been so close to it, caught up in it for so long that its simplicity struck him deep inside his chest: Trinity Site, where they exploded the first atomic bomb, was only three hundred miles to the southeast, at White Sands. And the top-secret laboratories where the bomb had been created were deep in the Jemez Mountains, on land the Government took from Cochiti Pueblo: Los Alamos, only a hundred miles northeast of him now, still surrounded by high electric fences and the ponderosa pine and tawny sandrock of the Jemez mountain canyon where the shrine of the twin mountain lions had always been. There was no end to it; it knew no boundaries; and he had arrived at the point of convergence where the fate of all living things, and even the earth, had been laid. (245–246)[27]

In the mouth of a uranium mine Tayo sees, finally, the overall pattern as he kneels and looks closely at a piece of ore: "The gray stone was streaked with powdery yellow uranium, bright and alive as pollen; veins of sooty black formed lines with the yellow, making mountain ranges and rivers across the stone" (246). Within the stone, inextricably intertwined, are the colors of good and evil. The uranium itself, essential to the most destructive idea man has yet conceived, is the color of life, "bright and alive as pollen." The uranium comes from mother earth and cannot, therefore, be evil. The evil results in separating the rock from the earth and in separating elements within the ore: "But they had taken these beautiful rocks from deep within earth and they had laid them in a monstrous design" (246). Separating and dividing are the tools of witchery. Auntie has sought to separate Tayo from the tribal community; Emo has not only sought to intensify Tayo's separation from the community but has also attempted to divide Tayo against himself by insisting upon Tayo's liminal mixedblood status. Ceremonies seek to heal by compelling wholeness within the individual and between the individual and his world, including the earth itself. Capable of seeing the truth at last, Tayo cries "at the relief he felt at finally seeing the pattern, the way all the stories fit together . . . to become the story that was still being told. He was not crazy; he had never been crazy. He had only seen and heard the world as it always was: no boundaries, only transitions through all distances and time" (246).

Just before the scene in which Emo brutally sacrifices Harley as

Tayo watches, Silko reintroduces the story/poem about witchery. This time, however, Arrowboy watches as the witches attempt to complete their ceremony and by watching he prevents the completion. "Something is wrong," the witchman exclaims. "Ck'o'yo magic won't work / if someone is watching us" (247). The clear message is that it is our responsibility to be conscious, to watch and thus control evil the way Francisco is acutely aware of the albino's evil presence in *House Made of Dawn*. Evil cannot be destroyed, and to attempt to do so is to commit a dangerous error that would upset the delicate balance of the world. Tayo's temptation to destroy Emo—a temptation to which he succumbed early in the novel— would have merely fueled the witchery: "Their deadly ritual for the autumn solstice would have been completed by him. He would have been another victim, a drunk Indian war veteran settling an old feud" (253).[28]

As he stumbles back toward the pueblo after Harley's murder, Tayo dreams a waking dream of remembrance and reintegration: "He dreamed with his eyes open that he was wrapped in a blanket in the back of Josiah's wagon. . . . Josiah was driving the wagon, old Grandma was holding him, and Rocky whispered 'my brother.' They were taking him home" (254). Like the narrator in *Winter in the Blood*, Tayo has finally come to terms with his brother's (or, in this case, cousin's) death and feels himself forgiven. At the same time, he realizes the meaning of his love for Ts'eh Montaño: "He thought of her then; she had always loved him, she had never left him; she had always been there. He crossed the river at sunrise" (255). The abandoned child on a circular journey in search of the mother, in search of the coherent center and sense of self located within community, Tayo has found what he sought. Laura, too, had crossed the river at sunrise, and now Tayo, like Hummingbird and Fly, has brought "our mother" home, a journey that will be repeated by Lipsha Morrissey at the end of Louise Erdrich's *Love Medicine*. In Laguna tradition the dead have a significant role as rain-bringers. As Tayo comes to understand his place in the ecosystemically determined "story" of Indian—and mixedblood—identity, his mother is reclaimed into a place within his personal story and the interdependent story of their tribal culture. Once Tayo is able to comprehend that "she" had never left him, had always loved him—once he overcomes his feeling of abandonment by his mother, by his family and culture, by the land itself, his dead mother returns in the rain that revitalizes the barren landscape, both internal and external.

And now Silko completes the story of Hummingbird and Fly's endeavor to have the town purified and thus bring the Corn Mother (and fertility) home again. "Stay out of trouble / from now on," she tells the people. "It isn't very easy / to fix up things again." Auntie, who has finally accepted Tayo into the community, comically repeats this refain at the novel's end: "I tell them, 'It isn't easy. It never has been easy,' I say" (259).

As a final act, the returning culture hero must deliver his new knowledge to the people, and Tayo does this when he is invited into the kiva by the elders. The spiritual center of the pueblo, the kiva indicates that Tayo has indeed come home; no longer alienated, or shizophrenic, he can tell his story and thus articulate his fragmented self. And when he speaks, the elders understand at once. "You have seen her" they cry, "We will be blessed / again." As the voice at the beginning of the novel warned us we must, the elders have remembered the story.

Like virtually every novel written by an American Indian, *Ceremony* describes a circular journey toward home and identity. For some protagonists too much has been lost for the journey to be completed; for those who succeed, the key is remembrance.

Erdrich and Dorris's Mixedbloods and Multiple Narratives

◆

Louise Erdrich

Despite the importance of N. Scott Momaday's Pulitzer Prize for *House Made of Dawn* in 1969, no American Indian author has achieved such immediate and enormous success as Louise Erdrich with her first novel, *Love Medicine*. A best-seller, *Love Medicine* not only outsold any previous novel by an Indian author, but it also gathered an impressive array of critical awards including the National Book Critics Circle Award for Fiction in 1984, the American Academy and Institute of Arts and Letters award for Best First Novel, the Virginia McCormack Scully Prize for Best Book of 1984 dealing with Indians or Chicanos, the American Book Award from the Before Columbus Foundation, and the *L.A. Times* award for best novel of the year.

Why such astounding success for an author writing about a subject—Indians—in which Americans had previously shown only a passing interest (and that predominantly in the romantic vein mined by non-Indian authors)? The answer to such a question delves into the heart of Louise Erdrich's achievement with *Love Medicine* as well as her very popular second and third novels, *The Beet Queen* (1986) and *Tracks* (1988). And to examine Erdrich's fiction closely is also to explore that of her husband/agent/collaborator, Michael Dorris, whose first novel, *A Yellow Raft in Blue Water* (1987), has also been received with enthusiasm by readers and critics.[1]

Like almost every other Indian novelist, Louise Erdrich is a mixedblood. A member of the Turtle Mountain Chippewa band, Erdrich is of German, French, and Chippewa descent. She was born in Minnesota and grew up in Wahpeton, North Dakota, where her parents taught in the Wahpeton Indian School. In her novels, Erdrich draws upon both her mother's Chippewa heritage and her experiences as the daughter of a Euramerican growing up in middle America. Both the wild reservation bushland and the weathered edge of the North Dakota prairie permeate her novels, stamping their character upon Indian and non-Indian alike. "When you're in the plains and you're in this enomous space," Erdrich has stated, "there's something about the frailty of life and relationships that always haunts me."[2]

In her published novels—the first three of a planned quartet—Erdrich weaves genealogies and fates as characters appear and reappear in successive, interconnected stories. This web of identities and relationships arises from the land itself, that element that has always been at the core of Native Americans' knowledge of who they are and where they come from. Central to Native American storytelling, as Momaday has shown so splendidly, is the construction of a reality that begins, always, with the land. In Erdrich's fiction, those characters who have lost a close relationship with the earth—and specifically with that particular geography that informs a tribal identity—are the ones who are lost. They are the Ishmaels of the Indian world, waiting like June Kashpaw to be brought home. Imagining her role as a storyteller, Erdrich has explained: "In a tribal view of the world, where one place has been inhabited for generations, the landscape becomes enlivened by a sense of group and family history. Unlike most contemporary writers, a traditional storyteller fixes listeners in an unchanging landscape combined of myth and reality. People and place are inseparable." In laying out her fictional terrain, a coherently populated geography often compared to that of William Faulkner, Erdrich tells stories of survival, as she has also explained: "Contemporary Native American writers have therefore a task quite different from that of other writers. . . . In the light of enormous loss, they must tell the stories of contemporary survivors while protecting and celebrating the cores of cultures left in the wake of the catastrophe (cultural annihilation). And in this, there always remains the land."[3] Perhaps it is, in part, Erdrich's positive emphasis upon survival that has endeared her to the reading public. Though the frailty of lives and relationships and the sense of loss for Indian people rides always close to the surface of her stories, Erdrich's emphasis in all three novels is upon those who survive in a difficult world.

Like every other Native American novelist, Erdrich writes of the inevitible search for identity. "There's a quest for one's own background in a lot of this work," she has explained. "One of the characteristics of being a mixed-blood is searching. You look back and say, 'Who am I from?' You must question. You must make certain choices. You're able to. And it's a blessing and it's a curse. All of our searches involve trying to discover where we are from." She has commented upon her own identity as a writer conscious of both her Indian heritage and her somewhat insecure place in the American mainstream: "When you live in the mainstream and you know that you're not quite, not really there, you listen for a voice to direct you. I think, besides that, you also are a member of another nation. It gives you a strange feeling this dual citizenship. . . . It's kind of incomprehensible that there's the ability to take in non-Indian culture and be comfortable in both worlds."[4]

The seemingly doomed Indian or tortured mixedblood caught between worlds surfaces in Erdrich's fiction, but such characters tend to disappear behind those other, foregrounded characters who hang on in spite of it all, who confront with humor the pain and confusion of identity and, like a storyteller, weave a fabric of meaning and significance out of the remnants.

Love Medicine is an episodic story of three inextricably tangled generations of Chippewa and mixedblood families: the Kashpaws, Morriseys, Lamartines, and Lazarres. In fourteen chapters, seven narrators weave their many stories into a single story that becomes, very gradually, a coherent fabric of community—a recovered center. Along the way, Erdrich's masterful use of discontinuous and multiple narrative underscores, formally, the displacement and deracination that dominate her narrators' tales while at the same time forcing upon the reader his or her own sense of radical displacement and marginality. Ultimately, however, the fragmented narratives and prismatic perspectives of the novel emphasize not the individual anguish of an Abel, Jim Loney, Cecelia Capture, Chal Windzer, Archilde Leon, or most other protagonists of Native American novels, but the greater anguish of lost communal/tribal identity and the heroic efforts of a fragmented community to hold on to what is left.

Love Medicine begins with an illumination of liminality—a confla-

tion of Christian religion and Native American mythology, of linear/
incremental time and cyclic/accretive time—on the "morning before
Easter Sunday." Like the traditional trickster narrative, the story
opens with the protagonist, June Kashpaw, on the move: "June
Kaspaw was walking down the clogged main street of oil boomtown
Williston, North Dakota, killing time before the noon bus arrived
that would take her home."[5] Soon, the character around whom this
novel will cohere is dead, and it is ironic that June is attempting to
"kill" time—to break the entropic grip of linear, Western time—
while it is precisely this time that is killing June, the historical time
that has eroded a Chippewa sense of identity just as it has overseen
the loss of the Chippewa's traditional homeland. Rather than return
from her desperate life to the reservation, June walks deliberately
into a blizzard and accepts her death. Like Tayo's mother and Helen
Jean in Silko's *Ceremony*, June is one of those women who have
washed up in the no-woman's-land of prostitution on the parasitic
edge of the reservation, displaced and alone. When she decides to
go with one of the roustabouts from a bar rather than return home,
she thinks, "The bus ticket would stay good, maybe forever. They
weren't expecting her up home on the reservation" (3). With a bus
ticket that will never expire, and no expectations, June assumes the
role—like trickster—of a permanent traveler, infinitely dislocated
with no family/community/tribe to expect her return. Her fragmentation is emphasized when Erdrich writes: "And then she knew
that if she lay there any longer she would crack wide open, not in
one place but in many pieces" (5). As with virtually every other
aspect of June, this fear of cracking into "many pieces" represents
a kind of dialogic, a hybridized utterance that can be read in two
ways. In a Euramerican context it underscores June's alienation,
approaching schizophrenia, her loss of a centered identity. Fragmentation in Native American mythology is not necessarily a bad
thing, however. For the traditional culture hero, the necessary
annihilation of the self that prefigures healing and wholeness and
a return to the tribal community often takes the form of physical
fragmentation, bodily, as well as psychic deconstruction.

With no family to draw her home, June deliberately chooses
death, for as Albertine Johnson tells us in the novel's second chapter, "June grew up on the plains. Even drunk she'd have known a
storm was coming" (9). Raised by her Great-uncle Eli, the one
character in the novel who never loses touch with either earth or
identity, June knows where, if not who, she is: "Even when it

started to snow she did not lose her sense of direction" (6). And Erdrich ends the first chapter with the words, "The snow fell deeper that Easter than it had in forty years, but June walked over it like water and came home" (6). She comes home to an "unchanging landscape . . . of myth and reality," the feminine Christ-figure resurrected as trickster, the fragmented culture hero made whole within memory and story, returning through the annual cycle of Easter/spring—death/resurrection—to her Indian community as mythic catalyst.

Erdrich begins *Love Medicine* with a subtle displacement of time and an invocation of peripatetic trickster, "going along." Just as the traditional trickster's role is not only to upset and challenge us but also to remind us—obversely—of who we are and where we belong, June will figure throughout the novel as a touchstone for the other characters. Just as the tribal community in *Ceremony* desperately wants Tayo's lost mother to come home, the response of characters throughout *Love Medicine* to June's loss will underscore each character's sense of identity within the tribal community and, concomitantly, each character's potential for survival. And just as trickster transcends both time and space as well as all other definitions, June does indeed "kill time" as she moves freely, after death, in the thoughts and stories of the other characters. Jay Cox has noted June's resemblance to trickster, suggesting perceptively that June is the "chaotic everything" to all the characters in *Love Medicine* and that "June's death in the first chapter does little to impede her spirit from going along throughout the novel."[6] When, at the end of the novel, Lipsha Morrissey crosses the water to "bring her home," we know that Lipsha has finally arrived at a coherent sense of his place within the community (including the land itself) from which identity springs. And at the novel's end another trickster will be on the move as Gerry Nanapush heads across the "medicine line" into the depths of Canada, telling Lipsha, "I won't ever really have what you'd call a home" (268). Lipsha, son of the two powerful characters with whom the novel opens and closes—June Kashpaw and Gerry Nanapush—ends the novel on a note of profound resolution of identity.

By the time June walks away from the car toward her death, it is very likely after midnight and therefore officially Easter Sunday, the day the "snow fell deeper . . . than it had in forty years." By invoking Easter, Erdrich brings into the novel the myth of the crucifixion and resurrection, an analogy ironically underscored when she writes that June's ejection (with her pants pulled halfway up) from the warm car into the cold "was a shock like being born" (5). By associating June with both Christ and trickster, Erdrich underscores the twin elements that will make whole the fragmented lives of the novel: the commitment beyond the self that lies both at the heart of the Christian myth and, very crucially, at the center of the American Indian tribal community where individualism and egotism are shunned and "we" takes precedence over the "I" celebrated in the Euramerican tradition, and, just as important, a refusal to acquiesce to static definitions of identity. When she writes that "June walked over it like water and came home," Erdrich merges an image of Christ with the primary element that will figure prominently throughout the book: water. Erdrich has said, "In *Love Medicine* the main image is the recurrent image of the water—transformation (walking over snow or water) and a sort of transcendence. . . . The river is always this boundary. There's a water monster who's mentioned in *Love Medicine*. It's not a real plot device in *Love Medicine*. It become more so in *Tracks*. . . . We really think of each book [of the planned quartet] as being tied to one of the four elements." In the same interview, Erdrich and Dorris point out that the central elemental image in *The Beet Queen* is air, while in *Tracks* it is earth.[7] As in *House Made of Dawn*, this beginning is also the novel's ending, a circularity familiar to Native American storytelling, and it underscores the important place of water imagery in Chippewa storytelling, an importance understandable for a people whose traditional homeland was once the region of the Great Lakes.

Our first encounter with a family in the novel comes through Albertine in the second chapter.[8] After describing her relationship with her mother as "patient abuse," Albertine arrives home simply to be ignored at first by both mother and aunt. Albertine is one-half Swedish, the daughter of a white father who abandoned his wife and child at Albertine's birth, an Anglo outcast "doomed to wander" (the quintessential Euramerican condition of eternal migration). Albertine's mother is Zelda, one of the daughters of Nector Kashpaw and Marie Lazarre. Marie, a mixedblood who insists, "I don't have that much Indian blood," is from a family considered white trash by their Indian neighbors. Albertine, who thinks of herself as "light, clearly a breed," is approximately one-quarter Chippewa, but she identifies as Indian, complaining bitterly about allotment and following Henry Lamartine down the street just because he looks Indian.

Though Albertine has run away in the past and has apparently flirted with the kind of disastrous life that killed June, she is the character in the novel who, among those of her generation, is most secure in her identity, a certainty provided, ironically, by her mother, who says defiantly, "I raised her an Indian, and that's what she is" (23). Zelda, married for the second time to a Scandinavian husband and living in a trailer on the edge of the reservation, is the one who has the strength and certainty to retrieve her father, Nector, from the clutches of Lulu Lamartine and the one capable of providing her daughter with a sense of self lacking in many of the novel's characters. Albertine's strength comes from this unshakable knowledge of who she is and from her awareness that the past is a formative part of the present. Albertine emphasizes the power of the past—through stories—to inform the present when she says of June: "She told me things you'd only tell another woman, full grown, and I had adored her wildly for these adult confidences. . . . I had adored her into telling me everything she needed to tell, and it was true, I hadn't understood the words at the time. But she hadn't counted on my memory. Those words stayed with me" (15–16). The past permeates the present, coexisting through cyclical temporality within the spatial reality of the Native American world, staying with us, telling us in a single breath where we have been, where we are, and where we are going. As nearly every Native American author has sought to demonstrate, the loss of the past means a loss of self, a loss of order and meaning in the present moment, and an inability to contemplate a future that is part of that moment. Storytelling serves to prevent that loss; it bears, as Michel Foucault has said, "the duty of providing immortality."[9]

It is Albertine who understands the motivation of her great-grandmother, old Rushes Bear, in keeping Eli at home while allowing Nector to be educated at the government school. "In that way," Albertine explains, "she gained a son on either side of the line" (17). And it is Albertine who points out that Eli, who "knew the woods," had stayed mentally sharp while Nector's "mind had left us, gone wary and wild" (17). When Albertine, always seeking stories of the past, asks Nector to "tell me about things that happened before my time," the old man just shakes his head, "remembering dates with no events to go with them, names without faces, things that happened out of place and time" (18). Schooled by the government to be a bureaucrat, Nector has been molded into chairman of his tribe by his ambitious wife, Marie, but he has retained only the meaningless ciphers of dates and names that have neither bearing nor mooring in Albertine's world. He has become a victim of mechanical, entropic, historic time, while his brother has remained alert to the reality of his more traditional life on the other side of the time-line. Finally, it is Albertine who puts June's (as usual, contradictory) accomplishment into perspective for us when she intones: "Her defeat. Her reckless victory. Her sons" (35). June's sons are King and Lipsha, one recognized and damned, the other abandoned and saved.

Lipsha is June's reckless victory, just as her legitimate son, King, epitomizes her defeat and the defeat of all the failed characters in the novel. Throughout most of the novel Lipsha does not know who his parents are; he lacks an identity and even believes of his mother that she "would have drowned me" (37). When Albertine comes close to telling him the secret of his mother, Lipsha refuses to hear, saying, "Albertine, you don't know what you're talking about." He goes on to declare, "As for my mother . . . even if she came back right now, this minute, and got down on her knees and said, 'Son, I am sorry for what I done to you,' I would not relent on her" (36). Ultimately, Lipsha will relent on her; like Tayo in *Ceremony*, he will forgive his mother for abandoning him; and by bringing her home, he will come home to a knowledge of who he is. When Albertine asks, "What about your father? . . . Do you wish you knew him?" Lipsha replies, "I wouldn't mind" (37). At the end of the novel Lipsha will meet his father, Gerry Nanapush, and he will realize that his own healing "touch" has descended most powerfully from Old Man Pillager, the shaman who is the trickster's father and who will figure prominently in *Tracks*.

Gerry Nanapush, described by Lipsha as a "famous politicking hero, dangerous armed criminal, judo expert, escape artist, charismatic member of the American Indian Movement, and smoker of many pipes of kinnikinnick in the most radical groups" (248), is the most unmistakable trickster of the novel, bearing the traditional name of the Chippewa trickster, *nanapush* or *nanabozhu*. Impossible to contain, a shapeshifter capable of impossible physical feats, when he arrives at King's apartment to confront the stoolie who has informed on him, Nanapush speaks the classic trickster line: "'I want to play,' said Gerry very clearly and slowly, as if to a person who spoke a different language. 'I came to play'" (262). Gerry Nanapush is "mainly in the penitentiary for breaking out of it," ("breaking out" is, of course, trickster's *modus vivendi*) and, according to Lulu, "In and out of prison, yet inspiring Indian people, that was his life. Like myself he could not hold his wildness in" (227). Nanapush is a culture hero and shaman/trickster. At the same time, Nanapush, who, according to Albertine "shot and killed . . . a state trooper" on the Pine Ridge Reservation (170), bears a strong resemblance to American Indian activist Leonard Peltier, imprisoned for the alleged murder of two FBI agents at Pine Ridge. In an interview, Erdrich described her response when she attended Peltier's trial: "When the jury came back with that guilty verdict, I stood up and screamed. It was a real dislocation growing up thinking there was justice, and then seeing this process and knowing they were wrong in delivering that verdict."[10]

Like so many other characters in fiction by Indian writers, Lipsha's quest is for a sense of self and authenticity. Lulu Lamartine, his grandmother (whom Lipsha describes as "the jabwa witch") and a female trickster, finally forces him to listen to the story of his parentage. About his mother, June, Lulu says, "She watched you from a distance, and hoped you would forgive her some day" (244). About his father, Lulu says, "There ain't a prison that can hold the son of Old Man Pillager, a Nanapush man. You should be proud that you're one" (244). Finally, Lulu sees directly to the heart of Lipsha's strangeness, saying, "Well I never thought you was odd. . . . Just troubled. You never knew who you were. That's one reason why I told you. I thought it was a knowledge that could make or break you" (244–45). Upon learning of his heritage, Lipsha muses: "I could not help but dwell upon the subject of myself. . . . Lipsha Morrissey who was now on the verge of knowing who he was" (244). Seeking his father, Lipsha declares, "I had to get down to the bottom of my heritage" (248), and once he sits down to play cards with his father, Lipsha says, "I dealt myself a perfect family. A royal flush" (264). Lipsha has learned to mark the cards from his grandmother, Lulu Lamartine, and Gerry recognizes the feel of trickery on the deck: "Those crimps were like a signature—his mother's" (260). And, as the patterns of his heritage and identity become clear, Lipsha deals, saying, "I dealt the patterns out with perfect ease, keeping strict to Lulu's form" (263).

Finally, when he learns that Lipsha is on the run from the military police, Gerry works his magic, beginning with an affirmation of his son's identity: "'You're a Nanapush man,' he said. . . . 'We all have this odd thing with our hearts.'" Nanapush reaches out a hand and touches his son's shoulder, and Lipsha says, "There was a moment when the car and road stood still, and then I felt it. I felt my own heart give this little burping skip" (271). With a "heart problem," Lipsha will fail his physical and be exempted from the military, and to his father's relief he will not have to become a fugitive. The "odd thing" about Nanapush hearts is, of course, their ability to care deeply for others, individuals and Indians as a whole. This is the "love medicine" of the novel, as Lipsha comes to realize after Nector's blackly comic death when Lipsha tells Marie, "Love medicine ain't what brings him back to you, Grandma. . . . He loved you over time and distance, but he went off so quick he never got the chance to tell you how he loves you. . . . It's true feeling, not magic" (214).

In the figure of Nector, tribal chairman and patriarch of the Kashpaws, who are "respected as the last hereditary leaders" of the tribe (89), Erdrich introduces the clichéd view of the "vanishing American." Nector has been in a Hollywood movie. "Because of my height," he says ironically, "I got hired on for the biggest Indian part" (89). The biggest Indian part, however, isn't much: "'Clutch your chest. Fall off that horse,' they directed. That was it. Death was the extent of Indian acting in the movie theater" (90). Nector escapes from cinema death to the wheat fields of Kansas, where he is paid to pose for a painter. "Disrobe," the artist says, and Nector, stalling for time, replies, "What robe?" The painting that results is entitled *Plunge of the Brave* and shows a naked Nector leaping to his death in a raging river. Nector, who possesses perhaps the most subtly ironic sense of humor in the novel, concludes: "Remember Custer's saying? The only good Indian is a dead Indian? Well from my dealings with whites I would add to that quote: 'The only interesting Indian is dead, or dying by falling backwards off a horse'" (91). Nector says finally, "When I saw that the greater world was only interested in my doom, I went home on the back of a boxcar. . . . I remembered that picture, and I knew that Nector Kashpaw would fool the pitiful rich woman that painted him and survive the raging water. I'd hold my breath when I hit and let the current pull me toward the surface, around jagged rocks. I wouldn't fight it, and in that way I'd get to shore" (91). Nector recognizes the epic and tragic role white America has reserved for the Indian, a role in which, as Bakhtin pointed out, the hero must perish. For Indians who go to the movies or read novels, it would indeed appear that the greater world is interested only in their doom, and Nector articulates the direction of Indian characters in nearly all novels by Indian authors when he says, "I went home." Going home to reservation, family, tribe, or simply an Indian identity is the way Native Americans create "another destiny or another plot."[11]

Nector also articulates here the strategy he will follow throughout the course of his life: he goes consistently with the current, never fighting very strongly if at all. Thus he ends up married to Marie Lazarre because she simply takes him, forcing him to abandon at least temporarily his true love, Lulu Lamartine. Thus he allows Marie to manipulate him into the tribal chairmanship and a somewhat stable and respectable life. And thus he is swept late in the novel into Lulu's passionate current for a brief time before being towed to anchorage at home by his determined daughter, Zelda. "Call me Ishmael," Nector says, taking the line from *Moby-Dick*, the only book he has read. "For he survived the great white monster," Nector explains, "like I got out of the rich lady's picture. He let the water bounce his coffin to the top. In my life so far I'd gone easy and come out on top, like him. But the river wasn't done with me yet" (91–92).

What Nector fails to understand about Ishmael is that Melville's narrator survives for two primary reasons. The first is that he alone is able to see both good and evil—he is the "balanced man" aboard the cursed Calvinist ship named for the Pequots, a tribe slaughtered by the colonists in the name of a monomaniacal Calvinist vision. And the coffin that bounces Ishmael to the surface of the sea belongs to Queequeg, the Indian to whom Ishmael is bound by a shared bed and pipe. Ishmael floats atop the symbol of Queequeg's doom as Melville's novel ends. If Nector is Ishmael the survivor, it is at the expense of his Indian self. And it is clear in the novel that Nector, though he is an effective bureaucratic leader for the tribe, has lost a great deal. When he signs the letter evicting Lulu from her home, he assumes no responsibility for the act, saying, "As tribal chairman, I was presented with a typed letter I should sign that would formally give notice that Lulu was kicked off the land" (104). Lulu is being evicted so that a factory making "plastic war clubs" and other false Indian "dreamstuff" (in Lulu's words) can be built. Lulu's perspective is the Indian one: "If we're going to measure land, let's measure it right. Every foot and inch you're standing on, even if it's on the top of the highest skyscraper, belongs to the Indians. That's the real truth of the matter" (221).

When he comes to the agonizing decision to leave Marie for Lulu,

Nector says, "It seems as though, all my life up to now, I have not had to make a decision. I just did what came along . . . But now it is one or the other, and my mind can't stretch far enough to understand this" (106). In coming to a decision, Nector has attempted to confront the monsters in his life for the first time when he takes off his clothes and dives into the lake: "I swam until I felt a clean tug in my soul. . . . I gave her [Lulu] up and dived down to the bottom of the lake where it was cold, dark, still, like the pit bottom of a grave. Perhaps I should have stayed there and never fought. . . . But I didn't. The water bounced me up" (103). In diving deep into the lake, Nector has dared the water monster, Missepeshu, who, according to Lipsha, "lives over in Lake Turcot" (194). And as a Chippewa he has asumed even greater risk, for as Lulu explains, "drowning was the worst death for a Chippewa to experience. By all accounts, the drowned weren't allowed into the next life but forced to wander forever, broken shoed, cold, sore, and ragged. There was no place for the drowned in heaven or anywhere on earth" (234).

In spite of his official position with the tribe, and despite the fact that he is, as Lipsha points out, a kind of Indian monument unto himself, Nector is, like the Ishmael with whom he identifies, one of the novel's cultural outcasts. Nector wanders mentally between Indian and white worlds, eventually retreating to a second childhood where responsibility will never be forced upon him. In contrast, Eli, who has lived closer to the traditional Chippewa ways, knows precisely who and where he is to the end. In Eli the past is alive, and King's white wife, Lynette, perceives this when she shrieks, "Tell 'em Uncle Eli. . . . They've got to learn their own heritage! When you go it will all be gone!" (30). It is Eli who shows Nector's progeny "how to carve, how to listen for the proper bird-call, how to whistle on their own fingers like a flute," and it is Eli who remembers how to hunt in the old ways.

In *Love Medicine*, the searing pain of Indian lives found in such novels as *House Made of Dawn*, *Ceremony*, *Winter in the Blood*, *The Death of Jim Loney*, *Sundown*, *The Surrounded*, *The Jailing of Cecelia Capture*, and others is not as immediately evident. Lives and loves fail in *Love Medicine*, but not with the whetted edge found in fiction by most other Indian authors. Deracination is the crucible in which identities are both dissolved and formed, but the suffering is kept at a distance through the constantly shifting narrative and surface complexity of the text. Caught up in the tangled lives of mixedbloods who have the foolishness, cruelty, and courage to love whom they will and abandon what they must, the reader experiences the human comedy of these generations. But the non-Indian reader is not made to feel acutely, as he or she is in other Indian novels, a sense of responsibility for the conditions portrayed. Unlike many other works by Native Americans, Erdrich's first novel does not make the white reader squirm with guilt, and this fact may well have contributed significantly to the book's popularity with mainstream American readers. However, to say that Erdrich does not foreground the oppression and genocide that characterize white relations with Indians over the centuries is not to say that *Love Medicine* ignores that aspect of Indian consciousness. Formally, the novel's fragmented narrative underscores the fragmentation of the Indian community and of the identity which begins with community and place; and the fragmentation of this community, the rootlessness that results in an accumulation of often mundane tragedies among the assorted characters, subtly underscores the enormity of what has been lost.

In addition to this subtle fabric of alienation, deracination, and despair that forms the backdrop for the often darkly comic drama in this novel, Erdrich provides brief glimpses of more pointed Indian resentment. Even Lipsha, troubled by a tangled identity but also perhaps the most compassionate character in the novel, can be very bitter, musing upon "the old time Indians who was swept away in the outright germ warfare and dirty-dog killing of the white," and admitting, "Oh yes, I'm bitter as an old cutworm just thinking of how they done to us and doing still" (195). Albertine, heading home, declares, "The policy of allotment was a joke. As I was driving toward the land, looking around, I saw as usual how much of the reservation was sold to whites and lost forever" (11). The Catholic Church itself comes in for a severe scourging in the form of Sister Leopolda, the mad nun who tortures Marie Lazarre and struggles with Satan. Leopolda, as we discover in *Tracks*, is the mother who abandoned and never acknowledged Marie, the Indian who denied her Indianness, the demented murderer of her daughter's father, and the Christian who never relinquished her belief in Missepeshu, the lake monster of Matchimanito. Though Father Damien in *Tracks* will redeem the church considerably, in Leopolda we are confronted with evidence as damning as that McNickle presents in *The Surrounded*. About this thread in *Tracks*, the "prequel" to *Love Medicine*, Erdrich has said, "There are two major

Catholic figures in *Tracks*, Pauline [Leopolda] and Father Damien. Pauline took over the book. She's every aspect of Catholicism taken to extremes. . . . There's no question that the church on reservations has become more tolerant, and that there have been many committed priests who fought for Indian rights. But the church has an outrageous view on women—damaging and deadly."[12]

Erdrich does not ignore the racism and brutality of Euramerica's dealings with Indian people, but for the first time in a novel by a Native American author, she makes the universality of Indian lives and tragedies easily accessible to non-Indian readers. Kashpaws and Morrisseys and Lazarres and Lamartines are people readers can identify with much more easily and closely than they can with an Archilde, Able, or Tayo. These tangled lives are not so radically different from the common catastrophes of mainstream Americans, certainly no more so than those dreamed up by a Faulkner or Fitzgerald. And yet no reader can come away from *Love Medicine* without recognizing the essential Indianness of Erdrich's cast and concerns.

Erdrich's second novel, *The Beet Queen* (1986), is a tighter and more polished work than *Love Medicine*, with a smooth style that led Leslie Silko to write: "Erdrich's prose is dazzling and sleek. Each sentence has been carefully wrought, pared lean and then polished."[13] In this novel, six narrators share the episodic narrative with a third-person narrator in a chronological sequence shifting over time from 1932 to 1972. The story is one of men and women without reservations, hung out to dry on the flat, dull edge of the Minnesota–North Dakota heartland in a small town that could be anywhere or nowhere. The story is told in a triangulation that zeros in on Argus, a town that seems almost an empty place on the map. Just as water was the primary natural element in *Love Medicine*, in *The Beet Queen* the unifying element is air.

At first or perhaps even second glance, "Indian" seems to mean very little in this novel. In the same review in which she praised the style of *The Beet Queen*, Silko criticized the novel for this very point, writing: "What Erdrich, who is half-Indian and grew up in North Dakota, attempts to pass off as North Dakota may be the only North Dakota she knows. But hers is an oddly rarified place in which the individual's own psyche, not racism or poverty, accounts for all conflict and tension. In this pristine world all misery, suffering and loss are self-generated, just as conservative Republicans have been telling us for years." Silko concludes that *"The Beet Queen* is a strange artifact, an eloquent example of the political climate in America in 1986."[14]

Oddly, in attacking the book for its refusal to foreground the undeniably bitter racism toward Indians in America's heartland, Silko seems to be demanding that writers who identify as Indian, or mixedblood, must write rhetorically and polemically, a posture that leaves little room for the kind of heterogeneous literature that would reflect the rich diversity of Indian experiences, lives and cultures—and a posture Silko certainly does not assume in her own fiction.[15]

Identity is confused in *The Beet Queen*. Celestine James, one of the novel's tellers and central characters, is half Chippewa, while her half-brother, Russell, is apparently a fullblood. Mary Adare, another narrator and the most central of the characters, is non-Indian, as are Sita Kozka, Wallace Pfef, and Karl Adare. The final narrator in the novel, Celestine's daughter, Dot, is one-quarter Chippewa and will grow up, as we have already seen, to marry Gerry Nanapush in *Love Medicine*.[16] Indian identity is not, however, at the heart of this novel, and cultural conflict here is never explicit; there is no overt racism, no jagged sense of lost Indian culture or identity. Everyone in *The Beet Queen* is in the same boat—Indian or white, hetero- or homosexual—and the boat is an emotional dinghy set adrift on the very mundane sea of mid-America, where the frailty of lives and relationships has never been more pronounced.

Just beyond Argus is the Chippewa reservation, from which Celestine's family has come and back to which her brother Russell flees from a trivial town and the government that has bought bits of bone and flesh from him with an array of medals. As his body disintegrates from a multitude of war wounds, Russell withdraws into a silence that comes, like the unobtrusive reservation, to stand for a kind of hauntingly mute Indian presence. Russell's inarticulateness underscores his physical dearticulation by American culture. Adding to this shadowy backdrop are other Indian characters such as Fleur Pillager and Russell's half-brother, Eli Kashpaw, who appear briefly in the novel and then withdraw as if in preparation for their more significant appearances in Erdrich's next novel, *Tracks*.

Unlike *Love Medicine*, *The Beet Queen* provides only faint glimpses of points of contact between Indian and white cultures in this country, a kind of no-man's land where margins on the map have blurred and it is every man and woman for him- and herself, where emotional toughness ensures psychic survival and losses are continually cut. The vulnerable ones in the novel—Russell Kashpaw in his mute willingness to be used up in white men's wars; Sita in her self-consuming desires to be elsewhere, anywhere; Wallace Pfef in his poignantly sublimated homosexuality; Karl Adare in his even more poignant and dangerous isolation and abandonment—are broken and pushed rather gently aside in the novel.

The Beet Queen begins with a prologue entitled "The Branch," a brief sketch that introduces Mary and Karl Adare, the brother and sister who have been abandoned by their mother and set adrift toward Argus. At fourteen, Karl is delicate and "sweet," while his eleven-year-old sister, Mary, is weighted with the adjectives "short," "ordinary," "square," and "practical." Karl's last word in the prologue is "Run!" as he and Mary flee in opposite directions, one toward a new family and the other toward permanent impermanence.

Throughout the remainder of the novel Mary will be consistently described as heavy, immovable, while Karl will be almost weightless. Mary will carve a place for herself within an adopted family through sheer force of will, while Karl will simply drift with no firm sense at all of his own identity. Karl will, in fact, inform the novel with a kind of trickster presence: an eternal wanderer, a lover of both men and women, a sexual shapeshifter alternately identified with both Christ and Satan. Karl embodies opposites, contradictions, and possibilities, and he fathers Dot, the center around which identity coheres in this marginalized community (the "Dot"-matrix of the text). In an interesting discussion of narrativity and liminality in this novel, Catherine Rainwater fails to recognize Karl's role as *The Beet Queen's* trickster, insisting instead upon Karl's resemblance to the Fool from the Tarot deck. While trickster and Fool are, of course, closely related and in no way mutually exclusive tropes, trickster is a much more positive and creative force in Native American cultures. To miss this fact is to undervalue Karl's paradoxically positive role in the novel.[17]

In contrast to Karl, Mary's weighted world is emphasized in the first chapter of the novel when she describes the birth of their mother's new baby. When something heavy hits the floor in the room above them, both children throw out their arms and Mary says, "I don't know what went through Karl's mind, but I thought it was the baby, born heavy as lead, dropping straight through the clouds and my mother's body."[18] It is Mary who describes the mother's desertion during the "Orphans' Picnic," an abandonment of maternal responsibility that occurs without "a backward look, without a word, with no warning and no hesitation" (12). And Mary describes Karl's reaction: "'Take me!' he screamed. . . . He stared at the sky, poised as if he'd throw himself into it" (12). From that moment on, Karl (later described by Mary as "flighty") will seek to join his mother in flight, while Mary dreams of her mother falling with a deadly weight: "All night she fell through the awful cold. Her coat flapped open and her black dress wrapped tightly around her legs. . . . My heart froze. I had no love for her. That is why, by morning, I allowed her to hit the earth" (16). Karl and Mary's younger brother, also abandoned by the fleeing mother, is stolen and raised by a couple who name him Jude after "the patron saint of lost causes, lost hopes, and last-ditch resorts" (45), a very appropriate naming for a character in a geography that seems even more god-forsaken than the terrain of *Love Medicine*.

Amidst this tangle of tentative relationships, Mary creates a home out of singular determination. "I planned to be essential to them all," Mary confesses early in the novel, "so depended upon that they could never send me off" (19). Later, she will declare, "The shop was my perfect home," and we realize that it is perfect because it is heavy, immoveable, built on one level with floors "of cast concrete," thick walls, and rounded doorways that made the house seem "like a cave carved out of a hillside." Even the light from outside "fell green and watery through thick glass window-blocks" (67). The butchershop-home is Mary's den, her inextricable link with the one element that will never abandon her: the earth.

In sharp contrast to his earthy sister, Karl is insecure in every way, so protean that after making love with Celestine he at once brings out his case of knives and begins to give his roadman's pitch, moving immediately into the identity of the moment. Even earlier, at the time of his first encounter with Wallace Pfef, Karl is traveling as a salesman for something called the "Air Seeder," a magical device that "assisted by a puff of the motorized bellows" gently blows seeds into the earth. The Air Seeder "does not disturb the soil . . . reducing your surface loss" (101). When Wallace asks him where he's from, Karl replies, "Here . . . different places." While this reply underscores his tricksterish transience, on a mundane, human level it is precisely Karl's desire to reduce his "surface loss" that prevents him from forming any attachments. When pushed,

Karl finally identifies "a Catholic home for bastards" as his place to be from, thereby clearly defining his rootlessness. Even Karl's temporary lover, Wallace Pfef, has a surname that mimics the sound of expelled air, suggesting weightlessness.

When, at one point, Pfef says abruptly, "Why don't you let me try to find your sister?" Karl is frightened. Mary represents the only thing Karl might still have to lose, and he had tried to cut his losses in that category when he ran away from Argus and jumped back aboard the boxcar in the novel's prologue. When Pfef interjects this possibility, Karls says, "I suddenly had the feeling that had always frightened me, the blackness, the ground I'd stood on giving way, the falling no place" (106). In response Karl says, "I had to stop myself from falling, so I jumped. I felt silly and light, bouncing in the air" (106). And as he lies on the floor after breaking his neck in the fall, Karl says his sister's name "out loud" to Pfef, adding, "And then the injection took hold, the black warmth. I realized the place I'd landed on was only a flimsy ledge, and there was nothing else to stop me if I fell" (107). The "injection" is Mary's name, the "black warmth" that tenuous hold on identity that she represents for her lost brother. Melodramatically perhaps, Erdrich is underscoring here the flimsy hold Karl has on his identity. With a dead father who never acknowledged him, a mother who vanished as a dot in the sky, an outcast and wanderer, Karl has no community that might confer authenticity upon him. Mary is all there is, and because of his own abandonment of her twenty years before, Karl recognizes the flimsyness of that support. It is therefore appropriate that when he finally appears in Argus to seek his sister, he finds Celestine instead, and rather than being reconciled with his sister, he becomes her friend's temporary lover. A kind of Anglo-American trickster always "going along," Karl enters the community of Argus sporadically and briefly, staying long enough to sadden Wallace Pfef, help drive Sita Kozka closer to insanity, and help produce Dot, Celestine's daughter, who will be the fraudulent Beet Queen and go on to bear Gerry Nanapush's child in *Love Medicine*. And it is in the creation of the determinedly alive and willful Dot that Karl most clearly mimics the trickster, who, though rootless and often destructive, including self-destructive, is also a creator.

All relationships are terribly frail in this novel. Erdrich's characters here seem to inhabit a kind of terminal liminality. Characters drift by one another like detached particles. Parent-child relationships are almost nonexistent. Mary and Karl are virtual orphans;

Celestine and Russell's parents are dead; and Sita has so little in common with her parents that they much prefer the intrusive Mary. There are no storytellers here to provide the significance and structure that is created in the living juncture of past and present. Karl drifts in his lightweight world, sending nonsense gifts to his daughter from nameless places, resisting definition, and confessing, "I give nothing, take nothing, mean nothing, hold nothing" (318). Wallace languishes alone in a house far outside of town, waiting for brief connections that come to him from the cold. Sita mourns lost beauty alone in an apartment in Fargo before marrying twice and escaping into the isolation of insanity. Russell moves aimlessly between reservation and town before being isolated with Eli in his paralysis. Celestine, ostracized by the town for her unusual marriage, lives in an uneasy truce with Mary. Mary has a solid home only because she has made herself so dense that no one can budge her, yet it is Mary who says, "We are very much like the dead" (263), and it is Mary who reads the Book of the Unfamiliar and dreams wonderfully of "insects made of blue electricity, in a colony so fragile it would scatter at the slightest touch" (204). Finally, Mary displaces Sita, who must drift off to Fargo and back before sheltering in madness. Eventually, dead and disguised and merely an encumbrance, Sita is trucked to the Beet Queen parade in Mary Adare's meat delivery van. Mocking her characters' inability to fuse past and present into a conceivable future, Erdrich writes, "Sita looked forward, sternly, into the distance."

Russell might be thought to have embraced a warrior's role in allowing himself to be whittled away in recurrent wars, but he is strangely dispassionate and disinterested in his own life. Russell's ultimate lack of control over his life is underscored in the parade when, a paralyzed participant, he is propped on the American Legion float. He glimpses his dead sister Pauline inviting him to follow her into the other world, "wearing a traditional butterfly-sleeved calico dress and quilled moccasins" (299). Russell realizes that his Indian sister is walking "the road that the old-time Chippewas talked about, the four-day road, the road of death" (300). But even this vision from a traditional Indian world capable of providing order and identity is denied Russell as a woman—in the authoritative language of the culture that has marginalized and deconstructed him—cries suddenly from the curb, "He looks stuffed," and Russell begins to laugh at his own epic reflection: "It struck him as so funny that the town he'd lived in all his life and the members of the American Legion were solemnly saluting a dead Indian, that he started to shake with laughter" (299–300). Russell falls off the traditional road and finds himself back in the mocking parade, isolated within his detached self.

Only Dot is capable of bringing about some kind of tenuous, fragile community within this world of otherwise lost souls. With a single, unforgettably beautiful image, Erdrich illuminates this essential quality in the mixedblood child of Celestine and Karl:

> One night Dot slept past her feeding time and Celestine woke in the half-light of dawn with full breasts. The baby clung like a sloth, heavy with sleep, and latched on in hunger, without waking. She drew milk down silently in one long inhalation. It was then that Celestine noticed, in the fine moonlit floss of her baby's hair, a tiny white spider making its nest. It was a delicate thing, close to transparent, with long sheer legs. It moved so quickly that it seemed to vibrate, throwing out invisible strings and catching them, weaving its own tensile strand. Celestine watched as it began to happen. A web was forming, a complicated house, that Celestine could not bring herself to destroy. (176)

As the image of the delicate, almost invisible web suggests, it is around the child that a community will form in this novel. With a fleeting suggestion of Spiderwoman's web of creation and connection—that web spun throughout *Ceremony* and again in Paula Gunn Allen's *The Woman Who Owned the Shadows*—Erdrich defines the delicate structure of relationshps that make up the story of this tenuous community. Erdrich has called this scene "the real heart of the book," adding, "Everything bounced off that little section. Somehow that's the emblem of the book."[19] Mary testifies to this growing structure when she says, "I'd taken to defending my brother, not that he would have cared or ever returned the compliment, but out of the sheer bond of blood. Maybe I was grateful that, however accidentally, he'd given me my one tie of kinship, to Dot" (194).

Finally, it is Dot, fated to become the angry Beet Queen, who brings about a strange convergence of community in the novel when all of the strands of the web are joined as she is ready to receive her crown. From Karl's characteristic "*I'm on my way*" to the dead Sita and paralyzed Russell, each of those caught up in Dot's web come together at the crowning. When Dot soars skyward in Tom B. Peske's plane and returns to earth again, she completes the novel's circular journey, repeating Adelaide's flight but returning to where she began and belongs. In the plane, Dot seeds the clouds with her identity: "My whole long awful name. Ten letters" (336). And, in contrast to all of the orphans in the novel, Dot is brought home by her awareness of a mother's love. After thinking everyone has gone away while she flew, Dot says, "It is a lonely thought, and not entirely true. For as I am standing there I look closer into the grandstand and see that there is someone waiting. It is my mother, and all at once I cannot stop seeing her. . . . In her eyes I see the force of her love" (337).

As the novel ends, Dot is lying in her room listening to the rain she has brought to the parched earth. "I breathe it in," she says, "and I think of her lying in the next room, her covers thrown back too, eyes wide open, waiting" (338). Just as it does in *Ceremony*, *Fools Crow*, and innumerable other stories, the rain symbolizes fertility and renewal. Celestine's "waiting" ends the novel on the note of hope and reconciliation. The fragile web of family and, therefore, identity is intact.[20]

Tracks (1988), the third installment in Erdrich's quartet, follows the pattern set by James Welch in moving backward in time to a more "Indian" world. In *Tracks*, Erdrich takes the reader back to the generation prior to *Love Medicine*, to the first decades of the twentieth century and that crucial moment in history when the Chippewa began to see with a grim finality the last portion of their traditional lives slipping rapidly away. Nanapush, one of two narrators in the novel, can remember the way it was, including his own complicity, declaring, "I guided the last buffalo hunt. I trapped the last beaver with a pelt of more than two years' growth. I spoke aloud the words of the government treaty, and refused to sign the settlement papers that would take away our woods and lake. I axed the last birch that was older than I."[21]

Nanapush, like his namesake Gerry Nanapush, is trickster, his name drawn from the Anishinabe trickster, *nanapush* or *nanibozhu*. "Nanapush. That's what you'll be called," his father has told him. "Because it's got to do with trickery and living in the bush. . . . The first Nanapush stole fire. You will steal hearts" (33). Responsible through his storytelling for remembering the way it was, and thus for preserving Indian identity, Nanapush clowns his way with wry and ribald humor through the tragic times for his tribe. "We started dying before the snow," he begins his story, "and like the snow, we continued to fall. It was surprising there were so many of us left to die" (1).

Although *Tracks*, rather like Welch's *Fools Crow*, goes back in time to fill in the blanks for the author's two previous novels, Erdrich has confessed in an interview that this wasn't originally the plan, explaining:

> There was no chronological plan to the books. They started with an idea. *Tracks* had been written years and years before. It was the first fiction I'd ever worked on. I tried for years to publish it. There were some good pieces in it but it didn't fit together as a whole. I knew it was a book that would require more in terms of craft. After I finished *The Beet Queen* I was feeling low, not knowing where to go next, and Michael [Dorris] suggested that I go back to the *Tracks* manuscript.[22]

Interestingly, this novel conceived first is the most thoroughly "Indian," in a traditional sense, of Erdrich's three fictions. Spanning twelve years, the novel is divided into nine chapters according to seasonal cycles, with Chippewa names for the each cycle. After being ravaged by war and smallpox earlier, the Chippewa are now dying wholesale from consumption. Not only are families and clans being erased by disease and starvation, but the reservation land itself is vanishing as the corrupt allotment policy transfers more and more Indian land to white ownership. Traditionals such as Nanapush and Marie Kashpaw (Rushes Bear) oppose the land sales and the logging that is devastating the reservation (cf. *Bearheart*), and the tribe is split by the greed engendered by federal policy. The world Erdrich conjures up is not only a very real world of oppression and corrupt federal policy, but also an Indian world of mythic realism resembling that of *Fools Crow*. In *Tracks*—primarily through Nanapush's vision—the natural and the supernatural interpenetrate with fluid ease. In this world, like that of Gabriel Garcia Marquez's Macondo, ghosts walk and gamble with the living, surprised at their own predicaments, while Missepeshu, the monster of Matchimanito, makes frequent appearances with his appetite for young girls. All the while, "medicine" brews both love and death for those too close to the powerful Pillagers. Within the confines of this Chippewa world, Indians conspire against one another and against the government, and bureaucrats conspire endlessly to steal Indian lands.

That structure of fragile relationships outlined in *Love Medicine* and illuminated in the web imagery of *The Beet Queen* becomes much clearer in *Tracks*. Beginning the novel with the word "We" ("We started dying . . ."), Nanapush directs his stories to Lulu, the child of Fleur Pillager and the trickster-matriarch of *Love Medicine*. Nanapush's goal is to explain to Lulu who she is, and the word *we* underscores Nanapush's profound sense of connectedness and tribal community. Above all, Nanapush wants Lulu to forgive her mother, Fleur Pillager, for having given Lulu up to the government schools and to Nanapush himself. In the old trickster's desire that Lulu forgive, Erdrich maintains the thread running through the two earlier novels—Lipsha's forgiveness of June, the mother who abandoned him, and both Karl and Mary Adare's refusal or inability to forgive Adelaide, the mother who left them to make their own worlds. In *The Beet Queen*, Dot's reconciliation with her mother, and her identity, provides for a positive sense of closure, but such closure won't come so neatly in *Tracks*, which ends with Nanapush's voice still pleading with Lulu.

Nanapush himself is isolated, the last of his family to survive the latest disease. His trickster antagonist, ally, and lover in the novel is old Marie, who is the Rushes Bear of *Love Medicine* and mother of Eli and Nector Kashpaw in both novels. It is Nanapush, we discover, who has taught Eli the traditional ways celebrated in *Love Medicine*. Lulu's mother, Fleur Pillager, is the sole survivor of her family of traditional Chippewas, feared for their knowledge of "medicine." The only other Pillager to survive is a distant relative named Moses, who makes and sells medicines and who is the powerful and feared "Old Man Pillager" and the father of Gerry Nanapush in *Love Medicine*. In this book, Erdrich gives us the resources to trace the tangled strands of connected lives in the previous novels, *Love Medicine* in particular. We learn that the ragged peddler with healing powers who rescues Karl Adare and mends his shattered ankles in *The Beet Queen* is Fleur, the beautiful wild witch of Matchimanito in *Tracks* and the grandmother of Gerry Nanapush and the rest of Lulu's boys in *Love Medicine*. Dutch James, the father of Mary's one friend, Celestine, in *The Beet Queen*, is also one of the violaters of Fleur and just possibly the father of Lulu. If this is the case, then Celestine and Lulu are, oddly, half-sisters who will never know that fact. It is also possible, of course, that Eli Kashpaw, the old man who sits in Marie's kitchen in *Love Medicine* and who watches in *The Beet Queen* as Russell is hoisted and carried away to the parade, is Lulu's father in *Tracks*. It is even possible, say Fleur's neighbors, that Lulu is the daughter of Missepeshu himself.

We learn even more amazingly here that Sister Leopolda of *Love Medicine* is Pauline, one of the two narrators of *Tracks*, and that Pauline/Leopolda's illegitimate daughter, whom Pauline refers to as "that bastard," is Marie Lazarre of *Love Medicine*. Just as Pauline has had a divine revelation that tells her she has no Indian blood, Marie Lazarre says, "I don't have that much Indian blood." It is the unrecognized daughter of Pauline and Napoleon Lazarre who snares Nector Kashpaw in *Love Medicine* in a heavily ironic reversal of Nanapush and Nector's snaring of Clarence Lazarre in *Tracks*. In *Tracks*, Nanapush says, "Power travels in the bloodlines, handed out before birth" (31). Power has come down to Gerry Nanapush in *Love Medicine* from Fleur rather than Nanapush, who, we discover, is Lulu's father only through his own claim. Gerry is thus even more than a "Nanapush man"; he is a Pillager on both sides of his bloodline and passes this power on to Lipsha.

Nanapush sums up Erdrich's undertaking in these novels when he says, "Only looking back there is a pattern. . . . There is a story to it the way there is a story to all, never visible while it is happening. Only after, when an old man sits dreaming and talking in his chair, the design springs clear" (34). The design that springs clear in *Tracks* is the pattern that has been laid for the confused lives and tangled identities of *Love Medicine* and, to a lesser degree, *The Beet Queen*. The knowledge of the inextricable interrelatedness of all things, and the need to articulate the patterns of things through stories—both qualities integral to Indian cultures and central to Indian literature—are further emphasized when Nanapush says, "I shouldn't have been caused to live so long, shown so much of death, had to squeeze so many stories in the corners of my brain. They're all attached, and once I start there is no end to telling because they're hooked from one side to the other, mouth to tail" (46).

Tracks is about the catastrophic losses that have left the characters of these earlier novels wandering in Erdrich's vaguely defined terrain. And it is about that web of fragile relationships that define family, tribe, and community. The disintegration that isolates the often desperate individuals of *Love Medicine* begins in the world Nanapush describes as, in this most overtly political of Erdrich's works, we witness the corrupt machinations of the federal and tribal bureaucrats to gain control over the allotted reservation and sell it for personal gain. On one level the division between those who would sell off tribal lands for profit and those who would keep it at all cost splits the tribe, as Nanapush says, "down the middle, through time" (109). On a deeper level, the people are self-destructing before the campaign of cultural genocide staged by the government. Just as Archilde in *The Surrounded* and Cogewea in Mourning Dove's novel found apt symbols in the vanishing buffalo, Pauline recalls Nanapush's story of the last buffalo: "He said that when the smoke [from hunters' rifles] cleared and hulks lay scattered everywhere, a day's worth of shooting for only the tongues and hides, the beasts that survived grew strange and unusual. They lost their minds. . . . They tried their best to cripple one another, to fall or die. They tried suicide. They tried to do away with their young. They knew they were going, saw their end" (140). Pauline further epitomizes the extremity of lost identity for Indian people when she describes her revelation: "He said that I was not whom I had supposed. I was an orphan . . . and . . . I was not one speck of Indian but wholly white" (137). Pauline's dissolution into madness parallels her surrender of identity as she exclaims, "Only I must give myself away. . . . I must dissolve. I did so eagerly. I had nothing to leave behind" (141).

Almost alone, Nanapush tells stories to prevent such dissolution and loss for his people, to convince them—as he is trying to convince Lulu with this narrative—of what they indeed have to leave behind. It is Nanapush's stories that save Lulu when, a child, she stumbles in from the snow. "Once I had you," he says, "I did not dare break the string between us and kept on moving my lips, holding you motionless with talking, just as at this moment" (167). Nanapush tries to keep the string unbroken for all Indians, even enemies such as the Morrisseys, of whom he says, "And yet we old-time Indians were like this, long-thinking but in the last, forgiving, as we must live close together, as one people, share what we have in common, take what we're owed" (180). Even Nanapush's hilarious taunting of Pauline throughout the novel, laden with sexual comedy, may even be seen as typical of trickster's attempts to destroy hypocrisy and delusion and bring about self-knowledge. Just as traditional tricksters taunt and trick toward health, Nanapush is not willing to give up on even one soul as deracinated as Pauline's, a fact underscored when it is Nanapush who has the skill and courage to reach Pauline in the middle of tossing

Matchimanito Lake. Pauline unknowingly illuminates Nanapush's role as creator-storyteller when she calls him the "smooth-tongued artificer" (196).

Pauline, who has drawn the name Leopolda from Superior's hand, almost has the last word in *Tracks*. Just as Nanapush strives through stories and trickery to hold the people together, Pauline imagines stories that separate them. "I see farther," she says, "anticipate more than I've heard. The land will be sold and divided. . . . The trembling old fools with their conjuring tricks will die off and the young, like Lulu and Nector, return from government schools blinded and deafened" (204–205). Pauline's story—like the stories of Emo in *Ceremony*—allows for the ultimate extermination of Indian culture by the authoritative machinery of colonial Euramerica.

It is Nanapush, however, to whom Erdrich gives the first and last words of the novel. Though he discovers that Marie and Nector have betrayed both him and Fleur, he forgives Marie and goes to live with her. Though Pauline imagines that the "old fools with their conjuring tricks will die off," we know already that Nanapush will endure through succeeding generations to Gerry, a hero to Indian people, and to Lipsha, a compassionate healer who bridges the water to a secure self-knowledge. "I have seen each of you since then," Nanapush tells Lulu, "in your separate lives, never together, never the way it should be. If you wanted to make an old man's days happy, Lulu, you would convince your mother and your father to visit me. I'd bring old times back, force them to reckon, make them look into one another's eyes again" (210).

Nanapush becomes tribal chairman, accepting his role as leader despite his sardonic declaration that the people have become "a tribe of file cabinets and triplicates, a tribe of single-space documents, directives, policy" (225). And he forges once again his link to Fleur and "the funnel of our history" by producing church records to prove that he is Lulu's father. Finally, Nanapush begins the last sentence of the novel just as he began the first sentence, with the word *We*: "We gave against your rush like creaking oaks, held on, braced ourselves together in the fierce dry wind." The novel goes full circle, from *we* to *we*, and it concludes with a sense that all the strings haven't been cut, that Indian people may yet be teased and tricked into self-knowledge and a more secure identity through the necessary storytelling.

Michael Dorris

At the end of Michael Dorris's novel *A Yellow Raft in Blue Water* (1987), one of the book's three narrators and protagonists, Aunt Ida, is braiding her hair as a priest watches: "As a man with cut hair, he did not identify the rhythm of three strands, the whispers of coming and going, of twisting and tying and blending, of catching and of letting go, of braiding" (343). The metaphor of braiding—tying and blending—illuminates the substance of this novel, for it is, like Erdrich's works, a tale of intertwined lives caught up in one another the way distinct narrative threads are woven to make a single story. Like Erdrich, Dorris—part Modoc and for many years a professor of Native American studies at Dartmouth College—constructs his novel out of multiple narratives so that the reader must triangulate to find the "truth" of the fiction. And like Erdrich and other Indian writers, Dorris makes the subject of his fiction the quest for identity through a re-membering of the past.

Yellow Raft is told in three parts by three narrators—daughter, mother, grandmother, beginning with the youngest generation—so that as we move through the novel, stories are peeled off one another like layers of the proverbial onion as blanks are gradually filled in and we circle in both time and space from an unnamed Montana reservation to Seattle and back, and from the present to the past and back again. As in so many other fictions by Indian writers, the women in this novel live oddly isolated and self-sufficient lives, raising their children and keeping their stories intact without the aid of the alienated males whose lives intersect briefly with theirs. These intersecting lives are caught up in pathos rather than tragedy, and though most of the events of the novel take place on a reservation and involve characters who identify primarily as Indian, Dorris succeeds in highlighting the universality of tangled and fragile relationships. For those who want to pin down the precise setting of this novel, Dorris has said, "The action takes place on a reservation in eastern Montana. There are about five reservations in eastern Montana. We have discovered that it's easier if nobody thinks it's about them. It's not. None of these books is about real people."[23] Though this book may not be about "real people," these characters suffer through many of the same confusions and conflicts, pleasures and pains that we might find in a Los Angeles barrio or a Chicago suburb. Like Erdrich, Dorris has succeeded in *Yellow Raft* in allowing his Indian characters to be human to escape from the deadly limitations of stereotyping.

The first narrator of *Yellow Raft* is Rayona, a young half-Indian, half–African American teenager with all the resiliency of the synthetic fabric for which she is named. Like most mixedbloods in fiction by Indian writers, Rayona is trying to comprehend her life, particularly her abandonment by her Black father and her strangely tenuous connections to her Indian mother, Christine.[24] Unlike *Tracks*, with its opening and closing repetition of *We*, *Yellow Raft* opens with the singular *I* as Rayona describes her position in her mother's hospital room. Though Rayona does not realize it at the time, her mother, Christine, is dying, having destroyed her internal organs through drinking and hard living. With an intensely undependable mother and a mostly absentee father, of whom she ironically says, "Dad was a temp," Rayona is cast back upon the *I* that is the novel's first word and the dangerous antithesis of the communal identity central to Native American cultures. Relying mostly upon her self, Rayona has achieved a precariously balanced sense of self that straddles what the lecherous Father Tom calls her "dual heritage."

The closest thing to a secure community Christina can offer her daughter is a lifetime membership at Village Video. "It's like something I'd leave you," Christina says in a statement that offers a brilliant contrast to the legacies of tribal identity left to other characters in such novels as *House Made of Dawn*, *Winter in the Blood*, or *Ceremony*. In somewhat the same way that the traditional stories permeate *Ceremony* and *House Made of Dawn*, video permeates *Yellow Raft*, to the extent that the old idea of an Indian "village" could be said to have given way to a more modern—and culturally bankrupt—"Video Village." Christine emphasizes this disturbing transformation when she looks at a videotape of *Little Big Man* and says, "I dated a guy who played an Indian in that movie."[25] We are left to wonder if the guy was an Indian "playing" what Hollywood defines as Indian or if he was a white man playing an Indian. Either way, there is an unmistakable suggestion that "Indian" is a role to be played and identity something conferred by script and camera. Dorris will reinforce this video omnipresence throughout the novel, with characters constantly referring to movies and television to reaffirm their shifting senses of reality. In this world, surface has replaced the depth found in *Tracks*, trivialized aesthetics displacing the ethics of traditionally ecosystemic Indian values.

Even Aunt Ida, a character with a strong sense of self, seems an MTV caricature when we first encounter her wearing overalls, a "black bouffant wig" tacked on by shiny bobby pins, a dark blue bra, sunglasses, and Walkman speakers. Pushing a lawn mower that has no effect upon the grass, Aunt Ida is belting out, like a Stevie Wonder imitation in the wrong tune, the words to what should be considered the novel's theme song: "I've been looking for love in all the wrong places" (27–28). For the rest of the novel, Ida will seldom be far from a television set, involving herself in the twisted lives of scripted characters of soap operas while living in virtual isolation from the rest of her family and tribe. And when Christine and Aunt Ida confront one another for the first time after many years, Rayona can only say, "I . . . watch as though I'm seeing this scene on an old movie and a commercial could come along any time" (28). Christine, in turn, says, "I couldn't guess what Ray had in mind for a grandmother. Probably somebody from TV, Grandma Walton or even Granny from 'The Beverly Hillbillies,' but they were a far cry from Aunt Ida" (205). These mixedblood characters suffer from a loss of authenticity intensified by an inability to selectively assimilate the words and images besieging them from the ubiquitous media. Bakhtin suggests that the

> tendency to assimilate others' discourse takes on an even deeper and more basic significance in an individual's ideological becoming, in the most fundamental sense. Another's discourse performs here no longer as information, directions, rules, models and so forth—but strives rather to determine the very basis of our behavior, it performs here as *authoritative discourse*, and an *internally persuasive discourse*.[26]

The characters in Dorris's novel, seemingly trapped in a dialectic that never moves toward *telos*, or resolution, incapable of dialogue and without significant community to aid them in developing a coherent sense of self, become comic reflectors for the monologic discourse of the privileged center beamed to them in their isolation. The result is poignantly funny, pathos pointing—like the narrator's frozen father in *Winter in the Blood*—toward cultural tragedy.

Despite her resiliency, Rayona is as lost between cultures and identities as any character in Indian fiction, truly a stranger in a very bizarre land. Father Tom, who is trying to convince Rayona to go back to Seattle and far from the reservation where she might tell about his sexual advances, says, "And you won't feel so alone, so out of place. . . . There'll be others in a community of that size who share your dual heritage" (58). In a nicely ironic testimony to her dilemma, the lascivious priest offers Rayona a cheap, pseudo-Indian medallion he has been wearing, saying, "Wear this. Then people will know you're an Indian" (58). Identity is all surface. The center is lost. With a medallion, Rayona may become Native American rather than African American. Rayona's predicament is underscored even more ironically when she stops beneath a sign that reads, "IF LOST, STAY WHERE YOU ARE. DON'T PANIC. YOU WILL BE FOUND" (61). Rayona takes this advice and stays at Bearpaw Lake State Park, where the ladies' restroom "has a cartoon picture of an Indian squaw on the door." She doesn't panic, though she does attempt halfheartedly to appropriate the identity—rich family and all—of a popular, spoiled white girl, and she is found by Sky, a good-hearted draft-dodger who doesn't notice trivial details like skin color, and his tough-as-nails wife, Evelyn. Appropriately, Sky and Evelyn—Father Sky, Mother Earth—subsist in the "video village" of contemporary America on TV dinners; and lying on their couch, Rayona muses upon her fragmented self: "It's as though I'm dreaming a lot of lives and I can mix and match the parts into something new each time" (80). Indian identity is further undercut when the wealthy white parents of Rayona's coworker talk of their "adopted" Indian son who lives on a "mission": "When he writes to us now he calls us Mother and Pops just like one of our own kids" (94). Such an image suggests the distantly marginalized voice, the "wilderness children" of McNickle's novels, writing back to the metropolitan center—"Pops," the white father—in a poignant imitation of the expected discourse.

Rayona returns to the reservation and her mother via an Indian rodeo, where she achieves a totally unconvincing bronc-busting triumph that reminds everyone of Lee, Christine's brother killed in Vietnam. And once she is back, the three strands of family begin to be woven into one thread. Rayona's mother, Christine, begins the second book of the novel by declaring, "I had to find my own way and I started out in the hole, the bastard daughter of a woman who wouldn't even admit she was my mother" (129). In a novel in which identity is obscure at best, Christine is actually the daughter of Ida's father and Ida's mother's sister, Clara; she is the half-sister of the woman she thinks of as her mother. It is ironic that among many tribes, as we have seen in James Welch's *Fools Crow*, it was once common for a man to take his wife's sisters as additional wives, especially if his first wife was in need of assistance and one of her sisters, like Clara, needed a home. According to traditional tribal values, at one time there might have been nothing at all improper about Clara bearing the child of her sister's husband had the situation been handled correctly. But that world is long gone, and Clara's pregnancy is a potentially damning scandal. In spite of the fact that Christine has taught Rayona to speak "Indian" and Ida still knows how to dance traditionally, most values have been lost in the confusion of a reservation where young girls mouth the lyrics to "Poor Little Fool" ("I felt like a fool," Welch's *Winter* narrator says) while awaiting Armageddon, grandmothers wear black wigs and Walkmans, and a talented boy is labeled "the Indian JFK" and ridiculed by his sister when he speaks of "Mother Earth and Father Sky."

Christine's "brother," Lee, is the son of Ida and Willard Pretty Dog. A warrior, Willard has come home, like Russell in *The Beet Queen* and all the other soldiers in Indian fiction, with hideous scars and no hero's welcome, taken in like a refugee by Ida. Out of pride, Ida has ultimately rejected Willard and never acknowledged him as her son's father. Thus while Christine mistakenly believes Ida to be her mother and Lee her brother, neither Christine nor Lee can claim a father. Noting her differences from Lee, Christine says, "We were so different I wondered if we had the same father. . . . I studied middle-aged men on the reservation for a clue in their faces" (131). At Lee's funeral, Christine observes, "A woman who was somehow related to us wailed softly," and of the crowd of men she says, "One of them was probably Lee's father, my father, but that was an old question that would never be answered" (189). When Ida finally takes Christine to visit Clara as Clara lies dying in a hospital, Ida drags Christine away quickly, obviously afraid that Clara will confess that she, not Ida, is Christine's mother. Christine, with little time left to live, will never learn the truth of her biological mother, but she will by the end of the novel be accepted once again as a daughter by Ida.

In the third book of the novel, Ida tells her story, and the threads of relationships in the novel become more clear. It is in this book that relationships are also reforged. Christine, who jealously hounded Lee into the military and toward his death, is forgiven by Ida and forgives the bitter old lady in return. Dayton, Lee's best friend, both forgives Christine and is in turn forgiven.[27] Rayona is reunited with Christine and taken in as a daughter by Dayton, the mixedblood with whom Christine lives out her final days. Father Hurlburt, silent witness and participant in all—who is vaguely part Indian and has learned to speak Ida's language—is there in the end to watch and approve. And most significantly, Ida becomes the novel's supreme storyteller, as befits the Indian grandmother. "I tell my story the way I remember, the way I want," she says, adding:

> I have to tell this story every day, add to it, revise, invent the parts I forget or never knew. No one but me carries it all and no one will—unless I tell Rayona, who might understand. She's heard her mother's side, and she's got eyes. But she doesn't guess what happened before. She doesn't know my true importance. She doesn't realize that I am the story, and that is my savings, to leave her or not. (271)

With Ida's acceptance of her crucial role as the storyteller who holds the meaning of past, present and future within her words, Dorris moves his novel closer to the mainstream of Indian fiction. Ida becomes, like Nanapush in *Tracks*, the grandmother in *Winter in the Blood*, Francisco in *House Made of Dawn*, and all storytellers, the bearer of the identity and order that are so fragile they may perish in a single generation if unarticulated. Within Ida resides the power to abrogate the authority of that "other" discourse assaulting Indians from the media of Euramerica: she can take off her earphones and wig, turn off the television soap operas, and become a storyteller, leaving her "savings"—a recovered sense of self, identity, authenticity—to Rayona.

Though resolution and closure come with a somewhat unpersuasive rapidity and ease in this novel, *A Yellow Raft in Blue Water* moves energetically into Welch's Montana terrain to illuminate the lives of Indians who live on vestiges of tribal identities and reservation fringes, bombarded by video and the American Dream. In choosing to write of a nameless tribe on a nameless reservation, Dorris deliberately emphasizes the ordinariness of these experiences for the great number of Native Americans who, in searching for a sense of self, must reach back even further and with much less hope of success than a Tayo or Abel or even the narrator of *Winter in the Blood*. Writing in a prose style that inundates the reader with an occasionally annoying plethora of incidental detail, Dorris forces his reader to share his characters' experience of incessant strafing by the foreign and the trivial. The world of permanence and signficance, where every detail must count and be counted— the Indian pueblo/village community portrayed so effectively in

Ceremony and *Fools Crow*—has given way to an Indian Video Village in which alien discourses assert a prior authority and resist, with their privileged cacophony, easy assimilation. The individual who would "be" Indian rather than "play" Indian is faced with an overwhelming challenge.

8

"Ecstatic Strategies"

Gerald Vizenor's Trickster Narratives

◆

Born in 1934, Gerald Vizenor has devoted an incredibly prolific career to exploring the place and meaning of the mixedblood in modern America. With more than twenty-five books and scores of essays, poems, and stories published, in addition to a movie (*Harold of Orange*, 1983), Vizenor is one of the most productive as well as one of the most radically imaginative of contemporary American writers. At the heart of Vizenor's fiction lies a fascination with what it means to be of mixed Indian and European heritage in the contemporary world—in Vizenor's terminology, a "crossblood." And out of this fascination arises the central and unifying figure in Vizenor's art: the trickster. In Vizenor's work the mixedblood and the trickster become metaphors that seek to balance contradictions and shatter static certainties. The mixedblood, that tortured Ishmael of the majority of novels by both Indian and non-Indian authors, becomes in Vizenor's fiction not a pained victim but a "holotropic" and celebrated shape shifter, an incarnation of trickster who mediates between worlds. In Vizenor's fictional world—a coherent and fully realized topography as complete as Faulkner's South or Garcia Marquez's Macondo—the tortured and torturing mixedblood represented so unforgetably in Mark Twain's "Injun Joe" and Faulkner's "Chief Doom" simply refuses to perish in the dark cave of the American psyche but instead soars to freedom in avian dreams and acrobatic outrage.

Harsh laughter is the matrix out of which Vizenor's fiction arises, the kind of laughter Mikhail Bakhtin finds at the roots of the modern novel. "As a distanced image a subject cannot be comical," Bakhtin writes; "to be made comical, it must be brought close." And he continues:

> Everything that makes us laugh is close at hand, all comical creativity works in a zone of maximal proximity. Laughter has the remarkable power of making an object come up close, of drawing it into a zone of crude contact where one can finger it familiarly on all sides, turn it upside down, inside out, peer at it from above and below, break open its external shell, look into its center, doubt it, take it apart, dismember it, lay it bare and expose it, examine it freely and experiment with it. Laughter demolishes fear and piety before an object, before a world, making of it an object of famliar contact and thus clearing the ground for an absolutely free investigation of it.

In Bakhtin's words—a remarkably accurate description of a raven examining and dissecting an object of interest—we find a precise definition of the humor and method of the Native American trickster, he/she who brings the world close and directs this "comical operation of dismemberment," laying bare the hypocrisies, false fears and pieties, and clearing the ground "for an absolutely free investigation" of worldly fact. This is the trickster Vizenor has taken to heart and to the heart of his fiction. Bakhtin's explanation of the effects of these parodic forms in ancient art applies equally well to Vizenor: "These parodic-travestying forms . . . liberated the object from the power of language in which it had become entangled as if in a net; they destroyed the homogenizing power of myth over language; they freed consciousness from the power of the direct word, destroyed the thick walls that had imprisoned consciousness within its own discourse, within its own language."[1] The liberation of language and consciousness is Vizenor/trickster's aim, particularly the liberation of the signifier "Indian" from the entropic myth surrounding it.

The trickster discourse of Vizenor's fiction resembles Bakhtin's definition of Minippean satire:

> The familiarizing role of laughter is here considerably more powerful, sharper and coarser. The liberty to crudely degrade, to turn inside out the lofty aspects of the world and world views, might sometimes seem shocking. But to this exclusive and comic familiarity must be added *an intense spirit of inquiry and utopian fantasy.* In Minippean satire the unfettered and fantastic plots and situations all serve one goal—to put to the test and to expose ideas and idealogues. . . . Minippean satire is dialogic, full of parodies and travesties, multi-styled, and does not fear elements of bilingualism.

Vizenor's "parodia sacra" is often shocking, his plots "unfettered and fantastic," "full of parodies and travesties," and designed to serve the one goal Bakhtin defines: to test and expose ideas and idealogues. The result is never nihilistic, a point Elaine Jahner has made well: "Vizenor's consistent contribution has been the way he shows us a way to avoid cynicism; and while he indulges extravagantly in irony, he does so in a manner that finally returns ideals to a purity that leaves no further need for irony." It is the utopian impulse that guides Vizenor's mythic parodies, a quest for liberation from the entropic forces that attempt to deny full realization of human possibilities. Vizenor discovers such utopian potential in American Indian mythologies; and in trickster—who overturns all laws, governments, social conventions—Vizenor finds his imaginative weapon. Simultaneously, his profound identification with the mythic trickster enables Vizenor—who writes even autobiography in the third person—to repudiate that "privileged moment of *individualization*" Foucault identifies with the "coming into being of the notion of 'author,'" and to write multivocal narratives that deconstruct the egocentric authorial presence conventional in the genre of the novel in favor of an ecocentric voice that springs from liminal thresholds.[2]

Vizenor was born in Minneapolis, the son of a half-Ojibwe father (or Chippewa or, as the tribal people call themselves, *anishinaabeg*). Vizenor's grandmother, Alice Mary Beaulieu, was born into the crane totem on the White Earth Reservation, a totemic identification that manifests itself throughout Vizenor's work in avian visions and trickster flights. Vizenor has written, "My tribal grandmother and my father were related to the leaders of the crane; that succession, over a wild background of cedar and concrete, shamans and colonial assassins, is celebrated here in the autobiographical myths and metaphors of my imagination; my crossblood remembrance. We are cranes on the rise in new tribal narratives." Moved from the White Earth Reservation to the city as a result of the federal government's ill-conceived Relocation Program, Vizenor's twenty-six-year-old father, Clement Vizenor, was found with his throat cut, the victim of a still unsolved murder. (Years later while a professional journalist, Vizenor attempted to investigate his father's murder but was told by a police official that nothing was known because no one paid much attention to the murder of an Indian in those days.) Not quite two years old at the time of his father's death, Gerald Vizenor grew up in a series of foster homes in the Minneapolis area close to the White Earth Reservation where his father's *anishinaabe* relatives lived. It was a peripatetic childhood that would echo the beginning of almost all trickster narratives in Native American tradition: "Trickster was going along." And as he was going along, Vizenor served in the U.S. Navy in Japan, where he became interested in both drama and haiku, studied at New York University, received a degree from the University of Minnesota, did graduate work briefly at Harvard, and carved out a successful career as a journalist and mixedblood provocateur with the *Minneapolis Tribune*. Always active in Native American concerns, Vizenor headed the American Indian Employment and Guidance Center in Minneapolis, organized protests, and wrote troubling articles and essays about injustices directed at Native Americans. All of this before he began his career as an academic culminating in his acceptance of an endowed chair at the University of Oklahoma.[3]

Mixedbloods, Vizenor has written, "loosen the seams in the shrouds of identities." The mixedblood, he adds, "is a new metaphor . . . a transitive contradancer between communal tribal cultures and those material and urban pretensions that counter conservative traditions. The mixedblood wavers in autobiographies; he moves between mythic reservations where tricksters roamed and the cities where his father was murdered."[4] Vizenor's poetry, fiction, and essays, and his novels in particular, are surely the products of such a coming of age, the creations of a "transitive contradancer" defining the places of the mixedblood in the modern world. The vision and voice are those of the trickster; the terrain begins with a baronage on the White Earth Reservation and a dynasty of mixedblood tricksters and expands around the globe.[5] In the process, Vizenor shifts American Indian fiction into urban cities as well as reservation woodlands, invading the privileged metropolitan center with mixedblood clowns, detectives, and "landfill reservations" that constitute a kind of Indian reinhabitation of stolen America.

Vizenor's first novel, *Darkness in Saint Louis Bearheart*, is a tale of agonistic celebration that charts a new course for American Indian fiction and American literature. Alan Velie was the first critic to recognize Vizenor's post-structuralist methodology and to point out the central thread in Vizenor's writing: "In this work, Vizenor . . . tries to celebrate the unique status of the mixed-bloods—to reverse the prejudice that has plagued them, to make a hero of the half-breed."[6] *Bearheart* is a postapocalyptic allegory of mixedblood pilgrim clowns afoot in a world gone predictably mad. This postmodern pilgrimage begins when Proude Cedarfair—mixedblood *anishinaabe* shaman and the fourth in a line of Proude Cedarfairs— and his wife Rosina flee their Cedar Circus reservation accompanied by seven clown crows as the reservation is about to be ravaged for its timber by corrupt tribal officials. The nation's economy has collapsed because of the depletion of fossil fuels, and the government and tribal "bigbellies" lust after the Circus cedar.

As the pilgrims move westward toward the vision window at Pueblo Bonito, place of passage into the fourth world, their journey takes on ironic overtones in a parody not merely of the familiar allegorical pilgrimage à la *Canterbury Tales* but also more pointedly of the westering pattern of American "discovery" and settlement. Very early in their journey, Proude and Rosina are joined by an intense collection of misfits, both mixedblood and white. Benito Saint Plumero, or Bigfoot, is a mixedblood clown and "new contrarion," a "phallophor" descended from "the hotheaded political exile and bigfooted explorer, Giacomo Constantino Beltrami" (68–69). Like James Welch in *Fools Crow*, Vizenor's fictional names often echo history and mythology, both Indian and non-Indian. Bigfoot, for example, is the translated name of the celebrated Ojibwa war chief, Ma-mong-e-se-da.[7] This fictional Bigfoot's pride, in addition to his huge feet, is an enormous and exuberantly active penis, named President Jackson by the appreciative sisters in the "scapehouse of weirds and sensitives," a retreat founded with federal funds by thirteen women poets from the cities. Another pilgrim, Pio Wissakodewinini, "the parawoman mixedblood mammoth clown," has been falsely charged with rape and sentenced to a not-quite-successful sex change. Inawa Biwide, "the one who resembles a stranger," is sixteen, "an orphan rescued by the church from the state and the spiritless depths of a federal reservation housing commune" (71). Inawa Biwide will quickly become the novel's apprentice shaman, eventually following Proude Cedarfair into the fourth world. Rescuer of Inawa Biwide from the state is Bishop Omax Parasimo, wearer of metamasks which allow him to pass from Bishop to Sister Eternal Flame and other transexual metamorphoses. Justice Pardone Cozener, a minor figure in this oddly Chaucerian pilgrimage of the outraged and outrageous, is an "illiterate law school graduate and tribal justice . . . one of the new tribal bigbellies . . . who fattened themselves overeating on expense accounts from conference to conference" (74). Justice Pardone is in love with Doctor Wilde Coxwaine, the bisexual tribal historian also along on this journey westward.

One of four consistently female characters journeying with Proude is Belladonna Darwin–Winter Catcher, the daughter of Old John Winter Catcher, Lakota shaman, and Charlotte Darwin, a white anthropologist. Conceived and born at Wounded Knee, Belladonna is a victim of rigid world views. Other female pilgrims include Little Big Mouse, "a small whitewoman with fresh water blue eyes" who rides in foot holsters at the waist of the giant Sun Bear Sun, "the three hundred pound seven foot son of the utopian tribal organizer Sun Bear" (74), and Lillith Mae Farrier, the white woman who began her sexual menage with two canines while teaching on an Indian reservation.

Unarguably the most radical and startling of American Indian novels, *Darkness in Saint Louis Bearheart* is paradoxically also among the most traditional of novels by Indian authors, a narrative deeply in the trickster tradition, insisting upon values of community versus individuality, upon syncretic and dynamic values versus the cultural suicide inherent in stasis, upon the most delicate of harmonies between humanity and the world we inhabit, and upon our ultimate responsibility for that world. At the same time, through the eclectic lenses of his caricatured pilgrims, Vizenor demonstrates repeatedly the truth of Paul Watzlawick's declaration that the real world "is an invention whose inventor is unaware of his act of invention . . . the invention then becomes the basis of his world views and actions."[8]

The fictional author of this novel-within-a-novel is old Bearheart, the mixedblood shaman ensconced in the BIA offices being ransacked by American Indian Movement radicals as the book begins. Bearheart, who as a child achieved his vision of the bear while imprisoned in a BIA school closet, has written the book we will read. According to William Warren, writing in 1885, "The No-ka or Bear family are more numerous than any of the other clans of the Ojibways, forming fully one-sixth of the entire tribe. . . . It is a general saying, and an observable fact, amongst their fellows, that the Bear clan resemble the animal that forms their Totem in disposition. They are ill-tempered and fond of fighting, and consequently they are noted as ever having kept the tribe in difficulty and war with other tribes. . . ."[9] Bearheart, whose totem is the bear, is somewhat ill-tempered in his response to the AIM radicals and, through his novel, to American culture, but, like Proude, he assumes the role of trickster and uses laughter as his weapon in his war against hypocrisy and "terminal creeds." "When we are not victims to the white man then we become victims to ourselves," Bearheart tells a female AIM radical with her chicken feathers and plastic beads, underscoring Indians' inclination to embrace their own invention from "traditional static standards" as "artifacts." He directs her to the novel locked in a file cabinet, the "book about tribal futures, futures without oil and governments to blame for personal failures." To her question, "What is the book about?" Bearheart answers first, "Sex and violence," before adding, "Travels through terminal creeds and social deeds escaping from evil into the fourth world where bears speak the secret languages of saints" (xii–xiv).

"Terminal creeds" in *Bearheart* are beliefs which seek to fix, to impose static definitions upon the world. Whether those static definitions arise out of supposedly "traditional" Indian beliefs or out of the language of privileged Euramerica, they represent what Bakhtin terms "authoritative discourse," language "indissolubly fused with its authority—with political power" as a prior utterance.[10] Such attempts to fix meaning according to what Vizenor terms "static standards" are destructive, suicidal, even when the definitions appear to arise out of revered tradition. Third Proude Cedarfair expresses Vizenor's message when he says very early in the novel, "Beliefs and traditions are not greater than the love of living" (11), a declaration repeated near the end of the novel in Fourth Proude's insistence that "the power of the human spirit is carried in the heart not in histories and materials" (214).

Within the idea of trickster that has evolved through Native American oral literatures, Vizenor finds an approach to both the phenomenal and noumenal that is distinctly "Indian." "In trickster narratives," Vizenor has written, "the listeners and readers imagine their liberation; the trickster is a sign, and the world is 'deconstructed' in a discourse."[11] *Bearheart* is such a liberation, an attempt to free us from romantic entrapments, to liberate the imagination. The principal target of this fiction is precisely the sign "Indian," with its predetermined and well-worn path between signifier and signified. Vizenor's aim is to free the play between these two elements, to liberate "Indianness," and in so doing to free Indian identity from the epic, absolute past that insists upon stasis and tragedy for Native Americans.

While the authorial voice explains that Rosina "did not see herself in the abstract as a series of changing ideologies" (35), most of the pilgrims in this narrative, to varying degrees, do indeed suffer from the illness of terminal creeds. Bishop Omax Parasimo is "obsessed with the romantic and spiritual power of tribal people" (71), a believer in the Hollywood version of Indianness. Matchi Makwa, another pilgrim, chants a lament of lost racial purity, "Our women were poisoned part white," leading Fourth Proude to explain, "Matchi Makwa was taken with evil word sorcerers" (55).

Belladonna Darwin–Winter Catcher, the most obvious victim of terminal creeds, attempts to define herself as "Indian" to the exclusion of her mixedblood ancestry and, more fatally, to the exclusion of change. "Three whitemen raped me," she tells Proude, "three evil whitesavages." Upon learning she is pregnant, Proude replies, "Evil does not give life" (65). Belladonna does not heed the warning Proude offers when he underscores the power of language to determine reality, saying, "We become the terminal creeds we speak" (143).

When the pilgrims come to Orion, a walled town inhabited by the descendants of famous hunters and western bucking horse breeders, Belladonna is asked to define "tribal values." Belladonna replies with a string of clichés out of the "Hiawatha" vein of romantic literature, stating, "We are tribal and that means that we are children of dreams and visions. . . . Our bodies are connected to mother earth and our minds are part of the clouds. . . . Our voices are the living breath of the wilderness. . . ." A hunter replies, "My father and grandfathers three generations back were hunters. . . . They said the same things about the hunt that you said is tribal. . . . Are you telling me that what you are saying is exclusive to your mixedblood race?" Belladonna snaps, "Yes!" adding "I am different than a whiteman because of my values and my blood is different . . . I would not be white." She blithers on, contradicting much of what we have witnessed thus far in the novel: "Tribal people seldom touch each other. . . . We do not invade the personal bodies of others and we do not stare at people when we are talking. . . . Indians have more magic in their lives than whitepeople" (190–91).

A hunter responds: "Tell me about this Indian word you use, tell me which Indians are you talking about, or are you talking for all Indians" (191). Finally, after trapping Belladonna in a series of inconsistencies and logical culs-de-sac, he asks the question which cuts through the heart of the novel: "What does Indian mean?"

When Belladonna replies with more clichéd phrases, the hunter says flatly, "Indians are an invention. . . . You tell me that the invention is different than the rest of the world when it was the rest of the world that invented the Indian. . . . Are you speaking as an invention?" (191). Speaking as a romantic invention indeed, a reductionist definition of being that would deny possibilities of the life-giving change and adaptation at the center of traditional tribal identity, Belladonna is further caught up in contradictions and dead ends. The hunters and breeders applaud and then deconstruct the invention, giving the young mixedblood her "just desserts": a cookie sprinkled with a time-release alkaloid poison. They have recognized their guest's exploitation of language as "the medium through which a hierarchical structure of power is perpetuated," the only difference from the usual colonial impulse being that Belladonna inverts the hierarchy by placing the static "Indian" at the top. "Your mixedblood friend is a terminal believer and a victim of her own narcissism," a breeder says to the pilgrims (194).

Belladonna Darwin–Winter Catcher is a clear example of what Vizenor has described in an interview as the "invented Indian." In the interview, Vizenor confesses his satirical, didactic purpose:

> I'm still educating an audience. For example, about Indian identity I have a revolutionary fervor. The hardest part of it is I believe we're all invented as Indians. . . . So what I'm pursuing now in much of my writing is the idea of the invented Indian. The inventions have become disguises. Much of the power we have is universal, generative in life itself and specific to our consciousness here. In my case there's even the balance of white and Indian, French and Indian, so the balance and contradiction is within me genetically. . . . There's another idea that I have worked into the stories, about terminal creeds. I worked that into the novel Bearheart. It occurs, obviously, in written literature and in totalitarian systems. It's a contradiction, again, to balance because it's out of balance if one is in the terminal condition. This occurs in invented Indians because we're invented and we're invented from traditional static standards and we are stuck in coins and words like artifacts. So we take up a belief and settle with it, stuck, static. Some upseting is necessary.[12]

Belladonna is obviously inventing herself from "traditional static standards." In its association with both beauty and deadly nightshade, Belladonna's very name hints at her narcissistic dead end. That the belladonna, or nightshade, plant is also associated historically with witchcraft implies the nature of evil witchery according to Native American traditions: the misuse of knowledge for the benefit of the individual alone rather than for the community as a whole. Her mixedblood surname, "Darwin," calls to mind also the scientist most responsible in the popular consciousness for the substitution of random event, or evolutionary chance, in place of a world of imagined structure and order. In the wake of Darwinian evolution, we were made capable of imagining ourselves as victims—pawns of chance—instead of creators of order from chaos in the tradition of storytellers. According to the Darwinian origin myth, as conveyed to the modern mind through the vehicle of naturalism, powerless humanity inhabits a world antithetical to that evoked in the Native American origin myths in which men and women share responsibility for the creation and care of the world. In her attempt to define herself and all Indians according to predetermined, authority-laden values, Belladonna has forsaken such responsibility. She is a victim of her own words. As Proude explains, "We become our memories and what we believe. . . . We become the terminal creeds we speak" (143).

Bearheart seems to embody dialectically opposed conceptions of chance, or random event. On one hand, a deconstruction of "terminal creeds," in trickster fashion, represents an insistence upon the infinite proliferation of possibility, including the polysemous text. This is the kind of celebration so common to postmodern literature and theory, an insistence that "coherent representation and action are either repressive or illusionary," and a reveling in what we might call chance. On the other hand, a mere capitulation to chance, or random event, would deny the emphasis upon our ultimate responsibility for ordering and sustaining the world we inhabit that is central to Native American ecosystemic cultures. For example, when Vizenor's pilgrims arrive at What Cheer, Iowa, to gamble for fuel with Sir Cecil Staples, the "monarch of unleaded gasoline," Proude declares flatly that "nothing is chance. . . . There is no chance in chance . . . Chances are terminal creeds." (107) With chance, responsibility diminishes, a criticism the novel's author voices early in the novel:

> Tribal religions were becoming more ritualistic but without visions. The crazed and alienated were desperate for terminal creeds to give their vacuous lives meaning. Hundreds of urban tribal people came to the cedar nation for spiritual guidance. They camped for a few days, lusted after their women in the cedar, and then, *lacking inner discipline, dreams, and personal responsibilities,* moved on to find new

word wars and new ideas to fill their pantribal urban emptiness. (12, emphasis mine)

The key to reconciling, or at least containing, this apparent dialectic lies once again in Vizenor's trickster pose. Embodying contradictions, all possibilities, trickster ceaselessly dismantles those imaginative constructions that limit human possibility and freedom, allowing signifier and signified to participate in a process of "continually breaking apart and re-attaching in new combinations." In "Trickster Discourse" Vizenor quotes Jacques Lacan, who warns us not to "cling to the illusion that the signifier answers to the function of representing the signified, or better, that the signifier has to answer for its existence in the name of any signification whatever."[13] At the same time, however, trickster shows by negative example the necessity for humanity to control and order our world. Within the straitjacket of a fixed, authoritative discourse the self is made lifeless, like Belladonna, by stasis; within the unordered infinitude of pure possibility, the self deconstructs schizophrenically, the way trickster's body is continually coming apart in the traditional stories. Through language, stories that assert orders rather than order upon the chaos of experience, a coherent, adaptive, and syncretic human identity is possible without the "terminal" state of stasis. Every such utterance then becomes not "the telling of a story" but "the story of a telling," with responsibility falling upon the teller.

At the What Cheer Trailer Ruins, the pilgrims encounter not only the chances of chance, but also additional victims of terminal creeds, the Evil Gambler's mixedblood horde: "The three mixedbloods, dressed in diverse combinations of tribal vestments and martial uniforms, bangles and ideological power patches and armbands. . . . Deep furrows of ignorance and intolerance stretched across their unwashed foreheads" (99). In an experience common to Native Americans, the three killers feel themselves, with some accuracy, to be the victims of white America. Cree Casket, the "mixedblood tribal trained cabinet maker with the blue chicken feather vestments," tells the pilgrims, "I was trained in the government schools to be a cabinet maker, but all the cabinets were machine made so making little wooden caskets made more sense" (101). Cree Casket, we discover, is also a necrophiliac, a literal lover of the dead past. Carmine Cutthroat, described by Justice Pardone as "the red remount . . . with the green and pink stained chicken feathers," cannot speak, the Papago and Mescalero mixedblood having had hot lead poured down his throat by "seven whitechil-dren" while he slept. Willie Burke, the "Tliingit and Russian mixedblood" with a "compulsive need to kill plants and animals and trees," is rendered unconscious by Pio before he has a chance to tell his story of victimage. Doctor Wilde Coxwaine, examining the three mixedbloods, labels them "breathing plastic artifacts from reservation main street," declaring, "Here stand the classic hob-bycraft mannikins dressed in throwaway pantribal vestments, pro-motional hierograms of cultural suicide" (100).

Even the Evil Gambler himself is a victim of modern America, having been kidnapped from a shopping mall and raised in a big-rig trailer on the road, his upbringing a distillation of the peripatetic American experience. Being raised outside of any community, Sir Cecil has no tribal or communal identity; he exists only for himself, the destructive essence of evil witchery. From being doused repeat-edly with pesticides, he has become pale and hairless, a malignant Moby-Dick of the heartland. He explains, "I learned about slow torture from the government and private business. . . . Thousands of people have died the slow death from disfiguring cancers because the government failed to protect the public" (123). Sir Cecil, the Evil Gambler, is the product of a general failure of responsibility to the communal or tribal whole.

Among the trailer ruins, Lillith Mae Farrier is selected to gamble for fuel with Sir Cecil, the Evil Gambler reminiscent of the tradi-tional Evil Gambler in American Indian mythologies. Because she "did not know the rituals of balance and power," because she has not been properly prepared according to tradition for her contest with the Evil Gambler, Lillith loses and destroys herself (112). Proude then tosses the four directions in competition with Sir Cecil and, because chance plays no part in Proude's vision, the Gambler loses and is condemned to death by Saint Plumero. Sir Cecil com-plains to Proude: "The pilgrims wanted gasoline which is part of the game, but you want to balance the world between good and evil. . . . Your game is not a simple game of death. You would change minds and histories and reverse the unusual control of evil power" (126).

From the Trailer Ruins, the pilgrims, whose postal truck soon runs out of gas, travel westward on foot, encountering hordes of deformed stragglers on the broken highways. This host of cripples and monsters are, in the words of Doctor Wilde Coxwain, "Simple cases of poisoned genes," all ravaged by pesticides, poisoned rain, the horrors of the modern technological world. The authorial voice describes this national suicide: "First the fish died, the oceans turned sour, and then birds dropped in flight over cities, but it was not until thousands of children were born in the distorted shapes of evil animals that the government cautioned the chemical manufacturers. Millions of people had lost parts of their bodies to malignant neoplasms from cosmetics and chemical poisons in the air and food" (142). Insisting blindly on identifying the cripples as romantic figures, Little Big Mouse is attacked and torn to pieces by a mob of technology's victims.

Following the canonization of Saint Plumero, a ceremony making Bigfoot a "double saint," the pilgrims arrive at Bioavaricious, Kansas and the Bioavaricious Regional Word Hospital, where terminal creeds—language whose meaning is fixed, language without creative play—are the goal of the hospital staff. In an attempt to rectify what is perceived as a national breakdown in language, the scientists at the word hospital are using a "dianoetic chromatic encoder" to "code and then reassemble the unit values of meaning in a spoken sentence"(163). We are told that with "regenerated bioelectrical energies and electromagnetic fields, conversations were stimulated and modulated for predetermined values. Certain words and ideas were valued and reinforced with bioelectric stimulation" (164). The endeavor at the word hospital suggests what Foucault has labeled an intention "to programme . . . to impose on people a framework in which to interpret the present."[14] The "Bioavaricious Word Hospital" seems suspiciously like a metaphor for the Euramerican colonial endeavor seen from the point of view of the American Indian. Certainly the entire westering impulse of American manifest destiny is indisputably bioavaricious, devouring the continent—and now the third world—as it attempts to re-form the world in its own image. Part of this avaricious attempt to subsume all of creation into its own destiny has involved—particularly from an Indian point of view—an assertion of the absolute privilege of English, "fused with authority" and monologically predetermined. In such a "hospital" the life of language is consumed and destroyed.

Such an endeavor stands in sharp contrast to the oral tradition defined in a description of life among *Bearheart's* displaced just a few pages earlier:

Oral traditions were honored. Families welcomed the good tellers of stories, the wandering historians of follies and tragedies. Readers and writers were seldom praised but the travelling raconteurs were one form of the new shamans on the interstates. Facts and the need for facts had died with newspapers and politics. Nonfacts were more believable. The listeners traveled with the tellers through the same frames of time and place. The telling was in the listening. . . . Myths became the center of meaning again. (158)

In the oral tradition a people define themselves and their place within an imagined order, a definition necessarily dynamic and requiring constantly changing stories. The listeners are coparticipants in the "behavioral utterance" of the story; as Vizenor himself has written elsewhere, "Creation myths are not time bound, the creation takes place in the telling, in present-tense metaphors." Predetermined values represent stasis and cultural suicide. Roland Barthes says simply, "the meaning of a work (or of a text) cannot be created by the work alone."[15]

Impressed by the word hospital, Justice Pardoner and Doctor Wilde Coxwaine remain at Bioavaricious while the remaining pilgrims journey onward toward New Mexico. As they move westward, the pilgrims and sacred clowns meet fewer deformed victims of cultural genocide until finally they encounter the modern pueblos of the Southwest and a people living as they have always lived. At the Jemez Pueblo, the Walatowa Pueblo of N. Scott Momaday's *House Made of Dawn*, the pilgrims encounter two Pueblo clowns who outclown with their traditional wooden phalluses even Saint Plumero himself. The clowns direct Proude and the others toward Chaco Canyon and the vision window where, finally, Proude and Inawa Biwide soar into the fourth world as bears at the winter solstice.

A great deal is happening in *Bearheart*, but central to the entire thrust of the novel is the identification by the author's author, Vizenor, with trickster, the figure which mediates between oppositions, and in the words of Warwick Wadlington, "embodies two antithetical, nonrational experiences of man with the natural world, his society, and his own psyche." Citing Wadlington, Vizenor stresses the duality of trickster's role as on the one hand "a force of treacherous disorder that outrages and disrupts, and on the other hand, an unanticipated, usually unintentional benevolence in which trickery is at the expense of inimical forces and for the benefit of mankind."[16]

In one of the epigraphs to *Earthdivers*, Vizenor quotes Vine Deloria, Jr.'s, declaration that life for an Indian in today's world "becomes a schizophrenic balancing act wherein one holds that the creation, migration, and ceremonial stories of the tribe are true and that the Western European view of the world is also true. . . . [T]he trick is somehow to relate what one feels to what one is taught to think." About this balancing act, Vizenor himself says in the preface to this same collection of trickster narratives:

> The earthdivers in these twenty-one narratives are mixedbloods, or Métis, tribal tricksters and recast cultural heroes, the mournful and whimsical heirs and survivors from that premier union between the daughters of the woodland shamans and white fur traders. The Métis, or mixedblood, earthdivers in these stories dive into unknown urban places now, into the racial darkness in the cities, to create a new consciousness of coexistence.

For Vizenor, trickster is wenebojo (or manibozho, nanibozhu, and so on), "the compassionate tribal trickster of the woodland anishinaabeg, the people named the Chippewa, Ojibway." This is not, according to Vizenor, the "trickster in the word constructions of Paul Radin, the one who 'possesses no values, moral or social . . . knows neither good nor evil yet is responsible for both,' but the imaginative trickster, the one who cares to balance the world between terminal creeds and humor with unusual manners and ecstatic strategies." Vizenor says in the same interview: "When I was seeking some meaning in literature for myself, some identity for myself as a writer, I found it easily in the mythic connections."[17] Central to these mythic connections is trickster, the shapeshifter who mediates between humanity and nature, humanity and deity, who challenges us to reimagine who we are, who balances the world with laughter.

Near the end of *Darkness in Saint Louis Bearheart*, Rosina and Sister Eternal Flame (Pio in the late bishop's metamask) encounter three tribal holy men "who had been singing in a ritual hogan. It was the last morning of a ceremonial chant to balance the world with humor and spiritual harmonies. . . . The men laughed and laughed knowing the power of their voices had restored good humor to the suffering tribes. Changing woman was coming over the desert with the sun" (239). Changing Woman is perhaps the most revered of the Navajo Holy People, the mother of the Hero Twins and one of the creators of humankind. Marked by a somewhat fluid identity and eternal youth, she taught humanity the ceremonial ways to keep the natural forces of wind, lightning, storms, and animals in harmony—to balance the world.[18]

Coming over the desert with the sun, from east to west, is Rosina herself, who, like Proude, has achieved mythic existence here near the end. "During the winter," we are told in the novel's final line, "the old men laughed and told stories about changing woman and vision bears." Translated through trickster's laughter into myth, Proude and Inawa Biwide and Rosina have a new existence within the ever-changing stories, the oral tradition. For all peoples, Vizenor argues, but for the mixedblood in particular, adaptation and new self-imaginings are synonymous with psychic survival. Those who would live as inventions, who, like Belladonna, would define themselves according to the predetermined values of the sign "Indian," are victims of their own terminal vision. Bearheart's mocking laughter is their warning.

If *Bearheart* takes an original path in the thickets of Native American fiction, eschewing the conventional agonies of the mixedblood trapped between cultures, Vizenor's next novel is more radical yet. In *Griever: An American Monkey King in China* (1987), Vizenor takes the trickster to Tianjin and forges a new fiction of nonmimetic monkeyshines that departs still further from the recognizable traditions of Native American literature while forging even deeper ties between the archetypal trickster figures that populate the literatures of divergent cultures.

In 1983 Vizenor and his wife, Laura Hall, traveled to China, where they served as exchange teachers at Tianjin University. In 1986, *Griever*, a product of that experience, won the 1986 Fiction Collective Award and was subsequently published in 1987 by Illinois State University and the Fiction Collective. In 1988 *Griever* won an American Book Award and was described by the *New York Times* as "experimental and . . . luminous."[19] Somewhat paradoxically autobiographical while at the same time determinedly nonrepresentational, *Griever* draws upon Vizenor's experiences within the rigid structures of the Communist state, where, as in *Bearheart*, it seems that "some upsetting is necessary." To accomplish this upsetting and liberation, Vizenor creates a mixedblood Native American trickster-teacher, Griever de Hocus, from the White Earth Reservation. Merging through dreams with the classical trickster of China, the Monkey King, Griever reimagines the world, attacking the hyposcrisies and empty dogma of his host country as well as the foibles of his fellow American exchange teachers and, in trickster tradition, all of humanity.

With Griever, Vizenor participates in reimagining spatial and temporal relations. If, as Foucault implies, the human body is ultimately the one irreducible element in the social scheme, and the body "exists in space and must either submit to authority . . . or carve out particular spaces of resistance and freedom—'heterotopias'—from an otherwise repressive world," in the figure of Griever de Hocus, an animated hybridization, Vizenor demonstrates the trickster's ability to transcend both spatial and temporal repressions.[20] Soaring through dream-visions, Griever escapes temporal and spatial categories, destroys the "chronological net" and finds his "heterotopia"—or particular space of resistance and freedom— to be the world without map or chronology.

Whereas the allegory of *Bearheart* is often intentionally obscure, in *Griever* the author is careful to provide signposts to direct us in our reading of another difficult fiction. The first of these hints comes in the novel's epigraphs. The first epigraph quotes Octavio Paz's *The Monkey Grammarian*: "Writing is a search for the meaning that writing itself violently expels. At the end of the search meaning evaporates and reveals to us a reality that literally is meaningless. . . . The word is a disincarnation of the world in search of its meaning; and an incarnation: a destruction of meaning, a return to body." And Vizenor follows with a second epigraph taken from James J. Y. Liu's *Essentials of Chinese Literary Art*: "Chinese drama is largely nonrepresentational or nonmimetic: its main purpose is expression of emotion and thought, rather than representation or imitation of life. In other words, it does not seek to create an illusion of reality, but rather seeks to express human experience in terms of imaginary characters and situations."[21]

Together, these quotations should alert us to the way *Griever* must be approached: as nonrepresentational, nonmimetic. Despite the temptation to read the novel as a stylized rendering of the author's experience in China—that is, as an imitation of that autobiographical reality—Vizenor wants us to read his trickster's antics as we would approach the mythic: as expressions of "human experience in terms of imaginary characters and situations." Furthermore, the epigraphs serve as a warning to readers not to seek a "meaning" from this novel, the implication being that there are infinite and contradictory meanings coexisting and multiplying toward ultimate liberation in the polysemous text. Vizenor resists closure in his fiction with a determination resembling that of the Mind Monkey himself, of whom Vizenor writes, "He was driven to be immortal because nothing bored him more than the idea of an end; narrative conclusions were unnatural" (128). Lest we be tricked into merely embracing the ephemerality and fragmentation of the text as its sole significance, however, we should bear in mind that it is precisely the resistance to structure, to "meaning" and closure, in the novel that conveys the sharpest political message: the fragmentation of the novel is meant to illuminate the necessity for resistance to the oppressive hegemony of the society depicted in the novel. Bakhtin has written, "A particular language in a novel is always a particular way of viewing the world, one that strives for social significance."[22] In this novel, the language of the text itself asserts its privileged authority—its social significance—over the subjects of the text. In short, *Griever* is a very political work aimed like an explosive mine at the great walls of totalitarian China as well as the strictures/structures of modernist literature. And, as always, Vizenor finds the source of his explosive force in the "holotropic" trickster of Native American myth.

To further direct us in our fictional exploration, Vizenor—a kind of Indian guide in this textual wilderness—provides an epilogue that informs the reader that the author and his wife indeed served as exchange teachers in Tianjin and did in fact invade Maxim's de Beijing in the guise of interior reproduction inspectors. However, just in case this confession causes us to read *Griever* as a kind of confessional-qua-trickster novel, Vizenor adds a list of works "the author has considered in the imaginative conception of this novel," including especially *The Journey to the West*, translated by Anthony C. Yu, and *Monkey*, translated by Arthur Waley (237).

Both *The Journey to the West* and *Monkey* are translations of Wu Ch'êng-ên's epic story of Tripitaka's pilgrimage to India to bring the True Scriptures of Buddha back to China. Highly featured in the tales is Monkey, the immortal trickster of Chinese mythology who wars against stasis and rigid order on earth and in Heaven. Like his brethren the world over, Monkey is a creature of insatiable appetite and whim, an incorrigible shapeshifter for whom rules exist only as challenges. Powerful and wise enough to challenge the Jade Emperor himself, Monkey nonetheless finds himself repeatedly in trouble brought on by sheer impulse, so that he exclaims, "Bad! Bad! This escapade of mine is even more unfortunate than the last. If the Jade Emperor gets to hear of it, I am lost. Run! Run! Run!" Arthur Waley's description of *Monkey* might well serve as an introduction to all of Vizenor's fiction: "*Monkey* is unique in its combination of beauty with absurdity, of profundity with nonsense. Folk-lore, allegory, religion, history, anti-bureaucratic satire and pure poetry—such are the singularly diverse elements out of which the book is compounded." Like Vizenor's American Indian trickster, however, Monkey is at core a satirical litmus test for hypocrisy and false value.[23]

Griever is dedicated "to Mixedbloods and Compassionate Tricksters," an announcement that underscores Vizenor's merging of the two figures that dominate his fiction. For Vizenor the mixing of bloods, cultures, and identities leads to liberation, a freeing of the individual from the masks of a fixed cultural identity. The mixedblood becomes the essential trickster, a transformationist between the icons of identity that limit the imagination. Neither "white" nor "Indian," neither Chinese nor English, the mixedblood is his/her own person, a "socioacupuncturist," to use Vizenor's term, a prick capable of puncturing facades and stereotypes, administering needles to free the flow of energy and balance the whole. Trickster/mixedblood is, therefore, the perfect adversary of a totalitarian state that finds its lifeblood in "terminal creeds."

Like other Native American authors, Vizenor divides his novel into four parts, a number especially powerful in Indian tradition. For Native Americans a four-part structure, paralleling the seasonal cycles, suggests completeness and wholeness as well as closure. Barre Toelken and Tacheeni Scott write that for a Navajo audience the sequence of four parts suggests "an automatic progression ending on something important at the fourth step." From a different perspective, David Harvey notes that "cyclical and repetitive motions . . . provide a sense of security in a world where the general thrust of progress appears to be ever onwards and upwards into the firmament of the unknown."[24]

Vizenor frames his novel with letters from Griever de Hocus to China Browne, a child of Luster Browne's mixedblood dynasty. China has come to China "to interview a warrior clown about Griever de Hocus, the trickster teacher who liberated hundreds of chickens at a local street market and then vanished last summer on an ultralight airplane built by her brother" (19). A fair-skinned mixedblood from the White Earth Reservation, like Vizenor himself, Griever is the son of a Gypsy who passed through the reservation with a caravan named "the Universal Hocus Crown" which sold "plastic icons with grievous expressions, miniature grails, veronicas, and a thin instruction book entitled, 'How To Be Sad And Downcast And Still Live In Better Health Than People Who Pretend To Be So Happy'" (50). From his itinerant father Griever inherits his name and his practice of "Griever Meditation." From his mother he inherits his identity as a mixedblood Native American.

As a mixedblood trickster, Griever has never fit conveniently into any niche. His tribal grandmother at home on the reservation pretends that she cannot understand him: "His urban mixedblood tongue, she snorted when he graduated from college, 'wags like a mongrel, he's a wild outsider.' Even at home on the reservation he was a foreigner" (42). "Griever has an unusual imaginative mind," a teacher writes of the child, "and he could change the world if he is not first taken to be a total fool" (49). Still another teacher declares, "The cause of his behavior, without a doubt, is racial. Indians never had it easier than now, the evil fires of settlement are out, but this troubled mixedblood child is given to the racial confusion of two identities, neither of which can be secured in one culture. These disruptions of the soul . . . become manifest as character disorders. He is not aware of his whole race, not even his own name" (50). Griever illustrates the radical dismemberment typical of both trickster and traditional satire. The teachers' words are a satirical echo of the standard lament for the poor mixedblood caught between cultures and identities. Ironically, this is in one form or another the lament of many Native American writers such as Mourning Dove, Mathews, McNickle, and even, to lesser degrees, Momaday, Silko, and Welch. In spite of the fact that Vizenor makes Griever, like Momaday's Abel and Benally, a victim of the federal government's misguided relocation policy, in satirizing the white teachers' words Vizenor once again makes it clear that he will have none of the sentimental posture that mourns the entrapment of the mixedblood.

An actor before the revolution, Wu Chou, whose name means "warrior clown," "is remembered for his performances as the Monkey King in the opera *Havoc of Heaven*. When he was too old to tumble as an acrobat, he studied the stories of tricksters and shamans in several countries around the world" (23). At the time the novel takes place, Wu Chou is the "overseer of the electronic portal at the main entrance to Zhou Enlai University" (23). The actor/trickster/scholar and keeper of the gateway to knowledge is the perfect character to recognize Griever's own acting out of the role of Monkey King.

"Griever was holosexual," the warrior clown tells China Browne, adding, "Griever was a mind monkey. . . . a holosexual mind monkey" (21). Griever carried a holster "To shoot clocks," Wu Chou explains, a holster containing "pictures from wild histories" (26). When the warrior clown shows the scroll from the holster to China, the pictures she sees on the scroll illustrate the events of the novel we are about to read. Filling out Wu Chou's definition of the trickster teacher, the narrator of the novel explains: "Griever is a mixedblood tribal trickster, a close relative of the old mind monkeys; he holds cold reason on a lunge line while he imagines the world. With colored pens he thinks backward, stops time like a shaman, and reverses intersections, interior landscapes" (34). Through stories, we escape from the tyranny of chronology, history: "The listeners traveled with the tellers through the same frames of time and place," Vizenor wrote of the oral tradition in *Bearheart*. "The telling was in the listening" (158).

As Wu Chou reconstructs Griever for China Browne, Vizenor adds casually, "Two spiders waited near the narrow crack in the pane" (26). Watching and waiting is the creative presence of Spider, from whom the stories are spun by which, like Momaday's man made of words and Silko's Ts'its'tsi'nako, we comprehend the world. With the incidental touch of Spider's presence, Vizenor underscores the mythic dimension and the underpinnings of the oral tradition.

In the opening letter to China, Griever declares that his fellow exchange teachers are "the decadent missionaries of this generation" and that postrevolutionary China is made up (like Belladonna's Indian identity) of "invented traditions, broken rituals." In Vizenor's fiction invented traditions are trickster's targets, and Griever assaults these inventions with the antic fury of the Monkey King disrupting Heaven. One of the trickster's first acts is to free chickens waiting for slaughter in the free market, a radical performance that the Chinese understand in the context of myth: "Chicken liberation, then, was better understood as a comic opera. The audience was drawn to the trickster and his imaginative acts, not the high cost of chicken breasts. Mind monkeys, from practiced stories, would have done no less than emancipate the birds in a free market. Those who liberate, in traditional stories, are the heroes of the culture" (40). And as they watch Griever's liberation, the people "whispered about scenes in the other mind monkey stories" (41). Implicit in this line is the fact that we are witnessing another in the tradition of mind monkey stories, that the novel we are reading has no more commitment to "realism" than do the traditional stories of mythic heroics.

Like the trickster of Native American stories, Griever is an imaginative shapeshifter and "holosexual." In his imagination, Griever invades the voluptuous Sugar Dee: "He became a woman there beneath her hair, and with thunder in her ears, she peeled the blossoms; she pulled her head down in the lambent heat, down on her breasts, dibbled and sheared her high nipples with the point of her tongue. She towed her flesh back from the cold and heard the cocks and animals on her breath" (55). Becoming Sugar Dee, trickster engages in erotic union with him/herself, an act fully in the tradition of Native American tricksters. And from the moment of his chicken liberation early in the novel, Griever is accompanied by Matteo Ricci, a cock named for an Italian Jesuit missionary. Perched on Griever's shoulder throughout the novel, Matteo Ricci allows Vizenor to pun unceasingly upon the liberated cock that distresses everyone with its refusal to conform to codes. Adding a disturbing element of energy and uncertainty, Griever's outrageous cock—just like that of the trickster in traditional stories—causes every situation to be unstable, unpredictable, fertile with potential. In one scene a female teacher, Gingerie, "brushed her hair back and watched the trickster and his cock circle back to the guest house. She waited at the window and waved to him when he passed. Matteo Ricci spread his sickle feathers and shook his wattles" (71). Hilariously, Gingerie and the trickster's cock appear to respond to one another in the author's word-play.[25]

Surrounding Griever is a cast of nearly allegorical figures, whom the author terms "eight uncommon teachers from east to west":

> Luther Holes, the valetudinarian and guest house sycophant; Hannah Dustan, the computer separatist; Carnegie Morgan, also known as Carnie, the tallest teacher with the widest mouth and a rich name; Gingerie Anderson-Peterson, place name consumer with a peculiar accent; Jack and Sugar Dee, the inseparable industrial management consultants; and Colin Marplot Gloome, the retired time and motion scholar. (66)

Hannah Dustan, the "computer separatist," is a "hereditist" who "withstands miscegenation, and neither speaks nor listens to people that she determines are mixedbloods" (77). Hannah explains that "when people can be recognized for what they are, then they do better in the world. Jews, like the Chinese and other races, achieve more and earn more in those countries where there is discrimination, but not mixedbloods because no one knows who they are. Mixedbloods are neither here nor there, not like real bloods" (77–78). A true believer in terminal creeds, Hannah is not aware of Griever's own mixedblood and thus tolerates the trickster. Hannah's dreams are racially disturbed: "In the first she is haunted by dark children who claim she is their mother; in the second, columns of silent immigrants stand in public welfare lines around her house. . . . In both dreams the children and immigrants are mixedbloods, their hands soiled and covered with mold" (77).

Like Hannah, Griever has a troubling dream, in the first part of which he hears slogans chanted by men and women who march in circles:

> "Remember our national policies, our proud new policies," the voices intoned, "we strive to better our lives, death to cats and dogs, one child, death to criminals, one child, death to venereal diseases, one child, death to capitalist roaders, one child, death to spiritual pollution, one child, no spitting, one child, no ice cream with barbarians, one child, no sex on the road, one child, no bright colors, one child, no decadent music, one child, no telephone directories, one child, the east is red." (57)

An unmistakable indictment, this aspect of Griever's dream underscores the terminal condition of the totalitarian mentality, the state that opposes creation with death. And immediately after this litany in the dream a mute child (one child) appears and follows the trickster through the streets like a shadow, the child's reflection rippling back at Griever from all surfaces. The trickster gives the mute child a pencil and the child draws pictures on the concrete: "First he outlined a prairie schooner pulled by a small horse, then a lake with an island and brick houses surrounded by several oversized swine. Near the screen door he made a man who wore a round mask with a wide evil smile. The man held bones in his hands" (58). The child is surrounded by a pale blue light, and as the dream ends the light shoots from the mute child to the trickster and to the telephone, and Griever explains in his letter to China Browne, "When the light passed through me, I became the child, we became each other, and then we raised the receiver to our ear" (59). A voice on the telephone then asks the awakened Griever if he is alone in his room, protesting that visitors are required to register before entering the guest house. When Griever describes the dream child to Egas Zhang, the corrupt director of the foreign affairs bureau at the university, Egas explains that the child is "Yaba Gezi, the mute pigeon. . . . Child from old stories, no one sees the mute, from stories before liberation" (60–61). Later, Griever finds the child's drawings on the concrete balcony.

Ironically, of course, the old stories—like all traditional trickster tales—are stories of liberation, of imaginative freedom opposed by the new "liberation" of Egas Zhang's postrevolutionary China. And as the repeated reflection and mirroring of the child's face suggests, Yaba Gezi springs from within Griever, the child of imagination and creation silenced by the totalitarian state.[26] The mute child's drawings depict key elements in the story we are about to read. The prairie schooner is the cart of the mixedblood, Kangmei, in which Griever will be smuggled to safety. It is also Kangmei who will soar to final freedom with Griever at the novel's end. The island drawn by Yaba Gezi will appear in the novel as Obo Island in the midst of Shuishang Water Park, "a tribal place where shamans gather and dream" and home to those who have escaped the terminal creeds of totalitarianism.

When Griever is welcomed to Obo Island, he discovers one of the inhabitants is the "mute pigeon," Yaba Gezi. In keeping with Native American cosmology, the dream world and the waking world once again are one, without boundaries. Dreams arise from the self defined in dreams. Also living on the island are Kangmei; Shitou, the "stone man"; Pigsie, who teaches his swine to play basketball; and Sandie, the government rat hunter. Both Sandie and Pigsie bear names drawn from the "comic opera" stories of the mind monkey. Sandie had studied at the University of California at Berkeley before falling afoul of the revolution and being demoted to rat hunter. Pigsie had gone to the United States to study the operation of ultralight airplanes and play basketball, but his lasciviousness had caused his downfall to swine herder. In the classic stories of the Monkey King, both Sandie and Pigsie are monsters fallen from grace and redeemed to accompany the monk, Tripitaka, on his journey to bring the holy scriptures to China. Sandie, like the rat hunter, is rather colorless and sincere in the mythic tale, while Pigsie, like his swine-herding namesake, is beset by appetites and a fondness for buxom young women.[27] Like Griever, the inhabitants of the island are too liberated to exist easily in a terminal state.

Kangmei is the daughter of Egas Zhang's wife and "Battle Wilson, Oklahoma-born Sinophile, poet, idealist, and petroleum engineer" (144). Like Tripitaka in the Monkey King stories, Battle Wilson comes to China with sacred scriptures. Wilson, however, has stolen his scrolls from the British Museum to return them to their rightful home in China, and Battle Wilson's scrolls will, at the novel's end, turn out to contain not terminal truths but a recipe for blue chicken.[28]

Griever de Hocus overturns the terminal creeds of his hosts, liberating not only chickens in the marketplace but also a caravan of condemned prisoners en route to execution. In a moment of surprisingly undisguised rhetoric for this trickster novel, Griever shouts at the convoy: "I would sooner be dead than submit to tyranny. A legal system that can try thirty people in half a day, and commit them all to their graves as a result of that trial, is a tryannical system" (150).

With his face painted like that of the Monkey King in the comic opera, Griever identifies himself first as "White Earth Monkey King" and then successively as Wei Jingsheng and Fu Yuehua, both actual, historical political prisoners in China, before leaping aboard a truck and racing to freedom with three rapists, a heroin dealer, a murderer, a prostitute, a robber, and an art historian who "exported stolen cultural relics"—a crime familiar to American Indians (153). Though the prostitute turns out to be simply an organizer of a homework business for nannies, trickster's prisoners prove to be a sordid lot. Only the rapists make a serious attempt to escape, and they are shot by the pursuing soldiers. The others wait tamely to be recaptured. As is often the case with trickster, Griever's heroic gesture results in anticlimax.

When his affair with Hester Hua Dan results in pregnancy, Griever rejoices, giving the unborn child the name of Kuan Yin, the Efficacious Bodhisattva from the Monkey King stories. However, while Griever is delivering mooncakes to the mixedblood Lindbergh Wang during the Marxmass Carnival, Hester drowns herself in the guest-house pond to escape the wrath of her father, Egas Zhang. A typical trickster, Griever in disguise has been fondling the breasts of Gingerie a few minutes earlier, but now he rages with loss and despair over the deaths of Hester and their unborn daughter. Finally he escapes from the terminal state in an ultralight airplane bound for Macao.

Just as the novel began with a letter to China Browne, it ends with a letter to China that concludes the book on a lyrical note of despondency surprising for a trickster narrative. "China opened in pale blue smoke on the night he arrived and closed now in dead water," the author writes (228). And Griever tells China: "The Marxmass Carnival was horrible this year, no more carnivals like that for me. No panic holes are deep enough to hold my rage over what happened that night" (232). Redeeming the narrative from despair, however, are both Griever's final words, "This is a marvelous world of tricksters. Love, Griever de Lindbergh" (235), and the fact that Griever and Kangmei soar in ultralight avian dreams toward ultimate liberation. That they have apparently never reached their proposed destination—Macao—underscores the story's refusal to end, Griever's resistance to narrative closure. Trickster is still "going along."

Griever is an intensely political text, both as an incomplete attempt to escape from the "readerly" novel and as a bitter indictment of the totalitarian state. Though he/she may assume the guise of hypocrisy and even repression in comic roles, as a trope, trickster abhors repression and hyprocrisy and challenges us to reimagine the world and liberate ourselves in the process. In his epilogue, Vizenor notes that "President Li Xiannian was in the United States to sign an agreement with President Ronald Reagan that allows the People's Republic of China to buy American reactors and other nuclear technology 'designed for the peaceful use, and only the peaceful use of nuclear materials.'" These are the book's final words, another skirmish in what Gerald Vizenor has called the "wordwars." Given the contents of the novel they conclude, their irony is devastating. In this novel, American Indian fiction soars free of rural reservation America, past the privileged metropolitan center, to the other side of the earth.

Vizenor's third novel, *The Trickster of Liberty* (1988), might be considered a prequel to *Bearheart* and *Griever*. In this brief and highly episodic work, Vizenor takes his readers back to the origins of the Patronia Baronage on the White Earth Reservation and introduces Luster Browne and Novena Mae Ironmoccasin, the founders of a mixedblood trickster dynasty that spawns Shadow Box Browne and his nine siblings. Shadow Box in turn marries Wink Martin and the two continue the trickster line with their own swarm of mixedbloods: China Browne, Tulip Browne, Tune Browne, Garlic Browne, Ginseng Browne, Eternal Flame Browne, Father Mother

Browne, Mime Browne, and Slyboots Browne. Part of the extended family through marriage or adoption are Mouse Proof Martin and Griever de Hocus.

Vizenor opens *The Trickster of Liberty* with a prologue entitled "Tricksters and Transvaluation," in which mixedblood trickster Sergeant Alex Hobraiser debates the nature of tricksters with cultural anthropologist Eastman Schicer while an implied author provides informative declarations and pertinent quotations from poststructuralists such as Barthes and Lacan as well as various authorities on Indians and tricksters. While the alien anthropologist attempts in the best modernist tradition to discover a "trickster code" in the sergent's words—that is, to decode the text—the reader is provided with Vizenor's most direct clues to the nature of the (inherently indefinable) trickster presence in his fiction. "The Woodland trickster is a comic trope; a universal language game," the third-person voice of the prologue explains. "The trickster narrative arises in agonistic imagination; a wild venture in a communal discourse, an uncertain humor that denies aestheticism, translation, and imposed representations. . . . The tribal trickster is a comic *holotrope*, the whole figuration; an unbroken interior landscape that beams various points of view in temporaral reveries."[29] Perhaps most to the point for Vizenor's trickster narratives, we are told that "the trickster is comic nature in a language game, not a real person or 'being' in the ontological sense. Tribal tricksters are embodied in imagination and liberate the mind; an androgyny, she would repudiate translations and imposed representations, as he would bare the contradictions of the striptease" (x). Quoting Lacan, the narrator points out that "every word always has a beyond, sustains several meanings." The narrator goes on to add succinctly, "The trick, in seven words, is to *elude historicism, racial representations, and remain historical*" (xi).

Though it may strike some as merely ducking a tough issue, it seems readily apparent that any attempt to explain with certainty Vizenor's conception of trickster would foolishly resemble Eastman Schicer's yearning to "decode" a trickster monologue. However, the prologue underscores the essense of the author's identification as trickster "crossblood": the trickster "holotrope" defies terminal creeds, demands a transcendent freedom that negates such reductionist historicisms as the concept labeled "Indian," a codified image that attempts to enforce conformity to preconceived and static concepts, or "racial representations." The "Indian" in the terminal

Euramerican imagination becomes an aesthetic artifact frozen on coins, "a designer brave engraved in a cultural striptease," as Sergent Alex Hobraiser puts it (ix). Tune Browne, an "intuitive scholar" and political candidate posing ironically in braids, ribbons, bones, and fur, explains this terminal state differently, pointing to a staged photograph by Edward Curtis and declaring, "Curtis has removed the clock, colonized our cultures, and denied us our time in the world" (45).[30] Curtis, we might add, aestheticized the Indian, decontextualizing his living models the way sacred fetishes have been routinely decontextualized into iconic "art" in the world's museums—like the Feather Boy bundle in McNickle's *Wind from an Enemy Sky*. Griever de Hocus, avian trickster and "an adopted heir to the baronage," demands this "time in the world," explaining in *The Trickster of Liberty* that "we wear the agonistic moment, not the burdens of the past" (19).

Quoting Joseph Meeker's *The Comedy of Survival*, Vizenor's prologue further asserts that "the comic mode of human behavior represented in literature is the closest art has come to describing man as an adaptive animal" (xvii). This is the comic mode described by Bakhtin, that which "works in a zone of maximal proximity," drawing the subject "into a zone of crude contact where one can finger it familiarly on all sides . . . dismember it. . . . making it an object of familiar contact and thus clearing the ground for an absolutely free investigation of it."[31] Vizenor's darkly comic art asserts precisely that syncretic, adaptive, investigative nature, a liberation for the "Native American" from artifact and fact. Characteristically illustrative of this metaphor is Slyboots Browne, "the most devious, clever, and artful of the tricksters at the baronage . . . a wild avian dreamer who assumes, surmises, and imagines a world with no halters" (17). It is Slyboots who develops a microlight industry on the reservation baronage and who ships two of the microlights to Griever in Vizenor's previous novel, one to facilitate Griever's escape and one to bribe the Chinese cadres.

Moving out from the reservation, Luster Browne's progeny populate the world with tricksters who challenge, moment by moment, the values and creeds of the worlds they invade. Griever, as Vizenor illustrated in his previous novel, goes to China. China Browne goes to China after Griever, and her adventure is recorded in both *Griever: An American Monkey King in China* and *The Trickster of Liberty*. Tune Browne graduates from the University of California along with Ishi, the captive, aestheticized "Indian" housed in the Berkeley museum, last of the Yahi and, in phrases Vizenor quotes in *Trickster*, the "ideal museum specimen" sought by anthropologists (47). As Vizenor views him, Ishi is the perfect Indian, a modernist icon, the "primitive" decontextualized and thus made an autonomous and collectible artifact. In the museum, Ishi becomes an illustration of the insidious Western impulse James Clifford has described: "We need to be suspicious of an almost-automatic tendency to relegate non-Western peoples and objects to the pasts of an increasingly homogeneous humanity."[32]

Tune founds the New School of Socioacupuncture on the Berkeley campus and liberates dogs from the medical laboratories. Tulip Browne makes windmills and practices her profession as a private detective in Berkeley, where in a Vizenoresque roman á clef she solves the mysterious disappearance of a computer from the Native American Studies offices. Eternal Flame, who also figures prominently in *Bearheart*, founds a "scapehouse for wounded reservation women," and in a scene from *Trickster*, Sister Eternal Flame listens as Griever tells the story of the "scapehouse of weirds and sensitives" from *Bearheart*, to which Sister Eternal Flame responds, "You are the weird one" (93).

One by one, Vizenor chronicles the trickster adventures of each of Shadow Box and Wink Browne's children as they travel their peripatetic paths. The harshest satire of the book is reserved for self-deluding Indians and would-be Indians in a chapter describing the Last Lecture, a "tavern and sermon center" opened by Father Mother. In the tavern, tribal people listen as individuals are allowed to give a final lecture before dropping over a short precipice named the "Edge of the White Earth" into new names and identities with legal papers provided by Father Mother. In the most pointed lecture, one uncomfortably pertinent to all of us who identify as mixedbloods and educators, Marie Gee Hailme, an urban mixedblood, confesses her sins:

> We were all mixedbloods, some light and some dark, and married to whites, and most of us had never really lived in reservation communities. Yes, we suffered some in college, but not in the same way as the Indian kids we were trying to reach, the ones we were trying to keep in school when school was the real problem. But there we were, the first generation of Indian education experts, forcing our invented curriculum units, our idea of Indians, on the next generation, forcing Indian kids to accept our biased views. (110)

In addition to chiding Indian educators (and everyone else), Vizenor launches another of his many attacks upon those he sees as hypocritical activists pandering to whites' conceptions of invented Indians, introducing Coke de Fountain, "an urban pantribal radical and dealer in cocaine." De Fountain is a paroled felon whose "tribal career unfolded in prison, where he studied tribal philosophies and blossomed when he was paroled in braids and a bone choker. He bore a dark cultural frown, posed as a new colonial victim, and learned his racial diatribes in church basements" (111). Sharply reminiscent of his published criticisms of American Indian Movement radical Dennis Banks, Vizenor's sketch of De Fountain is the most blunt and effectively uncomfortable moment in *The Trickster of Liberty*.[33] Comparatively mild is Vizenor's satire directed at Homer Yellow Snow, who gets up to confess in his Last Lecture that he is, in fact, a pretend Indian. Pointedly calling to mind published doubts concerning the authenticity of author Jamake Highwater's claim to an Indian identity, Homer Yellow Snow's confession lays bare the essense of such controversy when he says to his tribal audience: "If you knew who you were, why did you find it so easy to believe in me? . . . because you too want to be white, and no matter what you say in public, you trust whites more than you trust Indians, which is to say, you trust pretend Indians more than real ones" (117–18).[34]

In *The Trickster of Liberty*, as in all of Vizenor's fiction, it is obvious that "some upsetting is necessary" and that the author/trickster is again intent upon attacking terminal creeds and loosening the shrouds of identities. Shapeshifting across the middle ground long reserved for displaced and distraught mixedbloods, Vizenor is the first American Indian author to find "crossbloods" a cause for joyous celebration. The most ambitious and radically intellectual of American Indian writers, Vizenor has taken Indian fiction—and the figure of the mixedblood in particular—into the future. In the irresistible penetration of his satires, Vizenor insists upon ethics beyond aesthetics, upon the immutable values of spirit and heart articulated by Proude Cedarfair, and though he celebrates the liberated play of postmodernism, he nonetheless goes well beyond the "contrived depthlessness" that has been defined as "*the* overwhelming motif in postmodernism."[35] In so doing, Vizenor has produced one of America's most distinctive literary voices.

Notes

◆

Chapter 1. Other Destinies, Other Plots

1. Clifford, *The Predicament of Culture*, 285; Blue, *The Lumbee Problem* 25. William Loren Katz has dealt more broadly with this question in his book, *Black Indians: A Hidden Heritage*, while Jack Forbes offers a complex discussion of this subject in its broadest ramifications in his study, *Black Africans and Native Americans*. For excellent discussions of Americans' evolving attitudes toward Native Americans, the reader should consult Roy Harvey Pearce's *Savagism and Civilization*, Richard Drinnon's *Facing West*, and Robert Berkhofer's *The White Man's Indian*. It is worth noting here that even such a brilliant Native American writer as Leslie Marmon Silko can fall victim to the same stereotyping, evidenced when Silko complained in a review of Louise Erdrich's *The Beet Queen* that it is impossible to tell who is Indian and who is not; Silko erroneously suggests that Mary in that novel is "part Indian." See Silko, "Here's an Odd Artifact for the Fairy-Tale Shelf," *Impact Magazine Review of Books, Albuquerque Journal*, Oct. 7, 1986. As will become clear, in this study I see no value in questioning any author's declaration of Indian or, in the cases of every Native American novelist, mixedblood identity. To explore the tensions and even contradictions inherent in mixedblood identity is another and far richer issue and one I do take up when such exploration seems critically rewarding. To simply dispute any individual author's declaration of self or cultural identity strikes me (writing from the point of view of one who identifies as a mixedblood) as a pointless commodification of "Indianness," a translation of culture into symbol currency.

2. Peter Wild, "Visions of a Blackfoot," *New York Times Book Review* 91 (Nov. 2, 1986): 14. Emphasis mine.

3. Neal Bowers and Charles L. P. Silet, "An Interview with Gerald Vizenor," *MELUS* 8 (1981): 45–47; Gerald Vizenor, "Trickster Discourse: Comic Holotropes and Language Games," in *Narrative Chance*, 188.

4. Philip Lujan and L. Brooks Hill, "The Mississippi Choctaw: A Case Study of Tribal Identity Problems," *American Indian Culture and Research Journal* 4, no. 3 (1980): 57–53. The case of the Mississippi Choctaw underscores the complexity of Indian identity. In the Treaty of Dancing Rabbit Creek, in 1830, the Choctaw tribe ceded the last of their original 23,119,964 acres in Mississippi to the government and agreed to move to Indian Territory in the west. By the early 1900s, the two thousand

Choctaw remaining in Mississippi had suffered for nearly a century from the state and federal governments' refusal to recognize their status as Indian, thus denying them all privileges and services dependent upon that recognition. It was not until 1944 that the Mississippi Choctaw were granted reservation status. Throughout that century, however, the impulse to preserve Choctaw identity proved so powerful that as late as 1974 a survey showed that English was the first language in only 7 percent of Choctaw households in Mississippi. Today Choctaw schools offer bilingual programs (ibid., 40–41). For the many mixedblood Choctaws like my own father, raised away from the small Choctaw communities, however, such identification proved much more difficult, or less desirable, to maintain in the face of social pressures.

5. H. David Brumble's declaration that "Indian autobiography looks back to Eden" simplifies the syncretic impulse underlying contemporary Indian writers' attempts to reconstruct cultural identity, though such a statement has interesting implications for the Indian perspective on America's gothic sensibility. See Brumble, *American Indian Autobiography*, 165.

6. Clifford, *Predicament*, 10; "The Man Made of Words," in Abraham Chapman, *Literature of the American Indian*, 97, 103; Momaday, *The Names*, 25.

7. Louis Owens, "The Future's So Bright They've Got to Wear Shades," *New Mexico Magazine* 65 (Aug., 1987): 24.

8. Bakhtin, *The Dialogic Imagination*, 276–77. While I am aware of the increasing tendency by critics to consider Bakhtin as a topical ointment applicable to virtually any critical abrasion, Bakhtinian analysis strikes me nonetheless as a valuable tool in dealing with certain aspects of Native American writing. Obviously, like many others I do not agree with Paul de Man that "to imitate or to apply Bakhtin, to read him by engaging him in a dialogue, betrays what is most valid in his work." See de Man's "Dialogue and Dialogism" in Gary Saul Morson and Caryl Emerson, eds., *Rethinking Bakhtin*, 114. Thus far, only Arnold Krupat has done much of significance with Bakhtin and Native American fiction. See below.

9. Barre Toelken and Tacheeni Scott, "Poetic Retranslation and the 'Pretty Languages' of Yellowman," in Karl Kroeber, ed., *Traditional Literatures of the American Indian*, 80; Arnold Krupat, "An Approach to Native American Texts," in Andrew Wiget, ed., *Critical Essays on Native American Literature*, 118.

10. I am borrowing this distinction from Bill Ashcroft, Gareth Griffiths, and Helen Tiffin, *The Empire Writes Back*, 82.

11. Ashcroft, Griffiths, and Tiffin, *Empire Writes Back*, 5.

12. Hazel W. Hertsberg has written, "The tribe represented the way of life of the people; *Indian* was a way of differentiating aborigine from European" (*The Search for an American Indian Identity*, 2).

13. See Fraser, *The Warrior Queens*, 230, and Ashcroft, Griffiths and Tiffin, *Empire Writes Back*; Kurt Lucas, "Navajo Students and 'Postcolonial' Literature," *English Journal* 79, no. 8 (1990): 54–58.

14. Bakhtin, *Dialogic Imagination*, 333.

15. David Harvey cites both Lacan and Jameson on this issue in his own attempt to define postmodernism (*The Condition of Postmodernity*, 33). See my chapter on Momaday for further discussion of this point. Jameson has also suggested the possibility of a "collective subject" beyond both the bourgeois ego and the schizophrenic postmodern subject. This "collective subject" would be "decentered but not schizophrenic." Such a distinction would seem to apply to American Indian identity, but, as Arnold Krupat has noted, Jameson does not apply his category to American Indians (*The Voice in the Margin*, 132–33).

16. Ashcroft, Griffths, and Tiffin, *Empire Writes Back*, 7; Jahner, "Metalanguages," in Gerald Vizenor, *Narrative Chance*, 167.

17. Ashcroft, Griffiths, and Tiffin, *Empire Writes Back*, 81–82. Hayden White has suggested that it is "possible to view historical consciousness as a specifically western prejudice, by which the presumed superiority of modern, industrial society can be retroactively substantiated" (*Metahistory*, 1–2).

18. For discussion of the "unnatural" aspect of egocentric autobiography for Native Americans as well as the complexity of such an undertaking, see introductions in Gretchen M. Bataille and Kathleen Mullen Sands, eds., *American Indian Women Telling Their Lives*; Brian Swann and Arnold Krupat, eds., *I Tell You Now*; and H. David Brumble III, *American Indian Autobiography*.

19. Dennis Tedlock, "The Spoken Word and the Work of Interpretation in American Indian Religion," in Kroeber, *Traditional Literatures*, 48.

20. de Angulo, *Indians in Overalls*, 38–39.

21. For discussion of this phenomenon, see Jarold Ramsey, "From 'Mythic' to 'Fictive' in a Nez Percé Orpheus Myth," in Kroeber, *Traditional Literatures*, 25–44. The fact that a tribal audience would know the outline of each traditional story has interesting ramifications for Native American novelists relying upon traditional mythology as an informing structural principle. A Pueblo or Navajo audience, for example, would anticipate the cyclical structure of Silko's *Ceremony* and might therefore know in advance that Tayo and his lover would be reunited in the spring because that is the structure of the myth Silko is incorporating.

22. Foucault, "What Is an Author?" in Robert Con Davis and Ronald Schleifer, eds., *Contemporary Literary Criticism*, 263, 274; Bierhorst quoted in Krupat, "Approach to Texts," 121.

23. Watt, *The Rise of the Novel*.

24. Allen, "Special Problems in Teaching Leslie Marmon Silko's *Ceremony*," *American Indian Quarterly* 15 (1990): 379. It is worth noting that Allen herself incorporates essential elements from Laguna mythology in her novel, *The Woman Who Owned the Shadows*, a fact that puts her protest in a somewhat ambiguous light. During a March 7, 1986, reading at the University of New Mexico, the Kiowa author was asked by a member of his audience to comment upon dangers involved in incorporating bear ritual and mythology in his poetry and prose. Momaday responded by suggesting that the risk was entirely personal, adding, "It is a risk I am willing to take."

25. Foucault, "What Is an Author?" 274, 275; and Derrida, "Structure, Sign, and Play in the Discourse of the Human Sciences," in Davis and Schleifer, *Contemporary Literary Criticism*, 230.

26. Bakhtin, *Dialogic Imagination*, 341, 342.

27. N. Scott Momaday, "The American Indian in the Conflict of Tribalism and Modern Society," lecture at Colorado State University, Fort Collins, Jan. 31, 1971, quoted in Matthias Schubnell, *N. Scott Momaday*, 141.

28. Bakhtin, "Discourse in Life and Discourse in Art," in Davis and Schleifer, *Contemporary Literary Criticism*, 397; Hymes, "*In Vain I Tried to Tell You*," 5, 6; Chona, *The Autobiography of a Papago Woman*, 23; David Harvey, *The Condition of Postmodernity*, 51; Bakhtin, *Dialogic Imagination*, 346.

29. Bakhtin, "Discourse," 408.

30. Postmodern fiction may, in fact, represent a new elitism, as has been suggested of Roland Barthes's theorizing, a new technique contrived in order to distance the contemporary artist from the preceding generation and thus legitimize that artist's marketability in an intensely consumer-oriented society. See Harvey, *Conditions of Postmodernity*, 57–58.

31. Kroeber, *Traditional Literatures*, 1. A fascinating discussion of Native American humor can be found in Keith H. Basso's *Portraits of "The Whiteman."*

32. Velie, *Four American Indian Literary Masters.*

33. The question might be: Whom, among post-modern theorists, does Vizenor not cite at one time or another?

34. *The Empire Writes Back*, 160.

35. Harvey, *Condition of Postmodernity*, 25. For more elaborate discussion of this aspect of modernism, see Malcolm Bradbury and James McFarlane, *Modernism: 1890–1930* (Harmondsworth and New York: Penguin, 1976). Harvey has pointed out that the famous Karl Marx–Hof in Vienna was "designed not only to house workers but also to be a bastion of military defense against any rural conservative assault mounted against a socialist city" (*Condition of Postmodernity*, 33–34).

36. Krupat, *Voice in the Margin*, 22; Smith, "Contingencies of Value," in Robert von Hallberg, ed., *Canons*, 6.

37. Pearce, *Savagism and Civilization*, xvii. This is a revised edition of Pearce's seminal work *The Savages of America*, published in 1953. Bakhtin, *Dialogic Imagination*, 36. America's romance with the Indian is a long and torrid one, of course, and continues intensely today. Even those scholars most sensitive to and knowledgeable of American Indian lives and concerns apparently cannot escape from this romance, as the deeply affective titles of their critical studies and anthologies suggest: *Reading the Fire, Smoothing the Ground, Song of the Sky*, and so on. Ralph Ellison, whose novel *Invisible Man* defined brilliantly the linguistic marginality of black Americans, includes an interesting commentary upon the deadly epic, tragic stereotype in his novel. In the "Rainbow of America's Future" poster described in *Invisible Man*, we find "an American Indian couple, representing the dispossessed past," while Anglo, black, and mixed-race figures represent the present and future. Apparently Indians have no place in the present or future of the novel's "Brotherhood" (*Invisible Man*, 376).

38. Krupat, *Voice in the Margin*, 63. A noteworthy exception to this generalization, however, is Eliot's inclusion of American music within his fragments.

39. Clifford, *Predicament*, 5; Krupat, *Voice in the Margin*, 53, 54.

40. Louis Menand, *Discovering Modernism*, 19.

41. Harvey quotes Lacan and Jameson on this subject. See *Condition of Postmodernity*, 53.

42. Dorris, "Native American Literature in an Ethnohistorical Context," *College English* 41 (1979): 147–62.

43. As must already be obvious, I deliberately use these terms interchangeably. Like most of those who identify as Native American or mixedblood, I grew up with the term "Indian." Though it obviously reflects a history of oppression and appropriation, it is also a term that Indian people have taken to themselves and redefined and with which they are, for the most part, comfortable.

44. Benston, "I Yam What I Yam: The Topos of Un(naming)" in Henry W. Gates, Jr., ed., *Black Literature and Literary Theory*, 152; Clifford, *Predicament*, 14–15.

45. Lar Hothem, *North American Indian Artifacts*, viii.

46. Clifford, *Predicament*, 15.

47. Jack W. Schneider, discussing fiction about Indians by both Indian and Euroamerican authors, has written that "taken as a whole, the Indian fiction reveals a gallery of the dispossessed, who are, in the words of Matthew Arnold, 'Wandering between two worlds, one dead / The other powerless to be born.' " See Schneider, "The New Indian: Alienation and the Rise of the Indian Novel," *South Dakota Review* 17 (1980): 68.

48. See Standiford, "Words Made of Dawn: Characteristic Image and Incident in

Native American Imaginative Literature," in Wolodymyr Zyla and Wendell M. Aycock, eds., *Ethic Literatures since 1776*, 327.

49. It is appropriate that among Anglo-American writers Ken Kesey is the one trickster who would most consciously overturn the naturalistic vision of the vanishing American. Kesey accomplishes this in *One Flew Over the Cuckoo's Nest*, the novel that announces the end of naturalistic modernism, when he creates Bromden, or "Chief Broom," Kesey's trickster-narrator who seizes the control panel and hurls it through the asylum window before sprinting to freedom.

50. Louis Owens, "N. Scott Momaday," in John F. Crawford, William Balassi, and Annie Esteroy, eds., *This Is About Vision*, 63.

51. Pokagon's *Queen of the Woods* is problematic. According to James A. Clifton, *Queen of the Woods* was most likely written by the wife of Cyrus Engle, Pokagon's attorney, agent, publisher, and advisor. "Simon could not have written this drippingly romantic, late Victorian, frontier fantasy," Clifton insists. "Whatever his touted claims to higher education or his genuine talents at the podium, he was scarcely literate and had grave difficulty composing a simple letter." Clifton, "Simon Pokagon's Sandbar: Potawatomi Claims to Chicago's Lakefront," *Michigan History* 71, no. 5 (1987): 14.

52. Bakhtin, *Dialogic Imagination*, 345, note. In reading Momaday's fiction with the aid of Bakhtin, I cannot agree with Krupat, who, applying Bakhtinian dialogic, finds little to praise and much to dismiss in Momaday's work. See my chapter on Momaday below.

53. Ibid., 356, 358.

54. Even contemporary critics can unthinkingly reflect this deeply entrenched static sense of what "Indian" is supposed to mean, as when an otherwise very perceptive critic writes of Welch's *Winter in the Blood*: "So in a sense this novel is Indian in subject, but modern and essentially human, an integration of red and white laments." The unintentional implication here is, of course, that unlike novels about other groups, a work that is "Indian in subject" is not expected to be also "modern and essentially human." Kenneth Lincoln, *Native American Renaissance*, 153.

55. Clifford, *Predicament*, 231.

56. See, for example, Vizenor's "Bone Courts."

57. Pearce, *Savagism and Civilization*, 202, 255.

58. Hymes, "In Vain," 5.

59. Deloria, *God Is Red*, 88.

60. My primary source for the preceding historical information is Harold E. Fey and D'Arcy McNickle, *Indians and Other Americans*.

Chapter 2. Origin Mists

1. Edward Standiford, *The Pattern of California History*, 221.

2. Yellow Bird (John Rollin Ridge), *The Life and Adventures of Joaquín Murieta, the Celebrated California Bandit*, 4 (subsequent references to the novel will be to the University of Oklahoma Press reprint edition and identified by page number in parentheses in the text). For detailed discussions of Ridge's source materials and his radical distortion of "fact," see Joseph Henry Jackson's lengthy introduction to the reprinted novel. See also Franklin Walker, *San Francisco's Literary Frontier*, 51–54.

3. Walker, *San Francisco's Literary Frontier*, 47.

4. Mikhail Bakhtin, *The Dialogic Imagination*, 341, 342.

5. Bakhtin, *Dialogic Imagination*, 277. For discussion of the traditional trickster, see Paul Radin, *The Trickster*.

6. Boudinot himself was a prominent Cherokee, the first editor of the Cherokee Council's newspaper, the *Cherokee Phoenix*, and the author of *Poor Sarah; or, the Indian Woman* published in Cherokee characters in 1833. For further information regarding the Ridges and Cherokee politics during this time, see Grant Foreman, *The Five Civilized Tribes*, 281–421.

7. Walker, *San Francisco's Literary Frontier*, 46, 48; Foreman, *Five Civilized Tribes*, 401.

8. Bill Ashcroft, Gareth Griffiths, and Helen Tiffin, *The Empire Writes Back*, 9.

9. Foucault, "What Is an Author?" in Robert Con Davis and Ronald Schleifer, eds., *Contemporary Literary Criticism*, 272.

10. Foreman, *Five Civilized Tribes*, 400–401.

11. See David Farmer and Rennard Strickland, *A Trumpet of Our Own*.

12. Cherokee author Robert J. Conley has explored the conflicts within the mixedblood Ridge in a superb short story entitled "Yellow Bird: An Imaginary Autobiography," in Conley's *The Witch of Goingsnake and Other Stories*, 3–37.

13. The second has been Simon Pokagon's *Queen of the Woods*, in 1899. See note 51 in chapter 1, above.

14. Green, "Cogewea: The Half-Blood," *Tulsa Studies in Women's Literature* 1 (1982): 221.

15. Biographical information taken from *Mourning Dove's Life among the Columbia River Salish of the Inland Northwest*, edited by Jay Miller. In his introduction to this work, Miller suggests that "it is clear that she went to considerable effort to disguise and shuffle events so as to distance her writing from her family, both to shelter them from public scrutiny and to avoid criticism of her literary abilities." I am grateful to Jay Miller for allowing me to read and quote from an unpublished draft of this work, subsequently published as *Mourning Dove: A Salishan Autobiography*, edited by Jay Miller, Lincoln: University of Nebraska Press, 1990.

16. Ibid., 8, 36, 41, 42.

17. By "heteroglossia" I refer to the condition defined by Bakhtin as "that which insures the primacy of context over text" (*Dialogic Imagination*, 428).

18. Quoted in Dexter Fisher's introduction to *Cogewea, the Half-Blood: A Depiction of the Great Montana Cattle Range*, viii (subsequent references to *Cogewea* will be to the University of Nebraska Press reprint and identified by page number in parentheses in the text).

19. Miller, *Mourning Dove's Life*, 12.

20. Bakhtin, *Dialogic Imagination*, 276–77.

21. For this distinction between "english" and "English" I am indebted to Ashcroft, Griffiths, and Tiffin, who have suggested that "One way to demonstrate an appropriated english is to contrast it with another still tied to the imperial center," a contrast evident in this passage from *Cogewea* (*Empire Writes Back*, 59).

22. Green, "Cogewea," 220.

23. Ashcroft, Griffiths, and Tiffin, *Empire Writes Back*, 7.

24. Green, "Cogewea," 218.

Chapter 3. Maps of the Mind

1. Carol Hunter has written that "*Sundown* . . . is one of the earliest novels by an Indian author to present the theme of the assimilated or mixed-blood Indian as an alienated character." In summarizing fiction by Indian writers earlier than Mathews, Hunter seems to overlook the anguish of Mourning Dove's Cogewea, asserting incorrectly that neither Mourning Dove nor Simon Pokagon (in *Queen of the Woods*)

"focused on the American Indian as being alienated in American society" ("The Protagonist as a Mixed-Blood in John Joseph Mathews' Novel *Sundown*," *American Indian Quarterly* 6 [1982]: 319, 320). In her 1990 novel *Mean Spirit*, the Chickasaw writer Linda Hogan also focuses upon this violent period in Osage history. Hogan's novel pays more attention to the tribal community than does Mathews's and is considerably more romantic in its methods and conclusions. For an exhaustively accurate history of this period, and Osage history and politics in general, see Terry P. Wilson, *The Underground Reservation: Osage Oil*. For biographical information concerning Matthews, see Wilson's "Osage Oxonian: The Heritage of John Joseph Mathews," *Chronicles of Oklahoma* 59 (Fall, 1981): 264–93.

2. Mathews's father, William Shirley Mathews, was one-fourth Osage and the grandson of legendary mountain man Bill Williams. Mathews's mother was French. Guy Logsdon, "John Joseph Mathews—a Conversation," *Nimrod* 16 (1972): 70–75.

3. Wilson, *Underground Reservation*, 97; Logsdon, "Mathews," 70–71.

4. Bill Ashcroft, Gareth Griffiths, and Helen Tiffin, *The Empire Writes Back*, 9.

5. Subsequent references to *Sundown* will be to the 1979 reprint edition and identified by page number in parentheses in the text.

6. David Harvey, *The Condition of Postmodernity*, 53.

7. Wilson, *Underground Reservation*, 75, 76.

8. In her introduction to the 1979 reprint of *Sundown*, Priscilla Oaks suggests that John Windzer kills himself: "Betrayed and disillusioned when he discovers that his behavior endangers rather than helps his people, he commits suicide, giving impetus to the easy destruction of his son by leaving him enough money to drift and drink." All indications are, however, that Chal's father was killed by bandits, as Chal's mother explains, "He said that bad white mans would not come here now, 'cause civilization is here now. I said here is your pistol, but he said, this is not a wild country no more. But I said, you read in papers every day that bandit comes here to hide in hills. But he said, no, it is a civilized country now. He took that pistol, though. Now he is gone. Those white mans took that new car. That pistol is here. He had that pistol in his hand and one of those white bandits is not here, either" (*Sundown*, viii, 237).

9. Wilson, *Underground Reservation*, 156.

10. Ibid., 90.

11. Ibid., 201.

12. Ibid., 205.

13. D'Arcy McNickle, "The Hungry Generations," manuscript, no date; Charles A. Pearce to "Miss D'Arcy Dahlberg," April 6, 1929; and "Manuscript Report," October 23, 1934, author and publisher not identified, all in McNickle Papers, D'Arcy McNickle Center, Newberry Library.

14. McNickle to William Gates, March 25, 1934, McNickle Papers.

15. McNickle to John Collier, May 25, 1934, McNickle Papers. According to the Canadian government's Indian Act of 1875, all métis whose paternal lineage could be traced to European origins were legally classified as white. In the 1891 Canadian census, McNickle's mother's family were listed as white. Dorothy Parker, "Choosing an Indian Identity: A Biography of D'Arcy McNickle" (Ph.D. diss., University of New Mexico, 1988), 16.

16. McNickle had a contract with Covici, Friede dated October 29, 1934, for publication of "Dead Grass," but the novel was turned down in a letter from Covici, Friede to McNickle dated February 5, 1935, because of poor anticipated sales and poor "quality as a novel" (McNickle Papers).

17. McNickle to John Collier, May 4, 1934, McNickle Papers.

18. D'Arcy McNickle, *The Surrounded* (1978), 2 (subsequent references to *The Surrounded* will be to the 1978 edition and identified by page number in parentheses in the text).

19. This is the same buffalo herd that figures in Cogewea. The herd that both Mourning Dove and McNickle watched being rounded up was that begun by Michel Pablo, a rancher who married into the Flathead tribe and became one of the wealthiest men on the reservation. It seems probable that McNickle had Pablo in mind when he conceived the character of Max Leon in *The Surrounded*. In the penultimate manuscript version of this novel, titled "The Hungry Generations," McNickle initially wrote that Max sold "many buffaloes this year" before inserting "cows and" into the sentence. See John Fahey, *The Flathead Indians*, 271, 300–301. See also McNickle, "Hungry Generations," 13.

20. Mikhail Bakhtin, *The Dialogic Imagination*, 345.

21. Quoted in Ashcroft, Griffiths and Tiffin, *Empire Writes Back*, 167.

22. McNickle, "Hungry Generations," 56.

23. Bakhtin, *Dialogic Imagination*, 276.

24. McNickle may be indulging in irony here, since one of the original emissaries sent by the Flathead people to Saint Louis in 1831 to request that Catholic priests come to the tribe was named Narcisse. That Narcisse died in Saint Louis without having succeeded in his quest. Fahey, *Flathead Indians*, 64.

25. For an account of the Flatheads' eager reception of the priests finally sent by the church, see John Shea, *History of the Catholic Missions . . .* , 468. In a 1936 letter to McNickle, J. Verne Dusenberry, a resident of the Flathead area, wrote: "It is reported that Father Taelman read your book and has stated that he thinks you have gone completely mad. That [is] the one dissenting voice amid the cheers 'The Surrounded' has received. But after all, one would expect him to feel that way" (Dusenberry to McNickle, June 3, 1936. McNickle Papers).

26. Fahey, *Flathead Indians*, 270.

27. D'Arcy McNickle, *Wind from an Enemy Sky* (1988), 125 (subsequent references to this novel will be to the University of New Mexico Press reprint edition and identified by page number in parentheses in the text).

28. D'Arcy McNickle, speech given before the Northwest Indian Education Conference, Summer, 1977, 7, McNickle Papers; McNickle to the Commissioner of Indian Affairs, attention of Mr. E. R. Burton, July 20, 1934, McNickle Papers. For an intriguing discussion of this parent-child trope as a complex tool in America's disempowerment of the Indian, see Michael Paul Rogin, *Fathers and Children: Andrew Jackson and the Subjugation of the American Indian,*

29. Purdy, *Word Ways*, xiii, 6 (emphasis mine), 76.

30. James Ruppert, "Textual Perspectives and the Reader in *The Surrounded*," in Gerald Vizenor, *Narrative Chance*, 100; Jay Hansford C. Vest, "Feather Boy's Promise: Sacred Geography and Environmental Ethics in D'Arcy McNickle's *Wind from an Enemy Sky*" (paper presented at the 24th annual meeting of the Western Literature Association, Coeur d'Alene, Idaho, Oct., 1989). I am grateful to Jay Vest for permission to quote from his unpublished essay, which is forthcoming in *American Indian Quarterly.*

31. "The Hungry Generations," 302, 315–16.

32. Ashcroft, Griffiths, and Tiffin, *Empire Writes Back*, 7.

33. "The Hungry Generations," 319, 320.

34. Ibid., 330, 335–36, 337 (emphasis mine).

35. Pearce, *Savagism and Civilization*, 220.

36. E. H. Dodd, Jr., to Ruth Rae, Oct. 20, 1936; and Royalty statement from Dodd, Mead to Ruth Rae, Aug. 1, 1936, both in McNickle Papers.

37. E. H. Dodd, Jr. to Ruth Rae, Mar. 17, 1937; McNickle to E. H. Dodd, Jr., Mar. 22, 1940, and Apr. 11, 1940; and R. T. Bond to McNickle, May 12, 1944, all in McNickle Papers.

38. D'Arcy McNickle, *Runner in the Sun* (1987). Because of the usual constraints of space in a study such as this one, I am omitting discussion of this novel, which I, along with others, read as primarily a work aimed at juvenile readers. For full discussion of the novel, see Purdy, *Word Ways*.

39. Henry Dodd, Jr., to McNickle, Apr. 9, 1937, McNickle Papers.

40. McNickle to Douglas H. Latimer, July 6, 1976; and McNickle to Latimer, Mar. 23, 1977, both in McNickle Papers.

41. Malcolm Cowley to McNickle, Aug. 17, 1936, McNickle Papers. I have found no evidence that McNickle ever wrote the paragraph Cowley suggests. For firsthand information about dam controversy on the Flathead Reservation, see *Hearings*, 86th Cong., 1st and 2d sess., 1960.

42. From Fort Berthold, Office Records of Assistant Commissioner, Mr. Zimmerman, Correspondence, 1935–48, U.S. Department of the Interior, "Memorandum for the Press" December 31, 1937, McNickle Papers.

43. D'Arcy McNickle, "The Indian Agent," manuscript, no date, 293, McNickle Papers.

44. McNickle, "The Indian Agent—Resume of First Eleven Chapters," manuscript, no date, McNickle Papers.

45. Ashcroft, Griffiths, and Tiffin, *Empire Writes Back*, 7.

46. Elaine Jahner, "Metalanguages," in Vizenor, *Narrative Chance*, 167.

47. Bakhtin, *Dialogic Imagination*, 276.

48. Ibid., 343.

49. Ibid., 15.

50. In Pell, who changes from benefactor to well-intentioned villain between the early and final versions of the novel, McNickle may have had in mind a fusion of two figures he knew well: William Gates, a professor at Johns Hopkins University, and Oliver LaFarge, the author of *Laughing Boy* and supposed expert on Indians. Gates, with whom McNickle corresponded rather extensively in the 1930s, had worked widely with Indians in Central America and the American Southwest. LaFarge, whose biography McNickle had written, wrote, according to McNickle, as "an outsider looking in from a defined social position upon an alien world" (Parker, "Choosing an Indian Identity," 278).

51. James Clifford, *The Predicament of Culture*, 231, 246; Lyotard *The Postmodern Condition*, xxiv. Foucault's term for localized spaces is "heterotopia." David Harvey discusses the increasing ghettoization of American society which such concepts of "local determinisms" do nothing to discourage. See Harvey, 144 ff.

52. Ashcroft, Griffiths, and Tiffin, *Empire Writes Back*, 80.

53. Purdy, *Word Ways*, 132. Purdy makes this suggestion while admitting simultaneously that "Harper and Row assure 'that the corrections made on the manuscript were only the most minor grammatical changes.' "

Chapter 4. Acts of Imagination

1. Matthias Schubnell, *N. Scott Momaday*, 93; Lewis Gannet, review of *The Amerindians*, by Donald McNical, in *New York Herald Tribune*, April, 1937, McNickle Papers, D'Arcy McNickle Center, Newberry Library. In a review of McNickle's *The Surrounded*, Gannett wrote, "Perhaps, in literature as in politics and art, the American Indian is at last come into his own" (*New York Herald Tribune*, Feb. 14, 1936, McNickle Papers).

2. Bill Ashcroft, Gareth Griffiths, and Helen Tiffin, *The Empire Writes Back*, 7.

3. Matthews told an interviewer that, after the success of *Wah'Kon-Tah*, a Book-of-the-Month Club selection that sold fifty thousand copies, he was pressured to write a novel, "so I sat down and wrote it." "I've never read it since it was published" (Guy Logsdon, "John Joseph Matthews—A Conservation," *Nimrod* 16 (1972): 73.

4. Nigerian writer Chinua Achebe has quoted this famous phrase from James Baldwin to describe his own appropriation and transformation of the privileged language of the colonial power (Ashcroft, Griffiths and Tiffin, *Empire Writes Back*, 10).

5. Schubnell, *Momaday*, 15; Momaday, "The American Indian: A Contemporary Acknowledgement," *Intellectual Digest* 2, no. 1 (1971): 12; and Momaday, "The American Indian in the Conflict of Tribalism and Modern Society," lecture at Colorado State University, Fort Collins, Jan. 31, 1971, quoted in Schubnell, *Momaday*, 141.

6. Momaday, "The Man Made of Words," in Geary Hobson, *The Remembered Earth*, 167; Schubnell, *Momaday*, 44. During a 1985 reading at the University of New Mexico, Momaday was asked by someone from the audience whether McNickle had influenced his own work. Momaday replied in the negative, saying that he had not read McNickle's works. When, in a 1986 interview, I asked him about the influences of other writers, he replied, "I don't know many Indian writers who wrote early enough to be an influence on me. I keep up now with Jim Welch and some writers of my own generation and younger writers, but I think that when my literary intelligence was being formed I wasn't reading Indian writers. I just didn't know about them" (Louis Owens, "N. Scott Momaday," in John F. Crawford, William Balassi, and Annie Esteroy, eds., *This Is About Vision*, 64).

7. Ashcroft, Griffiths, and Tiffin, *Empire Writes Back*, 77 (for comment upon the "metropolitan" nature of modernism, see p. 160 ff.); Hogan, "Who Puts Together," *Denver Quarterly* 14 (1980): 103.

8. N. Scott Momaday, *House Made of Dawn*, 8 (subsequent references to this novel are to this edition and identified by page number in parentheses in the text); Momaday, "Man Made of Words," 168.

9. Peter Nabokov, *Indian Running*, 89; Schubnell, *Momaday*, 137.

10. For a discussion of postmodern schizophrenia as defined by Lacan and Jameson, see David Harvey, *The Condition of Postmodernity*, 53.

11. Carole Oleson has pointed out the emphasis in the prologue on "changeless change, the unending repetition of the seasonal cycle" ("The Remembered Earth: Momaday's *House Made of Dawn*," *South Dakota Review* 11 (1973): 60). For discussion of this element in traditional storytelling, see Jarold Ramsey, "From 'Mythic' to 'Fictive' in a Nez Percé Orpheus Myth," in Karl Kroeber, ed., *Traditional Literatures of the American Indian*, 25–44.

12. Harold S. McAllister, "Incarnate Grace and the Paths of Salvation in *House Made of Dawn*," *American Indian Quarterly* 2 (1976): 124–25.

13. Alan Velie has suggested that "Abel's problems stem more from intolerance on the part of Indians than whites" ("Cain and Abel in N. Scott Momaday's *House Made of Dawn*," *Journal of the West* 17 [1978]: 61). More recently, Paula Gunn Allen has noted that Abel "has exhibited symptoms of alienation throughout his youth" (*The Sacred Hoop*, 87). Harold S. McAllister declares that "Nicolás is a failure, by Catholic and by Pueblo standards: he is a priest with a son . . ." ("Be a Man, Be a Woman: Androgyny in *House Made of Dawn*," *American Indian Quarterly* 2 (1976): 18.

14. Scarberry-Garcia, *Landmarks of Healing*, 18–19.

15. Quoted in Schubnell, *Momaday*, 50.

16. Bakhtin, *The Dialogic Imagination*, 266–67. Momaday has said, "I knew an Abel

at Jemez who was a close neighbor. . . . I was thinking of him; he is one of the people who adds to the composite Abel" (quoted in Schubnell, *Momaday*, 57). Momaday's statement, however, does nothing to dampen the dialogical resonance of his character's biblical name.

17. Harvey, *Conditions of Postmodernity*, 53–54. Harvey's definition of this schiphrenic condition describes rather accurately the predicament of the unnamed narrator in James Welch's *Winter in the Blood*; however, as does Momaday, Welch allows his character to recover the displaced center and to assimilate past, present, and future into a coherent whole.

18. Ashcroft, Griffiths, and Tiffin, *Empire Writes Back*, 7.

19. See Owens, "N. Scott Momaday," 64; and Momaday, "A Love Affair with Emily Dickinson," *Viva: Northern New Mexico's Sunday Magazine*, Aug. 6, 1972, 2.

20. Velie, "Cain and Abel," 58.

21. Schubnell, *Momaday*, 121; McAllister, "Be a Man, Be a Woman," 15; Allen, *The Sacred Hoop*, 87.

22. Schubnell, *Momaday*, 97.

23. Melville, *Moby-Dick*, 16.

24. Rao quoted in Ashcroft, Griffiths, and Tiffin, *Empire Writes Back*, 39; Ortiz, "Towards a National Indian Literature: Cultural Authenticity in Nationalism," *MELUS* 8, no. 2 (1981): 8.

25. Four warnings of danger are supposedly "noise in the windpipe, ringing in the ear, twitching in the nose, and pricking of the skin on the body" (Clyde Kluckhohn and Dorothea Leighton, *The Navajo*, 183).

26. The atomic bomb will become a central symbol of this danger in Leslie Marmon Silko's *Ceremony*.

27. McAllister has suggested that, given the heavy emphasis throughout the novel on coincidentally Christian names, dates, and other details, "*House Made of Dawn* may be a Christian morality play; its subject is spiritual redemption in a squalid, hellish temporal world." McAllister goes on to suggest that Angela "represents a revision of the orthodox mother of God" (McAllister, "Incarnate Grace," 117, 119).

28. Momaday has said, "Lawrence was a man I liked as an undergraduate and read widely and I still admire Lawrence very much. He is more likely to have been a kind of influence on me than either Faulkner or Hemingway" (Owens, "N. Scott Momaday," 64).

29. Elsie Clews Parsons, *The Pueblo of Jemez*, 62.

30. D. H. Lawrence, *Studies in Classic American Literature*, 51.

31. Krupat, *The Voice in the Margin*, 177n14, 178, 187.

32. Owens, "N. Scott Momaday," 65.

33. Bakhtin, *Dialogic Imagination*, 358.

34. Momaday, "Man Made of Words," 162, 168; Momaday, "The Way to Rainy Mountain," *Reporter*, Jan. 26, 1967, 41–44.

35. Linda Hogan takes a different view of Tosamah, pointing out that "before Abel can be returned to balance, we are shown the many ways that he is undone by language." Hogan also says that in his sermon, Tosamah "speaks as an inspired poet" and that language "speaking through Tosamah, restores him to a unity with the world" ("Who Puts Together," *Denver Quarterly* 14 (1980): 104, 107).

36. Hirsch, "Self-Hatred and Spiritual Corruption in *House Made of Dawn*," *Western American Literature* 17 (1983): 313.

37. Owens, "N. Scott Momaday," 65.

38. For differing views of the traditional trickster, see Paul Radin, *The Trickster*; and Gerald Vizenor, "A Postmodern Introduction," in his *Narrative Chance*, 3–17.

39. The Forty-Niner is a fairly recent and primarily social dance form, probably

originating in Oklahoma, with songs sung in English in a light-hearted atmosphere. This dance furnishes a somewhat ironic backdrop for Benally's prayer. See Laubin.

40. Barry, "The Bear's Son Folk Tale in *When Legends Die* and *House Made of Dawn,*" *Western American Literature* 12 (1978): 386; Beidler, "Animals and Human Development in the Contemporary Indian Novel," *Western American Literature* 14 (1979): 137; Scarberry-Garcia, *Landmarks of Healing,* 56.

41. Leland Wyman points out that the Mountain Chant was originally designed to cure "Older Sister" of "the infirmities, swollen joints, pain . . . incurred during her various travels or to remove the evil alien influences from the captives of the Utes" (*The Mountainway of the Navajo,* 142).

42. Bakhtin, *Dialogic Imagination,* 345.

43. Deloria, *God Is Red,* 76, 82.

44. Interview with Gretchen Bataille, quoted in Schubnell, *Momaday,* 138.

45. Owens, "N. Scott Momaday," 66, 67.

46. N. Scott Momaday, *The Ancient Child,* 17 (subsequent references to this novel will be identified by page number in parentheses in the text).

47. Bakhtin, *Dialogic Imagination,* 343, 345n.

48. According to Schubnell, the original manuscript of Momaday's collection of poems, *The Gourd Dancer,* "includes, as its second part, a sequence of seventeen poems and four stories collected under the title 'The Strange and True Story of My Life with Billy the Kid' " (Schubnell, *Momaday,* 247).

49. William T. Morgan, Jr., "Landscapes: N. Scott Momaday," *Sequoia* 19, no. 2 (1975): 45.

50. Momaday, "Man Made of Words," 168; Bakhtin, *Dialogic Imagination,* 408; Schubnell, *Momaday,* 100.

51. Bakhtin, *Dialogic Imagination,* 408.

52. Ashcroft, Griffiths, and Tiffin, *Empire Writes Back,* 8–9.

53. What Dennis Tedlock has written about Zuni storytellers can be applied to Native American storytellers in general: "For the . . . storyteller-interpreter, the relationship between text and interpretation is a dialectical one: he or she both respects the text and revises it" (Tedlock, "The Spoken Word and the Work of Interpretation in American Indian Religion," in Kroeber, *Traditional Literatures,* 48).

54. Alice Marriott, *The Ten Grandmothers,* 4. Momaday has confided to his critical biographer, Schubnell: "When I think back on my education . . . I shudder; and I ask myself: How did I survive that? It was of course medicine. The bear was watching close by. The bear is always there" (Schubnell, *Momaday,* 177).

55. Deloria, *God is Red,* 84.

Chapter 5. Earthboy's Return

1. Like Momaday's Locke Setman, but in less obvious ways, Welch's narrator is involved in a modern-day vision quest, that search for identity essential to American Indian cultures. For discussion of the ritual of the Blackfoot vision quest central to each of Welch's novels, see William Thackery, "Crying for Pity in *Winter in the Blood,*" *MELUS* 1 (1980): 61–78. Welch has pointed out that his own family tree includes American Indian, English and Spanish forerunners. Among his relatives was Malcolm Clark, who figures significantly as the murdered trader in *Fools Crow.* See "An Interview with James Welch," in Ron McFarland, ed., *James Welch,* 13. Paula Gunn Allen places greater emphasis upon the "accretive narrative structure" of the novel, discussing the novel's relationship to the oral tradition in her critical study, *The Sacred Hoop,* 93–94.

2. John C. Ewers, *The Blackfeet,* 318.

3. David M. Craig has pointed out that this beginning "turns the novel inward, into the self" and that "there is a characteristic shape to Welch's fiction—a three-part story of estrangement, of search for self, and of return to the Indian world" in both *Winter in the Blood* and *The Death of Jim Loney*." Craig's "three-part story" fits the general pattern of American Indian novels rather neatly. Craig, "Beyond Assimilation: James Welch and the Indian Dilemma," *North Dakota Quarterly*, 53 (1985): 183.

4. John Joseph Mathews, *Sundown*, 274; Matthias Schubnell, *N. Scott Momaday*, 50. For Blackfoot naming, see George Bird Grinnell, *Blackfoot Lodge Tales*, 194–95. In a talk at the 1991 Newberry Library Native American Literature Summer Institute, Welch confessed that he had simply forgotten to name his narrator for the first thirty pages, and "At that point it seemed too late." (Author's notes.)

5. James Welch, *Winter in the Blood* (1974), 2 (subsequent references to this novel will be to the 1974 edition and identified by page number in parentheses in the text).

6. Harvey, *The Condition of Postmodernity*, 53–54.

7. Welch has admitted that in an early version of the novel he had named two of his great white hunters McGuane and Harrison, a not-very-subtle ribbing of fellow novelists Tom McGuane and Jim Harrison. Conversation with the author, Feb. 17, 1991.

8. Grinnell, *Blackfoot Lodge Tales*, 194–95.

9. A. LaVonne Brown Ruoff, "Alienation and the Female Principle in *Winter in the Blood*," *American Indian Quarterly* 4 (1978): 117.

10. Welch, *Fools Crow*, 27.

11. Grinnell says of the creator, Napi: "The animals understood him when he spoke to them, and he used them as his servants" (Grinnell, *Blackfoot Lodge Tales*, 142).

12. When Teresa says, "And Father Kittredge will want to say a few words over her" (p. 134), Welch is undoubtedly having fun with his friend and creative writing teacher at the University of Montana, William Kittredge.

13. John C. Ewers, *The Blackfeet*, 3–5. See also Grinnell, *Blackfoot Lodge Tales*, 137–44. For Blackfoot mythology, see also D.C. Duvall, "Mythology of the Blackfeet Indians," *American Museum of Natural History Anthropological Papers*, vol. 2, part 1.

14. Harvey, *Condition of Postmodernity*, 53.

15. Ibid., 54.

16. Andrew Horton, "The Bitter Humor in *Winter in the Blood*," *American Indian Quarterly* 4 (1978): 139; McFarland, *James Welch*, 9.

17. McFarland, *James Welch*, 31.

18. Terry Eagleton, "Brecht and Rhetoric," in Robert Con Davis and Ronald Schleifer, eds., *Contemporary Literary Criticism*, 415.

19. Welch's focus on a mixedblood protagonist in this second novel reflects a reality of modern Blackfoot existence. By 1950 it was estimated that 85 percent of the tribal membership of six thousand were mixedbloods. Citing these statistics, John C. Ewers comments, somewhat hyperbolically, "Neither by name nor by physical features do many of these people reveal their Indian ancestry" Ewers, *Blackfeet*, 326–27.

20. Harvey, *Condition of Postmodernity*, 48.

21. Isaiah 2:22: "Cease ye from man, whose breath is in his nostril: for wherein is he to be accounted of?" (King James Version).

22. James Welch, *The Death of Jim Loney*, 4 (subsequent references will be identified by page number in parentheses in the text).

23. This refrain from *The Waste Land* is also picked up by Fitzgerald in *The Great Gatsby* and Hemingway in *The Sun Also Rises*.

24. McFarland, *James Welch*, 10.

25. Harvey, *Condition of Postmodernity*, 53.

26. Paul Gunn Allen takes this approach to the novel, arguing that Loney's vision quest is answered and "he obtains a vision that becomes the guiding force in his life and his death, and he dies like a warrior in a place and a time of his own choosing" (Allen, *The Sacred Hoop*, 93).

27. Bakhtin, *The Dialogic Imagination*, 17, 36.

28. Sands, "Closing the Distance: Critic, Reader and the Works of James Welch," *MELUS* 14 (1987): 81.

29. Reviews of *Fools Crow* have noted this shift by Welch and almost universally praised the novel, one review describing the book as "a satisfying historical novel by a writer who . . . now goes beyond the portraits of desolation he's been so good at before, into the larger picture" (*Kirkus Reviews* 54 [Sept. 1, 1986], 1324). Another review called the book "both a novel and an expedition; for part of Welch's plan is quite clearly to try to reclaim a piece of this period and make it his own" (*Choice* 24 [Apr. 1987], 1223). Still another stated that "Welch's third novel . . . is like finding a lifestyle preserved for a century and reanimated for our benefit and education" (*Library Journal* 111 [Oct. 15, 1986], 112). Robert L. Berner called *Fools Crow* "the most significant event in the development of Native American literature," adding that "in telling the story of one Blackfoot warrior Welch has evoked the total culture of a tribe, an act of historical imagination unprecedented in our literature" (*World Literature Today* 61, no. 2 [Spring, 1987], 333). Another critic has suggested that the "cultural references scattered in the first two novels are in *Fools Crow* beautifully integrated into a complete picture of the Plains Indians civilization." This same essay, however, makes the misleading claim that in Welch's first two novels tradition plays little role and that in those novels "the tone of his narrative is totally contemporary and wanting in sacred respect toward what seems dangerously antiquated" (Roberta Orlandini, "Variations on a Theme: Traditions and Temporal Structure in the Novels of James Welch," *South Dakota Review* 26, no. 3 [1988]: 37–38, 46).

30. Bill Ashcroft, Gareth Griffiths, and Helen Tiffin, *The Empire Writes Back*, 8–9.

31. Bill Bevis, "Dialogue with James Welch," *Northwest Review* 20, nos. 2–3 (1982): 165; McFarland, *James Welch*, 4–5.

32. According to Ewers, "Napikwan," meaning "Old Man Person," was applied to the white men because of their impressive wonder-working powers. Ewers, *Blackfeet*, 13.

33. Ashcroft, Griffiths, and Tiffin, *Empire Writes Back*, 7, 10, 39.

34. James Welch, *Fools Crow*, 174 (subsequent references will be identified by page number in parentheses in the text). The "big treaty" referred to is "Lame Bull's Treaty" of 1855. Ewers, *Blackfeet*, 4–9, 29, 66, 205ff.; Grinnell, *Blackfoot Lodge Tales*, 208–25.

35. Ewers, *Blackfeet*, 307; Grinnell, *Blackfoot Lodge Tales*, 284.

36. Dreams were so respected that anyone having a dream portending disaster was privileged to turn back without ridicule. According to Ewers, "So great was Blackfoot respect for the messages received in dreams that they said any man who accused another of cowardice because he heeded his dreams and went home would surely be killed on the expedition" (Ewers, *Blackfeet*, 131). Fast Horse's "ghost shirt" or war shirt with "ragged holes and crude designs," a shirt given to him by his father and which had "once belonged to Head Carrier and had deflected many arrows and greased shooters," sounds much like the famous "Lord's shirt" which had originally belonged to Big Plume. After Christ had appeared to him four times in dreams wearing variations of the shirt, Big Plume had made the shirt with holes and crosses and had been rendered invulnerable to wounds in war and even invisible (Ewers,

Blackfeet, 192–93). Bull Shield, the Crow chief who mutilates Yellow Kidney, is not acting with unusual savagery. Mutilation and torture were apparently fairly common. Ewers recounts a story of a Blackfoot warrior, captured by the Cree, who was "scalped, his right hand cut off, and thus started back to his own nation to tell the news." Ewers also writes of a Cree pipe-stem carrier killed by the Blackfeet, who then skinned the victim and stuffed the skin with grasses, placing the figure "in a trail where the Crees were accustomed to pass in their hunting expeditions" (Ewers, *Blackfeet*, 138).

37. Ewers, *Blackfeet*, 29.

38. Ewers, *Blackfeet*, 247–48.

39. Estimates indicate that of 173 Indians killed in the surprise attack in the dead of winter, fifteen were "fighting men between the ages of twelve and thirty-seven." One U.S. soldier was reported killed. Joe Kipp, the half-Blackfoot son of trader James Kipp, would go on to become a notorious whiskey trader among the Blackfeet, founding Fort Standoff at the confluence of the Belly and Waterton rivers. Ewers, *Blackfeet*, 242, 250–51, 257.

40. Whenever a Blackfoot counted a new coup, or achieved a new exploit of note, he was entitled to a new name. Name changes were common, but always significant of actions or characteristics recognized by the community. Grinnell, *Blackfoot Lodge Tales*, 194.

41. According to Ewers, the actual chiefs Heavy Runner, Little Wolf, and Big Lake of the Piegans and the Blood chief Gray Eyes met with General Scully on New Year's Day, 1870. Welch includes the Kainah chief, Sun Calf; Big Lake and Little Wolf of the Pikunis; and Heavy Runner. Ewers says, "These friendly chief agreed to try to kill the murderers and to bring in their bodies and all the stolen stock they could find" (*Blackfeet*, 248). In actuality, the chiefs were unable to accomplish what they promised, just as Welch indicates in his novel.

42. Ashcroft, Griffiths, and Tiffin, *Empire Writes Back*, 82.

43. In an interesting parallel, Grinnell recounts a conversation with a Blackfoot man named Double Runner, who told Grinnell, "The old things are passing away, and the children of my children will be like white people. None of them will know how it used to be in their father's days unless they read the things which we have told you" (Grinnell, *Blackfoot Lodge Tales*, vii).

44. Traditionally, a straying wife could be severely punished by having the end of her nose cut off or even being killed. In 1833, Prince Maximilian claimed that clipped noses were common in Blackfoot camps: "When ten or twelve tents were together, we were sure to see six or seven women mutilated in this manner" (Ewers, *Blackfeet*, 101).

Chapter 6. "The Very Essence of Our Lives"

1. A number of critics have written about the nonlinear temporality in this novel. James Ruppert, for example, has suggested that the structure of *Ceremony* "discourages the reader from imposing a strict chronological order on the narrative, thus reinforcing the perception that the novel is a simultaneous, unified moment that circles like the waves around a rock dropped in a quiet pond, rather than a linear progression of events"—a way of testifying to the novel's place within the patterns of the oral tradition. James Ruppert, "The Reader's Lessons in *Ceremony*," *Arizona Quarterly*, 42, no. 1 (1986): 80. See Elaine Jahner, "An Act of Attention: Event Structure in *Ceremony*," *American Indian Quarterly* 5 (1979): 37–46; Jarold Ramsey, ed., *Reading the Fire*; and Carol Mitchell, "*Ceremony* as Ritual," *American Indian Quarterly* 5 (1979): 27–35.

2. In Joseph Bruchac, ed., *The Next World*, 1730.

3. Simon Ortiz, "Towards a National Indian Literature: Cultural Authenticity in Nationalism," *MELUS* 8, no. 2 (1981): 11.

4. For readings that do stress such distinctions, see Ramsey, *Reading the Fire*, 189ff.; Mitchell, "*Ceremony* as Ritual"; and Seyersted, *Leslie Marmon Silko*.

5. Leslie Marmon Silko, *Ceremony* (1977), 1 (subsequent references to the novel will be to the 1977 edition and identified by page number in parentheses in the text). "Keres" refers to the seven pueblos whose language is identified as Kersesan: Acoma, Laguna, Santa Ana, Zia, San Felipe, Santo Domingo, and Cochiti. The other two linguistic identifications among the pueblo are the Zuni and the Hopi. See Hamilton A. Tyler, *Pueblo Gods and Myths*, xix. For discussion of Thought-Woman, see Paula Gunn Allen, *The Sacred Hoop*, 13ff.

6. Allen, *Sacred Hoop*, 95.

7. See Foucault, "What Is an Author?" in Robert Con Davis and Ronald Scheifer, eds., *Contemporary Literary Criticism*, 263–75.

8. Tedlock, "The Spoken Word and the Work of Interpretation in American Indian Religion," in Karl Kroeber, ed., *Traditional Literatures of the American Indian*, 48; David Harvey, *The Condition of Postmodernity*, 51.

9. See Harold S. McAllister, "Be a Man, Be a Woman: Androgyny in House Made of Dawn," *American Indian Quarterly* 2 (1976): 14–22. See also Allen's discussion of pairing and balance in *Sacred Hoop*, 12ff; and Kenneth Lincoln, *Native American Renaissance*, 12.

10. Quoted in Peggy V. Beck and Anna Lee Walters, *The Sacred*, 38–39.

11. David Hailey, "Visual Elegance of Ts'its'tsi'nako and the Other Invisible Characters in *Ceremony*," *Wicazo Sa Review* 6, no. 2 (1990): 1–6.

12. Mitchell, "*Ceremony* as Ritual," 27–35; Lincoln, *Native American Renaissance*, 237.

13. Alfonso Ortiz, *The Tewa World*, 21. For a very useful discussion of traditional elements permeating the novel, see Edith Swan, "Laguna Symbolic Geography and Silko's *Ceremony*," *American Indian Quarterly* 12 (1988): 229–49.

14. Conversation with the author, Dec. 3, 1990.

15. Any critic should be hesitant, I believe—for propriety's sake and out of respect for Native American cultures, if not simply for fear of misrepresentation—to go very far in explicating sacred and ceremonial materials. However, for more thorough discussion of the Pueblo world view, the reader may consult Tewa anthropologist Alfonso Ortiz, *Tewa World* and *New Perspectives on the Pueblos;* and Hamilton A. Tyler, *Pueblo Gods and Myths*.

16. Mitchell, "*Ceremony* as Ritual," 29.

17. Harvey, *Conditions of Postmodernity*, 53.

18. Mikhail Bakhtin, *The Dialogic Imagination*, 342, 345.

19. Tyler, *Pueblo Gods*, 173.

20. For a discussion of gender and female significance in particular in Pueblo cultures, see Allen, *Sacred Hoop*. See also Paula Gunn Allen, *Studies in American Indian Literature*, 127–33; Paula Gunn Allen, "A Stranger in My Own Life: Alienation in American Indian Prose and Poetry," *MELUS* 7, no. 2 (1980): 3–19; Judith A. Antell, "Momaday, Welch, and Silko: Expressing the Feminine Principle through Male Alienation," *American Indian Quarterly* 12 (1988): 213–20; and Kristin Herzog, "Thinking Woman and Feeling Man: Gender in Silko's Ceremony," *MELUS* 12, no. 1 (1985): 25–36.

21. Tyler, *Pueblo Gods*, 105, 175. See also Edith Swan, "Laguna Symbolic Geography and Silko's *Ceremony*," *American Indian Quarterly* 12 (1988): 229–49.

22. Ron McFarland, ed., *James Welch*, 16.

23. Tyler, *Pueblo Gods*, 166. See also Swan, "Laguna Symbolic Geography," 243.

24. For a thorough discussion of this subject, see Susan Blumenthal, "Spotted Cattle and Deer: Spirit Guides and Symbols of Endurance and Healing in *Ceremony*," *American Indian Quarterly* 14 (1990): 367–77.

25. Ortiz, *Tewa World*, 21.

26. Tyler, *Pueblo Gods*, 167 (for the complete story, see 166–68). Silko has used this myth in a fascinating contemporary way in the short story "Yellow Woman" in her collection *Storyteller*.

27. For anyone who has spent a significant amount of time in and around New Mexico's pueblos—with their profoundly ecosystemic world-view—the irony of the region's involvement in nuclear technology strikes deeply. For the people of Laguna Pueblo and places near Laguna, living in sight of uranium tailings and the results of open-pit mining, the irony is a constant.

28. In an essay highlighting the humorous elements in this novel, of which there are many, one critic attempts to find humor even in this horrific inverse ritual, suggesting that "Tayo's refusal to be caught up in the dynamics of mutual destruction is comical because it seems cowardly, as whites judge bravery . . ." (Elizabeth N. Evasdaughter, "Leslie Marmon Silko's *Ceremony*: Healing Ethnic Hatred by Mixed-Breed Laughter," *MELUS* 15, no. 1 [1988]: 83–95).

Chapter 7. Erdrich and Dorris's Mixedbloods and Multiple Narratives

1. Despite obvious stylistic differences between *A Yellow Raft in Blue Water* and Louise Erdrich's three novels, both Erdrich and Dorris insist that each of their novels has been to some extent a collaboration. In a 1989 conversation with me, Michael Dorris said simply, "We've worked very closely together on each of the novels," and in a published interview, he explained: "The process of everything that goes out, from book reviews to magazine articles to novels, is a give and take" (Sharon White and Glenda Burnside, "On Native Ground: An Interview with Louise Erdrich and Michael Dorris," *Bloomsbury Review* 8 [1988]: 17).

2. J. H. Tompkins, "Louise Erdrich: Looking for the Ties That Bind," *Calendar Magazine*, Oct., 1986, 15.

3. Louise Erdrich, "Where I Ought to Be: A Writer's Sense of Place," *New York Times Book Review*, July 28, 1988, 1, 23.

4. Joseph Bruchac, ed., *Survival This Way*, 77, 79, 83.

5. Louise Erdrich, *Love Medicine*, 1 (subsequent references to the novel will be identified by page number in parentheses in the text).

6. Jay Cox, "Dangerous Definitions: Female Tricksters in Contemporary Native American Literature," *Wicazo Sa Review* 5, no. 2 (1989): 19.

7. Herta D. Wong, "An Interview with Louise Erdrich and Michael Dorris," *North Dakota Quarterly* 55 (1987): 210.

8. While it is tempting to see in Albertine a version of the author, Michael Dorris has declared, "There's the assumption that because this character has some education, she must be Louise. And it's certainly not" (Wong, "Interview," 206).

9. It should be noted, of course, that Foucault says at the same time that the "authored" work "now possesses the right to kill, to be its author's murderer" (Michel Foucault, "What Is an Author?" in Robert Con Davis and Ronald Schleifer, eds., *Contemporary Literary Criticism*, 264).

10. Tompkins, "Louise Erdrich," 15.

11. Mikhail Bakhtin, *The Dialogic Imagination*, 7.

12. Laurie Alberts, "Novel Traces Shattering of Indian Traditions," *Albuquerque Journal*, Oct. 23, 1988, G-8.

13. Leslie Marmon Silko, "Here's an Odd Artifact for the Fairy-Tale Shelf," *Impact Magazine Review of Books, Albuquerque Journal,* Oct. 17, 1986, 10.

14. Ibid., 10–11.

15. In a conversation prior to publication of *The Beet Queen,* Michael Dorris mentioned to me the negligible presence of Indians in the foreground of his wife's second novel, noting that they expected some readers to be surprised by this fact.

16. In an interview, Erdrich confessed that she and husband/collaborator Dorris only discovered that the Wallacette of *The Beet Queen* was Dot Adare of *Love Medicine* when the second novel was almost finished: "Then we were sitting at dinner one day, and Michael looked up in amazement and said, 'Do you know who she is?' So we went to check *Love Medicine* to see what the years were to see if they would work out. And indeed it turned out to be Dot Adare" (Wong, "Interview," 202).

17. See Catherine Rainwater's "Reading Between Worlds: Narrativity in the Fiction of Louise Erdrich," *American Literature* 62 (1990): 405–22.

18. Louise Erdrich, *The Beet Queen,* 8 (subsequent references to the novel will be identified by page number in parentheses in the text).

19. Tompkins, "Louise Erdrich," 15.

20. To Evelina Lucero, a wonderfully perceptive student in one of my graduate seminars, I owe the further observation that Dot's child by Jerry Nanapush in *Love Medicine,* a child who has more Indian blood than her grandmother, Celestine, suggests a kind of generational return home to a Chippewa identity.

21. Louise Erdrich, *Tracks,* 2 (subsequent references to the novel will be identified by page number in parentheses in the text).

22. Alberts, "Novel Traces," G-8.

23. Wong, "Interview," 207.

24. In the first published excerpt from this novel, the narrator was Raymond, a male version of Rayona, orphaned and shipped to the reservation "because the tribal council didn't say no" (Dorris, "A Yellow Raft in Blue Water," in Mary Bartlett, ed., *The New Native American Novel,* 93–107). Dorris has commented upon his own mixedblood upbringing: "My background was slightly more schizophrenic [than that of his wife, Louise Erdrich]. . . . It was a jolt to go from one family to the other. . . . I mean most mixed-blood people have experiences of this type. We're a kind of tribe in and of itself, almost" (Sharon White and Glenda Burnside, "On Native Ground: An Interview with Louise Erdrich and Michael Dorris," *Bloomsbury Review* 8 [1988]: 16). In a separate interview, Dorris described the sense of not belonging as "something that a lot of mixed-bloods relate to—going to a new situation always feeling peripheral . . ." (Wong, "Interview," 212).

25. Michael Dorris, *A Yellow Raft in Blue Water,* 23 (subsequent references to the novel will be identified by page number in parentheses in the text).

26. Bakhtin, *Dialogic Imagination,* 2.

27. The act of forgiveness is a motif in Native American fiction, as if indirectly Indian authors may be suggesting a potentially regenerative response, perhaps the only one possible, to the centuries of oppression and decimation the tribes have experienced.

Chapter 8. "Ecstatic Strategies"

1. Mikhail Bakhtin, *The Dialogic Imagination,* 23, 24, 60.

2. Ibid., 26 (emphasis mine); Jahner, "Review of *The Trickster of Liberty,* by Gerald Vizenor," *Wicazo Sa Review* 6, no. 2 (1990): 38; Michel Foucault, "What Is An Author?" in Robert Con Davis and Ronald Schleifer, eds., *Contemporary Literary Criticism.*

3. My information comes from numerous conversations with Vizenor, particularly

that of Aug. 1, 1989, as well as the manuscript of his autobiography, *Interior Landscapes,* which he generously allowed me to read in draft form. Concerning the murder of his father, in an autobiographical essay Vizenor quotes the *Minneapolis Journal,* which reported that "robbery was not the motive. . . . The slain youth was reported to have been mild tempered and not in the habit of picking fights. Police learned that he had no debts, and, as far as they could ascertain, no enemies" ("Crows Written on the Poplars," in Brian Swann and Arnold Krupat, eds., *I Tell You Now,* 101–102).

4. Swann and Krupat, *I Tell You Now,* 101.

5. Vizenor's work often has a disturbing effect on readers not prepared for its complexity and sophisticated application of trickster motifs. According to Vizenor, when first submitted to publishers the novel was permanently "lost" by editors on three successive occasions. Conversation with the author, Aug. 8, 1989; see also my essay, "Ecstatic Strategies," in Vizenor, *Narrative Chance,* 141–53.

6. Vizenor, *Darkness in Saint Louis Bearheart,* 1978 (references to this novel in this chapter are to the 1978 edition and identified by page number in parentheses in the text); Velie, *Four American Indian Literary Masters,* 138. Velie has followed this pioneering introduction to Vizenor's work with a second essay examining the trickster elements in Vizenor's work ("The Trickster Novel," in Vizenor, *Narrative Chance*). In one of the few book-length studies of contemporary American Indian poetry and fiction, Kenneth Lincoln's *Native American Renaissance,* Vizenor receives two lines of attention. In contrast, A. La Vonne Brown Ruoff has published extensive (mostly bibliographical) work on Vizenor in two essays: "Gerald Vizenor: Compassionate Trickster," *Studies in American Indian Literature* 9 (1986): 52–63; and "Woodland Word Warrior," *MELUS* 13, nos. 1 & 2 (1986): 13–43.

7. See William Warren, *History of the Ojibway People,* 52, 195, 218, 243, 248, 219, 220.

8. Quoted in Vizenor, *Narrative Chance,* 188.

9. Warren, *History,* 49.

10. Bakhtin, *Dialogic Imagination,* 341–42.

11. "Trickster Discourse: Comic Holotropes and Language Games," unpublished paper presented by Vizenor at the School of American Research in Santa Fe, New Mexico, June, 1986.

12. Neal Bowers and Charles L. P. Silet, "An Interview with Gerald Vizenor," *MELUS* 8, no. 1 (1981): 45–47.

13. See David Harvey, *The Condition of Postmodernity,* 49, 50; Vizenor, "Trickster Discourse," 4.

14. Michel Foucault, "Film and Popular Memory," an interview by Martin Jordin in *Radical Philosophy* 11 (1975): 29. It is quoted in Vizenor's "Trickster Discourse," 9.

15. Bakhtin, "Discourse in Life and Discourse in Art," in Davis and Schleifer, *Contemporary Literary Criticism* 397; Vizenor, *Earthdivers,* xii; Barthes, *Critical Essays,* xi.

16. Warwick Wadlington, *The Confidence Game in American Literature,* quoted in the epigraph to Vizenor's *The Trickster of Liberty.*

17. Vizenor, *Earthdivers,* xii; Bowers and Silet, "Interview," 42.

18. Clyde Kluckhohn and Dorothea Leighton, *The Navajo,* 181.

19. Trachtenberg, "A Trickster in Tianjin," *New York Times Book Reviews,* Jan. 10, 1988, p. 18.

20. For a discussion of this aspect of Foucault's thought and its relation to time-space measurement and social power/repression, see Harvey, *Condition of Postmodernity,* 213ff.

21. Gerald Vizenor, *Griever* (subsequent references to the novel will be cited by page number in parentheses in the text).

22. Bakhtin, *Dialogic Imagination*, 333.

23. Wu Ch'êng-ên, *Monkey*, 11, 57.

24. Toelken and Scott, "Poetry Retranslation and the 'Pretty Languages' of Yellowman," in Karl Kroeber, ed., *Traditional Literatures of the American Indian*," Harvey, *Condition of Postmodernity*, 202.

25. For examples of traditional trickster's uncontrollable sexuality and shapeshifting, see Paul Radin, *The Trickster*.

26. According to Vizenor, the mute child first appeared to him in a dream the night before Vizenor and his wife, Laura Hall, left for China: "We had just arrived in our apartment in China when a young mute Chinese girl was there. She had followed us, and now she wanted to live with us, she could communicate but she could not speak, we were drawn to her needs and love and attempted to adopt her" (from Vizenor's unpublished "Notes on Griever de Hocus").

27. See Wu Ch'êng-ên, *Monkey*, 80–82ff.

28. Vizenor may well be having fun here with his friend and colleague, Terry Wilson, chair of Native American Studies at the University of California, Berkeley.

29. Vizenor, *The Trickster of Liberty*, ix–x, xxiv (subsequent references to the novel will be identified by page number in parentheses in the text). Vizenor's concept of "universal language game" contrasts with the emphasis upon localized "language games" in the writing of Jean-François Lyotard, whom Vizenor often refers to. See Lyotard, *The Postmodern Condition*, xxiv.

30. Anyone who identifies as American Indian, full- or mixedblood, has surely had the experience, untold times, of being confronted by a non-Indian who says, "If you're Indian, why don't you have an Indian name?" or "I thought Indians couldn't grow beards" or "Indians never lose their hair." From other Indians may come the flipside question: "What's your enrollment number?" The sad response is often the individual who strikes a pose from an old coin, a joyless masquerade indeed.

31. Bakhtin, *Dialogic Imagination*, 23.

32. James Clifford, *Predicament of Culture*, 246.

33. For Vizenor's published indictment of Dennis Banks, see his essay, "Dennis of Wounded Knee," *American Indian Quarterly* 7, no. 2 (1983): 51–65. Vizenor anticipates Tune Browne's comments about Edward Curtis when he says in this essay, "The poses of tribal radicals seem to mimic the romantic pictorial images in old photographs taken by Edward Curtis for a white audience" (55). The AIM urban radicals also seem to be the targets of Vizenor's satire in *Bearheart* when he describes the Evil Gambler's mixedblood horde "dressed in diverse combinations of tribal vestments and martial uniforms, bangles and ideological power patches and armbands" (*Bearheart*, 99).

34. For background on the Highway controversy, see John Ashton's essay, "Tempest in a Teepee," *Westward* 7, no. 12 (1983), reprinted in *Talking Leaf: Los Angeles Indian Newspaper* 49, no. 2 (1984): 1–2, 15.

35. Harvey, *Condition of Postmodernity*, 58.

References

Alberts, Laurie. "Novel Traces Shattering of Indian Traditions." *Albuquerque Journal*, Oct. 23, 1988, p. G-8.

Allen, Paula Gunn. *The Sacred Hoop: Recovering the Feminine in American Indian Traditions*. Boston: Beacon Press, 1986.

————. "Special Problems in Teaching Leslie Marmon Silko's *Ceremony*." *American Indian Quarterly* 15 (1990): 379–86.

————. "A Stranger in My Own Life: Alienation in American Indian Prose and Poetry." *MELUS* 7, no. 2 (1980): 3–19.

————, ed. *Studies in American Indian Literature*. New York: Modern Language Association, 1983.

Antell, Judith A. "Momaday, Welch, and Silko: Expressing the Feminine Principle through Male Alienation." *American Indian Quarterly* 12 (1988): 213–20.

Ashcroft, Bill; Gareth Griffiths; and Helen Tiffin. *The Empire Writes Back: Theory and Practice in Post-Colonial Literatures*. London and New York: Routledge, 1989.

Bakhtin, Mikhail. *The Dialogic Imagination: Four Essays by M. M. Bakhtin*. Ed. Michael Holquist. Trans. Caryl Emerson and Michael Holquist. Austin: University of Texas Press, 1981.

Barry, Nora Baker. "The Bear's Son Folk Tale in *When Legends Die* and *House Made of Dawn*." *Western American Literature* 12 (1978): 375–87.

Barthes, Roland. *Critical Essays*. Trans. Richard Howard. Evanston, Ill.: Northwestern University Press, 1972.

Bartlett, Mary, ed. *The New Native American Novel: Works in Progress*. Albuquerque: University of New Mexico Press, 1986.

Basso, Keith H. *Portraits of "The Whiteman": Linguistic Play and Cultural Symbols among the Western Apache*. Foreword by Dell Hymes. Cambridge: Cambridge University Press, 1979.

Bataille, Gretchen M., and Kathleen Mullen Sands, eds. *American Indian Women Telling Their Lives*. Lincoln: University of Nebraska Press, 1984.

Beck, Peggy V., and Anna Lee Walters. *The Sacred: Ways of Knowledge, Sources of Life.* Tsaile, Ariz.: Navajo Community College Press, 1977.

Beidler, Peter G. "Animals and Human Development in the Contemporary Indian Novel." *Western American Literature* 14 (1979): 133–48.

Berkhofer, Robert F., Jr. *The White Man's Indian: Images of the American Indian from Columbus to the Present.* New York: Vintage Books, 1978.

Bevis, Bill. "Dialogue with James Welch." *Northwest Review* 20, nos. 2–3 (1982): 163–85.

Blu, Karen I. *The Lumbee Problem: The Making of an American Indian.* Cambridge: Cambridge University Press, 1980.

Blumenthal, Susan. "Spotted Cattle and Deer: Spirit Guides and Symbols of Endurance and Healing in *Ceremony.*" *American Indian Quarterly* 14 (1990): 367–77.

Bowers, Neal, and Charles L. P. Silet. "An Interview with Gerald Vizenor." *MELUS* 8, no. 1 (1981): 41–49.

Bruchac, Joseph, ed. *The Next World: Poems by Third World Americans.* Trumansburg, N.Y.: The Crossing Press, 1978.

———. *Survival This Way: Interviews with American Indian Poets.* Tucson: University of Arizona Press, 1987.

Brumble, H. David, III. *American Indian Autobiography.* Berkeley: University of California Press, 1988.

Chamberlain, J. E. *The Harrowing of Eden: White Attitudes Toward Native Americans.* New York: Seabury Press, 1975.

Chapman, Abraham, ed. *Literature of the American Indians.* New York: NAL, 1975.

Chona, Maria. *The Autobiography of a Papago Woman.* Memoirs of the American Anthropological Association, no. 46. Ed. Ruth Underhill. Menasha, Wisconsin. The Association, 1936. Reprinted as *Papago Woman,* New York: Holt, Rinehart, and Winston, 1979.

Clifford, James. *The Predicament of Culture: Twentieth-Century Ethnography, Literature and Art.* Cambridge: Harvard University Press, 1988.

Clifton, James A. "Simon Pokagon's Sandbar: Potawatomi Claims to Chicago's Lakefront." *Michigan History* 71, no. 5 (1987): 12–17.

———, *Being and Becoming Indian: Biographical Studies of North American Frontiers.* Chicago: The Dorsey Press, 1989.

Colonnese, Tom, and Louis Owens. *American Indian Novelists: An Annotated Critical Bibliography.* New York: Garland Publishing, 1985.

Coltelli, Laura. *Native American Literatures.* Pisa, Italy: Servizio Editoriale Universitario, 1989.

———, ed. *Winged Words: American Indian Writers Speak.* Lincoln: University of Nebraska Press, 1990.

Conley, Robert J. *The Witch of Goingsnake and Other Stories.* Norman: University of Oklahoma Press, 1988.

Cox, Jay. "Dangerous Definitions: Female Tricksters in Contemporary Native American Literature." *Wicazo Sa Review* 5, no. 2 (1989): 17–21.

Craig, David M. "Beyond Assimilation: James Welch and the Indian Dilemma." *North Dakota Quarterly* 53 (1985): 183–90.

Crawford, John F.; William Balassi; and Annie Esteroy, eds. *This Is About Vision: Interviews with Southwestern Writers*. Albuquerque: University of New Mexico Press, 1990.

Davis, Robert Con, and Ronald Schleifer, eds. *Contemporary Literary Criticism: Literary and Cultural Studies*. New York: Longman, 1989.

de Angulo, Jaime. *Indians in Overalls*. San Francisco: City Lights Books, 1990.

Deloria, Jr., Vine. *God Is Red*. New York: Dell Publishing Co., 1973.

Dorris, Michael. "Native American Literature in an Ethnohistorical Context." *College English* 41 (1979): 147–61.

Drinnon, Richard. *Facing West: The Metaphysics of Indian-Hating and Empire-Building*. Minneapolis: University of Minnesota Press, 1980.

Duvall, D. C. "Mythology of the Blackfeet Indians." *American Museum of Natural History Anthropological Papers*, vol. 2, part 1. Washington, D.C.: Government Printing Office, 1908.

Ellison, Ralph. *Invisible Man*. New York: Random House, 1952.

Erdrich, Louise. "Where I Ought to Be: A Writer's Sense of Place." *New York Times Book Review*, July 28, 1988, p. 1.

Evasdaughter, Elizabeth N. "Leslie Marmon Silko's *Ceremony*: Healing Ethnic Hatred by Mixed-Breed Laughter." *MELUS* 15, no. 1 (1988): 83–95.

Ewers, John C. *The Blackfeet: Raiders of the Northwestern Plains*. Norman: University of Oklahoma Press, 1958.

Fahey, John. *The Flathead Indians*. Norman: University of Oklahoma Press, 1971.

Farmer, David, and Rennard Strickland. *A Trumpet of Our Own: Yellow Bird's Essays on the North American Indians*. San Francisco: Book Club of California, 1987.

Fey, Harold E., and D'Arcy McNickle. *Indians and Other Americans: Two Ways of Life Meet*. New York: Harper and Row, 1970.

Forbes, Jack D. *Black Africans and Native Americans: Color, Race and Caste in the Evolution of Red-Black Peoples*. Oxford and New York: Basil Blackwell, 1988.

Foreman, Grant. *The Five Civilized Tribes*. Norman: University of Oklahoma Press, 1934.

Fraser, Antonia. *The Warrior Queens*. New York: Vintage Books, 1988.

Gates, Henry Louis, Jr., ed. *Black Literature and Literary Theory*. New York: Methuen, 1984.

Green, Rayna. "Cogewea: The Half-Blood." *Tulsa Studies in Women's Literature* 1 (1982): 217–21.

Grinnell, George Bird. *Blackfoot Lodge Tales*. New York: Charles Scribner's Sons, 1920.

Hailey, David. "Visual Elegance of Ts'its'tsi'nako and the Other Invisible Characters in *Ceremony*." *Wicazo Sa Review* 6, no. 2 (1990): 1–6.

Harvey, David. *The Condition of Postmodernity: An Inquiry into the Origins of Cultural Change*. Cambridge: Basil Blackwell, 1989.

Hertsberg, Hazel W. *The Search of an American Indian Identity: Modern Pan-Indian Movements*. Syracuse: Syracuse University Press, 1971.

Herzog, Kristin. "Thinking Woman and Feeling Man: Gender in Silko's *Ceremony.*" *MELUS* 12, no. 1. (1985): 25–36.

Hirsch, Bernard A. "Self-Hatred and Spiritual Corruption in *House Made of Dawn.*" *Western American Literature* 17 (1983): 307–20.

Hobson, Geary. *The Remembered Earth.* Albuquerque: University of New Mexico Press, 1981.

Hogan, Linda. "Who Puts Together." *Denver Quarterly* 14 (1980): 103–12.

Hothem, Lar. *North American Indian Artifacts: A Collector's Identification and Value Guide.* Florence, Ala.: Books Americana, Inc., 1984.

Horton, Andrew. "The Bitter Humor of *Winter in the Blood. American Indian Quarterly* 4 (1978): 131–39.

Hunter, Carol. "The Historical Context in John Joseph Mathews' *Sundown.*" *MELUS* 9 (1982): 61–72.

———. "The Protagonist as a Mixed-Blood in John Joseph Mathews' Novel: *Sundown.*" *American Indian Quarterly* 6 (1982): 319–37.

Hymes, Dell. *"In Vain I Tried to Tell You": Essays in Native American Ethnopoetics.* Philadelphia: University of Pennsylvania Press, 1981.

Jahner, Elaine. "An Act of Attention: Event Structure in *Ceremony.*" *American Indian Quarterly* 5 (1979): 37–46.

———. 1990. "Review of *The Trickster of Liberty,* by Gerald Vizenor." *Wicazo Sa Review* 6, no. 2 (1990): 38.

Jordin, Martin. "Film and Popular Memory." *Radical Philosophy* 11 (1975): 29.

Katz, William Loren. *Black Indians: A Hidden Heritage.* New York: Atheneum, 1986.

Kluckhohn, Clyde, and Dorothea Leighton. *The Navajo.* Garden City, N.Y.: Doubleday and Co. and the American Museum of Natural History, 1962.

Kroeber, Karl, ed. *Traditional Literatures of the American Indian: Texts and Interpretations.* Lincoln: University of Nebraska Press, 1981.

Krupat, Arnold. *The Voice in the Margin: Native American Literature and the Canon.* Berkeley: University of California Press, 1989.

Larson, Charles R. *American Indian Fiction.* Albuquerque: University of New Mexico Press, 1978.

Laubin, Reginald, and Gladys Laubin. *Indian Dances of North America: Their Importance to Indian Life.* Norman: University of Oklahoma Press, 1977.

Lawrence, D. H. *Studies in Classic American Literature.* Thomas Seltzer, 1923. Reprint, New York: Compass-Viking, 1964.

Lincoln, Kenneth. *Native American Renaissance.* Berkeley: University of California Press, 1983.

Logsdon, Guy. "John Joseph Mathews—A Conversation." *Nimrod* 16 (1972): 70–75.

Lucas, Kurt. "Navajo Students and 'Postcolonial' Literature." *English Journal* 79, no. 8 (1990): 54–58.

Lujan, Philip, and L. Brooks Hill. "The Mississippi Choctaw: A Case Study of Tribal Identity Problems." *American Indian Culture and Research Journal* 4, no. 3 (1980): 37–53.

Lyotard, Jean-François. *The Postmodern Condition: A Report on Knowledge.*

Trans. Geoff Bennington and Brian Massumi. Foreword by Fredric Jameson. Minneapolis: University of Minnesota Press, 1984.

McAllister, Harold S. "Be a Man, Be a Woman: Androgyny in *House Made of Dawn*." *American Indian Quarterly* 2 (1976): 14–22.

———. "Incarnate Grace and the Paths of Salvation in *House Made of Dawn*." *South Dakota Review* 12 (1974): 115–25.

McFarland, Ron, ed. *James Welch*. Lewiston, Idaho: Confluence Press, 1986.

McNickle, D'Arcy. McNickle Papers, Newberry Library, Chicago.

Marriott, Alice. *The Ten Grandmothers*. Norman: University of Oklahoma Press, 1945.

Melville, Herman. *Moby-Dick*. New York: W. W. Norton and Co., 1967.

Menand, Louis. *Discovering Modernism: T. S. Eliot and His Context*. Oxford: Oxford University Press, 1987.

Miller, Jay, ed. *Mourning Dove: A Salishaw Autobiography*. Lincoln: University of Nebraska Press, 1990.

Mitchell, Carol. "*Ceremony* as Ritual." *American Indian Quarterly* 5 (1979): 27–35.

Momaday, N. Scott. "The American Indian: A Contemporary Acknowledgment." *Intellectual Digest* 2, no. 1 (1971): 12, 14.

———. "A Love Affair with Emily Dickinson." *Viva: Northern New Mexico's Sunday Magazine*, Aug. 6, 1972, 2.

———. "The Way to Rainy Mountain." *Reporter*, Jan. 26, 1967, pp. 41–44.

Morgan, William T., Jr. "Landscapes: N. Scott Momaday." *Sequoia* 19, no. 2 (1975): 38–49.

Morson, Gary Saul, and Caryl Emerson, eds. *Rethinking Bakhtin: Extensions and Challenges*. Evanston, Ill.: Northwestern University Press, 1989.

Nabokov, Peter. *Indian Running: Native American History and Tradition*. Santa Fe, N.M.: Ancient City Press, 1981.

Oleson, Carole. "The Remembered Earth: Momaday's *House Made of Dawn*." *South Dakota Review* 11 (1973): 59–78.

Orlandini, Roberta. "Variations on a Theme: Traditions and Temporal Structure in the Novels of James Welch." *South Dakota Review* 26, no. 3 (1988): 37–51.

Ortiz, Alfonso. *The Tewa World: Space, Time, Being, and Becoming in a Pueblo Society*. Chicago: University of Chicago Press, 1969.

———, ed. *New Perspectives on the Pueblos*. Albuquerque: University of New Mexico Press, 1972.

Ortiz, Simon. "Towards a National Indian Literature: Cultural Authenticity in Nationalism." *MELUS* 8, no. 2 (1981): 7–12.

Owens, Louis. "Acts of Recovery: The American Indian Novel in the '80's." *Western American Literature* 22, no. 1 (1987): 53–57.

———. "Earthboy's Return: James Welch's Act of Recovery in *Winter in the Blood*." *Wicazo Sa Review* 6, no. 2 (1990): 27–37.

———. "Ecstatic Strategies: Gerald Vizenor's *Darkness in Saint Louis Bearheart*." *Narrative Chance: Postmodern Discourse on American Indian Literatures*, ed. Gerald Vizenor. Albuquerque: University of New Mexico Press, 1989, pp. 141–59.

———. "The Future's So Bright They've Got to Wear Shades." *New Mexico Magazine* 65 (Aug., 1987): 24.

———. "The Red Road to Nowhere: D'Arcy McNickle's *The Surrounded* and 'The Hungry Generations.' " *American Indian Quarterly* 13, no. 3 (1989): 239–48.

———. Review of *Darkness in Saint Louis Bearheart. Talking Leaf: Los Angeles Indian Newspaper* 48 (Sept., 1983): 9.

———. Review of *Fools Crow. Los Angeles Times Book Review*, Dec. 14, 1986, pp. 1, 6.

"The 'Map of the Mind': D'Arcy McNickle and The American Indian Novel." *Western American Literature* 19, no. 4 (1985): 275–83.

———. Review of *The Jailing of Cecelia Capture. Western American Literature* 4 (1986): 373–76.

———. Review of *The Woman Who Owned the Shadows. American Indian Culture and Research Journal* 8, no. 2 (1986): 61–63.

Parker, Dorothy, "Choosing an Indian Identity: A Biography of D'Arcy McNickle." Ph.D. diss., University of New Mexico, 1988.

Parsons, Elsie Clews. *The Pueblo of Jemez.* New Haven: Yale University Press, 1925.

Pearce, Roy Harvey. *Savagism and Civilization: A Study of the Indian and the American Mind.* Berkeley: University of California Press, 1988.

Purdy, James. *Word Ways: The Novels of D'Arcy McNickle.* Tucson: University of Arizona Press, 1990.

Radin, Paul. *The Trickster: A Study in American Indian Mythology.* New York: Schocken Books, 1972.

Rainwater, Catherine. "Reading Between Worlds: Narrativity in the Fiction of Louise Erdrich." *American Literature* 62 (1990): 405–22.

Ramsey, Jarold, ed. *Reading the Fire: Essays in the Traditional Indian Literatures of the Far West.* Lincoln: University of Nebraska Press, 1983.

Rogin, Michael Paul. *Fathers and Children: Andrew Jackson and the Subjugation of the American Indian.* New York: Alfred A. Knopf, 1975.

Ruoff, A. LaVonne Brown. "Alienation and the Female Principle in *Winter in the Blood.*" *American Indian Quarterly* 4 (1978): 107–22.

———. "Gerald Vizenor: Compassionate Trickster." *Studies in American Indian Literature* 9 (1986): 52–63.

———. "Woodland Word Warrior." *MELUS* 13, nos. 1 & 2 (1986): 13–43.

Ruppert, James. "The Reader's Lessons in *Ceremony.*" *Arizona Quarterly* 42, no. 1 (1986): 78–85.

Sands, Kathleen Mullen. "Closing the Distance: Critic, Reader and the Works of James Welch." *MELUS* 14 (1987): 273–85.

Satz, Ronald N. *American Indian Policy in the Jacksonian Era.* Lincoln: University of Nebraska Press, 1975.

Scarberry-Garcia, Susan. *Landmarks of Healing: A Study of House Made of Dawn.* Albuquerque: University of New Mexico Press, 1990.

———. "Sources of Healing in *House Made of Dawn.*" Ph.D. diss., University of Colorado, 1986.

Scheckter, John. "James Welch: Settling up on the Reservation." *South Dakota Review* 24, no. 2 (1986): 7–19.

Schneider, Jack W. "The New Indian: Alienation and the Rise of the Indian Novel." *South Dakota Review* 17, no. 1 (1980): 67–76.

Schubnell, Matthias. *N. Scott Momaday: The Cultural and Literary Background.* Norman: University of Oklahoma Press, 1985.

Seyersted, Per. *Leslie Marmon Silko.* Western Writers Series 45. Boise, Idaho. Boise State University Press, 1980.

Shea, John. *History of the Catholic Missions among the Indian Tribes of the United States, 1529–1854.* New York: Edward Dunigan and Brother, 1855.

Sherzer, Joel, and Anthony C. Woodbury, eds. *Native American Discourse: Poetics and Rhetoric.* Cambridge: Cambridge University Press, 1987.

Silko, Leslie Marmon. "Here's an Odd Artifact for the Fairy-Tale Shelf." *Impact Magazine Review of Books, Albuquerque Journal,* Oct. 7, 1986.

Smith, Henry Nash. *Virgin Land: The American West as Symbol and Myth.* New York: Vintage Books, 1950.

Standiford, Edward. *The Pattern of California History.* San Francisco: Carfield Press, 1975.

Swann, Brian, and Arnold Krupat, eds. *I Tell You Now: Autobiographical Essays by Native American Writers.* Lincoln: University of Nebraska Press, 1987.

———. *Recovering the Word: Essays on Native American Literature.* Berkeley: University of California Press, 1987.

Swann, Edith. "Laguna Symbolic Geography and Silko's *Ceremony.*" *American Indian Quarterly* 12 (1988): 229–49.

Thackery, William. "Crying for Pity in *Winter in the Blood.*" *MELUS* 7, no. 1 (1980): 61–78.

Tompkins, J. H. 1986. "Louise Erdrich: Looking for the Ties That Bind." *Calendar Magazine,* Oct., 1986, p. 15.

Turner, Katharine C. *Red Men Calling on the Great White Father.* Norman: University of Oklahoma Press, 1951.

Tyler, Hamilton A. *Pueblo Gods and Myths.* Norman: University of Oklahoma Press, 1964.

Velie, Alan. "Cain and Abel in N. Scott Momaday's *House Made of Dawn.*" *Journal of the West* 17 (1978): 55–62.

———. *Four American Indian Literary Masters: N. Scott Momaday, James Welch, Leslie Marmon Silko, and Gerald Vizenor.* Norman: University of Oklahoma Press, 1982.

Vizenor, Gerald. "Bone Courts: The Rights and Narrative Representation of Tribal Bones." *American Indian Quarterly* 10 (1986): 319–32.

———. "Dennis of Wounded Knee." *American Indian Quarterly* 7, no. 2 (1983): 51–65.

———. *Earthdivers: Tribal Narratives on Mixed Descent.* Minneapolis: University of Minnesota Press, 1981.

———. *Interior Landscapes.* Minneapolis: University of Minnesota Press, 1990.

———, ed. *Narrative Chance: Postmodern Discourse on Native American Indian Literatures*. Albuquerque: University of New Mexico Press, 1989.

von Hallberg, Robert, ed. *Canons*. Chicago: University of Chicago Press, 1984.

Walker, Franklin. *San Francisco's Literary Frontier*. New York: Alfred A. Knopf, 1939.

Warren, William. *History of the Ojibway People*. Minnesota Historical Society, 1885. Reprint, Saint Paul: Minnesota Historical Society Press, 1984.

Watt, Ian. *The Rise of the Novel*. Berkeley: University of California Press, 1957.

White, Hayden. *Metahistory*. Baltimore: Johns Hopkins University Press, 1973.

White, Robert H. *Tribal Assets: The Rebirth of Native America*. New York: Henry Holt and Co., 1990.

White, Sharon, and Glenda Burnside. 1988. "On Native Ground: An Interview with Louise Erdrich and Michael Dorris." *Bloomsbury Review* 8 (1988): 16–18.

Wiget, Andrew, ed. *Critical Essays on Native American Literature*. Boston: G. K. Hall, 1985.

Wild, Peter. "Visions of a Blackfoot." *New York Times Book Review* 91 (Nov. 2, 1986): 14.

Wilson, Terry P. "Osage Oxonian: The Heritage of John Joseph Mathews." *Chronicles of Oklahoma* 59 (Fall, 1981): 264–93.

———. *The Underground Reservation: Osage Oil*. Lincoln: University of Nebraska Press, 1985.

Wong, Herta D. "An Interview with Louise Erdrich and Michael Dorris." *North Dakota Quarterly* 55 (1987): 196–218.

Woodward, Charles L. *Ancestral Voice: Conversations with N. Scott Momaday*. Lincoln: University of Nebraska, 1989.

Wu Ch'êng-ên. *Monkey*. Trans. Arthur Waley. London: George Allen and Unwin, Ltd., 1942.

Wyman, Leland. *The Mountainway of the Navajo*. Tucson: University of Arizona Press, 1975.

Yellow Bird (John Rollin Ridge). *The Life and Adventures of Joaquin Murieta the Celebrated California Bandit*. 1854. Reprint, Norman: University of Oklahoma Press, 1955.

Zyla, Wolodymyr, and Wendel M. Aycock, eds. *Ethnic Literatures since 1776: The Many Voices of America, Part II*. Proceedings of the Comparative Literature Symposium, vol. 9. Lubbock: Texas Tech University Press, 1978.

Bibliography of American Indian Novels

◆

Allen, Paula Gunn (Laguna-Sioux). *The Woman Who Owned the Shadows.* San Francisco: Spinsters, Ink, 1983.

Bedford, Denton R. (Munsee). *Tsali.* San Francisco: The Indian Historian Press, 1972.

Bruchac, Joseph (Abenaki). *The Dreams of Jesse Brown.* Austin, Texas: Cold Mountain Press, 1978.

Chief Eagle, Dallas (Sioux). *Winter Count.* Colorado Springs, Colo.: Dentan-Berkeland Printing Co., 1967. Reprint, Denver: Golden Bell Press, 1968; Boulder, Colo.: Johnson Publishing Co., 1968.

Cook-Lynn, Elizabeth (Sioux). *From the River's Edge.* New York: Arcade, 1991.

Deloria, Ella Cara (Sioux). *Waterlily.* Lincoln: University of Nebraska Press, 1988.

Dorris, Michael (Modoc). *A Yellow Raft in Blue Water.* New York: Henry Holt and Co., 1987.

———, and Louise Erdrich. *The Crown of Columbus.* New York: Harper-Collins, 1991.

Erdrich, Louise (Chippewa). *The Beet Queen.* New York: Henry Holt and Co., 1986.

———. *Love Medicine.* New York: Holt, Rinehart and Winston, 1984.

———. *Tracks.* New York: Henry Holt and Co., 1988.

Hale, Janet Campbell (Coeur d'Alene). *The Jailing of Cecelia Capture.* New York: Random House, 1985. Reprint, Albuquerque, University of New Mexico Press, 1987.

———. *The Owl's Song* Garden City, N.J.: Doubleday, 1974. Reprint, New York: Avon, 1975.

Hogan, Linda (Chickasaw). *Mean Spirit.* New York: Atheneum, 1990.

King, Thomas (Cherokee). *Medicine River.* New York: Viking Press, 1990.

McNickle, D'Arcy (Cree/Métis, enrolled Salish). *Runner in the Sun: A Story of Indian Maize*. New York: Holt, 1954. Reprint with afterword by Alfonso Ortiz, Albuquerque: University of New Mexico Press, 1987.

———. *The Surrounded*. New York: Dodd, Mead and Co., 1936. Reprint with afterword by Lawrence W. Towner, Albuquerque: University of New Mexico Press, 1978.

———. *Wind from an Enemy Sky*. New York: Harper and Row, 1979. Reprint with afterword by Louis Owens, Albuquerque: University of New Mexico Press, 1988.

Markoosie [Markoosie Patsang] (Inuit Eskimo). *Harpoon of the Hunter*. Montreal: McGill-Queen's University Press, 1970.

Mathews, John Joseph (Osage). *Sundown*. New York: Longmans, Green and Co., 1934. Reprint, Boston: Gregg Press, 1979; with introduction by Virginia H. Mathews, University of Oklahoma Press, 1988.

Momaday, N. Scott (Kiowa). *The Ancient Child*. New York: Doubleday, 1989.

———. *House Made of Dawn*. New York: Harper and Row, 1968. Reprint, New York: Signet Books, 1969.

Mourning Dove [Hum-Ishu-Ma, Cristal Quintasket McLeod Galler] (Okanogan). *Cogewea, the Half-Blood: A Depiction of the Great Montana Cattle Range*. With notes and biographical sketch by Lucullus Virgil McWhorter. Boston: Four Seas Co., 1927. Reprint with introduction by Dexter Fisher, Lincoln: University of Nebraska Press, 1981.

Nasnaga [Roger Russell] (Shawnee). *Indians' Summer*. New York: Harper and Row, 1975.

Oskison, John Milton (Cherokee). *Black Jack Davy*. New York: D. Appleton and Co., 1926.

———. *Brothers Three*. New York: Macmillan Co., 1935.

———. *Wild Harvest*. New York: D. Appleton and Co., 1925. Reprint, Chicago: White House Book Club, 1925.

Owens, Louis (Choctaw-Cherokee). *Wolfsong*. Albuquerque: West End Press, 1991.

———. *The Sharpest Sight*. Norman: University of Oklahoma Press, 1992.

Penoi, Charles R. (Cherokee–Laguna Pueblo). *Indian Time*. Yukon, Okla.: Pueblo Publishing Press, 1984.

Pierre, Chief George (Okanogan). *Autumn's Bounty*. San Antonio: Naylor Co., 1972.

Pokagon, Simon (Potawatomi). *O-gi-Maw-Kwe Mit-i-gwa-ki (Queen of the Woods)*. Hartford, Mi.: C. H. Engle, 1899. Reprint, Berrien Springs, Mi.: Hardscrabble Books, 1972.

Ridge, John Rollin (Cherokee). *The Life and Adventures of Joaquin Murieta, the Celebrated California Bandit*. 1854. Reprint with introduction by Joseph Henry Jackson, Norman: University of Oklahoma Press, 1977.

Silko, Leslie Marmon (Laguna Pueblo). *Ceremony*. New York: Viking Press, 1977. Reprint, New York: Signet Books, 1978.

Smith, Martin Cruz (Senecu del Sur–Yaqui). *Canto for a Gypsy*. New York: Putnam, 1972.

———. *Gorky Park*. New York: Random House, 1981.

————. *Gypsy in Amber*. New York: Putnam, 1971.

————. *The Indians Won*. 1970. Reprint, New York: Nordon Publications, 1981.

————. *Nightwing*. New York: W. W. Norton and Co., 1977. Reprint, New York: Jove Publications, 1978.

————. *Polar Star*. New York: Ballantine Books, 1989.

————. *Stallion Gate*. New York: Random House, 1986.

Sneve, Virginia Driving Hawk (Sioux). *Betrayed* (juvenile). New York: Holiday House, 1974.

————. *The Chichi Hoohoo Bogeyman* (juvenile). New York: Holiday House, 1975.

————. *High Elk's Treasure* (juvenile). New York: Holiday House, 1972.

————. *Jimmy Yellow Hawk* (juvenile). New York: Holiday House, 1972.

————. *When Thunders Spoke* (juvenile). New York: Holiday House, 1974.

Storm, Hyemeyohsts (Cheyenne). *Seven Arrows*. New York: Harper and Row, 1972.

————. *The Song of Heyoekhah*. New York: Harper and Row, 1979.

Tucker, James (Choctaw-Cherokee). *Stone: The Birth*. New York: Zebra Books, 1981.

————. *Stone: The Journey*. New York: Zebra Books, 1981.

Vizenor, Gerald (Chippewa). *Darkness in Saint Louis Bearheart*. Saint Paul: Truck Press, 1978. Reprinted as *Bearheart: The Heirship Chronicles*, with afterword by Louis Owens, Minneapolis: University of Minnesota Press, 1990.

————. *Griever: An American Monkey King in China*. Normal: Illinois State University and Fiction Collective, 1987.

————. 1991. *The Heirs of Columbus*. Middletown, Conn.: Wesleyan University Press, 1991.

————. *The Trickster of Liberty*. Minneapolis: University of Minnesota Press, 1988.

Walters, Anna Lee (Pawnee-Otoe). *Ghost Singer*. Flagstaff, Ariz.: Northland Publishing, 1988.

Welch, James (Blackfoot–Gros Ventre). *The Death of Jim Loney*. New York: Harper and Row, 1979.

————. *Fools Crow*. New York: Viking Press, 1986.

————. *The Indian Lawyer*. New York: W. W. Norton, 1990.

————. *Winter in the Blood*. New York: Harper and Row, 1974. Reprint, New York: Penguin, 1986.

Williams, Ted C. *The Reservation*. Syracuse: Syracuse University Press, 1976.

Yellow Bird. *See* Ridge, John Rollin.

Index